The State Construction of 'Japaneseness'

JAPANESE SOCIETY SERIES
General Editor: Yoshio Sugimoto

Lives of Young Koreans in Japan
Yasunori Fukuoka

Globalization and Social Change in Contemporary Japan
J.S. Eades, Tom Gill and Harumi Befu

Coming Out in Japan: The Story of Satoru and Ryuta
Satoru Ito and Ryuta Yanase

Japan and Its Others:
Globalization, Difference and the Critique of Modernity
John Clammer

Hegemony of Homogeneity: An Anthropological Analysis of Nihonjinron
Harumi Befu

Foreign Migrants in Contemporary Japan
Hiroshi Komai

A Social History of Science and Technology in Contemporary Japan, Volume 1
Shigeru Nakayama

Farewell to Nippon: Japanese Lifestyle Migrants in Australia
Machiko Sato

The Peripheral Centre:
Essays on Japanese History and Civilization
Johann P. Arnason

A Genealogy of 'Japanese' Self-images
Eiji Oguma

Class Structure in Contemporary Japan
Kenji Hashimoto

An Ecological View of History
Tadao Umesao

Nationalism and Gender
Chizuko Ueno

Native Anthropology: The Japanese Challenge to Western Academic Hegemony
Takami Kuwayama

Youth Deviance in Japan: Class Reproduction of Non-Conformity
Robert Stuart Yoder

Japanese Companies: Theories and Realities
Masami Nomura and Yoshihiko Kamii

From Salvation to Spirituality: Popular Religious Movements in Modern Japan
Susumu Shimazono

The 'Big Bang' in Japanese Higher Education:
The 2004 Reforms and the Dynamics of Change
J.S. Eades, Roger Goodman and Yumiko Hada

Japanese Politics: An Introduction
Takashi Inoguchi

A Social History of Science and Technology in Contemporary Japan, Volume 2
Shigeru Nakayama

Gender and Japanese Management
Kimiko Kimoto

Philosophy of Agricultural Science: A Japanese Perspective
Osamu Soda

A Social History of Science and Technology in Contemporary Japan, Volume 3
Shigeru Nakayama and Kunio Goto

Japan's Underclass: Day Laborers and the Homeless
Hideo Aoki

A Social History of Science and Technology in Contemporary Japan, Volume 4
Shigeru Nakayama and Hitoshi Yoshioka

Scams and Sweeteners: A Sociology of Fraud
Masahiro Ogino

Toyota's Assembly Line: A View from the Factory Floor
Ryoji Ihara

Village Life in Modern Japan: An Environmental Perspective
Akira Furukawa

Social Welfare in Japan: Principles and Applications
Kojun Furukawa

Escape from Work: Freelancing Youth and the Challenge to Corporate Japan
Reiko Kosugi

Japan's Whaling: The Politics of Culture in Historical Perspective
Hiroyuki Watanabe

Gender Gymnastics: Performing and Consuming Japan's Takarazuka Revue
Leonie R. Stickland

Poverty and Social Welfare in Japan
Masami Iwata and Akihiko Nishizawa

The Modern Japanese Family: Its Rise and Fall
Chizuko Ueno

Widows of Japan: An Anthropological Perspective
Deborah McDowell Aoki

In Pursuit of the Seikatsusha:
A Genealogy of the Autonomous Citizen in Japan
Masako Amano

Demographic Change and Inequality in Japan
Sawako Shirahase

The Origins of Japanese Credentialism
Ikuo Amano

Pop Culture and the Everyday in Japan: Sociological Perspectives
Katsuya Minamida and Izumi Tsuji

Japanese Perceptions of Foreigners
Shunsuke Tanabe

Migrant Workers in Contemporary Japan:
An Institutional Perspective on Transnational Employment
Kiyoto Tanno

The Boundaries of 'the Japanese', Volume 1:
Okinawa 1868–1972 – Inclusion and Exclusion
Eiji Oguma

International Migrants in Japan: Contributions in an Era of Population Decline
Yoshitaka Ishikawa

Globalizing Japan: Striving to Engage the World
Ross Mouer

Beyond Fukushima: Toward a Post-Nuclear Society
Koichi Hasegawa

Japan's Ultra Right
Naoto Higuchi

The Boundaries of 'the Japanese', Volume 2:
Korea, Taiwan and the Ainu 1868–1945
Eiji Oguma

Creating Subaltern Counterpublics: Korean Women
In Japan and Their Struggles for Night School
Akwi Seo

Aftermath: Fukushima and the 3.11 Earthquake
Yutaka Tsujinaka and Hiroaki Inatsugu

Learning English in Japan
Takunori Terasawa

Others in Japanese Agriculture
Kenichi Yasuoka

Fighting Prejudice in Japan: The Families of Hansen's Disease Patients Speak Out
Ai Kurosaka

Living on the Streets in Japan: Homeless Women Break their Silence
Satomi Maruyama

U. S. Occupation of Okinawa: A Soft Power Theory Perspective
Hideko Yoshimoto

Social Stratification and Inequality Series

Inequality amid Affluence: Social Stratification in Japan
Junsuke Hara and Kazuo Seiyama

Intentional Social Change: A Rational Choice Theory
Yoshimichi Sato

Constructing Civil Society in Japan: Voices of Environmental Movements
Koichi Hasegawa

Deciphering Stratification and Inequality: Japan and Beyond
Yoshimichi Sato

Social Justice in Japan: Concepts, Theories and Paradigms
Ken-ichi Ohbuchi

Gender and Career in Japan
Atsuko Suzuki

Status and Stratification: Cultural Forms in East and Southeast Asia
Mutsuhiko Shima

Globalization, Minorities and Civil Society:
Perspectives from Asian and Western Cities
Koichi Hasegawa and Naoki Yoshihara

Fluidity of Place: Globalization and the Transformation of Urban Space
Naoki Yoshihara

Japan's New Inequality:
Intersection of Employment Reforms and Welfare Arrangements
Yoshimichi Sato and Jun Imai

Minorities and Diversity
Kunihiro Kimura

Inequality, Discrimination and Conflict in Japan:
Ways to Social Justice and Cooperation
Ken-ichi Ohbuchi and Junko Asai

Social Exclusion: Perspectives from France and Japan
Marc Humbert and Yoshimichi Sato

Global Migration and Ethnic Communities:
Studies of Asia and South America
Naoki Yoshihara

Stratification in Cultural Contexts: Cases from East and Southeast Asia
Toshiaki Kimura

Modernity and Identity in Asia Series

Globalization, Culture and Inequality in Asia
Timothy S. Scrase, Todd Miles, Joseph Holden and Scott Baum

Looking for Money:
Capitalism and Modernity in an Orang Asli Village
Alberto Gomes

Governance and Democracy in Asia
Takashi Inoguchi and Matthew Carlson

Liberalism: Its Achievements and Failures
Kazuo Seiyama

Health Inequalities in Japan: An Empirical Study of Older People
Katsunori Kondo

The State Construction of 'Japaneseness'

The Koseki Registration System in Japan

By

Masataka Endo

Translated by
Barbara Hartley

Edited by
Miriam Riley

Trans Pacific Press

Melbourne

First published in Japanese in 2013 by Akashi Shoten as *Koseki to kokuseki no kin-gendai-daishi.*

This English edition published in 2019 by:

Trans Pacific Press
PO Box 164, Balwyn North
Victoria 3104, Australia
Telephone: +61-(0)3-9859-1112
Fax: +61-(0)3-8611-7989
Email: tpp.mail@gmail.com
Web: http://www.transpacificpress.com

Designed and set by Sarah Tuke, Melbourne, Australia.

Distributors

Australia and New Zealand
James Bennett Pty Ltd
Locked Bag 537
Frenchs Forest NSW 2086
Australia
Telephone: +61-(0)2-8988-5000
Fax: +61-(0)2-8988-5031
Email: info@bennett.com.au
Web: www.bennett.com.au

USA and Canada
Independent Publishers Group (IPG)
814 N. Franklin Street
Chicago, IL 60610
USA
Telephone inquiries: +1-312-337-0747
Order placement: 800-888-4741
(domestic only)
Fax: +1-312-337-5985
Email: frontdesk@ipgbook.com
Web: http://www.ipgbook.com

Asia and the Pacific
Kinokuniya Company Ltd.
Head office:
3-7-10 Shimomeguro
Meguro-ku
Tokyo 153-8504
Japan
Telephone: +81-(0)3-6910-0531
Fax: +81-(0)3-6420-1362
Email: bkimp@kinokuniya.co.jp
Web: www.kinokuniya.co.jp
Asia-Pacific office:
Kinokuniya Book Stores of Singapore Pte., Ltd.
391B Orchard Road #13-06/07/08
Ngee Ann City Tower B
Singapore 238874
Telephone: +65-6276-5558
Fax: +65-6276-5570
Email: SSO@kinokuniya.co.jp

ISSN 1443–9670 (Japanese Society Series)

ISBN 978-1-920901-62-2

The translation and publication of this book was supported by a Grant-in-Aid for Publication of Scientific Research Results (Grant Number 17HP6002), provided by the Japan Society for the Promotion of Science, to which we express our sincere appreciation.

Contents

Tables

Introduction

Opening thoughts

Proof of being Japanese: Citizenship or koseki registration

How would a person respond if asked to provide proof of being Japanese? 'Hmm', they might reflect, 'I need to prove that I am a Japanese citizen'. This would be the most likely response, confirmed by the production of a Japanese passport. In legal terms, holding citizenship undoubtedly qualifies one to be a 'citizen' – a constituent member of a nation-state – and a passport is an official document with the power to prove the citizenship status of the holder.

What of the case, however, of a person with no passport? Given that this person would probably apply for a passport at some point, we will consider how the Japanese state processes such applications. Passport applicants must produce documentation that verifies that they are 'Japanese', namely, an entry from a koseki register record. According to the Passport Law of Japan (1951, Law No. 267), it is obligatory to provide either a copy or short form extract of a koseki register entry when lodging a passport application. Processing systems in Japan prevent the issuance of a passport without the lodgement of a koseki register entry, the proof that one is a citizen of Japan, as part of the application process.

We might therefore conclude that a koseki register entry, rather than a passport, is the official documentation that verifies that one is 'Japanese'. In other words, a koseki register entry constitutes formal proof of Japanese citizenship, because the ability to hold koseki registration is limited to those who hold Japanese citizenship. As discussed in Chapter Two, citizenship legislation in Japan has consistently valorised notions of bloodline – in legal discourse, the principle of *jus sanguinis*. Confirmation of whether or not a given individual holds Japanese citizenship is therefore verified by the individual's bloodline relationship with other 'Japanese' as recorded in the koseki registration system.

Yet, it is not necessarily the case that a person without koseki registration can never be 'Japanese'. There have been cases, for example, of individuals with no koseki register entry who are nonetheless presumed to be the children of 'Japanese' (that is, of people who hold Japanese citizenship). While the disadvantages faced by those without koseki registration will be discussed in detail in later chapters, we might briefly identify two here. The first is the fact that since, as noted above, a passport cannot technically be issued to a person without koseki registration, that person is unable to travel overseas. Secondly, such a person cannot in strict legal terms be entered into a resident record (*jūmin-hyō*), because this posssibility is only available to the people recorded in a koseki register (see, for example, Article 12, Clause 2, Section 1 of the Regulations for the Implementation of the 'Basic Resident Registration Law', *Jūmin kihon daichō-hō*).

The resident record provides proof of the circumstances of one's residence. In the absence of a record in this registration system, an individual is unable to do things such as register to vote, attend a school or receive public health insurance. Accordingly, without koseki registration an individual is not recognised by Japanese society as either a 'citizen' or a 'resident'. With the increasing circulation of information regarding the circumstances of unregistered children in recent years, general interest in this issue has grown. In the summer of 2012, the Fuji Television drama, *Iki mo dekinai natsu* (Breathless Summer), for example, featured a protagonist who did not hold koseki registration. Starring Takei Emi, this was possibly the first television drama to tackle head-on the problems faced by those without koseki registration (*mukoseki*).

Since, of course, one role of governance is to provide the relief measures necessary to ensure the rights of those without koseki registration, the disadvantages discussed above are largely confined to legal theory. Basic resident registers (*jūmin kihon daichō*) are administered by local governments that have official powers to create an exceptional resident record for people who do not hold koseki registration. In 2007, moreover, the Ministry of Foreign Affairs introduced processing exceptions so that even a person without koseki registration, who can nonetheless satisfy conditions such as confirmation of a parent–child relationship with a Japanese citizen, is now eligible for a passport. We might conclude then that the disadvantage of not holding koseki registration is markedly less significant than that of not holding citizenship.

Significant in terms of negative impact, however, is the social discrimination and prejudice suffered by those who do not hold koseki registration. Since its promulgation as an innovation of the modern nation-state in the form of a unified, national law in the early years of the Meiji era, the koseki registration system has continued to operate without interruption in Japan. In fact, for more than 140 years it has functioned as the official means by which an individual qualifies as 'Japanese'. Public opinion in Japan is steeped in popular notions decreeing that unregistered individuals fail to officially qualify as Japanese. This leads to damaging social censure of those without a koseki register entry. The prying eyes and unsubstantiated claims that often accompany this censure create social pressures that cast an oppressive pall over the everyday life of those without koseki registration.

What exactly, however, does it mean to be 'Japanese'? Is it a matter of 'Japanese ethnicity'? Is it having an entry in a koseki register record? Is it holding 'Japanese citizenship'? And for a person who is 'Japanese', moreover, what is the meaning of koseki registration?

Nation-state's citizen registration: Koseki system as use of power

Essentially an official document administered by the state at the national level, the koseki register record provides an account of changes in an individual's status relationships. Regardless of time or place, states around the world have compiled general registers of the people under their jurisdiction and administered these registers with various aims in mind. Such registers integrate the joint objectives of conducting a general survey to assess the mobility or immobility of the domestic population and gathering information on the status relationships of each individual in the wider group.

For states in ancient times, the population survey function was the most pressing registration requirement. In order to achieve the efficient imposition of state levies necessary for conscription, taxation and labour, it was sufficient to ascertain the simple population structure in terms of, for example, the number of men and of women, those who had reached the age of majority, those engaged in various occupations and the number of households. Prior to the emergence of 'citizenship' as a legal system in the modern era, moreover, entry into a koseki register record was seen as the state's authorisation of the individual as a 'citizen'.

By the beginning of the nineteenth century, however, the success of the Industrial Revolution and the growth of capitalism had fuelled the rise of the nation-state. The resultant diversification of work created social problems that called for the protection of workers and the provision of social security. Demands were accordingly made on the state to offer comprehensive guarantees in relation to the welfare and safety of the individual. Forced to expand its purview in terms of legislation and governance, the modern state transformed from 'custodian state' to 'welfare state'.

Parallel to this expansion of state responsibility was the need to develop an apparatus capable of conducting a detailed and precise assessment of the circumstances of the people. It was therefore necessary to establish a legal standard to determine the ways in which an individual might qualify as a constituent member of a sovereign nation-state. The need for such a system was not merely to facilitate the imposition of responsibilities on the 'citizen', the individual who fulfilled the fundamental legal criteria of citizenship. It was also necessary to enable the state to fully meet its obligations – such as guaranteeing suffrage, social security and education – regarding the welfare of the people. This called for much more than a mere population survey. It was now crucial for the state to gather information about the lived reality of the people in terms of family and residential relationships.

Thus, no longer content with merely assessing the numbers and locations of the people, the state set out to devise a system that could provide clear information regarding changes to status relationships throughout the life of the individual, such as birth, marriage, divorce and death. In order to achieve this, status registration systems were developed. These systems differed markedly, depending on whether the unit of registration was the individual or the family.

In Japan, the koseki registration system is the mechanism that records status relationship information. Koseki register records are compiled with the family – rather than the individual – as the basic unit and the system has the special characteristic of recording status in order to verify two aspects of an individual's life. The first is the private aspect including matters such as birth, death and family relationships, and the second is the public aspect that involves being a citizen of Japan.

Considered from a political science perspective, however, this kind of citizen registration mechanism developed in the context of the tense relationship between the state and the individual that has been in operation throughout modernity. As Maruyama Masao points out, the destiny of the modern nation-state involved two conflicting perspectives. These were unconditional state-ism – the desire for central control – that was the rationale for the emergence of the nation-state, and the notion of modern natural law, which gifted fundamental rights to the individuals recognised as the subjects of those rights.[1] Even with its expanding sphere of responsibility, it was considered natural in terms of the liberal thinking pioneered by Jeremy Bentham and John Stuart Mill for the modern nation-state to curtail its intervention into the private sphere, especially into the realm of the family and related matters such as marriage and divorce.[2] According to this thinking, state involvement in family life should be as non-interventionist as possible in order to guarantee the broadest possible freedom for each individual to develop her or his abilities and to undertake the actions necessary to achieve full self-actualisation. The role of the modern state, therefore, was limited to discouraging anti-social aspects of family life through, for example, promoting monogamy and prohibiting incest. It was, in other words, incumbent upon the state to respect the fundamental right of the family sphere to self-determination.[3]

With respect to the contradictions inherent in the power of the modern state, English political scientist Harold Joseph Laski (1893–1950) argued that by demanding that the people submit to its control, the state expressed a belief in its capacity to guarantee the fulfilment of the people's desires to the greatest possible degree.[4] In order to secure the norm of the people voluntarily submitting to its demands, however, the state needed to regularly reward those who deferred to its will and to extract agreement and approval through persuasion and indoctrination.

Koseki registration was grounded in a power relationship that compelled the individual to register.[5] Nevertheless, there was reluctance on the part of those who exerted this power to rely on the continuous use of force. Instead, the authorities encouraged voluntary submission by individuals who acknowledged that state control brought social stability. While koseki registration initially functioned as a system of voluntary information lodgement, it was necessary to provide incentives to ensure that individuals participated, and that effective compilation was accomplished. That is to say, it was necessary to cultivate a sense that koseki registration endowed the individual with a state of grace.

Thus, through promoting a formula that presented koseki registration as supporting the preservation of the state, while also guaranteeing various privileges for the individual 'citizens' who registered, the authorities fomented a pro-active stance towards the process. At the time of the operation of the Jinshin koseki registration system, compiled following the 1871 promulgation of modern Japan's first unified Koseki Registration Law, one legislator was moved to observe as follows: 'Our Koseki Registration Law is not merely proof of status. It is largely an administrative mechanism by means of which legislators are able to manage the people. In carrying out this task, the government is doing nothing other than fulfilling its obligations to ensure the happiness of the people'.[6] These words demonstrate that, while the principle function of koseki registers was to control and regulate, the people thereby incurred a debt of gratitude in appreciation of the fact that state control and regulation guaranteed their 'social happiness'.

In this way, koseki registration was transformed from its essential function of being a simple documentation of status into a process that demanded gratitude for the debt of favour incurred towards the state, which protected the people of the land through its law enforcement. Accordingly, the koseki registration system became a repository of information that operated across the entire spectrum of social relations.

'Japan's koseki registration system is supreme'

Every country has a fundamental system of civil law – often referred to as a 'civil code' – which administers changes to the private status of an individual in terms of being a wife, husband or child, including an adopted child. In modern Japan, the Koseki Registration Law has been administered as a subsidiary law of the Civil Code that implements the legal provisions relating to marriage, adoption for the purpose of maintaining the family line and other family relationships that pertain to the Code.

Notwithstanding the legal nature of koseki registration, however, how many people can clearly explain what this process actually is? There are few occasions in everyday life, such as confirming a register entry when inheriting property, during which an individual engages to any degree with the koseki registration system. Nevertheless, our lives proceed unimpeded by a lack of deep knowledge about the koseki registration process or its significance. Even in the pre-war era, when consciousness of koseki processes was likely to have been stronger than in the present, a government committee member felt it appropriate to declare that 'the most difficult problem associated with koseki registration is actually defining the system'.[7] It is as if koseki registration is a natural phenomenon that envelops people in Japan like air.

'Japan's koseki registration system is supreme throughout the world'. Yokoyama Minoru, a former justice bureaucrat who played a leading role in koseki registration administration, claimed that, so often were these self-congratulatory words repeated at meetings related to koseki administration, he tired of hearing them. But when asked, 'Why is this system supreme?' most bureaucrats were not able to provide an answer. One mayor responsible for overseeing koseki registration administration who was asked for an on-the-spot outline of the system could only declare that 'This is a very serious topic that is no laughing matter'.[8] As evident from the argument below, the majority of people – whether government officials or ordinary citizens – have limited personal engagement with the koseki registration system. In other words, awareness of the system is something inscribed externally. The underside of the self-congratulatory 'supreme throughout the world' discourse was that even those in official positions with responsibility for koseki registration administration fulfilled their duties without really understanding exactly how koseki registration procedures worked.

This hazy grasp of koseki matters in Japan is apparent even in legal discourse. The current Koseki Registration Law was promulgated as Law No. 224 on 22 December 1947. Common practice suggests that the first article of such a law will declare the objectives and spirit of the legislation. However, Article 1 of the 1947 Koseki Registration Law merely reads, 'The head of the municipality in question will have principal carriage of the administration of the koseki register'. In other words, nowhere in this legal document is there a definition of 'koseki register' or a statement outlining the purpose of the Koseki Registration Law. From a slightly different perspective, we might regard this as an expression of the extent to which people in Japan take the operation of the koseki registration system for granted, and how being entered into a koseki register is regarded as part of the 'natural' order.

Notion of the *ie* family embedded in koseki registration

Although, as noted above, koseki registration originated as a status registration system designed to track the mobility of the people and to maintain social order during the time of the ancient state, that very early system was not totally detached from moral norms and standards. In addition to its role in ensuring material welfare in terms of maintaining social capital and providing citizens with the means to live, the modern state naturally expanded its parameters to intervene in spiritual fields such as ethics, education, religion and customs and manners. In the 1945 publication *On Power: The Natural History of Its Growth*, French political scientist Bertrand de Jouvenel (1903–1987) argued that one of the most notable things about modern society is the magnificence of the state apparatus. Jouvenel went on to note that by effectively amalgamating moral and material control, this apparatus conditions the life of the individual and gives form to the activities of the private sphere.[9] That is to say, the state devises administrative mechanisms that promote moral and ethical ideals with a view to directing the behaviour and thoughts of individuals towards those ideals.

In modern Japanese society, the Koseki Registration Law has created a moral code that applies to both the 'citizen' and the 'family'. Long years of operation have effectively given rise to a collective koseki consciousness that unquestioningly accepts discursive claims that if one is 'Japanese' then one must hold koseki registration, and that those who have no 'koseki' entry are somehow deviant. Legal scholar Yamanushi Masayuki (1925–1964) referred to these kinds of legal and cultural assumptions as 'koseki registration consciousness'.[10] We can only conclude that underpinning this consciousness is the belief that being managed by the *koseki* registration system guarantees one's status as Japanese while also ensuring social order in the land.

'Koseki registration consciousness' is endemic throughout society, particularly apparent in everyday language. There are, for example, many instances in which lodgement of a marriage notice is referred to as 'entering a koseki register' (*nyūseki*). This is especially the case in media accounts of the lives of celebrities, where what should be referred to as 'marriage' or 'lodgement of a marriage notice' is now routinely reported, regardless of whether or not the persons involved use the term themselves, as 'entry into a koseki register'. Certainly, since people who marry are removed from their former koseki register record and entered into a new one that documents the details of the married couple only, the process can technically be referred to in this way. However, there are cases in which partner B is entered into a koseki register record for which partner A is the responsible party – in other words, cases in which partner A remarries. While on such occasions the use of the expression 'entering the register' is completely inappropriate, this is the term that is now likely to be used even when A is a celebrity whose situation is widely known. In the case of adoption to continue the family line, moreover, the used of the expression 'entry into a register' has become commonplace in reference to entering the adopted party into the adoptive parent's koseki register record. This occurs in spite of the fact that, because marriage relationships and koseki registration are conceptually connected, the term 'entry into a register' evokes the idea of 'marriage' rather than adoption.

Koseki registration consciousness is intimately connected to notions of male superiority. While marriage should ideally be a relationship between equals, a foundational principle of the *ie* family system of the Meiji Civil Code was the entry of a wife into the husband's *ie* family. Even in the post-war era when the *ie* family system no longer operated, in reality it remained commonplace for the wife to enter the koseki register record of her husband. Accordingly, notwithstanding the ideals and expectations of the parties concerned, public opinion can regard marriage as a husband 'taking' or 'receiving' a wife, while her parents 'give' a daughter to the husband's family. It is no surprise, moreover, that the practice of a wife calling her husband '*shujin*' (literally 'master') and of other people referring to the household head (usually the father) as '*danna sama*' (literally 'honourable master') is met by foreigners with bemusement.

The fact that even now the *ie* family system continues to exert influence clearly demonstrates just how deeply entrenched the notion of '*ie*' remains. As noted in Chapter Three, the essence of *ie* family system relationships lay in the authority of the dominant over the subordinate. Thus, the husband–wife relationship in the case of marriage and the adopted child–adoptive parent relationship in the case of adoption for the purpose of carrying on the family line became a mere 'means' to preserve the *ie* family. The free will of those in question was of no consequence. We might also note here that the Chinese character for '*yome*', the term for bride, is constructed from elements that indicate a woman attached to the *ie* family. Since the practice of assembling and recording all family members together in a single koseki register record has been consecrated as a 'beautiful custom', events such as divorce or the birth of a child outside legal marriage are regarded as 'a stain' on the record. Here we see the fabrication of a unique ethical standard that sanctifies the operation of koseki registration.

Rather than an actual living community, however, the 'family' in the context of the *koseki* registration system is merely the standardised unit of compilation. In the pre-war *ie* family system, any individual with a relationship to the legal household head (*koshu*) was recorded in the family's koseki register record in terms of her or his relationship over three generations. These koseki register records that crossed generations created the impression that the extended family spanning from grandparents to grandchildren was the norm in Japan. Although the 'three-generation koseki register record' was abolished in the present Koseki Registration Law, there are still instances of people being entered into a koseki register record alongside a person or persons they have not met for many years. On the other hand, as noted below, a foreign spouse is not entered into a koseki register record. There are therefore married couples who, despite being together for a long period of time, cannot in terms of koseki practice be regarded as members of the same 'family' because one is a foreigner. This example, in particular, clearly demonstrates the difference between the meaning of 'family' in terms of koseki registration and family as an actual living community. Awareness of this difference confirms the oppressive nature of koseki registration practices, which bear down upon the people of Japan from every direction.

Absence of 'foreigner' entries from koseki records

Koseki registration does not exhaustively apply to all who reside in territory under Japanese jurisdiction. For example, foreigners – those who do not hold Japanese citizenship – are not subjected to this process. There is, however, no article in the present Koseki Registration Law that directly states that those who do not hold Japanese citizenship are ineligible for koseki registration. Nevertheless, Article 6 stipulates as follows: Koseki register records are created for each unit consisting of a husband and wife and any of their children at their *honseki* address which exists within a district of a municipality, and each of the children is supposed to have the same *uji* family name as that couple. In the case, however, of the formation of a new koseki register record for a person who is married to a non-Japanese or a person who does not have a spouse, those people – and each of the children with the same *uji* family name – will be entered into the new record.

What this incredibly convoluted statement confirms is that since a foreigner does not formally have an *uji* family name, then that foreigner is essentially ineligible for entry into a koseki register record.

According to Toshitani Nobuyoshi, the koseki registration system is distinguished by the fact that 'The state, through the koseki register, determines the sphere of those who are under its control. Furthermore, by similarly distinguishing those who are outside its control, the state establishes social order and regulates stability'.[11] We can amplify Toshitani's ideas to conclude that in regulating the parameters of those whom it targets, the koseki registration system also exercises a distinct management function towards those who are unregistered (that is, who do not hold Japanese citizenship), thereby securing governance over the entire society.

On face value, the fact that the koseki registration system equally records the details of all individuals should produce the ideal format for guaranteeing the unity of the 'nation-state'. However, the processes required to ensure smooth enforcement of the system create the need to apply constant psychological pressure that imposes considerable disadvantage upon those without koseki registration. Accordingly, there has been an increasingly rigid exertion of control by the powers-that-be through the management of the koseki registration system, which operates as a compulsion mechanism that discriminates against foreigners and unregistered people.

Was there initially some positive reason for not registering foreigners in the koseki registration system? Explanatory notes to pre-war koseki register legislation state directly as follows: 'In this law, reference to those who are Japanese and those who hold Japanese citizenship indicates a person [*naichijin*] who belongs to the inner sphere [*naichi*, literally, inner land] of the Japanese state'.[12] In other words, the term 'Japanese' specified a person from mainland Japan. As seen in Chapter Four, the expression '*naichijin*' or 'person who belongs to mainland Japan' technically refers to someone who holds koseki registration in this inner sphere of mainland Japan and is used to indicate that an individual is innately Japanese. While some may think it self-evident that the koseki registration system records information only for those who are Japanese, as far as I am aware, there has never been any clear justification presented for this practice or any clear explanation offered of the relevant legislative background. Yet, as is evident from the example given below, the significance of this refusal to permit the entry of foreigner details into the koseki registration system cannot be overestimated.

Two thousand and twelve was the sixtieth anniversary of the San Francisco Peace Treaty (hereafter, the 'Peace Treaty'), which took effect on 28 April 1952. This was the day that Japan's independence as a sovereign state was restored after occupation by the Allied Powers. On 28 April 2013, the government of Japan sought to incite nationalistic sentiment among the 'Japanese' by organising remembrance ceremonies to celebrate 'Restoration of Sovereignty Day'. This day, however, was also the day on which, in one fell blow, those who had come to Japan from former colonial holdings – that is, Korean and Taiwanese people – lost their Japanese citizenship and were suddenly legally transformed into foreigners. This loss exemplified the operation of koseki registration principles – *koseki-shugi*. These principles became the means by which the Japanese state drew a line of demarcation between 'Japanese' and 'foreigner' according to whether or not an individual was entered into the koseki registration system of mainland Japan (see Chapter Five for further details).

In 1969, Song Dwoohoe (1915–2002), a Korean resident in Japan, challenged the way the Japanese government processed citizenship when the Peace Treaty came into effect. Lodging an objection declaring that he had, in fact, not lost his Japanese citizenship at that time, Song mounted a lawsuit against the government demanding that his citizenship be reinstated. On 8 September 2010, a century after the Japanese empire's annexation of Korea, second generation Korean resident in Japan Kim Myeonggwan (b. 1950) also mounted a lawsuit against the Japanese government calling for the confirmation of his Japanese citizenship. After twice being rejected by lower courts, the case proceeded on appeal to the Supreme Court where it was dismissed in December 2012. In Japan, citizenship became a mechanism used to deny access to civil rights. The fact that authorities stripped individuals of citizenship regardless of the will of those concerned cannot but cast a cloud over the country's validity as a democratic state. Moreover, the general disinterest shown by members of Japanese society towards the case mounted by Kim Myeonggwan demonstrates that, among the people of Japan, the significance of 28 April 1952 is largely restricted to memorialising the 'restoration of sovereignty'.

In July 2012, the Alien Registration Law was repealed, and a major reform of Japanese immigration and related procedures was carried out. In late 2011, approximately 2,080,000 resident foreigners were registered in Japan. Among those with '"South Korean" or "Korean" citizenship', 390,000 were born, or were the descendants of those born, in former colonies. These people therefore qualified administratively as 'special permanent residents' (*tokubetsu eijū sha*). This is a group whose circumstances were created, as discussed above, by the citizenship management policies of the Japanese government, which insists on a logic that marks members of this group as 'foreigners' and thus justifies treating them differently to 'Japanese citizens'. Throughout the post-war years, this difference has seen Japanese officialdom deny the rights of these 'foreigners' across a range of issues, including fingerprinting them, denying post-war reparation and discriminating against them in matters such as employment and attendance at Korean ethnic schools. It is arguable that, had the residents of Japan born in former colonies been given the freedom to choose Japanese citizenship on 28 April 1952, the malfeasance that has continued until the present day would not have become so entrenched in attitudes towards these people in Japan.

While the issue of citizenship management at the time of the Peace Treaty is addressed in greater detail in Chapter Five, one point needs to be emphasised here. This is the fact that, for reasons related to the manner in which koseki registration is administered, even among those who held what on the surface appeared to be identical 'Japanese citizenship', a legal boundary was established between 'Japanese' and 'foreigner'. The construction of the koseki registration wall that was reinforced as the norm at this time was, in fact, set in motion during Japan's imperial era control of its colonial holdings (refer to Chapter Four for further details). Yet, although any power to rule these former colonies had been completely extinguished, the massive force of pre-war administrative procedures during the era of the Japanese empire continued to carry weight even in 1952 when the Peace Treaty came into effect.

Once again, we should remind ourselves of the fact that holding an entry in a koseki register record is available only to those who are 'Japanese', and that this very point is used as the rationale to justify the importance of registration.

The problem of 'bloodline'

The mode of sovereignty that gained greatest momentum during the modern era derived from the concept of the 'nation-state' (*kokumin kokka*). The bedrock of the idea of 'nation' was the intimate connection that arose from 'common ethnic consciousness'. This consciousness was perceived to integrate the people into a polity by confirming a shared understanding that each individual member of a nation-state originated from a common bloodline. As Katō Takashi argued, however, there is a substantive slippage between the notions of 'nation' and 'ethnicity' that the state can never resolve.[13] This is fundamentally related to the fact that the catalyst for the concept of 'nation' is a type of enforcement disguised as inclusion through shared citizenship. This necessity to enforce ultimately reveals the state's inability to impose any common 'ethnic' essence – which demands unity around factors such common origin, language, customs, religion and place of residence – onto the identity of the individuals under its jurisdiction.

We might here consider the theory of the 'consciousness of commonality' (*dōrui ishiki*) developed by political scientist Ōyama Ikuo (1880–1955). According to Ōyama, the state encompasses complex elements comprised of countless individuals, classes and groups, each of which has competing personal and private interests. The single factor that 'maintains the honour and power of the unified substrate that becomes the state' is 'consciousness of commonality'. This 'consciousness' develops not merely through shared blood relationships but is also inculcated through shared historical narratives and religious beliefs, and through shared thought, language, customs and practices.[14]

The 'consciousness of commonality' promoted by the Japanese state sought to maintain unity through the preservation in the broadest sense of the 'bloodline' of its citizens. This is evident from the fact that since the Meiji era, citizenship policy in Japan has adhered to bloodline principles, the *jus sanguinis* of legal discourse. Under the rule of the Tokugawa Bakufu, Japan was an island state that for over 200 years maintained a closed-door policy (*sakoku*). As a result, when compared to China or the West, the country had almost no opportunity for exchange with people of different cultures and ethnicities. It was therefore easy for the belief to take hold at the core of Japanese society that common 'blood' ensured the maintenance of social order. Koseki registration demonstrated how Japanese citizenship was exclusively maintained through an individual's blood relations to other 'Japanese'. It was thus surely the koseki registration system that obsessively nurtured a 'consciousness of commonality' that demanded the creation of ties which single-mindedly promoted the unity of the people through 'bloodline'.

However, with the waves of globalisation that continue to gather force around the world today, the movement of people and things across national borders has become commonplace. The resultant political, economic and cultural opening of borders – borderlessness – has long seen a disintegration of the formula that sovereignty in the modern era must equal the nation-state. There are now countless people who live in a country outside that of their own nationality and countless people who hold dual citizenship. Many contemporary societies have responded to the rapid dissolution of national borders by permitting dual citizenship and by guaranteeing the rights of resident foreigners. The notion of citizenship has thus become increasingly flexible and no longer plays a defining role in individual identity. In Japan, too, where there are growing numbers of marriages between Japanese and non-Japanese, it is not so unusual to find a 'mixed household' in which a foreigner is the effective household head. However, in terms of the letter of the Japanese Koseki Registration Law, this sort of international family remains legally cleaved apart. Koseki registration obstinately demands identity through 'blood' among those whose status information is recorded. It remains doubtful, however, whether or not the 'blood' notarised by koseki registration was ever a means to regulate 'Japanese' purity in the first place.

The themes and structure of this book

The koseki registration system is no mere system of status registration. Rather, it has existed since the Meiji era as an apparatus designed to monitor and regulate the 'Japanese'. Not confined to the spiritual and ethical spheres, the significance of this system is the manner in which it has held sway over individual status at the judicial and international levels through the mechanism of citizenship. It is therefore vital that we understand the koseki registration system as an imposition of power that generates a fraught and incessant tension between both state and individual, and state and family. This is especially apparent when we consider the impact of the modern Japanese state's expansion of the territories under its control into an 'empire'. The mechanism that assimilated those of different ethnicities as 'imperial subjects' was the koseki registration system. This system, however, discriminated by creating different sorts of records for those who were Japanese by birth and those whose heritage lay in the colonies. Although administered externally in terms of citizenship as 'Japanese', those with colonial ancestry were administered internally in terms of koseki registration in a way that clearly marked them as different from those regarded as innately Japanese.

The application of Japan's policies of 'exclusion' and 'inclusion' has been comprehensively probed by Oguma Eiji in his 1998 work 'The Boundaries of the "Japanese": From the Colonial Control of Okinawa, Ainu People, Taiwan and the Korean Peninsula to the

Reversion Campaign' (*Nihonjin' no kyōkai: Okinawa, Ainu, Taiwan, Chōsen shokuminchi shihai kara fukki undō made*).[15] In my work entitled 'Citizenship and Koseki Registration During the Era of Colonial Rule in Modern Japan: Manchoukuo, Korea and Taiwan' (*Kindai nihon no shokiminchi tōchi ni okeru kokuseki to koseki: Manshū, Chōsen, Taiwan*) and published in 2010, I drew on the stance adopted in Oguma's 1998 publication while focussing more directly on the legal perspective. This approach provided a means of investigating the opportunistic intertwining of citizenship and koseki registration as mechanisms of control during the imperial era in Japan.[16] It is self-evident, moreover, that in the nation-state of modern Japan the koseki registration phenomenon embodied the *ie* family system. As many researchers have noted, far from being a mere legal device, the *ie* family was in fact a system of ideology and morality that supported state power while exerting control over the people of Japan.[17] How, then, did this *ie* family regulate the acquisition and loss of the citizenship that was the condition necessary for one to be a 'citizen' of Japan? The extraordinary degree of mobility in the space of 'empire' among, for example, immigrants and people from the colonies inevitably created citizenship problems for members of these groups. Yet, when they tried to solve the issues that confronted them, these people ran headlong into a system that demanded koseki registration as natural proof of 'Japanese citizenship'. There is currently no research which, in the context of the border-crossing of immigrants and residents of Japan's colonial holdings, considers from an international perspective exactly what koseki registration is or what the *ie* family was or is. The purpose of this book is to respond to this gap in the scholarship. In doing so, the discussion will draw attention not merely to the inclusionist/exclusionist function of the koseki registration system, but also to the external function that stipulated the legal position of a 'Japanese' citizen in the modern context, a context that generated ongoing tension between the individual and state.

The overarching concern in the chapters that follow is how factors such as 'ethnicity' and 'bloodline' – in tandem with notions of citizenship – influenced the policies of the modern state in a way that linked them so closely with the koseki registration system. The discussion accordingly provides a historical investigation that moves from the inception of the modern Japanese state through the post-war dissolution of empire and into the practices of contemporary times. The purpose is to determine the theory and function of koseki registration and its impact on both the ideal and reality of becoming 'Japanese'. In addition, the analysis will continue to question exactly what it means to be 'Japanese' and examine the meaning that koseki registration holds for those who are 'Japanese'.

The general structure of the book is presented below. Chapter One outlines how the koseki registration system originally operated and what this system provided proof of. The chapter problematises the kinds of power that the system exerts on the lives of individuals and how this system has been transformed into a mechanism to impose order and to restrict the options available to contemporary 'Japanese'. The particular characteristics of the system in Japan are profiled via comparison with the status registration systems of other countries.

Chapter Two begins with an overview of the significance of citizenship to the modern state in the context of modern thought. The chapter then reviews the history of citizenship law in Japan from Meiji times through to the post-war era. Here, focus is on the indivisible relationship between 'Japanese citizenship' on the one hand, and koseki registration and the *ie* family on the other. Consideration is also given to how and why the principle of bloodline or *jus sanguinis*, the keystone of the Japanese concept of citizenship, was deployed as a form of political power.

Chapter Three examines the history of how the koseki registration system under the modern Japanese state brought the 'Japanese' together as citizens. Here, a number of points are addressed. Firstly, attention is given to why the promulgation of the Koseki Registration Law was a necessary step in the creation of the 'citizens' of modern Japan. Secondly, the chapter examines the emergence of koseki registration as the norm for qualifying as 'Japanese'. Thirdly, consideration will be given to how koseki registration created a system and an ethics around 'bloodline' and the 'family' of 'Japanese' through associations with the *ie* family system. Conflict between this system of ethics and the value given by modern systems of thought to notions of individualism will also be examined. Finally, attention will turn to how, at the time of the demarcation of the boundaries of Meiji Japan, the Koseki Registration Law was introduced into the new territories of Hokkaido and Okinawa, and how Ainu and

Okinawan people resident in those new territories were incorporated into the koseki registration system of social control. The chapter will also seek to clarify the mechanism of the *ie* family system and the restraints that this placed upon the individual.

Chapter Four focuses on koseki registration and citizenship practices and policies at the time of the Japanese government's colonial rule. While foregrounding the spatial association with empire, including Manchoukuo (Mǎnzhōu Guó) and other areas of China that were subject to Japanese invasion, consideration will be given to how, in the context of Japan's external grab for territory, the people of the colonies were assimilated and controlled as 'Japanese'. Particular attention is given to clarifying how koseki registration policies, which were developed by government powerbrokers during the era of empire as essential measures of control grounded in notions of 'ethnicity' and 'bloodline', constructed the categories of 'Japanese', 'Korean' (*Chōsenjin*) and 'Taiwanese' (*Taiwanjin*).

Chapter Five examines how post-war government policy related to the reconstruction of the 'Japanese' remained in the thrall of pre-war koseki registration principles. The focus here is on the influence exerted by imperial era koseki registration policies on post-war citizenship management of those born in former colonies. Consideration will also be given to how, in a post-war Japan confronted with the unparalleled crisis of defeat in war and in which territorial and legal concepts became chaotically intertwined, the legal position of those repatriated from former colonies and former Manchoukuo was determined, and how koseki registration policies were used to rehabilitate these people as 'Japanese'. The chapter will similarly consider the situation of people who had been under American occupation in Okinawa.

In an increasingly diverse and rapidly globalising contemporary world, concepts such as 'international border' and 'citizen' are becoming more diverse and flexible. Drawing on the analysis in previous chapters, Chapter Six considers the reforms necessary to both the Koseki Registration Law and the Citizenship Law in Japan in order to ensure that these accommodate the needs of individuals who live in this increasingly diverse and globalised world. The chapter examines the situation in Korea and Taiwan, both of which operated post-war registration systems similar to that of Japan, and the reforms that have been undertaken in these countries in response to contemporary conditions. A comparison will be made between the current system in these countries and the koseki registration system of Japan.

Ultimately, this book seeks to determine how the koseki registration system, as an apparatus of the state, became an entity that constituted the 'Japanese' both inside and outside Japan. While reflecting on the manner in which concepts such as 'citizen', 'ethnicity' and 'bloodline' were strategically deployed to entrench political power, an attempt will be made to offer a template for constructing a new inclusive society in contemporary Japan.

1 Koseki Registration as Proof of 'Being Japanese'

What does koseki registration certify?

'Truth' and the koseki register record

This chapter begins by explaining the nature of the information that appears in the koseki registration system that records information about families. Article 6 of the Koseki Registration Law declares that the koseki register is an entity that officially systematises as one unit 'a single husband and wife, and also the children of that husband and wife, who share a common *uji* family name and *honseki* domicile address [hereafter *honseki* address, the meaning of which is elaborated upon below] in a given municipal jurisdiction'. Put another way, we can say that members of a 'family unit' that share the same *honseki* address and the same family name have entries in the same koseki register record. This is the principle of 'one family, one record' (*ikka isseki*).

What, then, is the nature of the information about the individual that appears in a koseki register record? According to Article 3 of the Koseki Registration Law, this information is as follows:

1. name;
2. date of birth;
3. reason for and date of entry into the koseki register;
4. *uji* family name of the individual's blood parents and place in the sibling order among children of those parents;
5. in the case of adoption, the family name of the adoptive parents and the place in the sibling order among children of those adoptive parents;
6. a record identifying the husband and the wife;
7. in the case of a person entered from a different koseki register record, the indicative information from that record; and
8. additional material as officially instructed.

Individuals are, of course, involved in an infinite number of family relationships as, for example, husbands and wives or adopted children, and each is recorded in its own way in the koseki registration system. Among the factors that might be included in point eight above, to be examined later in conjunction with point three and point seven, are matters for registration that are indispensable in terms of the family lineage function of the koseki registration system. We should, furthermore, clarify the meaning of the 'indicative information' from another koseki register referred to in point seven. Article 9 of the Koseki Registration Law stipulates the koseki register record shall be referred to by means of the name and *honseki* address of the person entered as the head of the register record. This official index is the mark or stamp of the governance authority that administers the koseki register in question. Since the person 'responsible for maintaining the koseki register record' is 'the individual whose name is listed first on that record', the family name and *honseki* address of this person are used as the 'indicative information' of the record in question.

In the pre-war era, koseki register information was not confined to the matters listed above, and included occupation or bureaucratic rank, status (e.g. commoner or peer), and even religious affiliation such as the Shinto shrine of the *ujigami* (local tutelary god) and the Buddhist temple parish to which those registered belonged. This deviation from the base legal aim of registering the identity of an individual was a carry-over from the fact that the so-called Jinshin koseki registration system – the Meiji era progenitor of the modern koseki registration system – was instituted as a population and household survey with a policing and surveillance function.

There is, nonetheless, no record in the pre-war koseki registration system of matters such as an individual's actual address or the names of those who share that address. Since the koseki register record ultimately was and continues to be a record of identity, residential address became the domain of the resident register. As discussed in Chapter Three, both Edo era family registers and the Jinshin koseki registration system of the early Meiji era recorded the residential address of the family and thus also operated as records of residence. With the compilation of the Meiji Civil Code, however, the koseki registration system was modified to become a record of identity in terms of one's position in the *ie* family. This was in accordance with the Code's stipulation of the importance of *ie* family grouping.

In a ruling handed down on 29 June 1932 by the Great Court of Cassation – the pre-war equivalent of the Supreme Court – the Japanese state declared that information recorded in a koseki register 'was assumed, in the absence of exceptional circumstances, *to accord with fact*' (emphasis added).[1] That is to say, the state accorded a 'truth' value to information recorded in the koseki registration system in terms of its role in publicly confirming the identity of an individual. Significant here is not the fact that the information in the register was necessarily an actual record of the 'truth', but that it was accepted as such. In this sense, it is perhaps no exaggeration to conclude that the koseki registration system constructed the 'truth'. This point, above all, reveals the manner in which the individual is largely powerless against the social control inherent in the workings of the koseki system.

The cross-referencing function of the koseki registration system

Given that life events such as marriage or adoption often require transfer from one koseki register record to another, it is extremely uncommon for a person to have the documentation of their identity confined to one record from birth to death. For example, newly married persons are removed from their previous record whereupon, as a couple, they create and have their details entered into a new koseki register record based on a mutually agreed-upon *honseki* address. Similarly, adopted children are transferred from their birth parents' koseki register record and entered into that of the adoptive parents. Furthermore, a child who has reached the age of majority can create a *bunseki* – branch family koseki register record – by declaring independence from the parental record and creating a new family group in which their new self assumes responsibility for maintaining the record. Changes of this nature are associated with the 'one family, one record' principle which defines the koseki register record as an entity comprised fundamentally of a married couple and their unmarried children.

The koseki registration system ensures ease of administration for the authorities of the various government policies built around the fundamental unit of the 'family' as listed in any given koseki register record. Over and above this, however, in the context of an individual's identity record, the state has equipped the system to be a multi-dimensional mechanism of control which, on the one hand, must include information transferred from previous koseki register records and which, on the other, requires the documentation of information relating to the current family grouping. This is referred to as the cross-referencing function of the koseki registration system.

To explain the meaning of this cross-referencing function we might consider the fact that following the death of an individual or the transfer of a child's registration at the time of adoption, the name of the person concerned is removed from the koseki register record on which she or he was originally entered. If the removal of every member of a given record occurs in this way, the record becomes inactive and is deleted from a governing authority's koseki register – the collection of all koseki register records that fall under that authority's jurisdiction – and transferred to an 'inactive koseki register record' (*josekibo*). With the transfer of an individual's details between koseki register records as outlined above, the records into which the person had previously been entered and that into which they are currently entered become linked in a way that permits the two to be mutually searched or referred to. In other words, cross-referencing between these two koseki register records is facilitated. This is because the old record documents the new information, such as current *honseki* address, while the new record lists the old information, such as previous *honseki* address. Furthermore, even if the old record is declared inactive, a 6 May 2010 Ministry of Justice directive saw the preservation period of inactive koseki register records extended from eighty to 150 years.

With effective use of this cross-referencing function of the koseki registration system, it is possible to go back in time from current koseki register records to the Jinshin koseki register records of the early Meiji era. At the time of the 1948 implementation of the current form of the Koseki Registration Law, Article 128 of that law supported the efficiency inherent in rolling over to the new post-war registration system the information contained in koseki register records compiled through the provisions of the pre-war Koseki Registration Law (Law 26, 1914). As a result, the new post-war records were built from, and thus reconfirmed the authority of, the information, including the *honseki* address, entered into pre-war koseki register records.[2] It is therefore currently possible to search a post-war koseki register record as a means of inquiring about the origins of a family back to the Taishō or even Meiji eras.

Hiraga Kenta (1912–2004), a Ministry of Justice bureaucrat who played a key role in the post-war revision of the Koseki Registration Law, proposed 'family lineage structure' as the special characteristic of koseki registration'.[3] This characteristic, he argued, emphasised the maintenance of the records of a family unit rather than an individual, and ensured the provision of a collective statement, rather than a mere list of life events, of every significant event in the life of a person between, and including, birth and death. Essentially, this 'family lineage structure' permits chronological knowledge of individual changes of identity and family relationships, thus providing a dimension of administrative convenience that is lacking in Western-style identity systems organised around the record of an individual.

Of course, rather than exemplifying a system that responds to the daily needs or interests of the people, the notion of 'one family, one record' that underpins the koseki registration system functions to enhance the surveillance power of the state and the effective management of individuals. This construction of people as '*ie* family members' rather than 'individuals' is a process that accompanies the compilation of a single chronological record of the identity changes that occur throughout an individual's life and is an essential feature that has permeated the modern koseki registration system through to the present day.

The singular quality of 'relationship connections'

There are surely few who could immediately explain the meaning of the term '*tsuzukigara*', or 'relationship connection'. In the koseki registration context, this term expresses the relationship between the individuals entered into the koseki register record and the person who compiles and maintains the record, where children are ranked in order of birth, for example, as eldest son/eldest daughter or second son/second daughter. Because the Meiji era Jinshin koseki registration system recorded the relationship between each person recorded and the *koshu* (legal household head), the idea of the 'relationship connection' to the legal household head took hold as the key determinant of an individual's significance in Japanese society. The notion of 'relationship connection' applies not only to koseki registration, but also to the certificate of residence and the national census (although, unlike the koseki system, in each of the latter the relationship is with the head of the residential rather than *honseki* address).

This notion of 'relationship connection' demonstrates the actual power that the koseki registration system exerts over the individual. First, as noted above, there is the matter of sibling or family position ranking. Also central is the discrimination that has been exerted against the so-called 'illegitimate' children born to a man and woman who are not legally married. The legal discrimination experienced by these children was evident in Article 900, Clause 4 of the Meiji Civil Code, which stipulated that 'illegitimate' children receive only half of the share of inheritance of their 'legitimate' siblings. Supporting the operation of this sort of socially prejudiced administrative process assisted the state, also seeking to accurately gauge the identity relationships of the individual in question, to hinder the likelihood of 'illegitimate' birth by inducing in the people a desire for 'right and proper marriage'. The display in the koseki registration system of the distinction between the 'legitimate' and 'illegitimate' child fomented a social consciousness that regarded failure to enter into a legal marriage as a form of social deviance.

The pre-war koseki registration system had two classifications for a child born to parents who were not legally married. A child whom the father refused to acknowledge was recorded as a '*shiseishi*' – loosely meaning 'a child born independently', in other words 'a child without male lineage connections'. A child born to unmarried parents but whom the father acknowledged was entered, with the father's permission, into the paternal koseki register record as a '*shoshi*', loosely meaning 'a commoner child'. The relationship connection entered into a koseki register record in the case of these children was either 'a male/female child born independently' or 'a male/female commoner child'. Thus, a quick glance at the koseki register record, which, like the birth report lodgement (*shusshō todoke*), identified the individual concerned as either 'without male lineage connections' or as 'a commoner child', made it possible to investigate 'legitimacy' in a way that reproduced social discrimination in matters such as marriage and employment.

In a 10 February 1942 revision to the Civil Code (1942, Law No. 7), the Ministry of Justice conceded that society 'must eradicate as far as possible the unjustified prejudicial attitudes towards, and discriminatory treatment of, "children born without male lineage"'.[4] Accordingly, the expression, 'commoner child or child born independently' became 'child not of a legal marriage', while 'child born independently' merely became 'child'. For example, Article 735, Clause 1 of the Civil Code, which read, '*A commoner child or child born independently* to a family cannot be given entry to that family without the agreement of the family head', was revised to read '*the child not of a legal marriage* to a family [...]' (emphasis added). As a result, any overt wording indicating that 'a child was without male lineage' was largely removed from legislative and regulatory systems related to the Civil Code, including the koseki registration system. With the 1948 enactment of the new post-war Civil Code, the term 'commoner child' was also excised from legal documents.

In the koseki registration context, however, problems remained for a child whose parents were not legally married. While children of a legal marriage were recorded by rank such as 'eldest son' or 'eldest daughter', children whose parents were not married were immediately identifiable by being recorded merely as either 'son' or 'daughter'.[5] Thus, through no fault of their own, children born to an unmarried mother and father were subject to legal and social discrimination. This situation persisted until November 2004 when amendments to Koseki Registration Law regulations stipulated that all children, regardless of parental marriage status, were to be listed according to sibling rank.

The initial justification for providing sibling relationship information in the koseki registration system was the need to determine *ie* family headship succession. First in line in this respect was the eldest son, followed by the second son, third son and so on. Since the notion of the legal household head was abolished in the post-war era, children should have been given parity in terms of property inheritance and maintenance obligations. Nevertheless, it is clear from everyday expressions such as 'she's married to the eldest son', or 'he's their second son', that sibling rank consciousness related to the old concept of relationship connection (*tsuzukigara*) lingers as a vestige of the putatively defunct *ie* family system.

The meaning of *honseki* address

In everyday life, people rarely consider the notion of *honseki* address. In addition to noting this on a résumé, providing one's *honseki* address is largely necessary only when applying for a passport or requesting a copy or short form extract of a koseki register entry. Given this limited everyday purpose, there are few people who can quote down to the apartment or street number their own *honseki* address.

Although a standard administrative unit of the koseki registration system, the *honseki* address has no other function than to act as the theoretical family location given in koseki register documentation. Since all those entered on a common koseki register record must share the same *honseki* address, this does not need to be either a particular individual's actual address or place of birth. In other words, it is an ideal address unrelated to the daily life of either the registered family or particular individuals in that family and does not imply communal living.

Koseki registration administration is one of a number of 'legally entrusted administrative matters' for which the central state delegates its substantive responsibility to local government. Local government, in turn, administers the Koseki Registration Law and regulations under the direction of the central state. The fact that it is the municipal authority within whose jurisdiction the *honseki* address is located that processes requests for copies or short form extracts creates the somewhat anomalous situation of the koseki register record generally being administered at a site that has almost no connection to the daily lives of those entered into it.

The notion of the significance of the *honseki* address for governing authorities has operated since the Meiji era. Once a family head nominated a *honseki* address, searching a koseki register for a particular *honseki* address and particular legal household head permitted access to the full range of family matters entered into the relevant record. Thus, in the past, as in the current day, the effective function of the *honseki* address was at best to supplement the cross-referencing function of the koseki registration system.

As long as the *honseki* address lies within a territory under Japanese jurisdiction, the person compiling the koseki register record can arbitrarily choose any place for this purpose, even one without direct personal connection. Permission has been given for certain families to record the Imperial Palace or the summit of Mt Fuji as their *honseki* address, while there is political efficacy, in terms of seeming to confirm Japanese ownership, in nominating a site of disputed governance such as the Senkaku Islands, Takeshima Island or the Northern Territories. Significant also in this respect is the fact that, since imperial subjects during the time of the 'Greater

Japanese Empire' were forbidden to move their *honseki* addresses between mainland Japan and its colonial holdings, this item became a means of distinguishing between the 'Japanese' and those born in the colonies based on ethnicity (see Chapter Four for further details).

Although, theoretically, at the time of the operation of the Jinshin koseki registration system one could freely nominate any *honseki* address, the choice advocated by the state as the ideal was a place with 'historical connection [to the applicant] such as the land where one was first bathed at birth or the *honseki* address of one's ancestors'.[6] In other words, people were officially urged either to maintain ties to the family line or to choose a place of life significance. Contrary to this, however, 'in an age during which there was a distinct social advantage to being born in Yamaguchi Prefecture, the homeland of many socially powerful figures, freedom of [*honseki*] choice led people from as far away as Ōshū (in present-day Iwate Prefecture) to transfer their koseki registration to Yamaguchi and to claim ties to that area'.[7] In the autocratic Meiji political landscape, dominated by the feudal cliques of the Edo era, enormous social advantage accrued to those from Yamaguchi – previously the Chōshū Domain. It was therefore not uncommon to find examples of people who nominated a place in that area as their *honseki* address. Here we see a clear slippage between traditional ideals as promoted by the system and the calculations and desires of the common people.

During the time of the Jinshin koseki registration system, authorities sought to curtail the mobility of the people. Thus, residential address was a significant item entered into that register. This suggested that, superficially at least, residential address equalled *honseki* address. However, as early as March 1873, Sugi Kyōji (1828–1917), the so-called father of statistical studies in Japan, noted in a proposal forwarded to the government that the Jinshin koseki system was overly complicated. Sugi argued that, since the primary mission of this register was to survey the 'continuation of families through the line of the father', the information gathered was of limited statistical significance. He urged reform of the koseki system so that, instead of merely recording family details, the information gathered would include practical statistical matters such as population, number of households and occupations.[8] In Sugi's opinion, a koseki register record that was organised around a *honseki* address could not adequately function as a source of population statistics (that is, as a census). He thus appealed for such information to be compiled separate from the koseki registration system.

By the time of the original 1890 version of the Meiji Civil Code (see Chapter Two for further information), however, acceptance of the fact that the *honseki* address was not necessarily the residential address was inferred in Article 266 of that Code, which stipulated, 'when the *honseki* address differs from the principle place of residence, this latter can be the address provided'. Even so, the so-called Meiji 31 Form koseki registration system clarified the doctrine of constructing the register with the *honseki* address as the document's fundamental address (see Chapter Three for further details). With the class divisions that accompanied post-Russo-Japanese War (1904–5) industrialisation, however, the population drift to urban areas became more pronounced. Faced with the reality of an increasing incongruity between the *honseki* and residential address, the Ministry of Justice had no option but to rule in 1916 that it was not necessary for the *honseki* to accord with the residential address.[9]

In order to also provide a record of population mobility, authorities introduced 'the temporary residence (*kiryū*) system' which supplemented the management function of the koseki registration system. 'Temporary residence' here referred to an address that, for a fixed period of time, was not the same as the *honseki*. The promulgation of the Temporary Residence Law (*Kiryū-hō*, 1914, Law No. 27), which stipulated that the temporary address must not be the same as the *honseki*, accompanied March 1914 revisions to the Koseki Registration Law. This required the registration on a 'temporary residents roll' of all people without a current *honseki* address, all whose *honseki* address was unknown and all foreigners who lived at a specific address for more than ninety days.

While the format has changed, the idea behind this temporary residents roll has been handed down to the present day in the form of the current residential registration system, which requires that each change of address by persons listed in a koseki register record be separately documented on an appendix attached to the record. This has created a mechanism that couples koseki registration with the resident certificate to facilitate knowledge of the residential circumstances of the person concerned.

Information lodgement as enforcement: Koseki as proof of existence

The power of koseki registration lies in the fact that it is structured to work against the individualisation of identity. According to the Koseki Registration Law, upon the advent of any event that leads to a change of identity, such as birth, death, marriage, divorce or adoption, the person involved is obliged to lodge notification of this event within a stipulated timeframe with the local municipal office. The lodgement process as stipulated in the Koseki Registration Law is essentially divided into two components: (A) the lodging of information that has previously been officially recorded, known as the information lodgement process, and (B) the initial lodging of information which then comes into legal effect, known as the establishment lodgement process.

Included in category (A) are matters regarded largely as objective fact, such as birth and death details, but also those that require approval or determination by legal or other official processes. This includes change of *uji* family name, naturalisation, being granted or stripped of citizenship, divorce that involves a court order, disappearance and a process known as *shūseki* – the creation of a new koseki register record for those without prior registration (see below). In the pre-war Koseki Registration Law this also included family headship succession, the creation of a new *ie* family, the succession or bestowal of a peerage and loss of social rank. Included in (B), on the other hand, are marriage, divorce by mutual consent, adoption, the dissolution of adoption, acknowledgement by a father of a child born to unmarried parents, entry into a koseki register record, transfer of *honseki* and the creation of a family branch record.

Since the processes designated in (A) are compulsory, both the lodgement period and the person responsible for lodgement are stipulated, with failure to comply incurring a fine. In contrast, (B) involves lodgement by choice and there are no provisions regarding the lodgement period or other conditions.

The lodgement process as stipulated in the Koseki Registration Law has two aspects, depending on whether an individual holds Japanese citizenship or resides in territory governed by Japan. An entry in a koseki register record must be compiled for every Japanese national. Thus, any event denoting a Japanese person's change of identity, such as birth, death or marriage, is subject to the lodgement process. Even if residing overseas, a Japanese person has an obligation to lodge the information at an overseas government office.

This principle is complemented by the notion that all people residing in a jurisdiction that is subject to the Koseki Registration Law have a legal obligation to lodge information relating to a change in identity status. The Koseki Registration Law does not apply to foreigners who are resident in Japan. Nevertheless, these foreigners are subject to the same legal conditions as Japanese nationals regarding changes of identity and therefore must lodge notification of matters such as the birth of a child or a death with the local municipal office. As long ago as August 1899, the Ministry of Justice issued a ruling which stated, 'When lodging a marriage notice, a foreigner must comply with the stipulations of the Koseki Registration Law and have this recorded on the identity register. Regardless of the difficulties involved, all foreigners should, moreover, lodge for registration other information required by law, such as the birth of a child or a death'.[10]

It is thus apparent that the principle of lodgement (*todokede shugi*) of individual identity changes permeates the Koseki Registration Law. Furthermore, once ratified by a municipal office, the information lodged comes into legal effect. With confirmation of its legal validity, even without entry into a koseki register record, there is no means by which such information can be withdrawn or revoked.[11] With the division of lodged information into the distinct categories of 'new' or 'previously documented', once information is lodged it attains the same status as an entry in a koseki register record from a legal perspective.

The principle of lodgement in the koseki registration system outlined above arises from the assumption that, out of necessity, all 'Japanese' hold koseki registration. What, then, happens in the case of a person who is not entered into a koseki register record? With the expectation that every person in Japan has an entry in a koseki register record, authorities have long been eager to capture the details of unregistered persons or those with an unclear *honseki* address.[12] Lack of clarity around *honseki* address was in the past not unusual in occupations such as day labourer or itinerant entertainer, where mobility was the norm. The process of newly creating a koseki register record for those without such record or for whom the *honseki* address is unclear is known as *shūseki*. Article 110, Clause 1 of the Koseki Registration Law stipulates, 'Within ten days of receipt of approval from the Family Court, a person who is not entered into a koseki register record may lodge a notice of intent to create a new koseki register record'. Once this intent to create is approved by the Family Court, an application for the creation of a new record can be lodged with the office of the municipality that administers the area within which the *honseki* address is located. Permission from the Family Court, however, does not make the application process obligatory. Accordingly, in spite of a person being Japanese there is no legal sanction if an unregistered person fails to apply to create a new koseki register record.[13] However, in response to a question from a presiding judge of the Shimonoseki District Court, in April 1921 the Ministry of Justice declared, 'when the *honseki* address is unclear, there is an obligation to apply for the creation of a new koseki register record'.[14] This plainly suggests that 'guidance' insisting upon participation in the koseki human management system was given to unregistered individuals. Nevertheless, application for the creation of a new koseki register record is ultimately the choice of the individual.

Rather than exercising concrete force, however, the state has taken the subtler step of creating social norms to ensure voluntary submission to this system based on the lodgement and entry of information into a koseki register. Specifically, the state has instilled everyday internal compliance by creating the understanding that failure to lodge material into a koseki register record results in a person lacking the necessary documentation to verify their existence as a Japanese. In this way, the state ascribes a moral function to lodgement and koseki registration.

As noted above, the actual everyday life occasions in which it is necessary to provide proof of koseki registration are few. However, the state has generated the consciousness that to dismiss the axiomatic truth of the necessity of registration is to have one's family regarded by society as 'improper' or 'illegitimate'. Rather than practical appeal or self-directed moral motives, it was a set of external standards that impelled the people to take out koseki registration. In this way, the power of the koseki registration system extended psychological force over the individual.

Koseki registration as surveillance

Range of individual information entered into a koseki register

Authorities often advocate for the logic and convenience of compiling a koseki register record as a family unit in terms of the fact that the wide range of information included about a family on any given record can be accessed at one time and in one location. This is the previously mentioned 'cross-referencing function'.

However, the record may contain information that some people do not wish to be publically accessible. This could include matters relating to divorce history, adoption or naturalisation. It might also relate to information from the pre-war koseki registration system, such as social status, or information that is no longer required on contemporary koseki register records, such as information related to a 'child without male lineage' or 'commoner child'. It is obvious that unlimited public access to information of this nature would be a serious violation of an individual's human rights.

The likelihood of this violation of rights is exacerbated by Article 39 of the Koseki Register Implementation Regulations, which stipulates that matters recorded in an old record must be carried across and recorded again during the compilation of a new koseki register record (this is referred to as 'item transference'). For example, it is stipulated that a person lodging notification of change of gender as the result of a sex change, and who leaves an old koseki register record to compile one anew, must document the change of sex on the new record. It is thus immediately apparent that this person was either 'formerly male' or 'formerly female' (for further information, see the first part of Chapter Six). We might regard the fact that, even if one begins a new koseki register record, prior surveillance continues as a 'special characteristic' of the koseki system.

There are other risks inherent in the information collection function of the koseki registration system. For example, the damage arising from mistaken entry or forgery of an individual's details on the register can impact on a wide range of people. As a corollary, when a record is lost in a disaster, it represents the loss of a massive information bank on an entire family. During the Second World War, aerial bombing by the United States Armed Forces over cities ranging from Tokyo to Okinawa saw koseki registers burnt to ash and scattered on the winds. According to official accounts, 357,081 koseki register records from 122 municipalities and 117,865 inactive koseki register records from 2,811 municipalities were destroyed.[15] In the chaos that ensued, there were many reported cases of identity theft in which one person appropriated the koseki register details of another and established themselves as that person. The blighted protagonist of the 1960 novel *Suna no Utsuwa* (lit. Container of

Sand, translated as *Castle of Sand* for the 1974 film adaptation) by crime writer Matsumoto Seichō (1909–1992), for example, takes advantage of the ruined post-war landscape to change his fortune and rise successfully in society by assuming the koseki identity of another.

Information captured in the koseki registration system covers a broad time span. Following the original compilation of a koseki register record, revisions to the Koseki Registration Law or associated regulations and ordinances result in format and style changes to the original record. Once these format changes occur, the old version is no longer used and assumes the status of 'revised koseki original'. In 1886, the Jinshin koseki registration system underwent large-scale revisions and was compiled in a new form (known as the Meiji 19 Form koseki registration system). At the time it was stipulated that, as the 'revised koseki original' for the new system, the Jinshin koseki registration system be preserved for a minimum of fifty years. However, since the Jinshin koseki registration system became the Meiji 19 Form koseki registration system, which in turn became the Meiji 31 Form koseki registration system, certain information that impacted strongly on koseki registration practice was retained in each version.[16] From that time, the absence of a truly comprehensive revision of the original Jinshin koseki registration system resulted in the continued use of discriminatory information in terms of matters such as social status and previous criminal record. This carried through in some cases into the Taishō or even Shōwa eras. As will be explained below, since in the past this material was available for public viewing, it long operated to incite social discrimination.

Background checks through koseki registration

The Jinshin koseki registration system content was markedly skewed towards a policing function, with emphasis on information relating to background checks. This included contemporary social class, such as commoner (*heimin*), peer or descendant of samurai (*shizoku*), and criminal record (for further information, see Chapter Three). Even after the Jinshin revisions, a column remained to indicate a person's commoner, peer or samurai status, or, in the case of those with a '*hisabetsu buraku*' background, to record a person as 'former Eta' or 'new commoner'.

However, with the post-First World War winds of 'Taishō democracy' championing greater individual equality and freedom, and the gathering of momentum of the Burakumin Liberation Movement through the efforts of the *Zenkoku Suiheisha* (National Leveller's Society, formed in 1922), trenchant criticism was directed towards the innately discriminatory nature of the koseki registration system. In response to such campaigns, March 1924 revisions to the Koseki Registration Law (1924, Law No. 26), stipulated that a koseki register entry regarding social status be made only in cases where the legal household head and her or his family had samurai or peer ancestry. In the case of a family holding a different rank to the legal household head, however, family rank was also to be entered, making the 1924 revisions completely inadequate as a means of abolishing discrimination. In response to this problem, Hiranuma Ki'ichirō (1867–1952), Chair of the Privy Council who also chaired the group known as the Central Society of Reconciliation, presented a 'Petition Concerning Names of Social Rank' to the Minister of Colonial Affairs. Advocating reconciliation, that is, social harmony, as a plank of the National Spiritual Mobilisation Movement in preparation for total war, Hiranuma acknowledged that the record of social status in various official documents was based on simple convention. He argued, nonetheless, that there was currently no particular benefit to this practice and that, in fact, it presented a not inconsiderable impediment to the promotion of social harmony. He therefore requested that the recording of such information in official documentation be abolished.[17] Upon receipt of this request, the Ministry of Justice duly rescinded the need to enter social rank into transcribed copies of koseki register records.

However, the elimination of discrimination from a system does not necessarily translate into the practice of everyday life. Social rank remained on the original record and on other previous koseki register records, with people continuing to note this information when submitting official documentation or even when compiling personal materials such as résumés or koseki register lodgement notices. Only when the post-war Constitution, which repudiated any system of social rank, brought an end to the need to enter information of this nature in any form into koseki registers did this product of the strict social hierarchy of the feudal era largely disappear from public and private documentation.

Table 1.1: Rescindment history relating to koseki register record transcriptions or short form extract privacy concerns

Issue	Rescindment details
Social rank	
Commoner	29 June 1938, Civil Matter No. 746, response by Director of Ministry of Justice Civil Affairs Bureau
Peer, samurai ancestor	16 April 1947, Civil Matter No. 317, directive by Director of Ministry of Justice Civil Affairs Bureau
The expressions 'child born independently' and 'commoner child'	18 February 1942, Civil Matter No. 90, notice by Director of Ministry of Justice Civil Affairs Bureau
The expression 'foundling', i.e. abandoned child	22 September 1928, Civil Matter No. 10395, response by Director of Ministry of Justice Civil Affairs Bureau
The name of the institution in the case of birth or death in either a public or private health facility or hospital	5 June 1941, Civil Matter No. 547, notice by Director of Ministry of Justice Civil Affairs Bureau, and 22 July 1941, Civil Matter No. 708, response by Director of Ministry of Justice Civil Affairs Bureau
The name of the institution in the case of either birth or death in prison; the occupation or bureaucratic rank of a person either lodging information or making a report	26 November 1926, Civil Matter No. 8120, notice by Director of Ministry of Justice Civil Affairs Bureau
Matters relating to crime	8/9 August 1963, resolution of joint Koseki Register Administration and Koseki Register Deliberative Committees, Gifu Prefecture

As apparent from Table 1.1, the pre-war koseki registration system required the provision of a wide range of background check-type information completely unrelated to identity verification. Typical was a person's criminal record, which appeared both on koseki register record transcriptions and in short form extracts, while birth or death in prison was noted down to the detail of the prison address, including the chief warden's name. Also recorded were loss of social rank and the deprivation of inheritance rights in the event of the imposition of the death penalty.[18] The practice of recording criminal records on koseki register record transcripts was not revoked until 1963.

The issue of criminality was further entrenched by a 12 April 1917 directive that ordered the heads of municipal authorities to compile a 'criminal roll' of people whose *honseki* address fell within a relevant municipality's jurisdiction. This roll was to be based on reports from the courts, the prosecutor's office, the military court-martial office and information from other municipal heads. Any registration transfer by a person on the roll was to be reported to the head of the municipality to which the individual in question relocated.[19] The municipal head was also obliged to compile a roll of itinerant criminals, that is, those not resident in the place of their *honseki* address, who were currently in that head's jurisdiction.[20] Since, as discussed in Chapter Four, people born in the colonies were not permitted to nominate a *honseki* address in mainland Japan, they were treated on the mainland as itinerant. Thus, the criminal record of a colonial-born subject became known on the mainland also. In addition to being used by police, prosecutors, courts and municipal authorities, these criminal rolls were used by corporations and detective agencies in marriage and employment background checks. In other words, the mediation of the koseki registration system created a social network by means of which those with a criminal record were subject to constant surveillance.

Recognition of the problem of public access to koseki registers

In spite of koseki register records being an accumulation of what might be termed 'excess information' concerning an individual, the right of public access to the system long remained intact, with unlimited access by the average person becoming an accepted element of the system. Public accessibility to the identity matters documented in a koseki register record provided information to third parties concerning proof of family relationships and proof of Japanese citizenship. The records also provided information employed in the drawing up of certificates of residence and statistics relating to population shift. As a result, public access to koseki register records became accepted practice and those included in the records conceded the right for their information to be used in this way.[21]

Historically, the first formal legal statement regarding koseki register records as publically accessible documents appeared in Meiji 31 (1898), when Article 13 of the Meiji 31 Koseki Registration Law declared, 'All persons, upon lodging the required fee, are able to view or request to be issued with either a copy or short form extract of the information recorded in a register entry'. The general application of this article also set in place the idea of public access to later forms of the koseki registration system.

While there are no legal notes explaining the position taken on public access appended to the Meiji 31 Koseki Registration Law, Article 11 of an earlier Ministry of Home Affairs 'Draft of the Koseki Registration Law', presented in 1890 to the first sitting of the Imperial Diet, stated, 'All individuals, upon lodging the necessary fee, can request to search or examine a koseki register record or a copy thereof'. Despite the fact that the draft never became law, this was the first hint that public access to koseki register records might eventually be systematised. Official explanatory notes relating to Article 11 of the Ministry draft argued for the necessity of public access to koseki registers. Those notes pointed out that, when entering into a contract, it was generally necessary to confirm the other party's current identity, including whether or not she or he was of age, was already married, or, indeed, was dead or alive. It was therefore, the explanatory notes declared, 'necessary to make *publicly available the document of records, that is, the koseki register*, which contains such matters related to identity, and furthermore *to let each person view these*' (emphasis added). This argument clearly carried weight with lawmakers and perhaps also explains the inclusion of the principle of public access in the later Meiji 31 Koseki Registration Law. Certainly, with the enactment of that legislation, the notion of koseki registers as publically accessible became inscribed in legal practice.[22]

Public access rights saw police agencies and prosecutors use the koseki register record of an individual in a manner conducive to maintaining social control and public security. Eager to ensure the thorough democratisation of Japan, Occupation authorities initially opposed public access to koseki register records on privacy grounds. In the final instance, however, the GHQ did not obstruct Koseki Registration Law revisions that sought to maintain or even strengthen the data collection and information provision functions of the koseki registration system.[23] As a result, Article 10 of the December 1947 Koseki Registration Law repeated the by now familiar statement that any person, upon paying the necessary fee, could view a koseki register record or request a copy of, or short form extract from, a record. In this way, the pre-war practice of public access persisted.

Although clearly violating privacy rights, there was widespread abuse of the right of public access to koseki registers even under the mantle of post-war democracy. This led to the constant undermining of the new Constitution by blatant acts of discrimination arising from the use of koseki register searches for employment and marriage background checks. According to Wada Mikihiko (b. 1957), distinguishing features of the *ie* family system were inextricably linked to both the compulsory declaration of data and public access to koseki register records. Thus, 'while erased in name, the *ie* family system very much remained in practice'.[24]

However, an increasingly mature human rights consciousness accelerated moves to demand limits to koseki register access. Accordingly, 1968 saw prohibitions on the viewing of Meiji era Jinshin koseki register records, while 1976 revisions to the Koseki Registration Law banned open access to both koseki register records and inactive koseki register records (although it was acknowledged that viewing them may be necessary for employment purposes). Justification was required when making a request for a full copy of or extract from a record and, if clearly unreasonable, such a request could be denied. The assessment criteria, however, were never clearly elaborated and since, as already stated, it was the practice in Japanese society to accord a priceless value to the koseki register record as a tool for investigating identity, it was difficult to fully bring to an end the unjust use of register information. Nevertheless, the notion of privacy as a basic human right developed and, following the enactment of the 2003 Personal Information Protection Law, the Koseki Registration Law revisions of May 2008 enshrined the private nature of koseki register records. Strict regulation of the issue of both copies and short form extracts ensued, and it became mandatory even for legal practitioners to document details of requests for koseki register information. To guard against false lodgement or the lodgement of fraudulent information, proof of identity became mandatory when submitting koseki register information.

These privacy reforms were nonetheless incompatible with the role played over many long years by the koseki registration system as an identity check apparatus. It proved challenging, therefore, to discourage people from the past practice of deploying register records to probe the background of a third party and thereby to 'expose hidden secrets'. Ultimately, the deeply rooted nature of this desire related directly to the fact that koseki registers provided an unnecessarily detailed record of individual information that far exceeded the function of identity systems in Europe or the United States. In the absence of reforms to the volume and type of information recorded, we must question whether the Japanese people's understanding of legal matters and human rights is sufficient to prevent koseki register abuse. Put another way, we might express concern regarding the level of maturity of Japanese democracy.

Significance of the *uji* family name in a koseki record

Whose name is the *uji* family name?

All people have their own name by means of which identity is clearly established in relation to others. Nevertheless, as demonstrated by the impact of legally changing one's name, we should not think that the Japanese *uji* family name is simply the name of an individual. The Koseki Registration Law stipulates that any change in *uji* family name generates koseki register record construction, entry or excision. In other words, a change in the *uji* family name is linked to some change to koseki registration. This intimate relationship between the koseki registration system and family name is the source of both the previously mentioned cross-referencing function and the genealogical structure of a koseki register record.

If the *uji* family name was essentially the name of an individual person, there would be a concomitant recognition of the right of the individual to select the *uji* family name as an arbitrary choice. However, this name is designated at birth from the *uji* family name of either the child's father or mother, with no option to freely change. Any change that does occur arises from a change in relationship between a husband and wife (such as marriage or divorce), or a change in relationship between a parent and a child (in cases such as adoption). There is also scope in Article 19 of the Koseki Registration Law for an individual to return to the use of the former *uji* family name following divorce. In other words, both the acquisition and change of an individual family name is confined to the types of koseki register record changes that mark relationship changes between a husband and wife or parent and child. From this it is clear that the *uji* family name is the ultimate unit around which the koseki registration system is organised. Thus, while there is a veritable galaxy of families with names such as Satō, Suzuki or Tanaka, and while these names might sound the same or might even be transcribed using the same characters, they most definitely are not the names of the same family.

Inherent in the notion of '*uji* family name' is the idea of 'family line'. Unlike one's given name, the essential character of the family name is determined by an objective set of facts unrelated to individual intent. The family name, however, is not merely a technical unit of koseki register record organisation. Because the unified identity suggested by the *uji* family name as inscribed in a koseki register record creates a sense of the family as bonded over and above any individual, these names evoke attachment to and nostalgia for the *ie* family. This, we might argue, is a key factor in the persistence of the *ie* family tradition in Japanese society.

From surname to family name and individual name to family name

Do the terms 'surname' (*myōji*) and 'family name' (*uji*) refer to the same thing? It is common for people to inquire upon meeting for the first time, 'What is your surname?' Yet, it is not that unusual to ask, 'What is your family name?' In terms of civil law, as noted, *uji* is used to indicate the surname of an individual on official documentation.

The '*uji* family name' system operative in Japanese society today did not emerge without coercion. Rather, its use and meaning came about through submission to the power of the state and various state directives and exhortations. Amino Yoshihiko (1928–2004) pointed out that all subjects, from aristocrat to farmer, recorded a family name in the koseki registration system of the Ritsuryō State (seventh to tenth century), and it is likely that the very fact of registration gave the people of the time an opportunity to decide upon a name for their family or clan. The family or clan name (*kabane*) was seen as a gift from the Emperor, and during the Nara era imperial permission was required to change this name.[25] Since these family or clan names were regarded as bestowed by the Emperor on the people as a whole, the individual – including members of the imperial family – was an entity that, of itself, had neither family name nor clan name.

With the tenth century dissolution of the Ritsuryō system, the koseki registration system, too, all but ceased to function. At this time, the common people took the name of their place of residence as their surname, with clan names remaining in use only for samurai and court nobility. By the close of the medieval era, a marked distinction had developed between the social status of samurai and common people, and when the Tokugawa administration established the samurai/farmer/craftsman/merchant class system (*shi-nō-kō-shō*), openly taking a surname was forbidden for all except samurai. Along with the right to carry a sword, the use of a surname as a samurai privilege was a symbol of the feudal social order.

However, even within the context of the strict order of samurai society, there is no single narrative to Japanese surname history. Yanagita Kunio (1875–1963) argued that from medieval times when the main house of a family divided into several branches (under siblings, uncles or nephews), it was customary for these branches to retain the surname of the main house. This was the case following the division and conflict within the Uesugi family at the time of the Ōnin War (1467–1477). There were certainly those, however, who saw the monopoly of the surname as the privilege of the main family house. Thus, the Tokugawa Clan created new family names for the Owari, Kii, Mito (Gosanke) and Tayasu, Hitotsubashi and Shimizu (Gosankyō) branch families of the household, while the many branches of the old Matsudaira family retained a single name. It is evident that, even in the same clan-based society, contradictory positions coexisted. On the one hand, these called for restrictions on the use of a family name as a means of confirming the standing of the main house, while on the other hand there was support for common surnames for branch families as a means of broadcasting the strength of the 'power network' of the clan.[26]

The ban on commoner public use of surnames following the social divisions of the Tokugawa era, moreover, did not necessarily mean that these people did not have surnames. Certainly, depending on the domain, there were examples of rural villages that prohibited farmers from using surnames in order to clearly distinguish those of samurai rank. Nevertheless, the widespread nature of this practice even among the common people is evident in the use of surnames among groups that range from village officials to landless peasants found in Edo era census records and in records of temple contributions of the time.[27] In the face of these official prohibitions, moreover, many responded to professional necessity by using trade and stage names as individual surnames.

Advancing 'equality of the four social classes' (*shimin byōdō*) as a Restoration slogan, the new Meiji government approved the use of surnames by commoners in September 1870 (Meiji 3); and, in line with the 'rich country, strong army' objective of the nation-state, these newly 'permitted' surnames quickly became compulsory as a means of facilitating army service. On 14 January 1873, three years after the compilation of Jinshin koseki registers, the Army Ministry advised the Grand Council of State that 'Commoners from remote areas without a surname are a cause of great inconvenience when checking the military register'. With the compulsory use of surnames now a function of military need, the government lost no time through Decree 22 of the Grand Council of State, issued on 12 February of the same year, in making the use of a surname an obligation rather than a right.[28] Since koseki registers were the fundamental documents from which the army roll was compiled, surname use on koseki register records also became compulsory in order to identify young men of conscription age. In other words, the management of the individual through the surname was essential for the development and maintenance of the military mobilisation required by the nation-state.

It was common practice due to the necessities of daily life for people to leave their *ie* family and move to another place to make a living. Often, an individual would change their name in accordance with the changing circumstances of daily life. This led to inquiries to the Ministry of Home Affairs, which had carriage of koseki administration, about the sorts of names suitable for the register. On 3 May 1875, Tsuruga Prefecture (largely present-day Fukui Prefecture) forwarded an inquiry regarding the appropriate response in terms of koseki registration for a person who, lacking a trade or stage name, wanted to use the name of a profession as a surname and thus be known, for example, as Carpenter someone-or-other. The directive came that, while it was possible to use a professional name for individual purposes, it was compulsory to use an actual surname for koseki registration.[29] On 2 June 1875, moreover, the Ministry issued a directive declaring that change was prohibited once a surname was decided upon, regardless of the fact that the existence of multiple people in a local area with the 'same surname and same given name' might impede business transactions.[30]

This directive impacted on the case of a man who had left his family home in Niigata in order to undertake medical training and was now working in Okayama Prefecture. While training, the man began to use a name related to his occupation as a personal name. Following this, in accordance with the 1870 edict noted above, the man's parental household decided upon a family name that differed from the one the man had chosen for himself. On 1 May 1876, Niigata Prefecture sent an inquiry to the Ministry of Home Affairs to ask whether or not it might be possible for the man to continue using his name of choice as already recorded on his résumé and other documentation. In its reply of 9 May, the Ministry declared that the presence of different surnames on the same family register was not permitted and that the man would accordingly need to change his own name to that of the family.[31]

In this way, both the compulsory use of a surname and the fact that this surname needed to accord with the name of the *ko* (the household) and ultimately the *ie* (the family) transfigured the name of particular individuals into the *uji* family name of the koseki registration system. During the inseparable process of the standardisation of the *ie* family and the compilation and maintenance of the military service roll, the state inverted the nature of the surname. In other words, the average person was forced to take the koseki register family name, not for any purpose related to their daily life or even to any social activity, but in order to facilitate state management of the individual members of each and every household.

Same family name for husband/wife as a Meiji-state construct

There are many who believe that the use of the same *uji* family name by a husband and wife is a tradition passed down from old Japan. However, the 'same family name for married couples' principle was, in fact, an initiative of the Meiji state. Even following the Meiji insistence of a surname for common people, there was no immediate demand for married couples to use the same family name.

On 17 March 1876, a decree from the Grand Council of State declared, 'When a woman marries, she should retain her own family name. She will, however, take her husband's family name if necessary for the succession of his family'. Thus, even after entry into her husband's family, a woman of the time was required to preserve her old surname. The August 1877 Ehime Prefecture 'Guidelines for Additions and Deletions to Koseki Register Records' in fact forbade a married woman from changing her surname, even when entered into her husband's koseki register record. These guidelines noted, 'When marrying into another family, a woman will always enter [on that family's koseki register record] the family name of her parents'.[32] That such an idea prevailed a relatively short time before the promulgation of the Meiji Civil Code, which entrenched the *ie* family system, can be read as a means of distinguishing between the long-standing and newcomer occupants of the household. Given that the priority was for the family name to indicate the family line, it was necessary to permit even a husband and wife to have separate family names.

In a statement of opinion forwarded in 1878 to the Ministry of Home Affairs, Meiji era legislative bureaucrat Inoue Kowashi (1844–1895) stated, 'While there can be one koseki register record only per family, it is not necessary to have only one surname for each family household. [...] This is because the use of several surnames in one family is a social norm'. According to Inoue, the use of the koseki registration process to insist upon a single family name in a way that did not concur with social practice was a recipe for 'widespread chaos'.[33]

The opportunity for the codification of the 'one family name for a husband and wife' principle came with the compilation of the Meiji Civil Code. Article 243 of the original 1890 Code, which dealt with civil status, stated, 'The legal household head and family members will each be known by the *uji* family name of that household'. According to the explanatory notes made at the time of drafting, the requirement for all who were related to a legal household head, including those who had entered the household from other families, to use the same family name was in marked difference to past practice. The statement went on to declare, '*Uji* family name in the past was determined by lineage, so that even when marrying into the Taira Clan, a Minamoto woman retained her family name. This practice will no longer occur'. The role of the *uji* family name was now 'not merely to distinguish between family A and family B, but to ensure correct family lineage'.[34] Thus, rather than designating only the individual, the *uji* family name came to indicate the family to which the individual belonged.

This notion of shared *uji* family names for married couples was carried over during the 1898 compilation of the Meiji Civil Code. Article 746 of the Code entrenched the principle of 'one family, one *uji* family name' by stipulating that 'the legal household head and all its members will each be known by that household's *uji* family name'. In terms of koseki registration, the *ie* family principle that each person be attached to a single household insisted both on a person having an *uji* family name, and on having one family *uji* name only (the so-called 'one person, one *uji* family name doctrine'). This also applied when a person entered or left a family. Thus, the Code stipulated, 'When a woman marries, she enters the *ie* family of her husband' (Article 788, Clause 1) and 'A child enters the household of its father' (Article 733). Furthermore, any change of *uji* family name necessitated a change to the koseki register record. Accordingly, when a woman from family A became a wife in the household of family B, or when the son of family C became an adopted son in family B, both took the name of family B. Any individual changing their *uji* family name needed the approval of the legal household head.

There is no doubt that, throughout their life, the individual carried the burden of family responsibility through their family name. Even today, the notion of married couples having the same surname is justified on moral grounds and according to the need to maintain the 'integrity' of the marriage. However, since this so-called 'integrity' results in the submission of the woman's subjectivity to that of the man, we can only regard this practice as a reflection of the putatively defunct *ie* family system.

Survival of the *uji* family name under post-war democratisation

Claims are often made that the new Koseki Registration Law proclaimed in conjunction with the post-war abolition of the *ie* family system released the *uji* family name from the shackles of the old system and transformed it into the name of the individual. Given that the individual still lacks the right to freely choose their name, however, questions remain regarding the extent to which a clean break was made with the undemocratic pre-war *ie* family system.

If we examine post-war Civil Code reform, it becomes apparent that, with respect to *uji* family name, precedence was repeatedly given to the custom of the *ie* family system. In October 1946, the Civil Code Reform Draft Committee, which included Wagatsuma Sakae (1897–1973), presented its outline for legislative reform. This document stated, 'A husband and wife will both have the *uji* family name of the husband, except in the case of objection when both will take the wife's *uji* family name'.[35] This statement strongly profiled notions of male lineage by suggesting the use of the wife's name as an exception only. In the United States, choice of surname was at the discretion of the individual, and, when a draft bill based on the Committee's recommendations was drawn up for Civil Code reform, the GHQ looked to abolish notions of shared *uji* family names for husbands and wives on the grounds of women's rights. Thomas L. Blakemore (1915–1994), of the GHQ's Legal Division, annotated the draft with a comment declaring the need for freedom of surname and noting a preference for mutual choice by married couples of the use of either partner's family name. Following this recommendation, the Committee inserted the phrase 'in accordance with the decision made at the time of the marriage' into the draft.[36]

As a result, Article 750 of the 1947 new Civil Code stipulated, 'A husband and wife, in accordance with the decision made at the time of the marriage, shall use the *uji* family name of the husband or of the wife'. The decision for the *uji* family name of one to become the family name of both was to be made cooperatively, with the original holder of the chosen name becoming koseki register record head. This removal of the compulsory *uji* family name of the *ie* family system did bring a faint whiff of democratisation to the post-war koseki system. Nevertheless, given that in actual fact even under the new Koseki Registration Law a husband and wife and their unmarried children had to have the same *uji* family name, the principle of 'same household, same *uji* family name' remained essentially unchanged.

The extent to which the old *ie* family system continues to permeate koseki register practice and the use of family names in Japan denotes the unrelenting ascendency of male lineage. While the post-war Civil Code should have rung a deathknell for the *ie* family system, the continued use of the family name consolidated the distinguishing feature of that system in the new Code. Constitutional scholar Miyazawa Toshiyoshi (1899–1976) summed this up in the well-known saying, 'the *ie* may have vanished but the *uji* family name remains'.[37] By 'ultimately approving an already existing common practice',[38] the imposition of the concept of the *uji* family name onto the post-war Koseki Registration Law guaranteed the retention in that law of the conventions of the Meiji state.

What becomes of the family name in the case of marriage between a Japanese and a non-Japanese? Article 750 of the Civil

Code stipulates that the need 'to take the *uji* family name of either the husband or the wife' does not apply to marriages of this kind. The fundamental absence in koseki register theory of any intent to require a foreigner to change their surname when marrying a Japanese is a function of the fact that notions of the *uji* family name are unknown outside Japan. However, May 1984 revisions to the Koseki Registration Law (1984, Law 45) made it possible for the child of a Japanese spouse and foreign marriage partner to use an overseas surname as the *uji* family surname for koseki registration purposes. Article 107 of the Koseki Registration Law stipulates that a Japanese person who wishes to change their surname to that of a non-Japanese spouse must request permission from the Family Court and then lodge a change of surname request with the relevant municipal authority within six months of the marriage. In other words, this change is not merely a matter of individual choice. Yet, in spite of the seeming impregnability of the use of the *uji* family name in the Japanese koseki registration system, the growing number of marriages between Japanese and non-Japanese may see the odd crack begin to appear in this system. Notwithstanding minor advances of this nature, this example of the options available to a Japanese and non-Japanese couple profiles the way in which koseki register theory assumes that use of an *uji* family name is a 'privilege' permitted only to those Japanese with a koseki register record.

Even among Western legal systems, however, there is no consistency regarding family names. In France, where notions of individual freedom are paramount, choice of surname is protected as a basic right. Thus, any decision by a married woman to take her husband's name is regarded not as an obligation but as a personal choice.[39] There is basically no country in the West that requires a woman to take her husband's surname upon marriage.[40]

Given that each is located in East Asia, there is an expectation that similarities will apply to the family systems of China, Korea and Japan. This, however, is not the case, particularly regarding the use of surnames and family names. The fundamental core of the family system in China is the patriarchal family clan, which confirms bloodline by passing down the *sei* family name from the ancestors as an indicator of male lineage. The *sei* family name, unchanging throughout one's life, is received from the father to signal the identity of the 'patriarchal family clan', and any 'change of surname' is a humiliating repudiation of one's self and one's ancestors.[41]

Accordingly, marriage legislation in China acknowledges the right of both the wife and the husband to retain their own surname. The family system in Korea, discussed in detail in Chapter Four, also regards the *sei* family name, passed down from the ancestors, as indicative of male lineage. Since this notion is even more ascendant in Korea than in Japan, the principle of forbidding marriage between people with the same family name operates in the former.

One index of democracy is the extent to which the everyday rights of the individual can be concretely manifested in terms of free will. We must therefore regard as undemocratic any system which, rather than permitting choice of name as an individual's civil right, restricts this in terms of bloodline or the old *ie* family system. As noted above, post-war democratisation should have heralded the end of that system. Nevertheless, the pre-war *ie* family retains its grip on Japanese society through the use of the *uji* family name which embodies the controls imposed by the koseki registration system.

Koseki registration as proof of citizenship

'Domestication', or 'naturalisation', and the koseki system

The process of a non-Japanese person being granted permission by the Japanese government to acquire Japanese citizenship is denoted in Japanese by the expression '*kika*', which literally translates as 'domestication' and also implies subjugation. This word, '*kika*', is equivalent to the English term 'naturalisation'. In order to understand why this process is labelled thus in Japan, we might return to the ancient past. It is from this era that the essence of the term 'domestication' derives.

Historical scholarship in pre-war Japan conventionally used the expression '*kika-jin*', or 'the domesticated', when referring to '*torai-jin*' – those persons who had literally 'crossed over from the continent and come to Japan'. These people made a huge contribution to the development of the ancient Ritsuryō State. Use of this nomenclature continued until as late as 1970. Included in this group were people from various places on the continent who, in terms of occupation, came not only from legal, diplomatic and military spheres, but also from economic, merchant, religious and cultural domains. In spite of their important state-building role, these people from outside Japan were referred to derogatorily as 'the domesticated'. In the words of Ueda Masa'aki (1927–2016), this term cravenly accorded with 'constructs that statesmen and politicians had exhumed from the abyss of ethnic discrimination'.[42] Ueda was instrumental in having the term '*kika-jin*' revised to '*torai-jin*' in recent history textbooks.

To find the origin of *kika-jin*, we might refer to the *Nihon shoki* (The Chronicles of Old Japan; approx. 720 AD). Here it is written that, during the reign of the Emperor Ōjin (said to have been the third to fourth centuries AD), Yuzuki no Kimi, descendent of the Hata clan, and Achi no Omi, descendent of the Aya clan, came to Japan leading a large contingent of people from the kingdom of Kudara (formerly Baekje in the south west of the present-day Korean Peninsula). This migratory journey was recorded as 'domestication'. The expression 'domestication' here implied the assimilation of 'people from benighted lands beyond the sphere of imperial rule' through submission to the benevolent authority of the Emperor and acceptance of the law of the land. The 'domestication' of these 'people who crossed over and came to Japan', furthermore, saw them assured of 'daily necessities, a safe abode, and registration as a subject' by becoming 'people inside the imperial sphere'.[43] This is to say that, in addition to receiving food, clothing and a place in which to reside, these people were entered into the registration system of the land. Once entered, they received an *uji* family name or '*kabane*' hereditary surname. From the end of the fourth to the end of the seventh century, various classes of people, ranging from royalty and aristocrats through to farmers, who came from places such the kingdom of Han (China) and the kingdoms of Baekje and Goguryeo (encompassing much of the present-day Korean Peninsula and Northeast China), became 'Japanese' through 'domestication' processes of this kind.

Accordingly, the term 'domestication' denoted the entry of those from different ethnic groups into the koseki registration system as evidence that they had submitted to the Japanese state. This practice of the ancient state was, of course, based on the assumption of the ascendency of the bloodline of one's own ethnic group and also carried suggestions of assimilation into the new Japanese nation.[44] Prevailing from the time of Yamato era imperial governance through the medieval era and into modern times, the term 'domestication', in the words of one legal bureaucrat, 'endured to become fixed as the contemporary naturalisation process that applies in current legislation related to both citizenship and koseki registration'.[45] Here we see the present-day state embracing a practice cultivated by the authorities of ancient Japan.

As stated in the following chapter, Japan's citizenship policies regard this 'domesticating' process of naturalisation as a privilege bestowed by the state rather than the right of the individual. Article 5 of the current Citizenship Law stipulates that the Minister of Justice can only approve naturalisation in the case of a foreigner who complies with a range of conditions, which include being resident in Japan for more than five years and being of good character. Regardless of whether the applicant meets these conditions, ultimate approval remains at the Minister's discretion.

Consideration of various Western legal codes suggests three variants to naturalisation doctrine. In the United States, for example, any person who fulfils the necessary legal criteria has the automatic right to be naturalised. In England, naturalisation is at the discretion of the state. In Germany, both rights and discretion apply.[46] Since any notion of rights is consistently absent from naturalisation policy in Japan, we might interpret this process as one of 'submission to the state' that takes its lead from the custom of ancient times.

Throughout the modern era, persons given permission to naturalise in Japan have been eligible for entry into a koseki register. However, those with a non-Japanese ethnic background remain subject to the register's discriminatory function. In terms of the Koseki Registration Law, the entry of a naturalised person into a koseki register comes either with the creation of a new record at the time of marriage or a change of record at the time of adoption. Once entered, the fact that a person is 'from outside the country' will be documented for the rest of their life, making it evident from a quick glance that the person in question is a naturalised citizen.

Acknowledging that this would foment persistent discrimination and disadvantage against the naturalised person in marriage and employment, the Ministry of Justice revised the Koseki Registration Law Regulation (Ministry of Justice Directive 40) in December 1960 in order to limit the practice of recording naturalisation to the first register into which the person's name was entered. The need to repeat this when transferring to or creating a new koseki register record no longer applied. Here we see naturalisation policy and in turn koseki registration policy attempting to give positive consideration to the circumstances of the naturalised person.[47] There also seems to be some recognition on the part of the Japanese government that the need to record naturalisation in the koseki registration system works against assimilation as a 'Japanese citizen'. Nevertheless, while naturalisation in Japan accepts the entry of the foreigner to the 'benevolent realm of the state', the tight connection between this process and the role of the koseki registration system continues the antiquated practice of placing the foreigner under surveillance as a 'person from a benighted land beyond the sphere of imperial rule'.

Why is koseki registration proof of being 'Japanese'?

Since being registered on a koseki register is restricted to 'citizens of Japan', it is axiomatic that all those who hold Japanese citizenship are entered into a koseki register. A person who takes foreign citizenship or who loses Japanese citizenship is removed from the register. In this way, the koseki registration system acts as a de facto 'roll of holders of Japanese citizenship'. The corollary to this is the presumption that a person without koseki registration is not a Japanese citizen.[48]

As explained in detail in the following chapter, because Japanese citizenship is based on the principle of bloodline (*jus sanguinis*), evidence must be provided in the case of those who acquire Japanese citizenship through birth of either a 'Japanese' mother or father. Theoretically, this might require proof going back through the generations to confirm that the grandparents, great-grandparents and so on were also Japanese. Since providing such strict, objective proof is next to impossible, the presence of a mother or father on a koseki register record also entitles the child to have an entry that operates as alternate proof of being Japanese.

However, *jus sanguinis* can become a trap with a follow-on effect.[49] What happens when a person who does not hold Japanese citizenship is mistakenly entered into a koseki register? In this instance, if the municipal authority that administers the relevant family registration processes remains unaware of the problem and fails to remove the person in question from the register, then their children and grandchildren will also be given a koseki register entry and be officially recognised as Japanese. If officialdom, however, discovers the original error and realises that the person concerned is non-Japanese, registration will be revoked and the person's name removed from the koseki register. Should that occur, there is a domino effect involving the revocation and removal of the entries based on the family lineage of that original person.[50]

Prior to the 1899 enactment of the Japanese Citizenship Law, customary law applied when seeking proof of Japanese citizenship by reference to koseki register records.[51] Koseki register entries continue to be used in this way even today. Since 1969, the Civil Affairs Bureau of the Ministry of Justice has issued a 'citizenship identification certificate' to Japanese people studying or conducting business overseas. When applying for this certificate, it has been necessary to produce a copy of a koseki register entry as proof of Japanese citizenship.[52]

Unregistered people and creating a koseki register record

Can we therefore claim that a 'Japanese' person who does not have koseki registration is in fact 'Japanese'? While it may be that in theory every Japanese should have an entry in a koseki register record, such entries are only possible once information is lodged. Lodgement might not occur for a range of reasons, however, leading to many being classified as 'unregistered persons' (*mukoseki-sha*), and having no information on record.

Principle among the reasons for non-koseki registration are the following: (1) parents fail to provide a birth notice for a child; (2) inability for a child to be registered because the parents themselves are unregistered; and (3) a person's *honseki* address is unknown. Of these, perhaps unsurprisingly, (1) is the most common. The usual means by which a person is first entered into a koseki register record is through lodgement of the birth report. Accordingly, when a parent for whatever reason fails to lodge this notice, the child becomes an unregistered person, that is, one who is not entered into a koseki register record. However, since birth, like death, is clearly a concrete reality, it is completely absurd to deny this fact on the grounds that no form was lodged with the authorities or that information was not registered.

Those with no entry in a koseki register record are regarded as having no proof of Japanese citizenship and must technically suffer the disadvantage of being unable to apply for either a passport or certificate of residence. As noted above, there is a process known as *shūseki* to assist these people to create a new record. However, a condition of that process is that the person lodging the request must be a Japanese citizen. In the case of reason (2) cited above, even unregistered parents may be able to prove their Japanese citizenship. If this is the case, the child, too, is a citizen of Japan and has the right firstly to apply to the Family Court to create a new koseki register record and secondly to create this record should the Court give its approval.

Creating an entry into a new koseki register record, however, is not a means by which one simultaneously acquires Japanese citizenship. In fact, the courts have specifically ruled that, 'With respect to the koseki register providing, in terms of Civil Law, proof of identity and also proof of citizenship, *koseki registration is not a mechanism to determine whether the person in question holds or does not hold citizenship*' (emphasis added). Thus, according to the courts, the koseki register record is merely a practical 'general identity document' that preserves – rather than actively promotes – the acquisition of Japanese citizenship.[53]

In Japan, 'proof of citizenship', as distinct from koseki registration, is not a concept with a historical tradition. However, in the draft 'Japanese Identity Law Manifesto', released in June 1943 by the joint government/private sector Japanese Principles of Law Research Group, a framework was proposed for establishing '*shinmin-shō*' (proof of imperial subject identity) as an alternative to either a koseki register record copy or short entry. To be issued by the municipal authority with responsibility for the individual's *honseki* residence, this document with photograph attached was to record *honseki* address, relationship to head of the koseki register family, sibling order and date of birth.[54] In the context of a national policy environment that sought to 'promote the establishment of a Greater East Asia New Order', the draft manifesto invoked the *Kokutai no Hongi* (1937, Cardinal Principles of the Essence of the National Body of Japan) in an attempt to reorganise the Civil Code and the Koseki Registration Law to overtly reflect the 'moral principles' that were characteristic of the Japanese legal tradition. This was to be done in order to 'strengthen the foundation of the nation-state for a system of total war and anticipating the perfection of our sophisticated method of national protection'.[55] Notwithstanding this ideological bias, the draft aimed to simplify koseki registration practice in order to make the koseki registration system a more functional entity, while also proposing groundbreaking reform aimed at preventing the severe social discrimination associated with the way in which the system recorded the family name. The 'Japanese Identity Law Manifesto' was never translated into practice, however, and there have been no other concrete proposals for a national identity system to replace the koseki registration system.

Status registration systems in Japan, the West and China

Citizen registration based on the individual as the unit

There is no one system of identity registration shared by the United States and the various countries of Europe, with each having regulatory specifics that strongly reflect local ways of thinking. Nevertheless, the following commonalities prevail, each of which is in marked contrast to the family registration system in Japan.

Firstly, these places register the identity of a single individual. More than half of current demands for reform – or, in some cases, abolition – of Japan's koseki registration system cite the need for Japan to also change from a system of family registration to one of registering individuals.[56] Secondly, European and United States systems compile independent registers for the various events that mark changes to identity. That is, rather than being compiled together on a single document, matters such birth, marriage, divorce and death are recorded as separate events on separate registers. While there are state-by-state differences, the system in the United States relies on the provision of birth, marriage and death certificates for each individual that are recorded in the relevant registry records. Thirdly, in comparison to Japan, there is a marked limit to the matters that are compulsorily recorded on an individual's identity register. While there are registers that record births, deaths and marriages in Europe and the United States, there is nothing equivalent to the Japanese koseki registration system that records an individual's family relations on a single document and that includes information concerning matters such as divorce, adoption or legal acknowledgement of a child born to parents who are not legally married. (As discussed below, however, there are countries where, in addition to separate registers for specific matters, family registers are also compiled.)

The adoption in Europe and the United States of an individual-based identity registration system has its historical antecedents in the fact that from ancient times to the Middle Ages the Christian Church established the norms and strictly administered the systems of

European society. In the fourth century AD, when the Roman Empire formally declared Christianity as the state religion, the authority of what is today the Catholic Church was broadly established. In Christian society, the life of the devotee was under the absolute control of the Church, which validated identity changes such as birth, marriage and death in terms of Christian teachings and thus tied these changes to religious ceremonies such as baptism. As long as such an event did not violate church doctrine, it was recorded in the church registers of births, marriages and deaths (a burial register was also kept). Since registration was only available to believers, these processes also served to expose heretics.

With the religious reforms of the modern era, the separation of church and state and the emergence of modern notions of 'the citizen', the state assumed responsibility for identity registration that had previously been managed by the church. Nevertheless, the state retained the practice of compiling a specific register for each identity-related event, leading to the contemporary Western systems based on the individual. The continued focus on the registration of births, marriages and deaths is undoubtedly a relic of the custom of taking church registers as records of religious ceremonies.

In addition to compiling registers based on individual life events, however, countries such as France, Germany and Spain operate family records (*kazokubo*). These are compiled upon marriage at the request of the parties concerned as a record of matters such as the surnames and parents of those being wed. Entries are updated with changes to family circumstances including divorce, death and the birth of a child. In Germany, while there is variation between each '*Land*' or German provincial municipal administrative unit, legal recognition of the family record system came in 1924.[57] When the Nazi Party assumed power, however, the system was constructed anew in line with the 1937 Nazi identity registration laws. Under the guise of recording family details, family records were grounded in racial ideologies derived from eugenics theory to provide information on 'bloodline' and family relations. Although completely unnecessary in terms of individual identity, religion was also recorded with the clear intent of discriminating against people of the Jewish faith. While the racial element was eliminated, the fundamentals of the system continued into the post-war era.[58]

At the time of the Meiji Restoration in Japan it was clear that the quickest road to becoming a modern nation-state was to emulate

Western legal systems. Nevertheless, with the push to change the Unequal Treaties as an essential embodiment of the independence of the Japanese state, lawmakers drew the line at adopting a system of identity registration from outside the country. At an 1882 meeting of the Council of Elders that discussed proposed changes to the Jinshin Koseki Registration Law (the draft of the Koseki Registration Regulations to be discussed further in Chapter Three), for example, the suggestion was made to discontinue the contemporaneous local koseki registration system in favour of a Western model. Against this, Council member Watanabe Kiyoshi (1835–1904) argued that each country had its own customs and that Japan, too, should retain existing customs of worth. Watanabe strongly argued as follows: 'Since the current family system exists in Japan alone, rather than adopting the practice of another country, we should retain the koseki register practices that have long operated here'. Dismissing the draft legislation as inappropriate, he emphasised that rather than becoming captive to the legal norms of various Western countries, members should regard the current koseki registration system as a traditional form of identity confirmation that should be protected because it is suitable for Japan.

The Meiji 31 Koseki Registration Law, enacted in 1898, did in fact draw on the Napoleonic Code, the so-called 'jewel in the crown' of the French Revolution, to introduce an individual registration system. This, however, was abolished before being given adequate time to function effectively (see Chapter Three for further discussion). That move extinguished any ideological spark of revolution regarding an individual registration system in 'modern nation-state' Japan, and thus kept alive a form of registration which validated individual identity merely in terms of family membership.

Koseki registration as unique to Japan

We might sum up the particular aspects of the Japanese koseki registration system in comparison to Europe and the United States as follows. Firstly, the unit of organisation is the family, secondly, the system valorises the unusual concept of place inherent in the *honseki* address and thirdly, the system notes the relationship connections – including the birth order of children – of the family members recorded. The first factor requires no further comment. On the third point we might observe that Western identity systems merely record the fact that an individual is the child of a parent or parents without reference to sibling birth order. The second point, *honseki*, calls for greater elaboration.

There is no Western concept that corresponds to the Japanese notion of *honseki* address, nor is there a concept of 'registration address' that is common to Western countries. France records the place of birth while Germany enters the place of marriage. In Switzerland, the registration address can be a hometown or place of residence. With a stretch of the imagination we might regard the Swiss 'hometown' as similar to the Japanese '*honseki*', although the former is a person's legally determined place of citizenship and transfer is regulated.[59] Regardless of differences, the base identity register address required in France, Germany and Switzerland has a concrete relationship to the real life of those concerned. In contrast, the Japanese *honseki* address need have no relationship to the lived experience of either the whole family or any individual member. Rather, it is freely determined and can be transferred at will by the individual whose name appears first on a particular koseki register record (*koseki hittōsha*). This individual, in pre-war parlance, was the legal household head.

Allied Occupation pressure for reform of the koseki registration system was accompanied by questions regarding the *honseki* address. Not surprisingly, the GHQ questioned a national identity system based on the *honseki* address that had no connection to the actual address of any registered individual. According to Aoki Yoshihito of the Ministry of Justice, Second Division, Civil Affairs Bureau, who was involved in post-war koseki registration system reform, one GHQ advisor argued that the requirement for every municipality throughout the land to have carriage of koseki registration matters was both inefficient and illogical. The GHQ therefore offered to provide budgetary support to have the system centralised in a manner similar to that of the United Kingdom or the United States. Against this, Aoki pointed out that, firstly, there were currently in excess of 40,000 staff involved in koseki registration administration, and secondly, that huge security problems would be created if records and registers were centralised. He also argued that centralisation would be contrary to the 'desire' of the people who sought to lodge their own family registration at a 'near-by municipal office'. Aoki refrained from referring specifically to the issue of *honseki* address, claiming

Table 1.2: Differences between China's population registration system and Japan's koseki registration system

	Population registration in China	**Koseki registration in Japan**
Registration target group	Chinese nationals resident in China	Holders of Japanese citizenship
Unit of organisation	Household – people living at the same address	Married couple (husband and wife) with the same surname and their unmarried children
Standard place of registration	Usual place of residence	*Honseki* domicile abode
Changes (including transfer) to standard place of registration	Restricted	Unrestricted
Administering body	Public Order Bureau (metropolitan and city dwellers); local 'People's Committee' (provincial and rural dwellers)	Local municipal authority

that 'the other party [GHQ] appeared to have no understanding whatsoever of that concept'.[60]

Clearly, this Ministry of Justice defence was nothing more than stopgap sophistry. In actual fact, koseki register administration did not occur at a 'near-by' municipality, but at the municipality in which the *honseki* address was located. Since the *honseki* address was a marker of the *ie* family system, these Ministry efforts to avoid raising that issue can be seen as a deliberate tactic to prevent the GHQ from taking the scalpel to the notion of the koseki registration system that was connected to the *ie* family.

Differences between registration systems in China and Japan

The koseki registration model is but one of an endless list of cultural reforms and systems that Japan has adopted from China throughout the centuries. In the Spring and Autumn era (770–476 BC) and then the Warring States era (475–221 BC), the equivalent of koseki registration was regulated in China principally to facilitate tax collection and military service records. As the feudal state developed, the registration system also came to have policing and population statistic collection roles, confirming its importance as a core administrative system.[61]

It is often noted that a koseki-like registration system continues to operate in China today, with Chinese authorities sometimes even using a Chinese word with equivalence to the Japanese word '*koseki*' when discussing the local system. However, the official name of the present-day system in China is the 'household registration system'.

Following its victory over the Chinese Nationalist Party, the Chinese Communist Party (CCP) established the People's Republic of China (PRC) on 1 October 1949. After the chaos of fifty years of internal conflict, which included the period of the invasion and occupation by the Japanese Imperial Army, the CCP sought to restore and maintain order in the new China. With family registration regarded as an indispensable element in the creation of an ideal socialist state, China's Ministry of Public Security devised a draft proposal for a household registration system. This was implemented in January 1958 through the People's Republic of China Household Registration System Ordinance, which stated its objectives as 'maintaining social order, protecting the rights and interests of the people and contributing to the formation of a socialist state' (Article 1).[62]

Not only did it become compulsory for every person in the PRC to have a household register entry as proposed in the ordinance, it also became the practice for information recorded in the household register and on the register roll to function as evidence of identity as a citizen of that country (Article 4). In the case of foreigners or stateless people, previous legal stipulations were voided with these persons also becoming subject to the Household Registration Ordinance (Article 2, Clause 3). All those who shared residence with a designated household head became members of a household unit – similar to the *setai* household in Japanese – with information for that household unit collated on a household registration roll (Article 5). Notification to the household registration authorities of any change to basic register information was required at times such as marriage, divorce, adoption, creating a new household, joining a household or disappearance.

Unlike the Japanese koseki registration system that sought to register matters concerning family relationships, China's household registration system recorded information in terms of one's place of residence. However, its function exceeded the parameters of mere residence registration to become a mechanism that worked to confine people to the location of their household registration address. Those with household registration in a rural area who sought to move to a metropolitan area required documentary evidence of employment from the Labour Bureau of that metropolis, documentary evidence of school qualifications and written permission to transfer from the metropolitan Household Registration Authority. They also needed to lodge registration transfer documentation with the Household Registration Authority responsible for their usual address (Article 10, Clause 2). In this way, movement of the population (that is, of households) from the country to the city was strictly regulated. Clearly, the state deployed the household registration system as a mechanism for imposing public order.

Explanatory notes to the draft proposal put forward by China's Ministry of Public Security justified the new system in terms of preventing a huge, unchecked flow of the agricultural labour force from the country to the city. This was opposed not only on the grounds of exacerbating transport, residence, employment and education problems, but also in terms of the negative influence on agricultural production and the construction of the new Chinese state. Strict administrative controls were therefore imposed on household registration in order to regulate rural population movement into cities.[63]

Since its inception, China's household registration system has confined the farm labourers on whose efforts the socialist state was founded to rural villages. Today, too, these people remain fixed for life as full-time agricultural workers. Even if a person with rural registration manages to relocate to a city, the absence of an official city household leads to discrimination in areas such as employment, education and marriage. There were also problems with planned economy era ration distribution. While technically 'Chinese', those born in rural areas are treated from birth as second-class citizens. The household registration system has created major inconsistencies that have hindered the liberalisation of post-economic reform Chinese society, impinged on the effective use of human resources in metropolitan areas and reproduced regional inequality.

Post-war democratisation and ideological reform via the individual

The question arises as to the degree of fundamental ideological reform that accompanied post-war democratisation. The litmus test in this respect is surely the extent to which that democratising process swept away the notion of the *ie* family system which had held Japanese individuals in its clutches since the Meiji era. We must thus consider whether or not there was full reform of the koseki registration system, the administration of which is a concrete expression of the *ie* family ideal.

As a member of the committee that drafted the post-war Civil Code, Wagatsuma Sakae (referred to above) was central to the process of sweeping post-war reforms. In 1948, on the eve of the implementation of that Code, Wagatsuma published a document entitled *Ie no seido, sono rinri to hōri* (The *Ie* Family System: Its Ethics and Jurisprudence). Here, he stated, 'It is no exaggeration to say that today the *ie* is nothing more than the existence of the koseki registration system'. As an example, he noted 'the problems that might arise if food rations were distributed with the *ie* family as the distribution unit'.[64] This was because the *ie* family of the koseki registration system had been mercilessly scattered during the 'Fifteen Years War' as a result of conscription, mobilisation and evacuation to the countryside to become a mere armchair concept with no relation to real life.

It is said that while the GHQ saw the obliteration of the *ie* family system as essential to Japan's democratisation, officials also grasped the tremendous convenience of a system that permitted oversight of a husband and wife, and parent and child, through a single koseki register record. This is not to suggest any significant level of support by the GHQ for the koseki registration system. American legal scholar Roscoe Pound (1870–1964) observed, 'what is peculiar to Anglo-American legal thinking, and above all to American legal thinking, is an ultra-individualism'.[65] Given the deeply entrenched nature of individualism in American society, the adoption of an identity system on the grounds of convenience or efficiency based on a group unit such as the family would almost certainly be regarded as a violation of individual rights.

Aware of the possibility that the term '*ko*' (literally door) in the expression 'koseki' was shorthand for the *ie* family system, the

GHQ expressed concerns at this nomenclature. In response, the Ministry of Justice claimed that the term 'door' literally referred to the door through which family members left and returned to a household. Claiming that the use of '*ko*' was therefore appropriate in the expression 'koseki', which used the family as the organisational unit, the Ministry won the argument of the day.[66]

It was through this sort of expedient rhetoric that the term 'koseki' was retained. There were nonetheless legislators who did propose a koseki registration system based on a separate card for each individual rather than recording all information on a single document. Such suggestions were, of course, opposed, although it is important to note that these objections were not merely related to administrative practicalities. According to debate participant Wagatsuma, there were two main points of view. One advocated 'staying with the koseki system', accepting the convenience of retaining its good points and later attempting to reform the assumptions on which it was based. The other, based on the belief that the likelihood of reform occurring in the context of an existing system was limited, sought to introduce an individual card system in spite of the work involved. This latter 'must have legal support if the assumptions of Japanese society are to be reformed'.[67] That is, one side prioritised the convenience of retaining the system and addressing the issue of reform at a later stage, while the other prioritised an immediate reform of the system, including the fundamental ideas on which this system was based, by undertaking a decisive renewal of all of the processes involved.

Ultimately, this difference of opinion over whether or not to adopt a method of koseki registration based on the unit of the individual goes to the heart of the ideological conflict that marked post-war democratisation. It is superfluous to point out that the koseki registration system preserved the ascendancy of the family unit into the post-war era. Over and above administrative convenience and efficiency, retention of this system was the result of a refusal, as elaborated upon in Chapter Three, to understand the damage caused by administrative practices rooted in notions of the *ie* family in operation in Japanese society. As a result, crucial attempts made at the time of the war's end to mount a spiritual revolution, which, as it were, interrogated the ideological beliefs that prevailed among Japanese people, came to nothing.

2 On Being a Citizen: The Close Nexus Between Japanese Citizenship and Koseki Registration

Modern-state citizenship: From allegiance to rights

Citizenship and the nation-state: From subject to citizen

The term 'citizenship' refers to the conditions according to which an individual holds membership of a given nation-state and is a method of distinguishing between nationals and foreigners. Codified in law during the modern era, citizenship expresses the state's connection to the individual while determining the individual's legal status vis-à-vis that state. Regarded as the bond between the individual and the state to which they are attached, citizenship is also seen as the wellspring of an individual's allegiance towards that state.

In medieval feudal society, the notion of 'citizen' referred to those with allegiance to the domain or fiefdom of a king or lord. In other words, it referred to a serf, one living under conditions of servitude, who through birth automatically fell under the jurisdiction of – that is, effectively became a 'citizen' of – a certain kingdom or domain. Since strict controls operated on movement across borders during feudal times, for the vast majority of people place of birth was place of residence. As a result, the formula birthplace = address = citizenship or nationality was the norm at the time. To be a citizen of a certain place was evidence that one was the personal possession of the ruler of that domain. Any notion of identity held by the individual was purely that of 'subject', that is, of being an object to be governed.

With the decline in Church authority that had swept the medieval world, the modern idea of 'nation' emerged. This adopted a new guise of politically unified 'sovereign state' over a defined territory or domain. Accordingly, thinkers such as John Locke (1632–1704) and Jean-Jacques Rousseau (1712–1778) developed the notion of the 'social contract', which argued that the individual possessed 'natural rights' by means of which they expressed allegiance to the nation-state through a voluntary or autonomous contract. This 'contract' gave people a degree of conscious attachment to that state. Thus, there was a shift from being a subject under the rule of a lord or king to being a citizen who participated autonomously in the governance process. This shift marked the rise of the nation-state as a homogenous and integrated community of 'citizens'.

Here the concept of 'citizen' made a clean break with any sense of unconscious allegiance to a lord or king to re-emerge as an individual who chose free and conscious allegiance to the nation-state. As a watershed in this respect, the French Revolution (1789–1799) promoted the notion of the citizen (*citoyen*) who, in contrast to one affiliated with the state through absolute allegiance to a monarch, stood in relation to the state as an active subject. The 1791 French Constitution and the 1804 Napoleonic Code (Code civil des Français) were the first legal documents to regulate citizenship by transforming an abstract concept into a working legislative system that clearly profiled the citizen as an entity holding concrete political rights.

Various nineteenth century Europeans states, including Austria, Greece and Germany, followed the French model by including citizenship provisions in their civil codes. Germany, in contrast, is regarded as the first jurisdiction to develop stand-alone systematic citizenship legislation. This was enacted in 1843 in relation to the acquisition or loss of citizenship rights vis-à-vis the Prussian empire.[1]

As the modern world entered the second half of the nineteenth century and European powers vied to 'carve up the world', notions of citizenship assumed new significance with the need to integrate the residents of newly acquired territories as 'citizens' of the power concerned. In the quarter century between 1875 and 1900, the amalgamation of various colonial holdings, largely located in Asia and Africa, saw 50,000,000 new English, 44,000,000 new French and 19,000,000 new Belgians incorporated into their respective domestic states.[2] The political conundrum of how these nation-states, which had grown to become powerful empires, would assimilate and grant the right of 'citizen' to members of the different ethnicities among the colonised drove the formulation of citizenship law that occurred in various European countries at that time.

Yet, even in contemporary times, the notion of citizenship as inseparable from allegiance to the state remains pervasive, with much citizenship legislation demanding an 'oath of allegiance' as a condition of naturalisation. Typical in this respect is Article 101 of the 1940 United States Nationality Act, which declared the 'citizen' to be a person who undertook 'perpetual allegiance to the United States'. Rather than legal significance, however, terms such as 'allegiance' convey strong moral meaning with distinctly ritualistic and formulaic dimensions.[3]

Citizenship as an individual right

In addition to being equivalent to the English term 'citizenship', the Japanese word '*kokuseki*' is also used to denote the English term 'nationality'. How, then, do these concepts differ? Scholar of international law Paul Weiss argues that the terms 'citizenship' and 'nationality' each stress a different aspect of the conditions necessary to qualify one as a member of a nation-state. Thus, while 'nationality' emphasises the external relationship between the individual and the nation, 'citizenship' highlights the internal bond. The latter, in other words, connotes an individual's competency to fully participate as a member of a nation-state, a competency that includes the exercise of political rights. In other words, if nationality marks a borderline between one's own and other countries, citizenship refers to one's concrete rights as a citizen – that is, as a participating member of the system of a state. According to Weiss, however, 'While every citizen is a national, not every national is necessarily a citizen of a given nation-state. Such matters, furthermore, lie within the realm of domestic rather than international law'. It is thus apparent that the notion of holding 'nationality' has a wider reach than the notion of 'citizenship'. As an example, we might consider a Filipino living under the colonial rule of the United States. Prior to independence in 1935, even if a person living in the Philippines took an oath of allegiance, that person might be granted nationality but could not become a citizen of the United States.[4] There are countries such as Japan, however, where even today legal thinking tends to collapse notions of citizenship and nationality, so that not holding 'nationality' fundamentally results in a person having no rights, including political rights, as a citizen.

On 12 April 1930, the first international legal agreement related to the citizenship of individuals, the Convention on Certain Questions Relating to the Conflict of Nationality Law (hereafter, the Hague Convention) was adopted through the auspices of the League of Nations. In its Preamble, this Convention stated, 'that it is in the general interest of the international community to secure that all its members should recognize that every person should have a nationality and should have one nationality only'. The Preamble further declared, 'The ideal towards which the efforts of humanity should be directed in this domain is the abolition of all cases of both statelessness and of double nationality'. The Hague Citizenship Convention came into effect on 1 July 1937. Japan signed but never ratified this Convention.

Supporting the notion that the conditions for membership of a nation should be decided domestically without external interference, Article 1 of the Hague Citizenship Convention stated, 'It is for each State to determine under its own law who are its nationals. This law shall be recognised by other States in so far as it is consistent with international conventions, international custom, and the principles of the law generally recognised with regard to nationality'. By stating, 'Any question as to whether a person possesses the nationality of a particular State shall be determined in accordance with the law of that State', the Convention confirmed that determinations of nationality, that is, of citizenship, should be based on procedures of law. Recognising the holding of citizenship as an individual right, the document cautioned against states making arbitrary decisions to change the citizenship of any individual.

The passport provided proof that one held citizenship of a particular state. Predictably, the passport system was developed in Europe, birthplace of the modern nation-state. Such a system had a policing and public order function that enabled both the surveillance of foreigners entering a country and the tracking of residents' movements. During the era of absolute monarchical rule, this tracking was necessary because the exit of subjects from a country was seen as weakening the strength of the military. In addition, as the expansion of nations created an urgent need for funds, issuing passports became a revenue raising measure.

When the flame of modern individualism shone bright following the French Revolution, however, many countries in Europe abolished the passport system on the grounds that it inhibited an individual's freedom of mobility.[5] Nevertheless, the international instability created by the First World War saw a revival of the system, which, in addition to confirming proof of individual identity, became widely adopted as a means of politically and diplomatically regulating departures from a country.[6] In this context, the passport indicated that a nation-state had granted political permission to the citizen to depart the country, with many states also making it obligatory for a foreigner entering their jurisdiction to hold a passport. After the First World War, the system that regarded the passport as proof of citizenship was commonly adopted.

Jus soli, jus sanguinis: Birthplace, bloodline

The principal, and most fundamental, means of acquiring citizenship is through birth, with states granting qualification for membership to a pre-determined range of people when they are born. The two basic elements that determine this range are place of birth and bloodline.

The notion that citizenship is determined by place of birth is referred to by the Latin term '*jus soli*'. *Jus soli* commonly operates in those countries, including the United States, England, Canada and Brazil, in which immigration policies have resulted in multicultural societies. This is because the notion of shared land of birth was seen as necessary to promote assimilation among citizens by imbuing a sense of common consciousness in the offspring of those who had relocated from another land.

On the other hand, the adoption of *jus soli* in English Common Law, the customary law of England, was grounded in feudal thinking from the Middle Ages. At that time, those born in territory under the dominion of a king became through birth a 'subject' of that king. In contrast, those born outside such territory, regardless of the citizenship status of their parents, were categorised as foreigners.[7] In the United States, too, the allegiance, duties and citizenship rights invoked by these Common Law traditions became the foundation of all legal regulations related to citizenship through the *jus soli* principles, which prioritised place of birth over bloodline.[8]

With the growing emphasis on individualism from the eighteenth century, however, protecting the natural rights of the individual became an inherent property of Common Law. Since legal systems in the United States were also based on British Common Law, procedures there, too, acknowledged the value of an individual's natural rights and the need to protect these from interference by society or the state.[9] There was also a practical sense of convenience in the principles of *jus soli* that bestowed citizenship on an individual according to where they lived and worked.

Jus sanguinis, the principle of the law of bloodline, on the other hand, was the means by which a child inherited citizenship from its parents at birth. This way of thinking is thought to originate in the types of ethnocentric values that advocated for the formation of a nation-state from a single ethnic group with a single culture.[10]

The first recorded legal stipulation of citizenship through *jus sanguinis* appeared in the 1804 French Civil Code, the so-called 'Napoleonic Code'. The principles of this code exerted widespread influence throughout Europe and were responsible for superseding the idea of *jus soli* that dominated until that time.

One intent of *jus sanguinis* was to act as a strong antithesis to the feudal era subordination of the individual. In contrast to the feudal conceptualisation, also the founding notion of Common Law, that nationality or citizenship was absolutely decided by place of birth, *jus sanguinis* sought to manifest principles that accommodated the essence of the free human being. This particularly included the notions that the individual should not be controlled by a connection to land and that no currently vested rights should be violated.[11]

Jus sanguinis can be patrilineal, where the child inherits the citizenship of the father only. It can also be either patrilineal or matrilineal, with the child inheriting the citizenship of either parent. In addition to there being almost no states which currently have a purely matrilineal system, in the first half of the twentieth century the notion of *jus sanguinis* was inevitably patrilineal. Japan, too, during the eighty-plus years between the 1899 instigation of citizenship legislation and legislative reforms undertaken in 1984, operated a patrilineal *jus sanguinis* system. Adoption of a patrilineal system was justified on the grounds that the state needed to make a consistent ruling in the case of parents with different nationalities in order to guard against the technical possibility of a child ending up with dual citizenship.[12] In deciding the legal conditions for citizenship at the time, however, legal systems throughout the world opted for what was then regarded as the natural prioritisation of patrilineal blood.

Whether or not a country adopted *jus soli* or *jus sanguinis* as a means of naturally bestowing citizenship depended on tradition and political need. While, as noted above, England's decision to adopt *jus soli* was related to its inheritance of a monarchical tradition derived from feudal times, decisions by continental countries such as France and Germany to adopt *jus sanguinis* as the foundational citizenship principle related to inherited traditions of Roman Law. Population policy could also exert an influence on this choice, as demonstrated by the fact that various South American countries which accepted migrants, including Brazil and Argentina, adopted *jus soli*. We might further note that, although French tradition valorised *jus sanguinis*, notions of birthplace were also drawn upon in the wider sphere as a means of bolstering population numbers in France.[13]

Since citizenship conditions inevitably differed according to local circumstances, it was difficult to establish a unified set of general principles pertaining to citizenship acquisition. Thus, as noted, citizenship decisions in international law have largely been relegated to the sphere of the domestic law of the states in question.[14]

Individual freedom to determine citizenship

A key issue relating to the acquisition of citizenship is the debate between the principle of sole nationality, which asserts that the individual should hold citizenship of one nation and one nation only, and the principle which respects the right of the individual to choose in this regard. The right to citizenship is linked to the sovereignty of the nation-state and, as noted, is a matter for the domestic governance of a given state. With the growing acknowledgement of individual autonomy in natural law during the modern era, however, it was argued that the state should cede to individual will and refrain from the forcible imposition of citizenship. On the contrary, the modern nation-state was urged to protect both 'the principle of freedom to change citizenship' and 'the principle of citizenship without force'.

We have seen how in the feudal states of the Middle Ages people were 'subjects' attached to a given domain. Changes to the ownership of that domain led to a natural change of the citizenship of resident 'subjects'. Notwithstanding the emergence of the modern nation, until the mid-nineteenth century a number of states continued to assert notions such as 'once a subject always a subject' and 'perpetual allegiance'.

One manifestation of this notion of 'perpetual allegiance' was the ruling in English Common Law that, notwithstanding the acquisition of foreign citizenship through naturalisation, a British subject could not renounce British citizenship.[15] Following independence from Great Britain, the United States also inherited these same principles of perpetual allegiance as part of Common Law and, reluctant to create an expatriation precedent – a precedent to renounce one's citizenship – sought to deter or at least strictly control citizenship renunciation.[16]

The strengthening of individualism in nineteenth century Common Law, however, saw post-Civil War (1861–1865) revisions to United States legislation, which in 1868 declared 'the right of expatriation' to be 'a natural and inherent right of all people'. Eighteen seventy legislation in England, too, refuted the long-standing principle of perpetual allegiance, recognising instead the right of British subjects to renounce their citizenship.[17]

While the individual right to free choice may have existed in theory, nation-states were in fact reluctant to wholly cede the power to acquire or renounce citizenship to the individual. This was particularly due to the fact that it was generally thought that to renounce one's citizenship implied the acquisition of the citizenship of another country, and the subsequent cutting of ties with the former state. This was perhaps a natural conclusion from the point of view of the need for single citizenship referred to above and from the fact that no state was interested in losing any 'citizen' who might contribute human capital to the national cause. Until at least the end of the nineteenth century, therefore, in many countries – England included – renouncing one's citizenship was less of a right than a process requiring legal permission.[18] Eager to guarantee the size of its military and concerned to ensure that all met their obligation to serve, Japan too, as detailed below, did not recognise free renunciation of citizenship in its previous citizenship legislation. Embedded in the spirit of citizenship was a notion of 'selfless devotion to the state', which did not permit foregoing the duty to serve.

Birth of Japanese citizenship law: Adoption of *jus sanguinis*

The necessity of defining 'citizen' through citizenship law

The stipulation of citizenship through legal ordinance in Japan resulted from Western encounters following the opening up of the country to the outside world (*kaikoku*). This saw a growing stream of Europeans ('*ijin*' or aliens) flow into Japan. These first substantive international contacts at the level of the people made it necessary to define the meaning of being 'Japanese' in law. With many foreigners now resident in Japan and marrying Japanese, two issues in particular arose. The first was foreigner acquisition of Japanese citizenship, and the second concerned the citizenship of children born from the marriage of a foreigner to a Japanese.

The first legal stipulation of citizenship in Japan came with the 'Regulation Regarding Permission for Marriage to a Foreigner' (Grand Council of State Declaration No. 103), promulgated on 14 March 1873. This document ruled, for example, that on becoming the wife of a foreigner a Japanese woman would lose her Japanese citizenship, while a foreign woman who became the wife of a Japanese would acquire Japanese citizenship. In establishing conditions for the acquisition or loss of citizenship through marriage between a foreigner and a Japanese, the regulations clearly promoted a paradigm of single citizenship for married couples based on the citizenship status of the male.

Various models existed for citizenship legislation. In France, for example, citizenship conditions were stipulated in the Constitution, the regulatory foundation of the French nation-state. In Japan, when the Imperial Rescript on the future opening of the National Diet was handed down in 1881, the Freedom and People's Rights Movement campaigned vigorously for a constitutional state. This saw a range of constitutional drafts, which stipulated citizenship conditions and rules for citizenship application, drawn up privately (prior to the Meiji Constitution) by various people's rights advocates. One such example is 'Draft for the Constitution of Japan', thought to have been composed around August 1881 by Ueki Emori (1857–1892), known for producing a radical private constitutional draft that was influenced by Western theories of natural rights. In Ueki's draft, the citizen was defined through principles of connection to place. Accordingly, Clause 40 read, 'A person who is in the political society of Japan is a Japanese'. Furthermore, the content of Clause 41, which deemed 'Japanese people, who shall not renounce their Japanese citizenship by choice or consent, shall not have their status rescinded', draws attention to Ueki's support for the freedom to renounce one's citizenship in a simple and straightforward manner.[19]

Stipulating citizenship requirements was also a conundrum that faced those who drafted the Meiji Constitution. As a key figure involved in this process, legal bureaucrat Inoue Kowashi (1844–1895) examined the constitutional models of existing states. In December 1886, Inoue consulted Hermann Roesler and Albert Mosse – German legal scholars employed by the Japanese government as foreign consultants – regarding the benefits or otherwise of including citizenship regulatory clauses in the constitution being drawn up by Meiji authorities. Both Roesler and Mosse were of the opinion that it was in the interests of Japan to develop stand-alone legislation.[20] Constitutional definitions, they argued, might become rigid and fossilised, whereas stand-alone legislation would have the flexibility to respond as required to changes in international and domestic circumstances.

On 11 February 1889, the Constitution of the Empire of Japan was promulgated as the fundamental legal framework of the Japanese state, and enacted from 29 November the following year. The Roesler and Mosse advice is evident from the fact that, while refraining from explicit stipulations related to citizenship, Clause 18 declared 'The conditions necessary for being a Japanese subject shall be determined by law'.

In line with Clause 18 of the Meiji Constitution, the original version (later modified) of the Meiji Civil Code, promulgated on 7 October 1890, provided the first comprehensive legal citizenship framework for Japan. Rather than creating stand-alone legislation, however, this document followed the French model of locating citizenship regulations within the Code itself. The original version of the Meiji Civil Code drew on a draft compiled by Gustave Boissonade (1825–1910), the French legal scholar and *o-yatoi gaikokujin* (foreign expert) employed by the Japanese government, and was modelled on the 1804 French Civil Code. This document ignited the so-called 'Civil Code debate' that raged both inside and outside the Imperial Diet. During the debate, conservative scholars such as Hozumi Yatsuka (1860–1912) protested that the influence exerted on this code by European individualism would damage the 'good morals and manners' evident in the family system of Japan since time immemorial. The generated heat resulted in a motion being put before the third session of the Imperial Diet in June 1892 to delay the implementation of the Civil Code in this original form. Never implemented, the proposed legislation is referred to as the 'original Civil Code'.

Reasons for the adoption of *jus sanguinis* in Japan

Is it a fact, however, that the content of the original Civil Code was based on individualistic thinking in any meaningful way? In the original Civil Code document, citizenship provisions made reference to a 'person's status'. Clause 7, which stipulated the conditions of citizenship acquired through birth, ruled that 'when the child of a Japanese is born overseas, that child is nonetheless Japanese'. This clause further confirmed the operation of the patrilineal principles that underpinned the legislation by stating, 'In the case of parents of different status, the status of the father will determine the status of the child'.[21]

Why, we might ask, did Japan select *jus sanguinis* over *jus soli*? That is, why choose blood over soil? Consider the statement made below by one of those who drafted that law, Kumano Toshizō (1855–1899). According to Kumano, 'rather than territory or place, the character of the people comes from race', and thus 'what is transmitted from parent to child has not the slightest connection to place of birth, but comes from the bloodline that is essentially an issue of race'.[22] Here, Kumano presents an ideal of the people based on a concept of race that is primarily connected to bloodline rather than implying any connection to land.

This ideal of the people that prioritised blood was intimately connected to the notions of bloodline that underpinned the *ie* family system. This was a system that demanded that all family members be 'Japanese'. The Meiji Restoration saw a rapid growth in resident foreigners, particularly Chinese people who entered Japan in large numbers after the 1871 Sino-Japanese Amity Treaty. By 1890, foreigner numbers had swelled to almost 10,000 (refer to Table 2.1), which saw policymakers anticipate a steep growth in Japanese households with local and foreign residents. According to Kumano, benchmarking a 'person's [citizenship] status' in terms of place of birth would result in a child born to a foreigner couple residing in Japan being designated 'Japanese'. Yet, although physically located in Japan, the child would be 'saturated' with the language, customs and thinking of the parent's homeland that must necessarily pervade the foreign parents' household. Reliance on place of birth as a determining citizenship principle 'would inevitably undermine family relationships by forcing a child and

Table 2.1: Breakdown by country of foreigner residents in Meiji Japan

Year	China	United States	England	Germany	France	Russia	Other	Total
1875	2,341	132	1,025	186	190	49	395	4,348
1890	5,498	972	748	559	353	50	527[a]	9,707
1910	8,420	1,633	2,430	782	534	117	981	14,897

Note: [a] Includes nine Koreans.
Source: Hōmu shō nyūkoku kanri kyoku, *Shutsu nyūkoku kanri to sono jittai* (The State of Immigration Control), Tokyo: Hōmu shō nyūkoku kanri kyoku, 1959, p. 8.

its parents to have different home countries'. Furthermore, in the event of war breaking out between the countries involved, a father and son 'might in extreme circumstances find themselves in the unhappy situation of being forced to take up arms against each other'. *Jus sanguinis*, in contrast, 'supported family unity' by ensuring that 'both parent and child were loyal to this land'. Adoption of *jus sanguinis*, Kumano therefore concluded, could only be seen as 'truly appropriate to people's emotions (*ninjō*) and in line with the natural order of things'.[23] Rather than any triumph of freedom and individualism, what we surely see here is the defeat in Japan of these modern concepts of natural law by a legislative spirit grounded in support for 'family unity'.

Wives, we might note, were expected to take the same citizenship as their husbands. This was evident in Clause 14, Section 1, which ruled that, 'If not continuously resident in Japan, the wife of a person who loses Japanese citizenship, or a child below the age of maturity of such a person, shall as a matter of course lose status as a Japanese person'. This principle was also apparent in the Clause 15, Section 1 declaration: 'A Japanese woman who marries a foreigner loses her status as a Japanese'. The operation of notions of male superiority argued that, 'Since a married couple are of one body and soul, the wife must subordinate herself to the husband and it is natural that this should apply also in matters of citizenship'. A husband and wife who held different citizenship would each have been subject to different laws. The claim, 'It was vital to maintain family unity by ensuring that married couples hold the same citizenship',[24] demonstrates how notions of family unity, grounded in a valorisation of the *ie* family, suffused even citizenship ideology.

Various ways of losing Japanese citizenship were canvassed in the legislation. Clause 12, Section 2, for example, noted that those who 'took a position with a foreign government or entered the military of a foreign power without Japanese government permission' would be penalised with loss of citizenship. While no similar ruling was evident in the later Citizenship Law in Japan, it was clear from this stipulation that, while bestowing suffrage and other privileges, the 'citizenship status' of the time imposed the duty to give one's all to the nation. Japanese who chose to devote themselves to the government or military of a foreign power were not only regarded as having abrogated their duty as citizens, but were also seen to present an active risk in terms of 'betraying their original homeland'.[25] The fact that citizenship in the original Civil Code was clearly imbued with the premodern ideal of eternal allegiance further suggests that there was never any real commitment to individualism in that body of legislation.

The establishment of citizenship law by the Meiji state

In March 1892, following the rejection of the draft of the original Civil Code, the Japanese government established the 'Legislative Investigative Committee', with Itō Hirobumi (1841–1909) as chair, as the body responsible for once more initiating deliberations into a replacement Code, Commercial Law and associated legislation. Drawing during its deliberations on the principles espoused in the original Civil Code, this Committee eventually submitted a new citizenship legislation draft in 1898 to the twelfth sitting of the Imperial Diet. While that initial draft was rejected, an amended version was accepted without major revisions by the thirteenth sitting of the Diet in December 1898. Promulgated on 16 March 1899 (Law No. 66, hereafter referred to as the former Citizenship Law), this legislation came into effect on 1 April that same year.

The opening clause of this first systematic law enacted on the subject of citizenship in Japan decreed the precedence of patrilineal blood by ruling that, 'If, at the time of birth, a child's father is Japanese, then that child too will be Japanese'. While bloodline became the foundation of citizenship acquisition, the actual evidence for this resided in the koseki registration system. Legislative Investigative Committee member Miura Yasushi (1828–1910) expressed concern that Clause 1 of the draft failed to express the idea that 'A person is seen to be Japanese by virtue of having an entry in a koseki register'.[26] He went on to argue that surely the overview regulations of the draft should endorse the fact that such registration would naturally confirm Japanese citizenship in terms of the registered person being 'of Japanese origin'. Miura's suggestion was never adopted. Nevertheless, his point of view confirms the tacit understanding that family bloodline, as authenticated by the workings of the koseki registration system, did indeed provide proof that one was 'Japanese'.

Strict reliance on the principle of patrilineal blood, however, was potentially problematic. What, for example, should be the ruling in a case where both the mother and father were unknown, or neither had citizenship? And what of the child of a Japanese father who was nonetheless born outside a formal marriage? Since a rigid bloodline interpretation would have resulted in the child in each case having no citizenship – that is, in the child becoming stateless – the following concessions were made.

Clause 4 of the legislation acknowledged the first example by stipulating 'In the case of a child born in Japan to parents who are unknown or who hold no citizenship, the child is deemed to be Japanese'. In other words, *jus sanguinis* was overridden here by *jus soli*. By conceding the significance of place of birth as a means of acquiring citizenship, this ruling avoided the problem of the stateless child.

The second issue outlined above was of the child born to a Japanese father outside a legitimate marriage. If the father acknowledged this child, she or he could be given an entry as a *shoshi* (commoner child) in the father's koseki register record and thus acquire Japanese citizenship. A child born outside marriage who was not recognised by the father, however, was entered into the mother's koseki register record as a *shiseishi* (illegitimate child). What was the citizenship process for such a child? Clause 3 of the former Citizenship Law stipulated 'If, in the case of the father being unknown, or not holding citizenship, the mother is Japanese, then the child also becomes Japanese'. The phrase, 'the father being unknown', referred to an 'illegitimate child', where the relationship between a child born outside marriage and its father could not be determined. If the mother in such a case was Japanese, however, Clause 3 of the legislation permitted the acquisition of Japanese citizenship at the time of birth.[27] The ruling that the citizenship of a child born outside a formal marriage without 'a legal father' would accord with that of the mother[28] arose from disquiet regarding the possibility of otherwise creating a stateless child – a child without citizenship.

From the perspective of the nation-state, moreover, strict reliance on *jus sanguinis* could, in fact, compromise its power by reducing the number of citizens available for mobilisation on its behalf. This was evident from the fact that military service could not be imposed on the children of foreigners who were resident in those countries that adhered to citizenship principles based on blood. France, for example, adopted a policy of *jus sanguinis*. However, when in 1851 there was an increase in the number of foreign residents exempt from military service, the law was revised to encompass what might be referred to as 'two-fold *jus soli*'. This meant that a child born in France to a foreign father who had also been born in France automatically acquired French citizenship. This, of course, was a dilution of the pure application of *jus sanguinis*.[29]

Clause 20 of the former Citizenship Law stated, 'any person who takes citizenship of a foreign country through their own will loses Japanese citizenship'. By stipulating that foreign citizenship through naturalisation led to a loss of Japanese citizenship, the ruling prevented the acquisition of dual citizenship by a Japanese. However, steps were taken to prevent those eligible for military service from renouncing Japanese citizenship through foreign naturalisation as a means of evading that service. To this end, Clause 24 stipulated that any male child 'over seventeen years of age' who was 'currently serving with the army or navy and including those who were exempt from serving in the military, could not renounce Japanese citizenship'. Thus, Japanese men of conscription age were forbidden to forgo their citizenship. Furthermore, because the legislation did not permit one to renounce one's citizenship by choice, Nikkei Nisei (second generation Japanese immigrants) children born to Japanese fathers in countries such as the United States, which relied on *jus soli* citizenship principles, inevitably acquired dual citizenship. The fact that Japanese people resident in the United States in the first half of the twentieth century were subject to ongoing taunts from the anti-Japanese movement was related to a fear that, although these Nikkei Nisei children were United States citizens by birth, as holders of dual citizenship they might take up arms against America in the event of war with Japan.[30]

No right to naturalisation

The former Japanese Citizenship Law exercised two forms of control over foreigners seeking to naturalise. Firstly, naturalisation as a right was denied. Sections 1 and 2 of Clause 7 of the legislation, which related to the naturalisation of foreigners from outside Japan, determined, 'A foreigner is able to naturalise with the permission of the Home Minister. The Home Minister is not able to permit naturalisation to a person who does not accord with the conditions outlined'. This was in contrast to the original government draft, which, rather than invoking the name of the Minister, merely read, 'The foreigner who complies with the conditions above can naturalise with the approval of the government office with the relevant judicial control'. However, Legislative Investigative Committee member Hozumi Yatsuka argued that making the foreigner the subject of the naturalisation action implied that, 'A foreigner who complied with the stated conditions had the right to receive permission to naturalise'.[31] In order to discourage any expectation on the part of foreigners of such a right, the words, 'with the permission of the Home Minister' were inserted into the law.

Section 2 of Clause 7 of the legislation listed five necessary conditions for those making an application for naturalisation. The third among these, which required the applicant to be 'of good conduct', clearly had strong political overtones. During Legislative Investigative Committee deliberations, Hozumi Nobushige (1855–1926) stated that although the term 'upright character' was 'vague', there was 'great appeal in this vagueness'. He went on to say, 'Given that it was not particularly desirable to have ruffian types becoming citizens of Japan, leaving [naturalisation] decisions in the hands of the Home Minister means that, even if other conditions are met, it will thankfully be possible to reject such a type'.[32] The intentional inclusion of the 'vague' condition of 'good conduct' expressed the lawmakers' intention to ensure that the right to select 'citizens' remained at the discretion of the Japanese state.

We might also remember that, in line with the principle that a married couple should hold the same citizenship, Clause 8 of the law stipulated that the wife of a foreigner could not naturalise independently, but only in concert with her husband.[33] This requirement further confirms that naturalisation was in no way an individual right.

The second limitation exercised with respect to naturalisation related to the types of public offices to which naturalised Japanese could be appointed. Clause 16 of the legislation forbade the naturalised person, the child of a naturalised person and the person who had acquired Japanese citizenship through becoming the adopted child or husband of a Japanese woman who was a legal household head from being appointed to the following positions: member of the imperial assembly, minister of state, general or admiral in the imperial army or navy, chair or deputy-chair of the Privy Council, councillor, imperial household official appointed by the Emperor, ambassador extraordinary and plenipotentiary, chair of the Great Court of Cassation, chair of the Board of Audit or chair of the Court of Administration. These restrictions were based on a perception that appointments to positions in what might be regarded as the engine room of the nation-state required the type of allegiance only found in those born as Japanese. It further implied a belief on the part of lawmakers that, title or process notwithstanding, patriotism could not be imbued overnight through naturalisation.

In Japan, citizenship governance fell under the jurisdiction of the Home Ministry – at least until its abolition at the end of 1947 – a fact that was undoubtedly related to the Home Minister's role in granting this right. It was also most certainly a function of the fact that, in the context of the weighty issue of the rights and responsibilities of the nation-state, there was a need to exercise political judgement in deciding who could and could not be a citizen of Japan.[34] The fact that granting permission to naturalise required a high level of political judgement concerning the potential of the person in question to assimilate into and contribute to the Japanese nation-state further explains how citizenship governance became the responsibility of the Home Ministry rather than the Ministry of Justice.

Citizenship as subordinate to *ie*: Unity of family 'blood'

Citizenship unity among married couples and family members

In the modern nation-state, it was seen as self-evident that married couples (and, indeed, all members of the one family) should hold the same citizenship. The notion of citizenship unity among married couples was adopted in the legal systems of many countries with particular influence from the 1804 French Civil Code.[35] This resulted from the belief that the absence of such unity would result in conflict over national allegiance that would in turn lead to a breakdown of the family, the fundamental unit of society. Until the First World War, therefore, many countries adopted the principle of married couples having the same citizenship in order to prevent a clash of national consciousness and thus maintain the unity of family life.[36] Since it was the wife, however, who was forced to change her citizenship at the time of marriage, there was no doubt that this notion of citizenship unity between a husband and wife had its origins in the belief in male superiority that permeated marriage traditions at the time.[37]

Eventually, however, two problems arose regarding the need for citizenship unity among married couples; both manifested as a result of changes in the relationship between the individual and the nation-state that came with the epoch-making events of the First World War.

The first problem arose from the perspective of nationalism that argued that individual allegiance towards the state should not be sacrificed in order to maintain fidelity between a husband and wife. This reflected the grave import attributed to citizenship during the national crisis of war. During the Great War, in spite of never losing love for one's original homeland, one could become 'the enemy' simply by the fact of marriage and thus have all rights in relation to one's home country stripped away. On the other hand, because a woman who became a 'foreigner' through marriage was no longer under the legal control of the country in question, she also evaded her responsibilities as a citizen and could not be penalised for treasonous acts. Many fake marriages during the war years saw manifestations of both possibilities. At the end of the First World War in countries such as the United States, moreover, women gained the right to vote. This led to a school of thought that argued that it was problematic to extend suffrage to a foreign woman, merely through marriage to a local man, whose self-awareness as a citizen and political consciousness might be questionable.[38]

Secondly, from the end of the nineteenth century there was a growing recognition of the equality of the sexes throughout the West. Accordingly, any need for a wife to subordinate herself to the citizenship of her husband was regarded as an outdated expression of male superiority that ignored the wife's free will. As the women's emancipation movement gathered momentum and flourished towards the end of the First World War, a growing number of voices called for independent citizenship, where applicable, for wives and husbands. In Russia, where the Bolshevik Revolution had been based on ideals of equality, freedom for women to choose in this respect was granted in 1918. Other countries then followed suit, including the United States in 1922 and France in 1927.[39] Accordingly, although the notion of unity of citizenship for married couples had been perceived as self-evident until that time, this was now overridden by the principle of the right of married couples to hold citizenship status independent from each other.

We might, however, caution against thinking that this push for citizenship choice among couples came totally from humanist principles of equality. Domestic ultra-patriots also stressed various points.[40] These zealots warned against the disadvantage accrued by the nation-state in granting political and other rights to a person who was unfit to be a 'citizen'. This group was also concerned by the disadvantage to the state that would result from abuses of the system that might occur when, in the name of being a 'foreigner', a person evaded their civil duties and any sanctions this evasion might incur.

Ie constraints on citizenship: Principle of family citizenship unity

Japan's 1899 former Citizenship Law operated within the strong constraints of the *ie* family principles woven into the Meiji Civil Code and Koseki Registration Law. Most conspicuous in this respect was the admonition to those who drafted the legislation that 'It must accord with the family system inherent to our country'.[41] As noted above, the words 'family system inherent to our country' came in the context of the *jus sanguinis* and bloodline values that required all family members to be 'Japanese'. As also noted, this resulted in the adoption of husband and wife citizenship unity and the need for the citizenship of the wife to accord with that of the husband. The citizenship of the child, furthermore, was required to accord with that of the father, unless the child fell into one of the exceptional categories outlined above. In those cases, the citizenship of the mother prevailed. Absent from the original Meiji Code but provided in detail in the former Citizenship Law were special stipulations (Clauses 5, 6, 18, 19 and 23) that spelt out the process relating to the acquisition or loss of citizenship based on personal status changes. These changes included marriage to a foreigner, acknowledgement by a father of a child, adoption of a son-in-law and marriage where the husband entered into a family with the wife as legal household head (refer to Chapter Three).

The background to these stipulations began in July 1894 when the Unequal Treaty with Great Britain was amended and extraterritorial rights for Western nations abolished. In addition to guaranteeing freedom of travel and residence for foreigners, the amendments soon saw the dissolution of boundaries between foreigner precincts and Japanese municipalities. The authorities accordingly recognised that this would lead to foreigners and Japanese freely sharing living quarters and that, particularly following the amended treaty coming into effect on 17 July 1899, there would be a rise in the number of events such as marriage and the acknowledgement of children by foreign fathers.

This was the social context within which the law stipulated, for example, that a Japanese woman who left her *ie* family to become the wife of a foreigner lost her Japanese citizenship, while a foreign woman who entered a family as the wife of a Japanese man acquired Japanese citizenship. These changes to citizenship were not the result of individual will. Rather, they were generated through changes made to a koseki register record when a woman left or entered an *ie* family. While such changes generally involved the woman or wife, the system also took into account the special cases of men adopted as sons-in-law or who married into families with women as the legal household head in order to preserve the family line.

Nevertheless, when a foreigner was adopted or married a female legal household head, over and above being a resident for more than one year and being of good moral character, the chief necessary condition to become a Japanese was the Home Minister's permission.[42] Of those who submitted an application and received citizenship in this way between 1924 and 1950, the year in which the new post-war Koseki Registration Law came into effect, seventy-one foreigners were adopted into families while thirty foreigners married women who were legal household heads. In both cases Republican Chinese made up seventy percent (forty-eight Chinese or seventy-one percent of the former, and twenty-one or seventy percent of the latter).[43]

As discussed in the following chapter, the Meiji Civil Code stipulated that the 'spouse was a family member'. Nevertheless, in the case of a foreigner married couple, even if the husband took Japanese citizenship the wife initially retained that of her original country. This resulted in an 'international marriage' in which the wife was a foreigner while the legal household head named on the koseki register record was Japanese. In the *ie* family system which prioritised bloodline above all else and which decreed that family unity be preserved through husbands and wives (and parents and children) holding the same citizenship status, such an option could not be countenanced. Accordingly, amendments were made. Furthermore, persons who acquired Japanese citizenship through entering a family would lose that entitlement as a matter of course if their personal status changed due to events, such as divorce or the departure of an adopted child from a family, resulting in them no longer being a member of the family. These cases demonstrate that the citizenship status of the individual was essentially subservient to the social order of the *ie* family.

Clear steps were taken, nevertheless, to ensure that children did not become stateless. Thus, in cases where a father who had been a Japanese citizen (making his wife and children Japanese) took a different citizenship, the wife and children could also take that new citizenship. However, in the event of their not following the husband's citizenship, the wife and children could retain Japanese citizenship status.[44]

The fact that many Western countries also followed the principle of citizenship unity among family members has been discussed above. However, the influence of the Koseki Registration Law and related policy demands gave the practice a different dimension in Japan. This is apparent in each of the instances below.

Firstly, prioritisation of the family in Japan overrode dual citizenship concerns. In the case of the entry into a family of a foreigner wife or child from a country that did not require a change of citizenship through marriage or adoption, the wife or child in question acquired Japanese citizenship while simultaneously retaining their former status in that respect. In the case especially of citizenship change through adoption, there was no other country outside Japan, with the exception of Republican China (1929 Citizenship Law), that required this. Japan, furthermore, was the only country that required such a change when a foreign man married a woman who was the legal household head.[45] In cases in which the former country did not require renunciation of the original citizenship, such people of necessity acquired dual citizenship. The fact that the former Citizenship Law made no stipulation to prevent

Table 2.2: Acquisition and loss of Japanese citizenship based on the ie *family system in the former Japanese Citizenship Law*

Reasons for foreigners to acquire Japanese citizenship	Reasons for Japanese to lose Japanese citizenship
Marriage to a Japanese (Clause 5, No. 1)	*All Japanese*
Acknowledgment of paternity by a Japanese father (Clause 5, No. 3)	Marrying a foreigner and taking the husband's citizenship (Clause 18)[a]
Married into a family with a female household head (Clause 5, No. 4)	Being recognised as the child of a foreign father (Clause 23, Section 1)
Wife following the lead of a husband who had taken Japanese citizenship (Clause 13, Section 1)	Wife following the lead of a husband who lost Japanese citizenship (Clause 21)
Child following the lead of a father who had taken Japanese citizenship (Clause 15, Section 1)[b]	Child following a father who lost Japanese citizenship (Clause 21)
	Divorcing a Japanese (Clause 19)
	Previous foreigners only
	Dissolution of previous adoption by a Japanese (Clause 19)

Notes: [a] Before revisions to the legislation in 1916, a Japanese woman who married a foreigner lost her Japanese citizenship; [b] Conditional on the child being below the age of majority in terms of the law of their former country.

the acquisition of dual citizenship in these cases was 'the result of prioritising concerns about the unique nature of our country's family system over and above any concern relating to dual citizenship'.[46]

The second special characteristic of the Japanese Citizenship Law that drew on koseki register policy and practice related to the restrictions noted above on the appointment of foreigners to public office who acquired Japanese citizenship through naturalisation (Citizenship Law, Clause 16). Such restrictions did not apply to a wife or child who acquired Japanese citizenship by conforming to that of a husband or father. Nevertheless, those who acquired citizenship through being adopted or through marriage into a family headed by a woman were subject to limitations in terms of public office appointments. This apparent anomaly is undoubtedly related to the fact that only men held suffrage in the pre-war era.

These examples point to the ways in which the Citizenship Law of the Meiji state subordinated the freedom of the individual to acquire or renounce citizenship to the principle of one citizenship for all members of the Japanese *ie* family, a family unit which pivoted around the father as the family head.

The *ie* family and control of individual citizenship

Deliberations by the Legislative Investigative Committee in 1898 on the Citizenship Law Draft included discussions on the principle of citizenship unity for married couples. Clause 12, Section 1 of the original draft stated, 'The wife of a person who has taken Japanese citizenship shall, with her husband, be a holder of Japanese citizenship. However, this is limited to those cases to which no objections are lodged within one month of the husband's acquisition of Japanese citizenship becoming known'. On this point, committee member Isobe Shiro (1851–1923) commented, 'It is not logical to forcibly naturalise by law a person who does not wish to be Japanese', for 'over and above merely being granted citizenship, the person to whom this right is extended must be one who feels that holding Japanese citizenship is an honour'.[47] In other words, making all family members have the same citizenship as a matter of course did not necessarily engender a sense of belonging to the nation-state, and may in fact have even created the anomalous situation in which those without love for country were embraced as 'citizens'.

Rather than any sense of individual belonging, however, it was ultimately the 'pure blood' of the family accepting the individual that was the primary factor upon which citizenship was based. As Legislative Investigative Committee member Ume Kenjirō (1860–1910) stated, 'While it is acceptable for an unmarried woman to not follow her partner's lead, marriage is a clear indication of her intent to accord with her husband's decisions, including in matters of citizenship'.[48] The formality of marriage was thus regarded as a vow of spiritual submission by a wife to her husband, an interpretation that was further supported by the fact that the legal systems of many countries at the time accepted the wife's deference to her husband in citizenship matters.

Nevertheless, debate around the definition of the 'family' presented unresolved problems for lawmakers both in the context of international marriage and in the case of a husband or father changing a family's citizenship through naturalisation. The Meiji Civil Code stipulated that 'Persons *in a given* ie *family* who are related to the legal household head of the *ie* family and the spouse of the legal household head of the *ie* family constitute the family [*kazoku*]' (Clause 732, emphasis added). Even among Legislative Investigative Committee members, however, there was conflict around the interpretation of the words, 'in a given *ie* family'. Committee member Hozumi Nobushige summed up the problem when he declared, 'Rather than referring to cohabitation or living together, the phrase "in a given *ie* family" refers to those entered on a single koseki register record'.[49] In other words, 'in a given *ie* family' came to signify being entered in the same koseki register record (refer to Chapter Three). Essentially, as evident from the statement, 'whether or not the foreigner in a family holds koseki registration',[50] the focus of lawmakers was on how to deal with citizenship in those cases in which a foreigner had been entered into a koseki register record after becoming a member of a Japanese *ie* family.

If a foreigner did take koseki registration after becoming a member of a Japanese *ie* family, it was necessary to ensure that this husband and wife, and also their children, held the same citizenship in order to protect the pure bloodline of that register. This accorded with the 'principle of family citizenship unity' that underpinned Japanese citizenship law. Thus, it is clear that the citizenship of the 'Japanese' was regulated by *ie* family principles.

Even prior to the establishment of the former Citizenship Law, the issue of whether or not the acquisition or loss of citizenship by an individual should be subordinate to the demands of the *ie* family system was the subject of considerable debate during Legislative Investigative Committee discussions around the establishment of a Civil Code. For example, according to the principle that said, 'the wife enters the *ie* family of the husband', in an international marriage the wife was required to change her citizenship to that of her husband. In discussions on the Civil Code held at the 128th meeting of the Legislative Investigative Committee (2 November 1895), however, committee member Ume Kenjirō expressed the view that 'while it is most certainly not desirable to have a husband and wife with different citizenship, just because a person is no longer Japanese does not mean loss of love for the country. This would be extreme. So if the husband in this case does not want to become Japanese, I do not think that the wife should be asked to comply with her husband and lose her Japanese citizenship'.[51] That is to say, it was Ume's opinion that if demanding koseki register unity on the part of a husband and wife in an international marriage meant a change of citizenship against the will of one of the parties involved, then a rift over conflicting allegiance would inevitably be generated between the pair.

In Legislative Investigative Committee discussions on the Civil Code, however, there was common agreement that legislation pandering to notions of individualism would damage the 'glorious custom' of the traditional family of Japan. Bloodline at birth notwithstanding, the principle that all members of an *ie* family, the unity of which was maintained through the koseki registration system, would hold Japanese citizenship was strictly applied until the system was dismantled after the war.

Post-war revisions to the Citizenship Law

The maintenance of bloodline and *jus sanguinis* in post-war Japan

The post-war Citizenship Law, promulgated on 4 May 1950 and brought into operation on 1 July of that year, followed a comprehensive revision of the former Citizenship Law conducted in line with the spirit of the new Constitution that came into force on 3 May 1947. This legislation, however, inherited the patrilineal principles of the pre-war era.

Clause 2 of the new Citizenship Law read as follows:

> The child, in the following circumstances, is a citizen of Japan:
> 1. when the father is Japanese at the time of the birth of the child;
> 2. when the father, having died prior to the child's birth, was Japanese at the time of his death; and
> 3. when the child is born in Japan and the identity of both the father and mother is unknown, or when neither holds any citizenship status.

That is to say, for a child to acquire Japanese citizenship, primarily the father and secondarily the mother needed to demonstrate proof of holding Japanese citizenship. If neither parent was entered into a koseki register, then the child naturally could not be registered since there was no register for them to be entered into upon birth. It was therefore theoretically impossible to prove that the child was Japanese.

While *jus sanguinis* and bloodline clearly dominated, the existence of a stateless child was nonetheless undesirable. To avoid this contingency, the third point in Clause 3 above – 'in the case of being born in Japan' – supplementarily accepts the principle of *jus soli*, the principle of place of birth. Such a concession avoided a child being born stateless and without citizenship. Patrilineal bloodline principles, nevertheless, dictated that even a child born to a Japanese mother and foreign father must take the citizenship of the foreign father. In the case of a stateless father and a Japanese mother, however, as long as the child was born to a formally married couple and was 'legitimate', then the third point of Clause 2 of the law could be applied. With the lodgement of a notice of birth, the child would acquire Japanese citizenship by being entered into the mother's koseki register record.[52]

The post-war Citizenship Law was drawn up cognisant of the spirit of Clause 24 of the new Constitution that valorised respect for the individual and gender equality. This legislation therefore abolished the process, which had operated in the former law, of citizenship acquisition for a child through acknowledgement by the father. There were two reasons for this. Firstly, the automatic citizenship changes recognised in the former law that accompanied changes in personal status – including marriage, adoption, divorce and acknowledgement by a father – resulted from the demands of the *ie* family system rather than any will on the part of a wife or child. A requirement for these changes was thus contrary to the spirit of Clause 24 of the new Constitution. Furthermore, in terms of legal precedent in other places, many countries in the post-war era made the shift from requiring unity of citizenship for family members to permitting independent choice.

However, research by Okuda Yasuhiro into the acquisition of citizenship by a child through acknowledgement by the father found that rather than abolishing that procedure, many countries that adopted bloodline principles when determining citizenship retained this process as a means of diminishing discrimination between 'legitimate' and 'illegitimate' children.[53] From this perspective, given that a child can be born outside a formal marriage regardless of the *ie* family system, the abolition of citizenship acquisition through acknowledgement by a father in Japan's post-war new Citizenship Law reproduced and thereby reinforced, with the distinction between 'citizen' and 'foreigner', the discriminatory categories of 'illegitimacy' and 'legitimacy' that the koseki registration system created.

Gender equality in citizenship law

The post-war era saw a growing trend towards the basic social principles of equality between women and men. This further accelerated advocacy for the right to freely chose citizenship status. Furthermore, in objective terms, the so-called precedence originally given in patrilineal thinking to the relationship between the father and the son was problematised by the nature of the mother–child relationship that was grounded in the real-life experience of birth. In other words, the putative rationality of patrilineal principles was unmasked.

Clause 9, Section 2 of the Convention Against the Elimination of All Forms of Discrimination Against Women (CEDAW), adopted by the United Nations in December 1979 and put into practice in September 1981, stipulated, 'States Parties shall grant women equal rights with men to acquire, change or retain their nationality'. This clearly required equal treatment of females and males in the application of citizenship acquisition principles. In accordance with the Convention, European countries such as Switzerland, Sweden, Austria and Italy followed each other in replacing patrilineal principles with principles that gave equal weight to the value of the mother and the father in citizenship legislation.

Furthermore, the maintenance of patrilineality caused the following problems in terms of the citizenship rights of the individual. In cases in which the country of a child's father drew on *jus soli* to determine citizenship while that of the mother operated according to patrilineal *jus sanguinis* principles, a child born in the country of the mother had no means of acquiring citizenship and therefore became stateless. This situation arose with respect to children born to one parent from Japan and one from the United States, which determined citizenship according to place of birth. In Okinawa, where the United States operated military bases even after the proclamation of the San Francisco Peace Treaty, children born to men in the American military and Japanese women (referred to as Amerasian children) were made stateless in terms of the situation outlined above.

In July 1980, in line with the influence of international legal trends and a growing domestic awareness of gender equity, Japan became a CEDAW signatory. This drove a change that moved away from the patrilineal principles in operation since the Meiji era. In preparation for Japan's June 1985 CEDAW ratification (1985, Treaty No. 7), 25 May 1984 revisions to the Japanese Citizenship Law saw the momentous shift to *jus sanguinis* based on either the maternal or paternal line. While the operation of patrilineal *jus sanguinis* required a child born to a foreign father and Japanese mother to take foreign citizenship, the 1984 revisions made it possible for the child to acquire Japanese citizenship. This undoubtedly broadened the means by which one could qualify as 'Japanese'. However, as will be discussed in Chapter Six, even with the embrace of these policies, strictly enforced regulations designed to prevent dual citizenship were incorporated into the Koseki Registration Law, giving new authority and power to the capacity of the koseki registration system to prove that one was 'Japanese'.

3 Modern Japan and Koseki Registration: The 'Japanese People' Defined by the *Ie* Family

Pre-modern history of koseki registration: Feudal society

Ancient Japan and koseki registration

While the emergence of the koseki registration system in Japan traces back to the Yamato Dynasty (approx. fourth to seventh century), the origins of this system lie, in fact, in China. In terms of 'historical records', statements in *Nihon shoki* (The Chronicles of Old Japan) to the effect that registers of the people were created and various duties imposed on them during the reign of Emperor Sujin (late third to early fourth century?) suggest the inception at that time of Japan's census for the purpose of koseki registration. It is said that in the fourth year of the reign of Emperor Ingyō (fifth century?), the system of family name (*uji*) and clan title (*kabane*) was consolidated and enforced as law, with the koseki registration system adjusted accordingly.

The Taika Reforms (*Taika no kaishin*), proclaimed in 645, established a Ritsuryō system of governance modelled on that of China's Tang Dynasty. This codification confirmed 'the Emperor's ownership of all land and all people' (*kōchi-kōmin*) as the basic principle of Yamato nation governance. Under this policy, the state proceeded to centralise power and enforce the 'law of the periodic reallocation of farmland' (*handen shūju no hō*), with the primary aim of securing tribute collection as a revenue source. Crucial to this process was the reorganisation of society around the unit of the household and the creation of the koseki registration system (*henko zōseki*). According to *Nihon shoki*, the first decree for establishing 'family registers [koseki] and yearly tax records [*keichō*]' came with the Taika reforms. However, the compilation of koseki registers was carried out in particular provinces for particular classes even before that time. The *Nihon shoki* statement is therefore generally understood as referring to the first unified administration of a nation-wide koseki registration system.[1]

The basis of the Ritsuryō State, founded by order of the 670 'Registration in the Year of Kōgo' (*Kōgo-nenjaku*), lay in the koseki registers and yearly tax ledgers that operated at the provincial level. Koseki registers were compiled every six years and included the clan name, title and real name of each individual in a household. Yearly tax ledgers, which held information such as sex and age and which permitted the imposition of taxes and levies, were prepared annually. Household heads were in principle male, and male lineage was generally observed through a system referred to as 'entry of the child into the father's koseki register record' (*fushi-dōkan*) – this is in spite of the fact that, as a rule, husbands and wives had different surnames.[2] Whether or not this signifies the emergence of male dominance or patriarchy during the time of the Ritsuryō State is beyond the scope of this discussion. Nevertheless, given that women were generally exempt from the levies and taxes imposed on adult men by the Ritsuryō authorities, they were almost certainly less important in terms of the relationship between the government and the people at the time. This is further suggested by the detailed koseki registration information available for males. According to a study by Kishi Toshio (1920–1987), for example, koseki registers and yearly tax ledgers compiled under both the Taihō and Yōrō Codes provide details for males only in terms of levels of ill health and disability, such as 'mild condition' (*zanshitsu*), 'serious condition' (*tokushitsu*) or 'incurable disability' (*haishitsu*). This is likely because the Ritsuryō State exempted those whose health or physical condition was 'serious' or 'incurable' from levies and taxes.[3]

The ancient koseki registration system thus functioned primarily as a population ledger for taxation purposes. Nevertheless, it was also deployed as a means of identifying rank and class. In addition, the registers played a role in maintaining social order by preventing vagrancy and brigandage. During the late Nara to early Heian periods, however, it became increasingly difficult to control the people through the register system. Farmers, for example, found the heavy taxes increasingly intolerable, and there were many who abandoned their farmland, absconded, refused to enter a register or falsified a register entry. At the same time, there were increasing numbers of private estates (manors) under the control of aristocrats, temples and shrines or local powerful families that received tithing from the common people. With the tax base limited in this way to the wealthy, the Ritsuryō system founded on the *kōchi-kōmin* principle began to break down. Following the tenth century rise of government by Fujiwara regents whose power base lay in private land holdings, the koseki registration system lost its original function of universal levy and tax collection.[4] By the Kamakura and Muromachi eras, koseki registration operated as a process in name only.

In the Warring States era, however, new conditions saw a revival of the koseki registration system. As the various fiefdoms entered the all-out war that raged at the time, there was a need to mobilise farmers as troops for battle and labourers to construct civil works and fortifications. In order to gather information on the numbers of people and other resources at their disposal in their domains (*han*), some feudal and liege lords conducted censuses to identify taxpayers, dwellings and numbers of livestock.[5] While the substance of koseki registration was largely lost under warrior class rule, feudal lords seeking a tax system that could be smoothly administered continued to rely upon some form of population status register.

Tokugawa shogunate-domain system and koseki registration

Established in 1603, the Tokugawa shogunate set itself the task of rebuilding the moribund koseki registration system. Groundwork for this revival was laid by the previous Toyotomi Hideyoshi (1537–1598) regime which had surveyed farmland, enforced comprehensive tax collection and corvée contribution, mobilised samurai warriors for military service and introduced policies that clearly distinguished between warriors and peasants as a means of suppressing peasant revolts. Under the 'population census' (*hitobarai*) edict of 1591 (Tenshō Year 19), this administration also conducted a nation-wide door-to-door survey known as the 'survey of population, livestock and dwelling numbers' (*jinchiku yakazu aratame*).[6] Like the Toyotomi regime before it, the Tokugawa government sought to maintain koseki registers in order to control the people, to ensure the separation of warriors and peasants and to consolidate its territorial control.

The equivalent of the koseki registration system under the shogunate-domain government was known as the 'religious affiliation register' (*shūmon ninbetsu chō*) system. In 1641 (Kan'ei

18), following the 1637 (Kan'ei 14) Shimabara-Amakusa Rebellion, the Tokugawa government decreed a nation-wide ban against Christians and embarked on the eradication of Christianity across Japan. As a means of thoroughly enforcing this ban, especially in rural areas, the authorities created the '*terauke*' system that required Buddhist temples and Shinto shrines to verify that affiliated individuals were not Christian. This was the substance of what was referred to as the 'religious affiliation census' (*shūmon aratame*).[7]

The basis of this religious affiliation census was the 'population register' (*ninbetsu chō*) compiled for each village. Information in this register came from a government census that collected personal information such as birth, death, sex, age and status (wife, servant etc.) for all members of each household. It is thus apparent that the '*shūmon aratame*' or religious affiliation census and '*ninbetsu aratame*' or village level population register had different purposes. The aim of the former was the elimination of 'heretics' from Japanese society, while the latter surveyed the people with a view to imposing tributes and extracting labour services.

During the Kyōhō period of the early eighteenth century, however, religious persecution became less severe. Accordingly, the *shūmon aratame* and *ninbetsu aratame* were amalgamated and administered nation-wide as the *shūmon ninbetsu chō* or *shūmon ninbetsu aratame chō*.[8] In the city of Edo, however, the *ninbetsu aratame* was also used for policing purposes, such as cracking down on vagrancy, controlling immigrant workers and searching criminals.

It is commonly known that a joint responsibility scheme known as the 'five households group' (*gonin gumi*) was established in rural villages for the purposes of ensuring good order through mutual surveillance, collecting annual tributes and prosecuting Christians. Initially, the *gonin gumi* scheme had its own registers known as '*gonin gumi ninbetsu chō*' that were independent from the *shūmon ninbetsu chō*. It appears, however, that the population register function of the *gonin gumi* scheme was gradually assumed by the *shūmon ninbetsu chō*, while the *gonin gumi* register developed into bylaws for *gonin gumi* members.[9] Of interest is the fact that the concept of 'family' subject to registration varied between the *ninbetsu chō* and the *shūmon aratame chō*.[10]

Koseki registration under the shogunate government, however, remained fraught with imperfection. To some extent this was because, in the absence of unified law, census procedures as administered by the individual domains varied between provinces. Confirming the pluralistic nature of early modern society, there was also discrimination on the basis of status and occupation in register compilation systems. Exemption from the household survey was granted both to the Buddhist monks and nuns who had carriage of the religious affiliation census and to members of the ruling warrior class. Furthermore, according to work by Ishii Ryōsuke, in addition to nuns, certain categories of religious workers and religious entertainers, such as Shintō priests, Buddhist ascetics (mountain monks), fortunetellers, buskers or other itinerant entertainers and Shintō dancer-actors were generally not permitted to live in the townships of Edo. The registration of these groups, unlike that of the common people, was accordingly administered by temples and shrines.[11] In addition, the *koseki* registration of 'humble and nonperson' (*eta-hinin*) people, who were regarded as below the warrior, farmer, artisan and merchant (*shi-nō-kō-shō*) classes, was administered by the individual referred to as 'Danzaemon' who was appointed by the Tokugawa government to act as the leader of the *eta-hinin* class.

Thus, although its function centred on both the religious affiliation survey and population census, the major purpose of the *shūmon ninbetsu chō* system, like that of the ancient koseki registration system, was to police. Yet, the *ninbetsu aratame* was not a comprehensive resident registration system covering all ranks and classes. In the late Edo period, severe famine and rising immigrant worker numbers saw a marked increase in population mobility between rural villages and cities. This led to the flow of homeless people and immigrant workers from farming villages into Edo. While the *ninbetsu chō* became an important source of information in both controlling and repatriating those who were part of this influx,[12] the koseki registration function of surveying and recording residential matters was to some extent compromised.

Meiji era koseki registration: Defining 'authentic Japanese'

The Meiji Restoration and deserters

Upon signing the 1854 Japan–US Peace and Amity Treaty and opting to 'open the country', Japan's political leaders faced the threat of external pressure from major Western powers. Seeking to protect the country's independence during this tense international situation, the country's leaders came to realise the importance of the rise of nationalism at the local level and of coming together as a people under the common consciousness of 'one nation'.

Symbolising the unity of the 'Japanese' nation was none other than the Emperor. With the Tokugawa shogunate ceding political power to the throne, Japan entered the period of 'restoration of imperial rule'. In 1868, the Meiji Emperor accordingly promulgated 'The Charter Oath of the Five Articles of the Imperial Covenant' (*Gokajō no goseimon*) and proclaimed Japan as a theocracy under the rule of a 'living god' (*arahito gami*). The modern Japanese state was further set on its course with a return to the mythical narrative that the nation had been founded by the legendary Emperor Jimmu.

Following the 'Decree for the Restoration of Imperial Rule' (*Ōsei fukko no daigōrei*), former shogunate territories came under the direct control of the imperial court and, in accordance with the new three-jurisdiction system of 'urban prefecture-domain-rural prefecture' (*fu-han-ken*), were reorganised into *fu* or *ken*. Japan's national legal system remained in transition, however, with individual domains continuing to enforce various shogunate era laws and regulations. The *shūmon ninbetsu chō* system also remained in use for the purpose of koseki registration.[13] With the spread of social disorder at the time of the Boshin Civil War (January 1868; Keiō 4) and the increasingly fluid political and social situation that followed the opening of the country to the outside world, there was a marked increase throughout the country in the numbers of people leaving their registered domiciles or deserting their domains.

The disintegration of the koseki registration system around the time of the Meiji Restoration was an expression of the strained relationship between individualism and political integration during the emergence of the modern Japanese state. Removing oneself from a koseki register was to remove oneself from the group to which one belonged. According to Maruyama Masao, changes to traditional relationships in the life of an individual leads to a loss of a sense of connection to the group and the values to which the 'self' was previously attached. This, in turn, generates a deep and painful sense of estrangement that triggers 'rebellion or displacement of the existing object of loyalty'. For the political class in Japan, the restoration of imperial rule brought a time during which 'internal tension and conflict between loyalty and rebellion in the individual reached a scale and height unprecedented in the country's history'.[14] This was because exiting a koseki register or domain led to an individual relinquishing community and value attachments, a process which in turn exacerbated the instability of their political sentiment.

Viewing re-registration as a priority both in terms of suppressing pluralistic identities and radicalisation among deserters and bringing them back under 'imperial power', the new government frantically sought to have deserters entered once more into the koseki registration system. On 7 March 1868 (Meiji 1), the authorities accordingly proclaimed a comprehensive crackdown on desertion that applied to all social ranks, from warriors down to peasants and servants. However, the proclamation notably stated, 'Since, in fact, it was *the policy error of suppressing free speech that led to people fleeing their places of residence*, those who voice opinions in an attempt to benefit the empire and their masters must, as a means of preventing social division, enjoy *an open channel of dialogue* [*genro-dōkai*] and be dealt with fairly' (emphasis added).[15]

Here, the expression '*genro-dōkai*' conveys a sense of political participation. The political ideology of 'public opinion' (*kōron*), in circulation since the dying days of the Tokugawa shogunate, promoted political integration through 'freedom of speech' as a means of nation building. Against the background of a growing desire for national unity in the face of external pressure, those who advocated for public opinion ideology as a way to abolish the existing status hierarchy and ensure the ideal of government based on free speech ranged from shogunate cabinet officials down to low-ranking warriors.[16] Succumbing to the popularity of these ideas, the new government acknowledged that the increase in deserter numbers was caused by policy incompetence on the part of the authorities. The authorities also supported the pluralisation of the political process through 'freedom of speech' as a means of ensuring that government administrative processes would advance 'the empire' (*kōkoku*) by benefiting even the bottom rungs of society.

Given that the adoption of a public opinion policy clearly prevented the categorical ostracisation of deserters as outlaws, the government faced something of a dilemma. The main advocates of 'public opinion' among the political classes during 'the restoration of imperial rule' were the samurai who had participated in the overthrow of the Tokugawa shogunate. Their forerunners in the anti-shogunate movement were the lordless *rōnin*, or wandering samurai, from various domains who had previously gathered in Kyoto. The tremendous energy of these restoration era deserters was noted with awe by Fukuchi Gen'ichirō (1841–1906) who observed, '*Those who left the service of various domains* gathered in the name of vagabondage with other volunteers to assert their radical political views; their influence reached as far as the Kanto region and was unstoppable once the situation erupted' (emphasis added).[17] Opting out of the registration system and taking a position free of domain or class interests was a necessary step for warriors seeking to use 'public opinion' to reform the political regime.

The government's indecisive response to the issue of desertion was apparent in an ordinance issued on 14 August 1868 (Meiji 1), stating as follows:

> Owing to unavoidable circumstances, [these men] *separated themselves from their respective domains, moved in all directions, advocated justice, gave their lives for a nation in crisis, transformed the ethos of indolence that had prevailed for several centuries and in no small measure helped the nation survive.* The successful restoration of imperial rule today is largely attributable to the contributions of these leaders. (emphasis added)[18]

In other words, the authorities were forced to acknowledge the fact that those who had freely left their domains to traverse the country following the emergence of a modern political consciousness were the driving force behind the political changes that, with the fall of the shogunate and the restoration of imperial rule, brought an end to the stagnation that had marked the end of several centuries of feudal governance.

Nevertheless, the disruption to social order caused by non-conformist deserters was considered inimical to the higher purpose of ensuring the stability of the imperial regime (*goseitai*). The new government frequently sounded warnings to this effect and issued 'proclamations' (*tasshi*) ordering the arrest and re-registration of deserters. These measures were also motivated by a desire on the part of policymakers to maintain order in cities, especially the imperial capital. From the final days of the Tokugawa government, Kyoto, Japan's political centre, had been the stage for the loyalist anti-shogunate movement and therefore naturally had a high concentration of deserters. To the Kyoto prefectural government, fundamental koseki register reform was essential as a means of repairing an ineffective residential registration system and also as a way of ensuring the reliable status registration that would assist in restoring social order. In October 1868 (Meiji 1), the Kyoto prefectural government enacted the 'Kyoto Prefecture Koseki Register Administration Law' (*Kyoto-fu koseki shihō*). This notably expounded the significance of household records in terms of status registration and genealogy on the grounds that 'Koseki registers contain wide-ranging and detailed information about age, death, birth, residence and occupation'. The law particularly emphasised the fact that registration confirmed those registered as 'upstanding citizens of the capital and not suspicious drifters'. That is to say, koseki registration provided valuable evidence of people being members of 'the public'.[19]

Edo, the previous seat of the shogunate that was renamed Tokyo once the imperial capital transfer was announced in July 1868 (Keiō 4), experienced a huge influx of deserters and vagrants from all over Japan. This led to a rise in the numbers of the 'property-less and homeless' in the imperial capital and confronted policymakers with serious problems related to order and public morals. On 22 March 1869 (Meiji 2), the new government issued the Tokyo prefectural government with a 'Proclamation of the Grand Council of State' (*dajōkan tasshi*) promoting the 'repatriation and registration' of 'those who have fallen out of the registration system'. Emphasising the virtues of koseki registration from a patronage point of view, the proclamation stressed the urgency of the situation by declaring '*Koseki registers are the foundation of governance* on which all administrative matters are based' (emphasis added). Furthermore, the statement asserted that, without reliable koseki registration, 'the ideal of edification and benevolent rule' could not be achieved.[20] Ultimately, this document argued that the koseki registration system was the basis of all government decision-making.

Support for the need to improve the Koseki Registration Law is also evident in 'A Proposal to Clarify National Polity and Establish a Form of Government' (*Kokutai shōmei seitai kakuritsu ikensho*), thought to have been prepared by Iwakura Tomomi (1825–1883) in August 1870 (Meiji 3). A prolonged peace had prevailed in the 'three major cities' of Tokyo, Kyoto and Osaka, and Iwakura argued that this had attracted large migrant populations. As a result, these cities were rampant with 'indolence and immorality'. Noting that Koseki Registration Law inadequacies and poor policing had impeded progress in the urgent task of re-settling vagrant migrants back into rural areas, Iwakura recommended that each city 'should, for the time being, permit people to leave while forbidding people with no good reason from entering'.[21] According to Iwakura, without the operation of a viable koseki registration system it was not possible to prevent the flow of drifters that was compromising law and order in the three major cities. His argument recalls the 'repatriating the people to their villages' (*hito gaeshi*) policies of the Tokugawa shogunate period.

On 4 September 1870 (Meiji 3), after carrot-and-stick attempts to encourage the re-registration of deserters by publicising the political significance of koseki registration, the new government finally issued 'Rules for the Re-registration of Non-Registered Property-less Persons' (*Dassuseki musan no yakara fukuseki kisoku*). These rules stipulated that all deserters, 'whether warrior or civilian', should be returned to their original place of registration at the expense of either their families or the local community. Nonetheless, believing that the movement of people could be restricted under the crumbling koseki registration system was a regression to feudal thinking, and relying on village self-government to enforce such restrictions was completely unrealistic.[22] These re-registration rules reveal the frustrations that resulted from the contradictory demands that beset those in power who, in spite of the fact that population flow from rural villages into cities was an inevitable phenomenon in a modern society embracing capitalism, tried to bind people to their places of birth under an outdated koseki registration system.

Restoration era koseki registration: A 'register of subjects'

It is clear from the above that the measures promoted by the new government to re-register deserters relied on both an outdated koseki mechanism and a class system based on feudal principles. Needless to say, modern democracy rejects restrictions on individual freedom for reasons of status and family background.

As is widely known, Fukuzawa Yukichi (1834–1901) argued for the 'break-down of social class' (*monbatsu daha*) as a necessary condition for the realisation of political and social democracy in Japan. In the opening passages of his *Seiyō jijō* (Conditions in the

West), published in 1866 (Keiō 2), Fukuzawa argued for the right of people to choose, in contrast to the hereditary occupation system of the feudal era, an occupation free of legal restrictions by the state. He further emphasised that there should be 'no discrimination between the warrior, farmer, artisan and merchant classes, no emphasis on people's family background and no respect for people on the basis of their rank at court'. This, he argued, would 'allow people of all classes to find their own stations in life, and prevent any obstruction whatsoever from impeding either the freedom or rights of others to develop their own natural abilities'.[23] Fukuzawa's ideal was to allow individuals to develop their 'abilities' as members of a classless society with freedom in choice of work. An essential move in achieving this ideal was the abolition of a koseki registration system that entrenched the class hierarchy of 'warrior, farmer, artisan and merchant' that underpinned the feudal society of the early modern era.

Contrary to Fukuzawa's exhortation for what might be referred to as an 'internalised modernisation process', and determined to establish centralised power structures in the true meaning of the restoration of imperial rule, the new government sought a drastic overhaul of the koseki registration system. In order to dismantle the shogunate-domain regime and create in its place a central mechanism, the authorities needed to submit the general population to a unified national koseki register framework. The first task in this project was to transfer the administration of koseki registers from individual domains to the direct control of the central government.

Official advocacy for 'the return of the domains and people to the Emperor' (*hanseki hōkan*) sought to have all feudal domain lords submit to the Emperor's authority. The 'Return of the Domains Memorandum', submitted in January 1869 (Meiji 2) and jointly signed by the domain lords of Satsuma, Chōshū, Tosa and Higo, admonished the 'private ownership' of land and people by liege lords. This memorandum stressed that a move away from the medieval feudal regime and a return to the ancient 'imperial ownership of land and people' was a prerequisite for national unification. To this end, the document reflected as follows: 'Where your loyal subjects reside is the Emperor's land, the loyal subjects whom you govern are the Emperor's people. Why, then, should these subjects be privately owned?'[24] When, following the Memorandum, a total of 262 domains proposed to return to the imperial fold, the new government implemented 'the return of the domains' from June

1869. Yet, rather than constructing individuals as modern 'citizens', this concentration of power at the centre saw people integrated into the new system as mere 'subjects' who were denizens of the Emperor's land.

Having achieved the critical objective of the submission of liege lords to the rule of the Emperor, in March 1869 (Meiji 2) the government announced guidelines for a new local government administrative framework through the 'Prefectural Administration Order' (*Fuken shisei junjo*). This order stated, 'The enumeration of households is the foundation of prosperity for all, while the organisation of five-household groups forms the basis for harmony among the common people'.[25] Once the government distributed a model law in the form of the 'Kyoto Prefecture Koseki Register Administration Law' referred to above, Tokyo and other prefectures began to enact similar koseki register legislation.

While the new government initially delegated deserter re-registration responsibility to local authorities, it now decided to facilitate the centralisation of power by setting up a unified national koseki registration system that integrated koseki register administration into a single operation under direct control at the national level. Established in August 1869 (Meiji 2), *Minbu-shō* (Ministry of People's Affairs) assumed responsibility for koseki registration administration. In December of that year, the new ministry prepared a set of 'Draft Regulations for the Compilation of Koseki Registers' (*Koseki hensei shokisoku an*).[26] These draft regulations are notable for the intention to enter all nationals, with the exception of the imperial family, into koseki registers based on place of residence '*without reference to social class or official rank*' (emphasis added). In this way, the koseki registration system, or 'register of subjects', was to be a tool for national unification. The regulations nevertheless retained various conspicuous elements of hierarchical feudal ideology. These included division of those registered into the three categories of nobility, warrior and commoner, and the omission from the general register of people from *eta-hinin* communities.

Establishing the Jinshin koseki registration system

Etō Shinpei (1834–1874), the Minister of Justice spearheading government efforts to modernise the early Meiji legal system, stressed that a koseki registration law was a necessary element of a modern nation-state governed according to the rule of law. Etō also argued that the registration system created by such a law should be based on accurate information about those registered. Aware that all Western nations had some form of status or identity registration system, Etō saw the need for Japan, too, to enact 'stringent laws on marriage, birth and death'.[27] He advocated for status registration under a systematic koseki registration law because '*accurate knowledge of the location of the citizen*' (emphasis added) was critical if the newly modernising state was to grow its 'prosperity and power' on par with major Western countries.

Taking these factors into account, the Ministry of People's Affairs drafted a national Koseki Registration Law, promulgated on 4 April 1871 (Meiji 4) as Decree No. 170 by the Grand Council of State.[28] The Jinshin koseki registration system was the entity created under this law. By bringing together the various registers previously compiled at the prefectural level, the Jinshin survey sought to produce 'a koseki registration procedure for the entire nation' (preamble to Decree No. 170).

The preamble to the Decree declared the political significance of the Jinshin system as follows.

> Ascertaining the koseki registration and its registered numbers in detail is a matter of the highest priority among the affairs of state. It goes without saying that protection of all nationals is an essential duty of the government. How can the government provide protection without ascertaining who the people to be protected are? It is for this reason that the government must maintain detailed koseki registers. Any person who leads a healthy and peaceful life is necessarily receiving the benefits of protection by the government. Conversely, *any person who avoids registration and remains unaccounted for is naturally akin to a non-national as he is not under government protection.* It is for this reason that people must submit to koseki registration. (emphasis added)

In other words, the preamble sought to mount a compelling argument for koseki registration by emphasising the fact that such registration was a key state policy and that people would be recognised as 'nationals' only when entered into a koseki register. Those not registered would be cast 'out of the nation' without state protection.

American political scientist James W. Garner (1871–1931) argued that a fundamental and necessary function of a state is the attempt to justify its own existence.[29] In order to consolidate itself as a legitimate institution, the new government of Japan adopted the tactic of impressing upon its people the disadvantages of falling outside state protection. At a later meeting of the 'Council of Elders' (*Genrōin*), Sano Tsunetami (1822–1902) praised this tactic as 'the wisdom of benevolent rule by a sacred Emperor', noting that 'A government could not be said to be fulfilling its duty if it did not take care of its people, who are its children, or make sure the people are in safe hands'.[30] The parent (government) could only protect its children (people) through the device of a koseki registration system that provided information on numbers, status and relations. By likening the relationship between the government and people to that of a parent and child, government paternalism drew on comforting language to disguise the coercive nature of registration procedures.

Jinshin koseki registration was compiled with each household under the direction of a '*koshu*' (legal household head). These household heads were answerable to '*kochō*' (government officials in charge of administering koseki registration). The '*ko*' (household) here was a real living community, conceptually different from the *ie* family in law (see below). In other words, the subject of this census was the 'home' (*kaoku*). The adoption of a koseki registration survey that was similar to a census in method was the result of the Restoration lifting the previous ban on migration. Under the Jinshin system, each household head had an obligation to report the name, age, relationship and religion of every member of their household. Under the 'Outline of the New Code' (*Shinritsu kōryō*) (Decree of the Grand Council of State No. 944) enacted on 20 December 1870 (Meiji 3), as the new state's first criminal code, concubines, too, were legally recognised as relatives and thus entered into early koseki register records. The demands of the Revision of the Unequal Treaties, however, and a desire to have parity with the West resulted in monogamy becoming the norm in Japan. Reference to concubines as family members was thus removed from the revised Criminal Code of 1880, after which these women also disappeared from koseki register records. The new system called for all koseki documents to be updated every six years.

What, then, does the Jinshin koseki registration system tell us about the social organisation of the 'Japanese people'? This can be summarised in three main points, the first two of which are apparent from Rule No. 1 of the Decree of the Grand Council of State No. 170, which stated, 'The purport of the formulation of this law is *to govern without exception the general subjects* (*from nobles through to warriors, soldiers, priests, officials, monks and commoners*) *at their places of residence*' (emphasis added).

Firstly, the Jinshin system attempted to achieve '*shimin byōdō*' (equality of the people) by entering individuals in a non-discriminatory manner that would lead to the aggregation of all into a horizontal relationship as 'subjects' of the Emperor. In response to a Kyoto Prefecture inquiry regarding the actual intent of the Jinshin system, the Ministry of People's Affairs stressed on 17 June 1871 (Meiji 4), two months after the proclamation of Decree No. 170, that replacing existing 'class and status-based' records with the new Jinshin koseki records would release people from the ties of the feudal class system and ensure 'the equal rights of all'. Given that the household registers which had been compiled for different 'classes and statuses' were not consistent, the Ministry further declared that, in keeping with 'the objectives of modernisation', it was 'the aim of the current government *to break down the familial relationships inherent in class and status and to give all people equal rights*' (emphasis added).[31]

The Jinshin koseki registration system deviated in major ways from the Edo era *ninbetsu aratame* system, which embodied the status hierarchy of the shogunate-domain political regime. For example, while Buddhist monks had previously received special treatment as 'unworldly people' and were therefore not entered into the 'secular' ledgers of Edo times,[32] the Jinshin system merely registered monks as 'general subjects'.

Yet, as evident from the treatment of *eta-hinin*, it was an exaggeration to say that the Jinshin system upheld 'equality of the people'. Rule No. 32 of Decree No. 170, for example, stated that *eta-hinin* shall 'not be recorded in the same register as commoners'. In terms of registration procedure, this clearly created a division between *eta-hinin* and 'general subjects'. On 28 August 1871 (Meiji 4), a proclamation of the Grand Council of State officially abolished the *eta-hinin* designation, a move that saw this group included in regular koseki registers.[33] Nevertheless, registers had a section in which 'class designation' was entered, and information such as 'former *eta*' or 'new commoner' continued to be recorded. While the government promulgated 'one monarch only under whom all subjects are equal' (*ikkun banmin*) as the first principle of the Restoration, it was nonetheless convenient to maintain discriminatory feudal conventions in the practice of day-to-day governance.

In order to reinforce the sanctity and inviolability of the Emperor as the ruler of all 'general subjects', it was necessary to place the Emperor – and the imperial family – above the koseki register system of 'commoners'. For this reason, the phrase 'demoted to the status of subject' came into circulation in the case of the creation of a new koseki register record for an imperial family member who joined an aristocratic family through marriage or adoption.

A second key point was the definition of 'Japanese national' according to the notion of residence. This led to the emergence in the modern Japanese state of the concept of 'original Japanese people' (*ganso Nihonjin*). The new government announced that those residing in a territory under the jurisdiction of the Emperor would become imperial 'subjects' of equal standing and that koseki registration would serve as official verification of this fact. Legal historian Fukushima Masao (1906–1989) referred to this as 'bondage to the koseki register instead of bondage to the land'.[34] Foreigner enclaves such as open ports, however, enjoyed extraterritorial rights and were excluded from the household census.

The third point was the intent to bring 'subjects' under Shinto control through koseki registration. In the early Meiji era, in conjunction with the government campaign that accompanied the Imperial Ordinance on the Establishment of Shinto, the Jinshin koseki registration system was assigned the role of indoctrinating the people through the dissemination of State Shinto. Rule No. 20 of Decree No. 170 stipulated that, when conducting a survey, census officers should check the 'talismans' (*mamorifuda*) of an individual's 'local patron deity' (*ujigami*). On 4 July 1871 (Meiji 4), the Grand Council of State made three proclamations relating to religion. These were 'Regulations for Local Shinto Shrines' (*Gōsha teisoku*), 'Procedures for Shinto Shrine Parishioner Surveys' (*Daishō jinja ujiko shirabekata*) and 'Rules for Shinto Priests when Issuing Talismans' (*Daishō jinja shinkan mamorifuda sashidashikata kokoroe*).[35] Each household census district was assigned one local Shinto shrine and all 'Japanese people' within the district became 'parishioners' (*ujiko*) of that shrine. Residents were accordingly entered into the parishioner register and issued with talismans from the district registration officer. This 'parishioner talisman', to be held by the individual from birth to death, was to serve along with koseki registration as a 'certificate of nationality as an imperial subject'.[36] Issuing an individual parishioner talisman, however, was inconsistent with the focus in registration law on the household. Since it was necessary to prioritise koseki registration, parishioner survey regulations were hastily abolished in May 1873.

While the parishioner registration system may have come to a premature end, the Jinshin koseki registration system continued to record the name of the 'patron shrine' (*ujigami jinja*) of each district until 1885.[37] The intent was to reorganise the Shinto shrine network to correspond to the administrative unit for koseki registration. There was also a need to strengthen the vertical relationship between the Emperor and his 'subjects' under 'the way of being with the gods' (*kannagara no michi*), which taught that all things were guided by divine providence.[38]

As noted above, the spirit of the Jinshin system indicated a shift from the previous security and policing purpose of the registration system, including deserter or drifter control and population mobility regulation, to the more sophisticated political goal of reorganising the 'Japanese people'. Yet, while notions of modern democracy are built around the idea of 'citizens' who, no longer beholden to feudalistic status relationships, participate voluntarily in political decision-making as constituents of the state, the political integration promoted by the Jinshin system merely affirmed the status of individuals as passive, subservient 'subjects'. There was no scope for the type of independence that was the true attribute of the 'citizen'.

The downfall of the Jinshin koseki registration system

The purpose of the Jinshin system, which came into effect on 1 February 1872, was to provide the government with basic information about available human resources in order to facilitate the policy development required to enhance the wealth and military prowess of the nation. This development related to matters such as land tax reform, the introduction of conscription and education system reform. The implementation of the Jinshin system marked the point at which, in addition to supporting the historical objective of policing, the administration of koseki registers promoted the rise of a bureaucracy with the ability to centralise government authority in Japan. Koseki register administration responsibilities were given to the Ministry of Home Affairs (*Naimu shō*), newly established in November 1873 as 'the body to administer the country's affairs of public peace and security' (Ministry of Home Affairs Staff Organisation – *Naimu shō shokusei*), through its Koseki Registration Office (renamed the Koseki Registration Bureau in April 1896). In addition to matters relating to policing, local government and the Shinto religion, the Ministry took control of the administration of the koseki registers that recorded the status of the 'Japanese people'.

By March 1873 the nation-wide compilation of the Jinshin survey was complete. According to a report by the Koseki Registration Bureau of the Ministry of Home Affairs, within the amazingly swift timeframe of fourteen months from the commencement of the compilation process, 'a total of over 31,000 koseki register volumes were put in order across the country'. Accordingly, the 'National Koseki Register Chart of Meiji 5' (*Meiji 5-nen no zenkoku koseki hyō*) was compiled for distribution in March 1873.[39] The undoubtedly rushed nature of the process, however, led to substantial omissions and errors. Given that the contents were far from 'in order', the requirement for a sexennial update of Jinshin koseki records (Decree No. 170) was suspended in July 1873.

Nevertheless, the promulgation of the 1873 Conscription Ordinance made it crucial for the government to determine the numbers available to be mobilised for 'universal conscription' (*kokumin kaihei*). A decision was therefore made for the Koseki Registration Bureau to conduct a nationwide annual census commencing on 1 January 1874. The Ministry of Home Affairs remained alarmed, however, by the large number of omissions from the koseki registers at the town and village level. On 19 December 1876, shortly before the conduct of the proposed 1 January census of the forthcoming year, Minister of Home Affairs Ōkubo Toshimichi (1830–1878) suggested to the Prime Minister (*dajō daijin*), Sanjō Sanetomi (1837–1891), that the Koseki Registration Law be revised. Ōkubo acknowledged that, as was apparent from the fact that similar legislation operated in advanced nations throughout the world, the Koseki Registration Law was indispensable for administering policies of state. Laws of this nature, he further noted, had operated from ancient times in Japan. While considerable progress had been

Table 3.1: National surveys of numbers of households, household heads and population (1872–1876)

Year	Households[a]	Household heads[b]	Population	Population change
1872	7,107,841	6,945,204	33,110,825	–
1873	7,101,325	6,987,368	33,300,675	189,850
1874	7,131,070	7,054,442	33,625,678	325,003
1875	7,220,548	7,167,887	33,997,449	371,771
1876	7,293,098	7,263,478	34,338,404	340,955

Notes: [a] Temples excluded; [b] Monastic household heads excluded.
Sources: 'Naimu kyō dai 3 kai nenpō' in *Naimu shō nenpō hōkokusho*, Vol. 5, p. 35, and 'Naimu kyō dai 4 kai nenpō furoku 2' in *Naimu shō nenpō hōkokusho*, Vol. 6, p. 351.

made in this respect in the several years since the post-Restoration institution of a new koseki registration law, koseki registration procedures in regions of high population mobility had lacked due diligence. As a result, significant 'problems of neglect and carelessness' had occurred. Arguing ominously that these matters would only be aggravated by annual data collection, Ōkubo suggested that census surveys instead be conducted at intervals of five or ten years. Given the unsatisfactory results produced to date by the current law, he further proposed that the government should halt the 1877 census and swiftly embark on legislative reform.[40] On 5 February 1877, the Grand Council of State responded to Ōkubo's suggestions by notifying all prefectures that the annual census was suspended pending the formulation of new koseki register rules.[41]

Given that the Jinshin koseki registration system lacked deadlines or penalty provisions for non-registration, it was natural from an institutional perspective that householder self-reporting was slow and inaccurate. Even within the government, Jinshin register entry procedures were criticised as 'destined to become a process in name only'.[42] Table 3.1 provides information on the census results reported by the Ministry of Home Affairs. Firstly, it is clear that in some years the number of households exceeds the number of household heads by more than 100,000. Such discrepancies can be partially explained by the use of undefined census criteria, which could see uninhabited dwellings classified as 'households'. The table furthermore indicates that there was a population increase of more than 300,000 over the three years from 1874. This is notwithstanding other Ministry data that reports birth and death numbers in 1876 as 869,126 and 654,562 respectively, making natural population growth for that year about 214,000.

The Ministry's Koseki Registration Bureau suspected that issues relating to 'population growth' figures resulted from incremental reporting by those who had initially been omitted from the registration system. Yet, while acknowledging the need for revisions to the Koseki Registration Law, the Bureau lamented that 'While some might attribute this [discrepancy] to household census process inadequacies, there is no doubt that the real reason is careless self-reporting by people ignorant of the existence of koseki register rules'.[43] In spite of repeated exhortations in the preamble to the implementation of the Jinshin system, the masses had clearly failed to heed arguments promoting the benefits of koseki registration.

Jinshin system revision demands: Conflict over military service

While the Jinshin survey was clearly ineffective as a population census, the Ministry of Army (*Rikugun shō*) identified further shortcomings regarding status registration. Expressing particular dissatisfaction that defective koseki register records made it impossible to enforce the 1873 Conscription Ordinance, thus permitting many to evade the draft, the Ministry demanded sweeping changes in order to achieve state goals of increasing wealth and military power (*fukoku kyōhei*).

The possibility that an only child might die in battle after being drafted presented a threat to the continuation of that family line. Since families were the very source of future soldiers, this would defeat the purpose of the Conscription Ordinance. To protect the continuation of families, household heads (that is, eldest sons) were exempted from military service. This demonstrated that even the power of the state could be forced to make concessions to the family.

There were families, however, who tried to exploit this provision by having a younger son adopted as the eldest son of another family, or by establishing a 'branch family' to permit a younger son to gain household head status. In this way younger sons were able to evade conscription.

The Meiji government originally established the koseki registration system as a means of authoritatively furnishing an official record of the 'registration of imperial subjects'. Adding the conflicting function of enlistment register to this base purpose was, not surprisingly, one reason that draft evasion became rampant. This was because once a person was recorded in the register as household head or eldest son, such information became an officially recorded fact that even the state lacked the power to override.

It was impossible, however, for the state to turn a blind eye to such flights from 'dedication to the nation' (*hōkoku*). In 1878, therefore, the government banned the creation of a branch family as a means of draft evasion, while in October 1879 the Conscription Ordinance was revised to place limits on exemptions for household heads and adopted sons. Nevertheless, Minister of Army Ōyama Iwao (1842–1916) expressed deep frustration at the fact that draft evasion continued to occur across the country due to lax koseki register management. He therefore proposed drastic revisions to the Koseki Registration Law. 'Most draft evasion occurs', he observed, 'due to a lack of rigor in the process of reporting to the koseki register, which is the primary source of Ministry data'. Unleashing a blistering critique, Ōyama observed that the high incidence of 'incorrect ages and the omissions of surnames or given names' rendered the register 'not much better than scrap paper'.[44]

Besieged from all sides, the Ministry of Home Affairs drafted a set of 'Koseki Registration Regulations' (*Koseki kisoku*) as a proclamation of the Grand Council of State tabled at the July 1882 Council of Elders. Renamed and passed as the 'Koseki Registration Law' (*Koseki hō*), this legislation had much more stringent reporting regulations than the former Jinshin Koseki Law. Despite Council approval, however, concerns regarding the financial impost of enforcement meant that the law was never promulgated.[45] Regional governments, too, were displeased with the disorderly nature of the Jinshin koseki registration system and also submitted requests for revision. In 1886 (Meiji 19), the authorities finally implemented sweeping koseki registration system reforms that took the shape of institutional rather than legislative changes through the proclamation of new regulations. These were the September 1886 'Procedures for the Reporting of Birth, Death, Transfer and Temporary Residence' (*Shushō shikyo shutsunyū kiryūsha todokekata*) (Ministry of Home Affairs Ordinance No. 19 of 1886), the October 1886 'Procedures for the Management of Koseki Registers' (*Koseki toriatsukai tetsusuki*) (Ministry of Home Affairs Ordinance No. 22 of 1886) and the October

1886 'Koseki Register Format' (*Koseki tōki shoshiki*) (Ministry of Home Affairs Ordinance No. 20 of 1886). The registration system that operated following these revisions is generally referred to as the 'Meiji 19 Form' koseki registration system (*Meiji 19-nen shiki koseki*).

The Meiji 19 Form system entailed the following revisions aimed at modernising registration law.

1. Procedures for stricter supervision of koseki register administration by prefectural governments, including standardised administration procedures and typography.
2. The establishment of a 'register list' (*tōki mokuroku*) of koseki registers and a collection of 'inactive koseki register records' (*josekibo*). There were three categories of registration – 'additions', 'removals' and 'transfers' – to be actioned upon receipt of notification.
3. Revisions to register format to ensure the inclusion of a 'remarks section' in which reason and date were entered when a register entry was made or changed.[46]

Through the implementation of these revisions, the koseki registration system achieved an improved level of accuracy as a record of status. Furthermore, in comparison to the time when implementation of the system varied from one prefecture to the next, the system moved one step closer to becoming nationally standardised.

The Meiji Civil Code and the Koseki Registration Law

Initially, law relating to koseki registration was procedural law attached to the Civil Code, the drafting of which was commenced by the Ministry of Justice in September 1876. As noted in the previous chapter, French jurist Gustave Boissonade (1825–1910), employed as a Japanese government advisor, supervised the first draft of the Civil Code, modelled on the Code developed in France. Following the Napoleonic Wars of the early nineteenth century, the individualism that marked the French Civil Code swept across Europe prior to belatedly reaching Japan. After teaching law at the University of Paris, Boissonade came to Japan in December 1873 to take a position with the Ministry of Justice Law School as a lecturer in French law. In many ways, it was Boissonade's influence that ensured that French law would become the basis for the Code in Japan. Support for the French Civil Code model was further guaranteed by the fact that many in early Meiji legal circles, including Mitsukuri Rinshō

(1846–1897), were scholars of French law who had studied in France. As a result, there was overwhelming support for French law within Ministry of Justice ranks.[47]

During July 1882 Council of Elders deliberations on the Civil Code, Mitsukuri, a central figure in the formulation of the Code, questioned the worth of enacting the Koseki Registration Law when a French-style civil code was being formulated. Dismissing koseki registration as a peculiarly oriental relic of feudal society, Mitsukuri noted, 'Koseki registration, which may have been useful in feudal times, is *something inherent to the Orient only.* While some claim it is necessary, I believe it is of little benefit under today's system of government [...] Laws of this nature are unheard of in Western nations'[48] (emphasis added). Mitsukuri believed that once a French-style identification document providing information such as inheritance and marriage was put in place under the new Civil Code, the koseki registration system would become superfluous.

Civil Code articles relating to civil affairs were promulgated on 7 October 1890. Nevertheless, following fierce attacks from conservative jurists during the Civil Code controversy referred to above, these came to an early demise. Those articles are now generally referred to as 'the civil affairs articles of the original Civil Code' (*kyū minpo jinji hen*).

In spite of criticisms of unacceptable levels of Western influence, the civil affairs articles of the old Code in fact gave considerable value to notions of family. This included the statement, for example, that 'The so-called *ie* family cannot be extinguished'. Individualism was also upheld, evident in the declaration that 'The foundation of the state lies in the individual; individuals shall be the holders of rights'. Ultimately, however, the legislation gave primary emphasis to familism, with individualism playing a secondary role. This is clear from a statement that reads, 'In formulating provisions relating to civil affairs and inheritance, our legislators largely maintained conventional familism, while also including some small measure of individualism'.[49]

Parallel to the drafting of the Civil Code, the Ministry of Home Affairs embarked on a revision of the Koseki Registration Law in order to pare down the registration system to one that operated purely for the purpose of individual status identification. A koseki register bill drafted by the Ministry of Home Affairs was introduced to the Imperial Diet in December 1890. Although passed by the

House of Peers, it was voted down in March 1891 by the House of Representatives. In April 1893, the Legislative Investigative Committee (*Hōten chōsa-kai*), presided over by Itō Hirobumi (1841–1909), began to formulate a new civil code based on German rather than French law. On 21 June 1898, articles relating to relatives and inheritance were enacted in this new 'Meiji Civil Code' (Law No. 9 of 1898). In addition, the Koseki Registration Law that was an integral part of the Code was finally enacted. The Meiji Civil Code established the *ie* family system and clearly defined the nature of koseki registration.

Koseki record embodying the *ie* family

The meaning of the *ie* family

In the general text *Koseki seido* (The Koseki Registration System), published in 1933 before the Second World War, Seki Kōjirō (1898–1944) concisely states, 'It should suffice to say when explaining the concept of koseki register that this is a document that records status-related matters for each *ie* family unit'.[50] Let us consider, then, what this '*ie* family' might be.

While the term '*ie* family' as given in the Meiji Civil Code has been interpreted differently by different scholars, Kawashima Takeyoshi (1909–1992) gives a very clear definition based on the belief that constituents of a family must be of the same bloodline, as a 'bloodline group' (*kettō shūdan*), with no need for a shared household. While generally physiological, this bloodline can also be fictitious, as in the case of adoption, with the paternal being the primary bloodline.[51] Under the Citizenship Law in Japan, the concept of 'identity through bloodline' underpinned the principle of married couples and all members of their family having the same citizenship.

The *ie* family as defined above is a concept created, so to speak, by the Meiji state. Watanabe Hiroshi points out that in Tokugawa era society people also lived as *ie* family members, engaged in family businesses or trades and owned assets or property as members of a family. Each family was represented by the head, who inherited the family name (surname or trade name) across the generations. This situation applied more or less across warrior, townsman and peasant classes. In Tokugawa times, however, kinship was not a necessary condition of family formation. Rather, the key elements were succession of the family business or trade and of the surname.[52]

The Meiji Civil Code, then, transformed what had been the relatively spontaneous and flexible Tokugawa era notion of '*ie* family' into a codified legal system. Article 732 of the Code stated, 'Any relatives, and their spouses, of a legal household head who belong to the *ie* family of that head are deemed to be family members'. At a meeting of the Legislative Investigative Committee, Tomii Masa'aki (1858–1935), a member of the Civil Code drafting committee, stated, 'It stands to reason, as well as custom, to deem only those referred to in [Article 732] as members of a family'.

According to Tomii, under the Meiji Civil Code the *ie* family 'is referred to by the term "*seki*" (membership) and does not, of course, imply a tangible building' (emphasis added).[53] When asked to clarify the phrase '[people who] belong to the *ie* family', Tomii responded that '*ie* family means koseki register record' and those who 'belong to an *ie* family', therefore, are those included on a koseki register record.[54] In other words, for Tomii, the concept of '*ie* family' was completely synonymous with the idea of the 'koseki register record'.

This is the thinking that informed the principle of 'one family, one record' (*ikka isseki*), according to which all those who were members of a particular *ie* family were to be recorded in a single koseki register record. Thus, the expressions 'entering the *ie* family' (*nyūka*) and 'leaving the *ie* family' (*kyoka*) came in fact to mean being entered into or removed from a koseki record, while 'branching the *ie* family' (*bunke*) referred to the creation of a separate koseki record. Even members of a group that lived and worked independently of other family members could not be regarded as a 'branch family' if still documented in the same koseki record as the original group.

Naturally, the concept of '*ie* family' under the Meiji Civil Code could not exist independently of the existence of a legal household head. The status of 'legal household head' itself was not necessarily determined by bloodline. That is to say, through adoption or marrying into an *ie* family, a person who was not a blood relative of the present legal household head could in fact inherit the family property and become legal household head in the future.

It is clear, therefore, that rather than being based on pure bloodline, the 'family' under the Meiji Civil Code was a legal relationship recorded on the document known as the koseki register record. The key device that held this formal and technical 'family' together was the *uji* family name. Through use of an *uji*, designated as such by the family, individuals were perpetually bound in their daily lives to the traditions and status of that family.

Ancestor worship and the *ie* family

The accumulation over time of these formal family relationships came to appear to the individual who belonged to the family as naturally acquired power relationships. Ancestor worship was the particular device that maintained these power relationships and passed them on to future generations. It was considered proper that veneration for the ancestors extend to the current household head who was thought to be the bridge connecting the ancestors to future generations.

The assertion from *Kyoto-fu koseki shihō* of October 1868, citied in the first section of the chapter, that 'Koseki register records [...] serve as individual genealogies for commoners and as important records in perpetuity for upper class perpetuity', confirms the key role of koseki register records as 'genealogies for commoners' in a manner reminiscent of continuous imperial lineage. Research by Ueda Masa'aki, however, confirms the presence of a 'crossing of bloodlines' with foreign visitors from the continent among the imperial and aristocratic families of ancient Japan. This is evident, for example, in the case of the mother of Emperor Kanmu, who was related by blood to a naturalised clan that originally came from the ancient Korean kingdom of Kudara (Baekje).[55] This and other examples suggest the fictive nature of any 'pure blood' tradition emphasised as the basis for continuous imperial lineage.

Under the pre-war Koseki Registration Law, matters for entry into the register included the name of the previous legal household head and the relationship between the current and previous head (Article 18 of the pre-war Koseki Registration Law). Recording this relationship permitted family members to confirm the unbroken line of inherited family headship and to recognise both the current and previous household heads as objects of worship. Hozumi

Yatsuka (1860–1912), a leading *ie* family ideologue, declared that the religious services associated with ancestor worship vertically connected past and present family constituents. According to Hozumi, since 'the *ie* family is a continuous worship of ancestors', it was the role of 'the household head to both celebrate the spirits of the ancestors and represent the authority of ancestors in the present day as a means of protecting future generations'.[56] The fact that koseki records confirmed ancestral 'bloodlines' gave these documents added value as genealogies of the common people.

The authority to preside over religious services for ancestors was vested in the household head. Under the Meiji Civil Code, it was the privilege of those who assumed the headship of a family to inherit ownership of the genealogy, ritual utensils and family tomb that were the items required in order to conduct the religious services associated with ancestor worship (Article 987). Yanagita Kunio argued that the relationship that had pertained since ancient times between governance and ceremony was also applicable on a smaller scale to families.[57] Certainly, the power phenomenon of 'governing the people' originated with the family, while ancestor worship services passed down from one generation to the next served to instruct family members in the nature of their power relationship with the legal household head.

Kokutai no hongi (Cardinal Principles of the National Polity of Japan), published by the Ministry of Education in 1937, famously declared the rule of the Emperor through the unbroken imperial line to be Japan's 'everlasting *kokutai*' (national polity). This document stressed as follows:

> Family life in our country began with our distant ancestors and, not limited to the lives of parents and children in the present day, will be continued by future generations for all eternity. Present-day family life links the past with what is to come by inheriting and advancing the aspirations of the ancestors and passing these on to the family members of the future. This is one reason why from ancient times the *uji* family name in our country has been held in such high regard.[58]

In other words, Japanese notions of 'family' were based on glorification of the family line in accordance with the principles of 'unity of the ancestors and the descendants' (*soson ittai*). According to these principles, the *uji* family name became an expression of the honour of the family accumulated by ancestors across past generations. When this view of family was aligned with notions of 'imperial line', which integrated the past and future in perpetuity through the idea of 'the eternity of heaven and earth' (*tenjō mukyū*), a direct link was created between the family and 'national polity'. In terms of this worldview, the koseki register record clearly became a symbol of the history of the family, from ancestors past through to present members and on to generations as yet unborn.

Rule by the legal household head, gatekeeper of the family

The legal household head was the master of the house who commanded the family. As noted above, Article 732 of the Meiji Civil Code stated, 'Any relatives, and their spouses, of a legal household head who belong to that head's family are deemed to be family members'. In other words, 'the family' was defined as those who have entered into the same *ie* family as the household head. According to Shinmi Kichiji (1874–1974), the term '*koshu*', which originally referred to an entry item in ancient koseki register records, was replaced during the Edo period by expressions such as 'principal' (*honnin*), 'head of the family' (*tōshu*) or 'owner of the house' (*ienushi*). The Jinshin koseki registration system, however, reinstated the use of the term '*koshu*'.[59]

The 'Koseki Registration Rules Draft' (*Koseki kisoku an*), tabled at an 1892 meeting of the Council of Elders, stipulated that 'Matters for entry in the koseki register must be reported by the legal household head' (Article 4). According to Sano Tsunetami, member of the Council of Elders, this assignation of self-reporting responsibilities to the legal household head was 'a desirable custom akin to the natural law' of Japan from ancient times, the benefits of which surpassed those of Western identity papers. Sano furthermore saw the legal household head's responsibility to manage the family's koseki register record as a 'moral and legal' obligation that was, in fact, a symbol of modern 'civilisation'. 'Since the head of a country governs all state affairs', Sano expounded, 'it is only to be expected that the head of a household should manage family affairs. In barbarous times there was no such custom, without which a society cannot be said to be civilised'.[60] From the perspective of 'law' and 'morals', the legal household head's responsibility for the family's koseki record was a given.

An individual could only form a new family relationship with the approval of the legal household head. Without the head's permission, no such change was possible. Article 750 of the Meiji Civil Code stipulated that any marriage or adoption arrangement which the legal household head refused to report could not be legally acted upon nor recorded in the koseki register. The legal household head had the power to enact 'separation from the koseki record' (*riseki*) and to refuse to approve 'restoration to the koseki record' (*fukuseki*) in the case of any person who married or entered into an adoption arrangement without consent. While *riseki* literally meant 'leaving the koseki record', it was in practice a sanction imposed by the legal household head to 'sever family ties'. Ume Kenjirō explains as follows: 'Once a person left the koseki record [as a result of *riseki*], all legal ties with the *ie* family were completely cut'. According to the drafters of the bill,[61] 'Since those who are not part of a family cannot expect family support [...] [*riseki*] serves as a sanction'.[62] Given that acceptance as a 'family member' depended on the legal household head's judgement, the individual who held this position was, to borrow the insightful expression used by Wagatsuma Sakae, the 'gatekeeper' of the family.[63]

The primary condition for succession to the role of legal household head was lineal descent with priority given to male, legitimate children. In the rare instance of there being no male successor, a female child might assume the legal household headship. In such a case, her husband was required to marry into her *ie* family. This form of marriage, unique throughout the world, is known as 'marrying a woman who is the legal household head' (*nyūfu kon'in*). When a marriage of this kind occurred, the woman's role as head was short-lived. As noted in Article 736 of the Meiji Civil Code, 'When a female household head takes a husband into her *ie* family, that husband shall assume the household headship'. Accordingly, except where the parties indicated contrary intention, the woman would in principle hand over the headship to her husband. The patriarchal idea persisted that, as ruler of the *ie* family, the household head should be male. Furthermore, through the idea that submission to the household head was analogous to the power relationship between the individual and the state, the 'family state' form of rule was established.

The link between the koseki registration system and 'national polity'

After the Meiji Restoration, the word 'national polity' (*kokutai*) came into common use in imperial ordinances and official documents and eventually entered into the vernacular. Satomi Kishio (1897–1974) argued that the term first appeared in August 1868 (Meiji 1) in an official notice from Emperor Meiji to the warriors and common people of Mutsu and Dewa Provinces. This notice declared, 'If a government does not earnestly inspire confidence in the minds of its people, how can it maintain its national polity and enforce public discipline?'[64]

The relationship between the Emperor and the people was clearly defined in a 'Letter Written in the Hand of the Emperor' (*Goshinkan*)[65] issued on 14 March 1868 (Keio 4) together with 'The Charter Oath of the Five Articles of the Imperial Covenant'. The document declared that administration of the country of the Emperor – referred to as 'the father and mother of the people' (*okuchō no fubo*) – was an expression of 'the imperial heart' (*ōmigokoro*) of 'the successive ancestors' (*retsuso*) since the time of the Emperor Jimmu. Accomplishing the peace and safety of all the people – the Emperor's 'infants' (*sekishi*) – would ensure the success of the 'restoration of imperial rule' (*chōsei isshin*). The *Goshinkan*, in other words, effectively declared the spirit of the Meiji Restoration. In this way, the true aim of the 'national polity' founded on the principle of 'the way of being with the gods' (*kannagara no michi*) was clarified. As Maki Kenji (1892–1989) noted, 'The gist of the spirit of Japan's national polity lies in a belief in an "unbroken imperial lineage"' (*bansei ikkei*).[66]

Hozumi Yatsuka is widely known for supporting the central role of 'unbroken imperial lineage' in the national polity of Japan. After arguing strongly against the civil affairs section of the original Civil Code in his April 1898 essay, 'The Legal Concept of the *Ie* Family' (*ie no hōriteki kannen*), Hozumi declared the 'family' to be a microcosm of national polity in the private domain. He further stated, 'Since remote antiquity, our national polity has modelled the family system. While a nation is a large-scale family, a family is a small-scale nation. A clarification of the family system, therefore, is a clarification of national polity'. He went on to argue that the family, which unified both ancestors and descendants, was a folk tradition and custom endemic to the national polity. 'Under the idea of family', he wrote, 'both ancestors and descendants are identified as one single and immortal entity'.[67] To support the family was to support stable social morals. In order to preserve the national polity underpinned by imperial lineage, it was necessary for all Japanese to both cultivate and attain a spirit of self-sacrifice.

The association between national polity ideology and the imposition of social order on the family through the koseki registration system was expressed in 1890 at the time of deliberations on a koseki register bill during the first session of the Imperial Diet. Here, the claim was made that 'The importance of Japan's koseki register legislation lies in the fact that this is a very significant aspect of Japanese custom. *In terms of the national polity, venerating bloodline and showing respect for the household head have very much been customs from the beginning of Japan*'[68] (emphasis added).

Modern nation-states in the West also saw ideological opposition emerge against the infiltration of individualism as a factor in family disintegration. By the end of the nineteenth century, the simplification of the husband–wife relationship through the spread of contract marriage based on the individualism advocated in the French Civil Code had seen the divorce rate soar.[69] From the state's point of view, the spread of divorce and de facto marriage made it difficult to gain an accurate picture of status relationships between people and thus hindered the compilation of the accurate records needed to facilitate conscription, the imposition of taxes and levies and the delivery of welfare. Against this backdrop, around the turn of the twentieth century, forms of conservatism emerged in Europe and the United States that attempted to prevent the spread of individualism and to reinforce national reunification through family community-based social reorganisation.[70] These Western ideologies saw the marital relationship as the key to renewing community bonds based on the family.

In Japan, however, the concept of 'family community' centred on the parent–child relationship. This relationship was also the keystone of the 'one nation, one family' (*ikkoku ikka*) paradigm that provided spiritual support for the Emperor system and also for the 'patriarchal state ideology' (*kachōteki kokka shisō*) which held the ruler to be the patriarch of the nation.[71] Not all commentary relating to Japan's 'national polity', however, supported the concept of a family state underpinned by an 'unbroken imperial lineage'. Kita Ikki (1883–1937), for example, believed that the sense of 'family' based on kinship had existed only in times of primitive social organisation. Developing his own theory of 'national polity' premised on the establishment of the personalities of individuals, Kita criticised Hozumi Yatsuka's advocacy for ideas such as 'unbroken imperial lineage' and 'the Emperor and subjects comprising one family' as a 'national polity theory based on ancient myth' (*takamagahara teki kokutai ron*).[72]

Nevertheless, the fictitious idea of 'the family state' built on ideas of 'one nation, one family' in which 'the ruler and subjects' were 'as one entity' was certainly the orthodox position in national polity discourse. It was this view of the 'state as family nation' which expanded, as is well known, into the spirit of 'all nations and states of the world unifying as one family' (*hakkō ichiu*) and which advocated the coexistence and co-prosperity of 'East Asian peoples' (*tōa minzoku*). Slogans such as '*daitōa kyōei ken*' (the Greater East Asia Co-Prosperity Sphere) and '*daitōa shin chitsujo*' (New Order in Greater East Asia), each of which was proposed as part of an international ideal to counter the new push for decolonisation led by the United States and Britain during the Second World War,[73] also derived from the fictitious idea of 'the family state'.

A manifesto entitled 'The Path of the Subject' (*Shinmin no michi*), published by the Ministry of Education in July 1941 when Japan was strengthening its national defence regime, proclaimed, 'The way of imperial subjects, which originates in our national polity, is for all people to unite their spirits as one and to discharge their duties in support of the Imperial Throne'.[74] Interestingly, the manifesto also stated, 'The family of our country is formed by the connection between ancestors and descendants and by unity around the family head. In other words, the primary relationship is *the parent–child relationship* centring on the family head, which is essentially different from *the form of assembly centring on the husband and wife* found in Western nations'[75] (emphasis added). The 'New Order in Greater East Asia' was designed as a pseudo parent–child relationship in which the 'empire' of Japan was to be venerated as 'the family head'. In the ultimate iteration of this New Order, the Emperor would rule the 'empire' and the Asian subjects who were also his 'children' (*sekishi*) would support his rule. Needless to say, the koseki registration system was to serve as the genealogical proof of an unbroken family line in which ancestors and descendants were integrated as a single entity.

Blood purity and family unity in the koseki system

Preserving 'pure blood': 'Anti-foreign' ethics in koseki law

In line with the process of enacting the Meiji Civil Code, the Koseki Registration Law (Law No. 12 of 1898) was finally proclaimed on 15 June 1898 (Meiji 31) and, together with the Code itself, implemented on 16 July. This law, which resulted in the creation of the Meiji 31 Form koseki registration system, is notable for clarifying eligibility for entry into a register. From that perspective, Article 170 of the new law stated, 'A koseki register record shall be created for *persons who have a settled* honseki *address* within the area of koseki registration jurisdiction'. The same article declared, '*A person who is not a Japanese national is not eligible to decide upon a* honseki *address*' (emphasis added).

In other words, the primary element in the compilation of a koseki register record was an individual's *honseki* address (Article 170, Section 1). As previously noted, the term '*honseki* address' refers to the designated location of an *ie* family and is not necessarily the same as the current residential address. The fundamental organising factor of koseki registration, nevertheless, was the *honseki* address principle according to which the koseki register record was the nodal point for those who constituted the notional 'family' documented in that record. The contradictions involved in the government adopting the *honseki* address as a reference value for koseki registration were discussed in Chapter One and will not be repeated here.

Secondly, the new law took a 'racial purism' stance in that it sought to restrict koseki registration to Japanese nationals (Article 170, Clause 2). This was in spite of the fact that, since the Jinshin koseki registration system recorded those who resided in Japanese territory as 'original Japanese people', it was self-evident that the koseki registration system would record the details of 'Japanese people'. That this was the case is apparent from comments made by Hijikata Yasushi (1859–1939), a member of the Legislative Investigative Committee, at a koseki register bill deliberation meeting on 7 May 1898. On this occasion, Hijikata declared, 'There is little need for stating that a non-Japanese national cannot decide upon a *honseki* address [...]. On the contrary, making such a statement may give rise to unnecessary questions relating to this law'.[76] Why was this point, which had formerly been a matter of tacit agreement, articulated in such direct language in the Meiji 31 Koseki Registration Law?

The answer to this question lies in the wording of the Citizenship Law that was being drafted at the time. According to the minutes of the second meeting of deliberations on the Koseki Registration Law held by the Legislative Investigative Committee on 7 May 1898, Kuratomi Yūzaburō (1853–1948), head of the Civil and Criminal Bureau at the Ministry of Justice, made an explanatory statement on this matter. Kuratomi pointed out that while the Civil Code stipulated that 'the wife shall enter her husband's *ie* family' and 'children shall enter their father's *ie* family', the Citizenship Law draft did not require a wife to necessarily hold the citizenship of her husband or children to hold the citizenship of their parents. 'Under the provisions of the Civil Code, [regardless of citizenship] those people who are in a marriage relationship or a father–child relationship will be considered as members of the same *ie* family. This could result in cases where such people are entered into a koseki register as a single family'. Out of fear of such a development (i.e. a non-Japanese being entered into a koseki register), a stipulation was added to ensure that the situation did not arise in which a household consisting of a mix of foreigners and Japanese was recorded as a family in the koseki registration system .[77] This move was in line with an agreement reached at an earlier committee meeting that 'the matter be clarified in koseki register legislation'.

The provisions in question given in the Citizenship Law corresponded to the following articles listed in 'Annotations to the Koseki Registration Law' (*Koseki hō shōkai*) prepared by a Ministry of Justice official.[78] Article 13 of those annotations stated, 'The wife of a person who takes Japanese citizenship shall obtain Japanese citizenship along with her husband. The previous provision shall not apply if the law of the wife's original country provides to the contrary'. Article 15 stipulated, 'Where the children of a person who takes Japanese citizenship have not yet reached the age of majority under the law of their original country, they shall obtain Japanese citizenship along with their father or mother. The previous provision shall not apply if the law of the children's original country provides to the contrary'.

Given that a wife entered her husband's *ie* family and that children entered their father's *ie* family, those in father–child or husband–wife relationships were naturally to be entered into the same koseki register record. Under Articles 13 and 15 above, however, there may have been cases in which a husband obtained Japanese citizenship while his wife did not, or cases of parents who took Japanese citizenship without a similar change by their children.

> This may result in the strange situation in which the wife or child without Japanese citizenship becomes a member of the *ie* family of the husband, or of the father or mother, by being entered into the relevant koseki register under the provisions of the Civil Code. Therefore, *Clause 2 of this article specifically provides that those who do not hold Japanese citizenship cannot decide upon a* honseki *address* and thus, even if in a parent–child or a husband–wife relationship, are in effect not permitted to become members of the *ie* family involved as far as koseki registration is concerned. (emphasis added)[79]

It is obvious that the provisions referred to in Article 170, Clause 2 of the Koseki Registration Law were added in order to ensure the uncompromising enforcement of the principle of family unity through shared citizenship of members of a single family. This was a means of maintaining the 'pure blood' of the koseki register record, which equalled the *ie* family.

Article 170, Clause 2 of the Koseki Registration Law read, 'A person who is not a Japanese national is not eligible to decide upon a *honseki* address'. In the revised Law of 1914 (Law No. 26), this was replaced with a new article, Article 9, which stated, 'A koseki record shall be created around the axis of a legal household head for each household which has decided upon its *honseki* address within the area of a given municipality'. The Ministry of Justice justified this revision on the following grounds: 'As long as "around the axis of the legal household head" is stated, it is no longer necessary to make reference to "foreign nationals". This is understood as a matter of course'.[80] In other words, the original provisions of Article 170 were deleted because it was obvious that a foreign national could not become a legal household head in Japan. This was confirmed in the declaration that stated, 'The koseki register record is compiled for the purpose of officially recording and officially displaying evidence of the status and family relations of an individual who holds Japanese citizenship'.[81] In this way, the notion of 'national purity' perpetuated in the koseki registration system was established as a self-evident unwritten law to be guarded as the foundation of the imperial state.

Status register demise: Individualism/familism conflict

The Meiji 31 Form koseki registration system included the following important additions to the registration system. The first was the adoption of a status registration process. A status register, which recorded information about an individual relevant to their status in terms of the Civil Code, such as birth, death, marriage and divorce, was established distinct from the koseki register. The koseki registration system was then reorganised accordingly. The adoption of a status registration system suggests the influence of Western legal principles, which drew on the individual as the unit of registration. In this sense, the Meiji 31 Form koseki registration system exhibits the strong influence of Boissonade's Civil Code with its emphasis on modern individualism and associated notions of the autonomous 'citizen'.

Secondly, the judicial aspect of the koseki registration system became more pronounced. This is closely related to the fact that the introduction under the Civil Code of a separate process of status registration into koseki registration procedures made the recording of such matters essential. The primary role of koseki registration shifted from the traditional administration of policing functions related to military service, sanitation and social order to judicial administration that focused on notarising personal status and relationship matters such as birth and marriage. Consequently, jurisdiction over koseki register administration was transferred from the Ministry of Home Affairs to the Ministry of Justice. Supervisory authority was accordingly transferred from municipal governments to district courts. As mentioned in the second section of Chapter One, however, the koseki registration system continued to be used by the authorities for policing purposes at the operational level.

This status registration process was abolished, however, in the 1914 revisions to the Koseki Registration Law and the associated detailed enforcement regulations (Ministry of Justice Ordinance No. 7) introduced at the time. This occurred due to the fact that the similarity between items entered into an individual's status register record and koseki record meant that there was little real purpose in maintaining the process introduced by the Meiji 31 Law.[82] The only information that was entered solely into the status register concerned the acknowledgement or its cancellation of an 'illegitimate child', denial of a child's legitimacy and appointment of an heir. Therefore, especially in regional areas, the status register was largely redundant. To continue maintaining these records would merely 'waste considerable money and labour over the decades'.[83] With the abolition of the status register, the koseki register once more became the sole system that recorded all status relationships.

During the February to March 1914 House of Representatives sitting of the thirty-first Imperial Diet that deliberated revisions to the Koseki Registration Law, requests were voiced from two different perspectives regarding the abolition of the status register. The first, which focused on convenience, suggested that, in light of the failure of the status register, information concerning military service, vaccination and criminal record be included in future in the koseki registration system as a means of improving social management expediency at the national level. It was also suggested that fingerprints of the legal household head and *ie* family members should be recorded. In spite of these arguments, the decision was ultimately made that it was not appropriate to record matters in the register that were outside the true spirit of the Koseki Registration Law.[84]

A different request, raised by Rikken Seiyū Kai Party Representative Shimada Toshio (1877–1947), concerned the harmonious balance between the koseki registration system and individualism. In the words of Minister of Justice Okuda Yoshito (1860–1917), the Meiji 31 Koseki Registration Law, which required both a status register record and koseki register record, was 'a law that amalgamated the individualistic ideal of Europe and the family-based ideal of Japan'. That is, the law very much embodied the 'clash of ideals'[85] that existed between Europe and Japan.

At the time of the enactment of the Meiji Civil Code, Shimada had argued for a status register that would record information concerning the individual. Since the spread of capitalism would lead to a greater expression of individualism in Japanese society, Shimada saw the 'collapse of the family system as envisioned by the Civil Code' as inevitable. He went on to argue, 'If before this collapse we abolish the status registration system, established out of necessity, we will merely end up having to reinstate that system in the not-too-distant future'. Shimada was sharply critical of the fact that the reality of social progress would betray 'the government's desire to give a greater profile to the family system and to enforce this system more strictly'.[86] Distinguishing between 'the status register that records individual relationships and the koseki register that records family relationships', he noted how difficult it was to achieve 'the perfect *ie* family system as expected by government officials and as stipulated in the current Civil Code'. Shimada ultimately concluded that, in light of the reality of the present-day economy and society, retaining the status register was a pragmatic decision. This was because the need for a status registration system would necessarily increase given that the government could only achieve its wish to prevent the family system from collapsing and to perfect and stabilise the family by paradoxically accommodating the spread of individualism.[87]

However, the intention of the Japanese government in making these Koseki Registration Law revisions was, in fact, to curtail the emergence of individualism and to push back against such a development by deploying the familism said to be inherent to Japan. This is evident in comments made by government committee member and Vice-Minister of Justice Suzuki Kisaburō (1867–1940) to the effect that 'It would be more sensible to moderate individualism and to further develop notions of familism'.[88] Accordingly, since the dual koseki registration and status registration system was a product of a 'clash of ideals' between the *ie* family system and individualism, abolition of the latter was the only outcome if the family comprised of 'Japanese people' was to be maintained.

With the abolition of the status register, the Koseki Registration Law was cleansed of all individualistic elements and transformed into a legal system, which, underpinned by the *ie* family system, now governed the status of the Japanese people. The revised law came into effect on 1 January 1915, (Taishō 4) and is known as the Taishō 4 Form Koseki Registration Law. Although simplified, Table 3.2 summarises the main koseki registration law revisions made up to that point. Since no other fundamental revisions to the Koseki Registration Law were made until 1947, the status of the 'Japanese people' was defined for several decades in terms of the Taishō 4 Form koseki registration system.

Table 3.2: Pre-war changes to the Koseki Registration Law

Version	Coverage	Governing agency	Main changes
Jinshin Koseki	Domestic residents	Ministry of Home Affairs (Ministry of Finance until 1872)	
Meiji 19 Form	As above	Ministry of Home Afairs	Register format revision. New list of registrations and book of decommissioned records. Unified administrative supervision by prefectural governments.
Meiji 31 Form	Japanese nationals	Ministry of Justice	New status register. Transfer of supervision to courts of law.
Taishō 4 Form	As above	Ministry of Justice	Abolition of status register.

Japan's territorial outline and expansion of the 'Japanese'

Ezochi incorporated into 'Japan': Hokkaido koseki system

In the Keichō period at the end of the sixteenth century, the Matsumae clan was given control of Ezochi (present-day Hokkaido) and implemented a household census for that territory. In 1855 (Ansei 2), Ezochi came under the direct control of the Tokugawa shogunate, which, as it did on the mainland, introduced the *ninbetsu chō* (population register) system as a form of koseki registration to facilitate 'assimilation'. However, due to the special circumstances of Ezochi, including the vastness of the territory and the presence of indigenous Ainu people, census information was largely only collected from '*wajin*' (Japanese settlers from the mainland) (see below).

In 1869 (Meiji 2), the Meiji government designated Ezochi as 'Japanese territory' and, under the new name 'Hokkaido', reorganised the area into eleven provinces and eighty-six districts. The Hokkaido Development Commission (*Hokkaido Kaitaku Shi*) was established in Sapporo in July of the same year as the body responsible for implementing the central government's 'domesticating Hokkaido policy' (*naichika*). Again, the koseki register was to be the main tool in this process. One purpose of conducting a household census in Hokkaido was to register local residents as 'Japanese subjects' in order to demonstrate that Hokkaido was an inherently Japanese territory over which Japan had effective control. In October, the Hakodate branch office of the Commission announced, 'Those who are not *residents under the Hokkaido koseki registration system* shall not be eligible to receive welfare assistance in times of need' (emphasis added).[89] It is notable that, once again, the benefit of 'assistance' for the impoverished was used as an attempt to enforce koseki registration.

With the 1871 promulgation of the Decree of the Grand Council of State No. 170 announcing the introduction of the Jinshin koseki registration system, the Ministry of People's Affairs instructed the authorities in Hokkaido to conduct a household census. As discussed earlier, the Jinshin koseki registration system was in principle compiled as a register of 'authentic Japanese people', with the current residential address as the *honseki* address. Because Hokkaido was still in the process of being settled by *wajin* Japanese, the new government issued a Grand Council of State Directive on 22 March 1873 entitled 'Special Measures for Koseki Registration Procedures in Hokkaido and Sakhalin Province' (*Hokkaido oyobi Karafuto shū ni kansuru koseki toriatsukaikata no tokurei*). This directive stated that, given the high concentration of deserters in Hokkaido since the end of the Edo period, including the many 'wanderers' from all over Japan with no *honseki* address making a living as fishermen, the Hokkaido Development Commission should compulsorily register those who had not committed serious crimes at the places at which they were currently sojourning.[90] In this way, the authorities sought to use koseki registration to tie drifters to the locations in which they were dwelling in order to secure as many human resources as possible for the development of Hokkaido.

The Conscription Ordinance enacted in 1873 on the principle of 'universal conscription' (*kokumin kaihei*) was not immediately enforced in Hokkaido. Instead, in June 1874, the Meiji government instituted the *tondenhei* (farmer-soldier) system as a means of recruiting soldiers for military service who could also be tasked with frontier development. Unlike universal conscription, the *tondenhei* system was used partly as a means of providing gainful activity for propertyless former warriors and the unemployed. In order to settle these people and thus identify them for *tondenhei* service, the government considered it necessary to have them permanently domiciled in Hokkaido. Proclaimed on 29 July 1890, the revised *tondenhei* regulations (Imperial Ordinance No. 102

of 1890) stipulated as follows: 'A *tondenhei* shall transfer his permanent domicile to Hokkaido where he will settle with his family and engage in military service'. This was a sign of the government's expectation that the principle of 'agreement between the permanent *honseki* address and residential address' (*honseki jūsho icchi shugi*), according to which a family resided at its *honseki* address, would continue to have the same value as it did at the time of the Jinshin system.

Seeking to source labour from overseas, in March 1873 the Hokkaido Development Commission proposed to the Grand Council of State that the territory accept Chinese immigrants as members of the workforce for the development of Hokkaido. This plan, modelled after the late nineteenth century United States policy of accepting an immigrant workforce from China, entailed naturalising the remaining two Chinese from ten who had been employed from 1875, and entering them into the Hokkaido 'commoner register' (*heiminseki*) with the objective of 'arousing the interest of people from other prefectures in settling in Hokkaido'.[91] Although never adopted, the aim of the plan was both to promote the naturalisation of Chinese immigrants as members of the Hokkaido development workforce and to provide impetus to the recruitment of migrant labour from the mainland. It should be noted that entry into a koseki register was the customary formal procedure for an individual to become 'Japanese'.

Ainu koseki registration: Former aboriginals as imperial subjects

When the Matsumae Domain controlled Ezochi, the indigenous Ainu were treated as 'benighted people beyond the sphere of imperial rule' (*kegai no tami*) and not permitted to live among Japanese residents. After Ainu resistance to the Japanese abated during the late Edo period, the Tokugawa shogunate allowed Ainu people to 'Japanise' (*kizoku*) and entered them into koseki registers as proof. Work by Kaiho Yōko indicates that compilation of *ninbetsu chō* books exclusively for the registration of Ainu people (referred to at the time as 'Ezo') began in various parts of Ezochi from the early nineteenth century.[92] An Ainu person who had taken a Japanese name, spoke Japanese and wore Japanese clothes was treated as an assimilated person and entered into a koseki register. The registers, however, callously referred to such a person as one who was 'newly incorporated into the Japanese state' (*shinpu no tami*) and managed the individual in a discriminatory manner. Even 'Japanised' Ainu people, for example, were identified as 'aboriginals' in koseki registers. In other words, koseki registration of the Ainu in Ezochi was the product of territorial expansion policies that forcefully integrated Ainu people into the shogunate-domain regime as 'people inside'.[93] This practice denied the autonomy of Ainu society.

In the first year of Meiji, when Ezochi was declared a territory of Japan and renamed 'Hokkaido', the new government cast the net of koseki registration in order to integrate Ainu people into the nation-state as 'imperial subjects of Japan'. With the 1871 promulgation of the Jinshin koseki registration system, the Hokkaido Development Commission (*hokkaido kaitaku shi*) proclaimed that Ainu throughout Hokkaido would be registered as 'commoners'. Although registration of Japanese residents in Hokkaido was completed in 1873, the entry of Ainu people into koseki registers appears to have taken until 1876.[94] In 1873, noting 'that the former beach and mountain dwellers held obligations as imperial subjects', the Hakodate branch office asked the Hokkaido Development Commission whether or not 'these Ezo people should be recorded as commoners in the general koseki register'. Confirming that this was the case, the Commission's response indicated that, once registered, Ezo people were free to enter into a marriage or similar arrangements with 'commoners'. This ruling permitted freedom of 'association' between Japanese and Ainu.[95]

It goes without saying that the process of entering non-Japanese people into a koseki register involved 'Japanisation' (*naiminka*), which included various changes to manners and customs. In order to inculcate the idea of the '*ie* family' into Ainu people in a manner that transformed them into 'imperial subjects', the Meiji government enforced the use of the *uji* family name, as it had with *wajin* Japanese, as proof of 'Japanese national' status while also administering the family on the basis of the 'household' (*ko*). A Development Commission proclamation insisted that the general Ainu population should take an *uji* family name, forcing indigenous names to become Japanese-style *uji* family names and given names that accorded with koseki registration practice. In July 1876, the Nemuro Branch Office accordingly directed that 'aboriginals adopt an *uji* family name'. This 'creation of a family name' (*sōshi*) policy, however, had little consistency. While the Hakodate branch office drew on

Chinese characters that were phonetic equivalents of the name of Ainu household heads to indicate family names, the Sapporo main office in many cases gave a single family name to all residents of a hamlet and then designated the original indigenous name as the given name.[96] In January 1912, on the grounds of diplomatic inconvenience, the Director of the Ministry of Justice Civil Affairs Bureau instructed the Nemuro District Court to also order the designation of new koseki register *uji* family names for those Ainu persons with Russian names.[97] This standardisation of Ainu manners and customs according to koseki register specifications in many ways recalls the treatment of naturalised people in ancient times, when koseki registration served as proof of 'assimilation under imperial rule' (*ōka*).

Although, as noted above, entry to the Jinshin koseki registration system was promoted under the slogan of dismantling the feudal era 'warrior, farmer, artisan and merchant' (*shi-nō-kō-shō*) hierarchy and thereby creating 'imperial subjects' of equal status, it was inconvenient for the ruling authorities to completely eliminate subordinate/dominant power relationships from the koseki registration system. Thus, despite the Japanese names and 'commoner' status given to Ainu people, through the use of the 'vernacular term' 'former aboriginal', the government sought in various ways to administer even those Ainu who had been entered into koseki registers differently from other Japanese. On 4 November 1878, government Notice No. 22 stated that there was, of course, no difference between the manner in which Ainu and other Japanese were dealt with in terms of registration or similar administrative matters. The claim was made, however, that it was sometimes necessary to distinguish this group from the general population. 'The absence of an established designation for [Ainu people]' had led to the use of various terms such as 'primitive people, aboriginal people or former aboriginals'. Given the confusion that this created, the Notice directed that the term 'former aboriginals' should now be used.[98] According to the Notice, 'former aboriginal' was an unofficial term that was not recorded in the koseki registration system and was only to be used for various administrative procedures. As a result, there was no discriminatory difference between the treatment of these people and general commoners. However, a document entitled, 'Business Report of the Development Commission' (*Kaitaku shi jigyō hōkokusho*), published in November 1878, stated, 'While former aboriginals receive the same treatment as other commoners, when necessary to distinguish them in the koseki registration system, they are referred to as former aboriginals'. Yearly koseki register surveys also recorded statistics for categories that included 'warrior class', 'commoners' and 'former aboriginals'.[99] While entry into a koseki register may have been meant as proof that Ainu people had been subsumed as 'imperial subjects', as 'newly ruled people' they were in fact clearly distinguishable from other 'Japanese' by being referred to in the koseki registration system and official documentation as 'former aboriginals'.

Enacted on 1 March 1899, the 'Hokkaido Former Aboriginal Protection Law' (*Hokkaido kyū dojin hogo hō*) (Law No. 27 of 1899) granted some farming land to Ainu people on the pretence of 'protection'. Until its repeal in 1997, this law helped entrench throughout Japanese society the derogatory view of Ainu as 'former aboriginals'. It is no exaggeration to say that koseki registration practices contributed to the enduring use until very recent times of this discriminatory designation. As outlined above, the process of having Ainu people entered into the koseki registration system demonstrates the double-edged sword of assimilation and discrimination wielded by the authorities.

'*Ryūkyū shobun*' and the koseki registration system

The term, 'Ryūkyū Disposition' (*Ryūkyū shobun*), refers to the various administrative manoeuvres by means of which the Japanese state assumed control of the Ryūkyū Kingdom. Founded in 1429, and originally subject to 'the Sino-centric order of China and other countries' (*kai chitsujo*) that dominated East Asian international relations, the Ryūkyū Kingdom was a vassal state within the tributary systems of both the Ming and Qing dynasties. In 1609, the kingdom also came under the control of the Lord of the Shimazu Clan of the Satsuma Domain and was thus subject to governance by both Qing and Satsuma. In the early Meiji years, the new government proposed incorporating the Ryūkyū Kingdom into the nascent Japanese state. Despite ongoing conflict with the Qing over attribution, annexation was effectively achieved in 1872 when Japan renamed the kingdom 'the Ryūkyū Domain'.

The compilation of a koseki register in Okinawa by the Meiji state began during the time when the territory was still referred to as the 'Ryūkyū Domain'. According to Kinjō Masaru, following the 1872 nationwide implementation of the Jinshin koseki registration system, 'Ryūkyū Domain Koseki Registration Statistics' (*Ryūkyū han koseki sōkei*) and 'Ryūkyū Domain Employment Statistics' (*Ryūkyū han shokubun sōkei*) were prepared under the instruction of the Grand Council of State and submitted to the Meiji government in 1873. These, however, were merely statistical tabulations of household data rather than information compiled in koseki register format.[100]

Jurisdiction over the Ryūkyū Domain was transferred from the Ministry of Foreign Affairs to the Ministry of Home Affairs.[101] This indicated that matters related to the territory were regarded as 'domestic' rather than 'diplomatic' issues. According to the 'Comparison Table of Population, Births and Deaths Surveyed on 1 January, Meiji 12' (*Meiji 12-nen 1-gatsu 1-nichi shirabe jin'in oyobi shusshō shibō hikaku hyō*) compiled by the Koseki Registration Bureau of the Ministry of Home Affairs, in that year the population of the Ryūkyū Domain was 310,545 (154,394 men and 156,151 women). This was 142,973 more than in January 1876.[102] The 1876 figures appear to have been based on koseki register statistics similar to those mentioned above.

On 4 April 1879, the Meiji government announced Promulgation No. 14, which stated, 'The Ryūkyū Domain shall be abolished and replaced by Okinawa Prefecture'. This change was achieved under the tacit threat of military action. As part of the 'Ryūkyū Disposition', the government indicated that it would retain Ryūkyū's previous municipal and land holding systems. In order to embrace the residents of the islands into the territory of Japan, nascent koseki registration procedures commenced. The most difficult task in applying the Koseki Registration Law to another ethnic group was how to make that group's traditions and customs match the system. For instance, while the Jinshin system required a 'class name' (*zokushō*) entry, the Ryūkyū Dynasty was structured around uniquely detailed classes and ranks. The royal family held the ranks of '*ōji*' and '*aji*', while aristocrat ranks included '*uēkata*', '*pēchin*' and '*chikudon*'. In a request dated 2 November 1876 to the General Affairs Bureau of the Ministry of Home Affairs, Tomori Uēkata of Ryūkyū Domain inquired whether, in a koseki register tabulation being submitted to the Ministry, '*aji*' should be entered as 'nobility', 'warrior' or 'commoner' class. The response ruled that 'The legitimate child of a prince or a member of the domain royal family should be entered as warrior class for the purpose of koseki register surveys to the Ministry of Home Affairs'.[103] This ruling confirms the inferior position assigned to Ryūkyū's allegiance by the Meiji state. Here, a group that should have been administered in an identical manner to that of the imperial family in Japan had their privileged status downgraded to warrior class.

On 18 January 1879, the Ministry of Justice issued 'Guidelines for Managing the Status of the People of the Ryūkyū Domain' (*Ryūkyū han jinmin mibun toriatsukaikata kokoroe*) to facilitate the processes involved in abolishing the Ryūkyū Domain and establishing Okinawa Prefecture. In line with these guidelines, the Ministry of Home Affairs reported to the Grand Council of State that, when entering people into the koseki registration system, Ryūkyū Domain would be instructed to 'record titles such as warrior class and commoner' in accordance with the traditional ranking system of the Ryūkyū Dynasty.[104] This suggests the approach of gradually integrating old customs into koseki registration practice.

In Okinawa, the compilation of koseki registers based on a Jinshin koseki register format began in 1880 when the Okinawa Prefecture municipal government system began operation.[105] On 3 September 1880, Minister of Home Affairs Matsukata Masayoshi (1835–1924) sent an 'Enquiry Regarding Official Expenditure for the Compilation of Koseki Registers in Okinawa Prefecture' (*Okinawa kenka koseki hensei kanpi shishutsu no gi nitsuki ukagai*) to Prime Minister (*dajō daijin*) Sanjō Sanetomi. This was prompted by a 3 May submission from Hara Masayori (1834–1894), an Okinawa Prefecture junior secretary. Hara observed that in Okinawa during the Ryūkyū Domain era, census surveys were poorly conducted and marked by 'corrupt practices such as concealing family members to escape capitation tax and levies and abandoning seriously ill people to become beggars on the streets'. There were also many aristocrats who had changed residence and whose place of domicile was no longer known. Given the confusion caused by these problems, there was a pressing need to conduct a more detailed census for the compilation of the new koseki registers. Since it was impossible to force the financial burden of such a process onto the people, Hara petitioned the government to bear the costs.

Matsukata responded by conceding that 'A prefecture such as yours has no standardised system for compiling a population register and has inaccurate household survey data'. The Minister also noted the 'bad practice of hiding or falsifying population figures'. While acknowledging that there was, therefore, a need to reorganise the koseki registration system in conjunction with the implementation of 'prefectural government', Matsukata concluded that further compilation should be put on hold until a review had been conducted of the Koseki Registration Law. On 6 October, Sanjō was also of the opinion that 'the matter be put on hold until discussions can be held at a later date'.[106] With the laborious task of compiling the Jinshin koseki registers incomplete even on the mainland, the reorganisation of the Okinawan koseki registers in accordance with mainland standards did not occur until revisions to the Jinshin koseki registration system were introduced in the Meiji 19 Form Koseki Registration Law.[107]

From around 1830 (Tenpō 1), the Ogasawara Islands saw the arrival of settlers seeking a new life from the United States and Britain. These Western immigrants were the first 'residents' of the islands. After the Meiji government claimed possession of the Ogasawaras in 1876, there was a growth in the numbers of Japanese immigrants from the mainland. One means by which the Japanese government established effective rule was by transforming the people who lived there into Japanese nationals. Between 1877 and 1882, sixty-four islanders from twenty-two families were permitted to 'naturalise' on the condition that they reside permanently on Ogasawara.[108]

Nevertheless, the Citizenship Law that governed 'naturalisation' was not enacted until 1899. Once again, in the absence of other legislation, it was the Koseki Registration Law that functioned to interpret citizenship-related legal matters. In September 1877, Minister of Home Affairs Toshimichi Ōkubo sent the Prime Minister an inquiry regarding the 'naturalisation' of foreign immigrants on Ogasawara. Here, the Minister implied the significance of koseki registration as 'naturalisation' in his use of the phrase 'entry in the register of subjects'.[109] In modern Japan's process of territorial expansion it was necessary to establish the presence of as many 'Japanese' residents as possible in the territories being appropriated. In the case of the Ogasawara Islands, koseki registration was an expedient measure by means of which the blue-eyed residents could be instantly transformed into 'Japanese nationals'.

'*Sōshi*' for Ryūkyūan people

The issue of how to convert both the 'family names and given names' (*shimei*) of Ryūkyūan people to a Japanese cultural equivalent was naturally pertinent to the enforcement of the Koseki Registration Law in Okinawa. Ryūkyūan family customs were completely at odds with the practice of compiling a koseki register record, the base unit of which was an *ie* family in which each member had the same *uji* family name.

There was no Ryūkyūan tradition of equating surname with '*kamei*' (family name). While aristocrats and the privileged classes in feudal Ryūkyūan society used the family name as the equivalent of a '*myōji*' (surname), this was derived from the name of the relevant fiefdom. Accordingly, the name changed when the family moved to a different fiefdom.[110] Common people generally had no family name. When permitted to use a surname, they also often made use of a place name as their family name. Farmers, too, used a '*yagō*' (house name derived from a place name or topographic feature) rather than a surname.[111] Thus, most Ryūkyūan family names were based on territorial or land connections rather than blood relationships.

Higashionna Kanjun (1882–1963), a Japanese scholar who specialised in the history of Okinawa, pointed out that the '*uji* and *kabane*' system, which articulated the names of clans and hereditary titles, was not a feature of traditional Ryūkyūan manners and customs. Instead, it was common practice for both aristocrats and commoners to use a given name as their main name. Thus, aristocrats and commoners generally had a given name followed by a family name, as in 'Tarō Yamashiro' or 'Jirō Kaneshiro'.[112] In written materials, it was customary for aristocrats and those of higher rank to place a 'hereditary title' indicating consanguinity before a personal name, and a 'family name', 'rank' and '*nanori*' (Japanese-style name) after their personal name. The family name was generally referred to as '*ya no na*' and was derived from a place name. For example, the name 'Shō Yūkō Ginowan Ueekata Chōho' consists of Shō = title, Yūkō = given name, Ginowan = family name, Uēkata = rank and Chōho = *nanori*. The 'Shō Yūkō' section of this name was known as '*kara na*', which was a Chinese-style name used in official documents written in classical Chinese. The *nanori* section was known as '*yamato na*', or Japanese name.[113] In other words, aristocrats and those of higher rank used their own Okinawan 'name', while also having formal designations in both Japanese and Chinese styles. In addition to names for official use, all people regardless of rank or class were given a '*warabena*' childhood name at birth. This was the name used by family members and close friends.[114]

With the ongoing 'Japanisation' of Okinawa that followed the Ryūkyū Disposition, the Okinawan status order was reorganised to correspond to the Japanese koseki registration system. This led to the standardisation of what had been the diverse Ryūkyūan naming culture according to koseki registration procedures. In February 1880, it was promulgated that Ryūkyūan aristocrats and commoners would in future place the given name after the surname. This was nothing less than the imposition on the Ryūkyūan people of the forced 'creation of an *ie* family name and change of given name' (*sōshi kaimei*) for the purpose of assimilation.[115] In spite of the fact that Ryūkyūan names were a source of pride that created a strong sense of community among people, these names were modified to suit the koseki registration policies imposed by a ruling race.

4 Colonial Holdings and the 'Japanese': Koseki Register Control of 'Ethnicity', 'Citizenship' and 'Bloodline'

Colonial 'Japanese citizenship': The logic of the powerful

Assimilating colonial residents: 'Citizenship' defined by ruler

From the time of the Meiji Restoration and the unification of the nation as a modern sovereign state, Japan blindly followed the Great Powers of Europe by forging ahead to acquire colonial holdings in Asia. How were the residents of territories subsumed into the Japanese 'empire' assimilated as 'Japanese'?

In 1895, Japan triumphed over the Qing state, the so-called 'sleeping lion', in the Sino-Japanese war. The terms of the Sino-Japanese Peace Treaty (*Nisshin kōwa jōyaku*, hereafter the Treaty of Shimonoseki) ceded Taiwan from the Qing state to Japan. Article 5, Clause 1 of the Treaty stipulated that residents of Taiwan who did not leave the ceded territories within 'a period of two years from the date of the exchange of ratifications' were, 'at the option of Japan', 'deemed to be Japanese subjects'. Entirely contingent on the discretion of the Japanese government, these people might have Japanese citizenship approved.[1] This stipulation, however, applied only to people of ethnic Han background. No clear policy was articulated by the Japanese authorities concerning the legal position of indigenous peoples, referred to by the Japanese as '*banjin*' (savage natives). Officials such as Yasui Katsuji, a judge of the Taiwan High Court, took the position that, since *banjin* were not included among the 'residents' (*jūmin*) of the treaty,[2] they did not acquire Japanese citizenship through Japan's acquisition of the territory. Initially, indigenous people were regarded, like the early immigrants to Japan from the continent referred to in *Nihon shoki* (The Chronicles of Old Japan), as 'people from benighted lands beyond the sphere of imperial rule' (*kegai no tami*). Nevertheless, it was thought that once they were civilised as people of the empire, these indigenous people would incrementally be treated as 'subjects of Japan'. This process was to occur through a policy referred to as 'enlightening the savages' (*riban seisaku*).

Victory in the Russo-Japanese War saw Japan became the first-ranked state in Asia. On 5 September 1905, the Russo-Japanese Peace Treaty (hereafter, the Portsmouth Treaty) enabled Japan to acquire from Russia the region of the island of Karafuto south of the fifty degrees north parallel (hereafter, Karafuto). Article 10 of the Treaty stipulated that 'Russian subjects' who were 'inhabitants of the territory ceded to Japan' could choose to either remain in situ after the cession or return to their home country, Russia. Although those who choose to remain were required to acknowledge the jurisdiction of the Japanese state, there was no stipulation mandating a change of citizenship.

Debate around whether or not Ainu or other indigenous residents of Karafuto who did not return to Japan at that time acquired Japanese citizenship had its origins in the historical circumstances of the reversion of the island. The Karafuto and Chishima Exchange Treaty, concluded between Japan and Russia on 7 May 1875, resulted in Russia, which previously had possession of Chishima, and Japan, which previously had possession of Karafuto, mutually ceding these territories to each other. In other words, Karafuto came under Russian administration, while Chishima became a Japanese territory. According to the Treaty, residents of both territories were given the right to retain their original citizenship and to continue to reside in the newly administered region. However, Article 4 of the Treaty's Appendix indicated that Ainu and other indigenous peoples would be given a three-year period of grace from the day of proclamation during which to choose either Russian or Japanese citizenship. Those who continued to remain in Karafuto after this three-year period would automatically acquire Russian citizenship. As a result, approximately 850 Ainu people relocated to Hokkaido where they qualified for Japanese citizenship. Even if they subsequently returned to Karafuto, their 'Japanese' status was preserved.[3]

Matters such as the above were concluded by the Portsmouth Treaty. The Japanese government's position was that the indigenous residents of Karafuto were not included among the 'subjects of the Russian empire' to whom Article 10 of the Treaty gave the option of choice of citizenship. Therefore, once the Treaty came into effect and the administration of the territory changed hands, the citizenship of these people would naturally change from Russian to Japanese.[4]

There was no difference in the stipulations in each of the treaties relating to Japan's acquisition of territory in Taiwan and Karafuto regarding residents' choice of citizenship. Respect for individualism emerged in the West during the eighteenth century. By the mid-nineteenth century, this had resulted in a maturation of legal thinking that acknowledged 'the non-compulsory principle' in matters of possible citizenship changes when territory changed hands. Even in the eighteenth century, it was not unusual for treaties related to such matters to feature a clause or article permitting choice of citizenship. These precedents were acknowledged in both the Taiwan and Karafuto agreements, and thus the freedom to choose citizenship was taken for granted.[5] We need to be cognisant, however, that 'the principle of citizenship without force', a modern legal concept used to judge the level of civil society in a state, carried no value in the case of indigenous peoples.

Unlike Taiwan and Karafuto, where a territory of state was ceded, Japan acquired Korea through the annexation of an entire state. Article 1 of the Korean Annexation Treaty (Japan–Korea Treaty of 1910), concluded on 22 August 1910, stipulated, 'His Majesty the Emperor of Korea makes the complete and permanent cession to His Majesty the Emperor of Japan of all rights of sovereignty over the whole of Korea'. Here, Korea acknowledged the complete transfer of governance authority over both the territory and people of Korea to the Japanese state. The absence in this treaty of any stipulation regarding citizenship is interpreted as a tacit understanding that through annexation all residents of Korea automatically acquired Japanese citizenship.[6]

In addition to gaining control over Taiwan and Korea, Japan acquired the Kwantung Leased Territories through the Portsmouth Treaty and the 1905 Sino-Japanese Treaty Relating to Manchuria (*Nisshin kan Manshú ni kan suru jōyaku*). Japan was also given a mandate over islands in the South Seas – the so-called 'South Pacific Mandate' – according to 'Articles Giving the Empire a Governance Mandate for the South Sea Islands' (*Nanyō guntō ni tai suru teikoku no inin tōchi-ryō jōkō*), drawn up by the Council of the League of Nations in December 1920. According to the strict letter of international law, however, the former was on lease from the Qing authorities, while the latter was a mandate entrusted by the League of Nations. In other words, neither was technically a holding of Japan. Therefore, Japanese citizenship legislation applied in neither site. As a result, rather than having residents change their citizenship status to Japanese, Japan legally designated the people who lived in these places as 'foreigners'.[7]

It is useful here to consider the system of mandated territories. This was introduced after the end of the First World War in relation to colonial holdings liberated from both Germany and the Turkish Ottoman Empire with the understanding that countries subject to mandated governance would eventually assume independence. Until such time, the territories concerned were subject to a period of 'guardianship' (*kōken*). Depending on the degree of 'civilisation' (*bunmei-ka*) as perceived by the Great Powers, mandated territories were classified as one of three categories – A, B or C. The South Sea Islands mandated to Japan were rated as C, 'the lowest level of civilisation with absolutely no likelihood of becoming a nation-state in the future'.[8]

Nothing concerning the citizenship of the residents of these mandated territories was stipulated in the League of Nations articles. However, at the first meeting of the League Committee Responsible for Mandated Territories, the committee chair observed, 'In the operation of the mandate system, there is a strict distinction between those territories in which the level of cultural development is high and those in which this development is low. Were we to treat alike the citizenship of both, this essential distinction would be extinguished'.[9] Accordingly, there was general agreement that the citizenship of the residents of mandated territories would not, as a matter of course, be changed. This was because, depending on the level of 'culture' of the residents of the mandated territory in question, these people might be regarded as unworthy of the privilege of being granted citizenship of the 'civilised' state responsible for their guardianship.

Considering this advice, on 23 April 1923, the Council of the League of Nations resolved that, while residents of mandated territories should be distinguished in status from the citizens of the nations with mandatory responsibilities, these people could voluntarily naturalise if approved to do so by the country administering the mandate in question. When the Council requested feedback to this resolution from administering nations, Japan responded at a 13 June 1928 Council meeting that the 'islanders' (*tōmin*) who were residents of the mandated territories under Japanese guardianship would be treated differently to 'subjects of the empire' (*teikoku shinmin*). Accordingly, Japanese citizenship would not be granted except in cases of marriage or naturalisation.[10]

The 1934 'Mandated Territories Annual Report' (*Inin tōchi nenpō*), submitted by the Japanese government to the Council of the League of Nations, noted that since Japan had assumed its mandate for the South Seas territories, 'three island women of Kanak ethnicity' (*tōmin Kanaka zoku onna 3 nin*) had become the wives of Japanese and acquired Japanese citizenship. The women had also been entered into Japan's koseki registration system.[11] In 1943, two residents of the islands acquired Japanese citizenship through adoption for the purpose of continuing the name of a Japanese family,[12] as per former citizenship legislation (see the third section of Chapter Two). Nevertheless, the vast majority of people resident on the islands mandated to Japan never became Japanese. The issue of citizenship in the context of mandated territories, like the citizenship of the indigenous people of Taiwan and Karafuto, throws into relief the fact that in the imperialist international order of the day citizenship was a construct contrived through the 'civilising' perspective of the powerful (*kyōsha*).

As demonstrated above, while the residents of colonial holdings were regarded as 'subjects of Japan' in formal citizenship terms, the governance of the 'Japanese citizenship' granted to these people differed significantly from that held by ordinary Japanese. This is apparent in an opinion paper entitled, 'The Issue of the Citizenship of the People of Korea after Annexation', submitted to the Governor-General of Korea, Terauchi Masatake (1852–1919), by scholar of international private law (*kokusai shihō*) Yamada Saburō (1869–1965) on 15 July 1910, immediately prior to Japan's annexation of Korea. Yamada was a significant figure who was involved at various levels in the development of imperial Japan's citizenship policies and colonial legal policies, including the drafting of the 'Law of Mutuality' (*Kyōtsū-hō*), a law that links different jurisdictions, discussed in detail below. In the concluding section of the opinion paper, Yamada stated as follows:

> Even if upon annexation former Korean nationals acquire Japanese citizenship, this in no way implies that a Korean person will be the same as a Japanese, and we must caution that such a situation will be no more than a mere foreigner acquiring Japanese citizenship. We are faced with the problem in national law of how to distinguish in legal terms between a Japanese on mainland Japan and a Japanese in Korea (that is, between a Japanese and a Japanese who is a Korean).[13]

In other words, together with the discrimination practised against residents of the colonies in terms of the way they were treated in comparison to those born in Japan, the Japanese citizenship that these people acquired was little more than an international and domestic marker which announced that these 'citizens' (*kokumin*) were subject to the exclusive jurisdiction of the sovereign state, Japan. Thus, we might regard the Yamada opinion paper as a document that presented the Japanese government with a utilitarian policy approach that understood citizenship as a legal entity that operated to maximise the national benefit. In other words, the paper presented citizenship as little more than a tool of governance.

Koreans bound to Japanese citizenship: Citizenship law in Korea

As problems with citizenship legislation became all the more pressing in the newly acquired territories, there was a need to develop legal processes to accommodate both the citizenship of children born in those territories and the naturalisation of foreigners. From this perspective, 20 June 1899 saw the promulgation of 'The Issue of the Implementation of Citizenship Law in Taiwan' (*Kokuseki-hō wo Taiwan ni shikō suru ken*; 1899, Imperial Ordinance No. 289), while 16 April 1923 saw the promulgation of 'The Issue of the Implementation of Citizenship Law in Karafuto' (*Kokuseki-hō wo Karafuto ni shikō suru ken*; 1923, Imperial Ordinance No. 88). These ordinances enabled the Japanese Citizenship Law to operate in both places. Even so, there was no application of this law to indigenous peoples in either Taiwan or Karafuto and changes of citizenship in those cases were dealt with by drawing on 'custom and reason' (*kanshū to jōri*).[14]

Korea was the sole colonial location in which the Citizenship Law was never implemented. The acquisition or loss of Japanese citizenship by the people of Korea was also ultimately decided upon by the application of custom and reason.[15] It should be noted that, during the imperial era, those to whom citizenship law applied had the advantage of the right to change citizenship. As noted in the second section of Chapter Two, as a necessary condition of the dual citizenship that resulted when a Japanese person naturalised as the citizen of another country, Article 20 of the former Citizenship Law required that person to rescind their Japanese citizenship. Korean people who naturalised, however, were never permitted to do this. In other words, they were fated to remain interminably Japanese.

In spite of Korea becoming a territory of Japan, the lack of implementation of citizenship legislation meant the acquisition or loss of Japanese citizenship did not occur in this region. The former Citizenship Law featured multiple references to 'Japan' and the 'Japanese'. For example, the first point listed in Article 7, Clause 1, which stipulated the conditions of applying for naturalisation, was 'more than five years residence in Japan'. This 'Japan', however, was legally interpreted as not including Korea.[16] Accordingly, residing for more than five years in Korea did not satisfy the first necessary condition for applying for naturalisation.[17] In terms of the Citizenship Law Korea was a legal anomaly among the territories of imperial Japan.

Why was Korea the only Japanese colonial holding in which the Citizenship Law was never implemented? As I noted in an earlier work,[18] in order to answer this question we first need to revisit Japan's annexation of Korea. 'Policy for the Annexation of Korea' (*Kankoku heigō hōshin*)[19] was a document presented by Korean Governor-General Terauchi Masatake to the second Katsura Tarō (1848–1913) Cabinet and ratified by that cabinet on 8 July 1910. Concerning the legal status of the people of Korea, the document declared, 'Until the implementation in due course of citizenship legislation in Korea, those who have naturalised with a foreign country and currently hold dual citizenship will, in the interests of our country, be considered subjects of Japan'. We can read this statement as signalling the intention of the Japanese authorities at that point to implement the Citizenship Law in Korea at some point in the future. Nevertheless, what is important here is the pragmatism of a citizenship policy, which, in terms of national interest, classified those Koreans with dual citizenship as 'Japanese subjects'.

Furthermore, in terms of the governance of Korea, Terauchi's submission stated as follows:

> There are not a few among Korean people in America or in Russia who engage in words and deeds that damage social order and who, in concert, in both the domestic and international spheres sometimes plan illegal activity. *In terms of conducting surveillance, it will be very inconvenient* if, after naturalising, these Koreans return to their home country and *exercise their rights and duties as foreigners.* We must therefore authorise an effective plan to ensure that Koreans who have naturalised in a foreign country are not permitted to renounce Japanese citizenship. (emphasis added)

In other words, there were fears that public order would be compromised if overseas Koreans were able to extinguish Japanese jurisdiction over them as persons of the Japanese state by rescinding Japanese citizenship upon naturalisation in their country of residence. Thus, regardless of whether or not they naturalised and became citizens of the country in which they were residing, overseas Koreans were not permitted to renounce Japanese citizenship. Instead, the policy insisted that they remain 'Japanese subjects'.

Although the application of the Citizenship Law to Korean people was rarely a subject of debate in the Imperial Diet, the 'Fifty-first Imperial Diet Explanatory Document' (*Dai-51-kai teikoku gikai setsumei shiryō*), compiled in November 1925 by the Office of the Governor-General of Korea, provides a brief explanation as follows of the reasons the Citizenship Law was not being implemented in Korea:

> Once they [Korean people] acquire Chinese citizenship and whip up anti-Japanese activity – including promoting and participating in the independence movement – in Chinese territory, there is no way for us to keep them in check .... Since in districts near the [Korean] border [with China] it is difficult to distinguish between Korean nationals and Koreans who have naturalised, 'the inconvenience and difficulty of enforcement' [*torishimari jō no fuben konnan*] will be inestimable and therefore *we adopt the advantageous policy of not formally recognising the naturalisation [as Chinese] of Korean people resident in Manchuria.* (emphasis added)[20]

As evident from the words, 'Korean people resident in Manchuria', the territory in which the consequence of the legal status of Korean people was regarded with greatest gravity was Manchuria. This was especially so with respect to Jiandao, the region near the border of

China and Korea, where there had been an extraordinary degree of movement by Korean farmers and peasants since before the annexation. One explanation for this spike in the level of mobility lay with the 'Land Survey Project' (*Tochi chōsa jigyō*) conducted between 1910 and 1918 by the Office of the Governor-General of Korea. This survey, which set out to 'modernise' the traditional land ownership relationships that had previously operated in Korea, led to the requisition of the arable land and land suitable for development of many Korean farmers. They were accordingly forced to leave their villages and make their way as migrants either to mainland Japan or Manchuria. As a result, approximately 230,000 Korean people flowed through the Jiandao border region from 1910 until about 1925.[21]

In the 'Agreement Relating to Jiandao' (*Kantō ni kan suru kyōyaku*), which was concluded with the Qing administration in 1909, Japan sought above all else to secure approval for Korean people residing in Jiandao to hold the right to reside and acquire land in China on the condition of submitting to the legal authority of the Qing. As a result, Jiandao became a foothold which strengthened the 'Special Rights and Interests' (*tokushu ken'eki*) of the Japanese in Manchuria. On the other hand, China was on the alert in case Korean people resident in Manchuria were being used as an advance guard for a Japanese invasion of Manchuria.[22] Even from the point of view of a third party country such as the United States, the existence of Koreans who were resident in Manchuria was seen as 'protecting the rights and interests' of Japan, and in that way was a convenient excuse for the development of Japan's military activities there.[23] Those Korean people whom the Japanese authorities regarded as a crucial vanguard in the expansion of Japan's rights and interests in Manchuria could not be permitted to rescind their Japanese citizenship.

At the same time, however, Jiandao was regarded as a core site for Korean anti-Japanese activity that had been central to the sudden eruption of the March First Independence Movement (Samil Movement). In October 1920, the Hara Takashi (1856–1921) Cabinet despatched approximately 10,000 troops to Jiandao in order to eliminate 'outrageous Koreans' (*futei Senjin*). Jiandao thus became a territory where, in the name of stabilising the governance in Korea, Japanese authorities had to be always on the alert. Concerning prosecutions against Koreans who were in that territory, through the previously mentioned Jiandao agreement, Japan had acquired the right to common courts. In order to apply this right effectively as a means of thoroughly controlling anti-Japan Koreans in Chinese territory, it was a legal necessity for these Koreans to have Japanese citizenship.

The first point to note here is that Japan sought to control as its own citizens those Korean people involved in the anti-Japan independence movement outside territory under its jurisdiction. On the other hand, Japan emphasised the right to diplomatic protection for Korean people as a strategy to maintain and expand the economic rights acquired by Koreans resident in Manchuria, who came to represent the rights and interests of Japan. In meeting these contradictory objectives of suppression and protection, imperial authorities bound Koreans tight within the constraints of Japanese citizenship and thereby ensured that, as people attached to Japan, they also remained under the administrative jurisdiction of Japanese officialdom.

In the West, stripping a person of citizenship is generally a political means of eliminating anti-establishment individuals.[24] In contrast, however, Japan sought in terms of its control over Korea to deprive these types of people of the right to rescind Japanese citizenship. In this way, Japan trussed up Korean people as 'Japanese citizens' in order to suppress anti-Japanese elements. Here, citizenship became a political mechanism that enhanced the power of the nation-state.

The koseki registration mosaic of empire

Colonies as 'territories not subject to mainland Japanese law' (*gaichi*)

There is a common understanding that 'assimilation policy' (*dōka seisaku*) was a strong feature of all aspects of Japan's colonial control. Japan, however, did not initially set out along this path. Rather, having observed the existence of traditions and customs in the various holdings that did not match Japan's systems of legal culture, the country's colonial administrations became concerned that applying the Meiji Constitution or other forms of Japanese law in a new territory in a manner similar to that which operated in mainland Japan could have a negative effect on successful governance. It is widely known that the territory of the 'Greater Japanese Empire' (*Dai Nippon Teikoku*) was legally divided into the '*naichi*', mainland Japan or literally 'inner territories', and '*gaichi*', the territories not subject to mainland Japanese law or literally 'outer territories'. The standard distinguishing between these two sites originated in the ethnic customs that characterised the colonies.

Scholar of constitutional law Kiyomiya Shirō (1898–1989) argued that since the colonies were 'currently unable to be incorporated into the domestic territory' of Japan, they should be recognised as 'an exception outside unified governance' (*tōitsu-teki tōchi no jogai-rei*). Each colonial holding thus became a site that required a special legal system that applied only in that particular territory.[25] This view, which constructed the colonies as 'exceptions outside unified governance', arose principally from the fact that various practices were particular to each colony. The construction of a legal system that stipulated and approved the operation of special laws that corresponded to local custom was fundamentally a means by which the Japanese government stabilised colonial governance.

One of the first steps in this stabilisation process was the 'Law Relating to Ordinances to be Implemented in Taiwan' (*Taiwan ni shikō subeki hōrei ni kan suru hōritsu*) (1896, Law No. 63), promulgated in Taiwan on 15 March 1896. This law, often referred to as 'Law No. 63', acknowledged that ordinances such as the Constitution that had been enacted by the Imperial Diet would not be immediately implemented in Taiwan. Instead, legal matters fundamentally concerning that territory would fall under a special system regulated by 'codes' (*risturei*) established by order of the Governor-General of Taiwan. Korean governance, too, fell under a similar law of expedience. Here, the 'Law Relating to Ordinances to be Implemented in Korea' (*Chōsen ni shikō subeki hōrei ni kan suru hōritsu*) (1911, Law No. 30), promulgated and brought into force on 25 March 1911, ruled that, rather than Imperial Diet legislation, Korean governance would comply with 'regulations' (*seirei*) issued by the Office of the Governor-General of Korea. Karafuto, however, was a slightly different case. Here, the majority of the population was comprised of immigrants from mainland Japan. Thus, the 'Law Relating to Ordinances to be Implemented in Karafuto' (*Karafuto ni shikō subeki hōrei ni kan suru hōritsu*) (1907, Law No. 25), promulgated on 29 March 1907, stipulated that any 'imperial ordinance' (*chokurei*) arising from this law would only apply to special Karafuto-specific issues such as 'matters related to indigenous peoples' (*dojin ni kan suru koto*).

In this way, not only did a different legal system operate between the mainland and the colonial holdings of Taiwan, Korea and Karafuto, but a different system operated in each of these three territories. In other words, the empire was comprised of various sites that operated under a range of differing legal regimes. Sites with a different legal system to that of mainland Japan were referred to as '*gaichi*' – literally 'outer territories'. In administrative terms, however, this word referred to those territories not subject to mainland Japanese law.

The existence of different legal systems in mainland Japan and each of the colonies resulted in the legal and governance systems of each being administered in complete isolation. Thus, the irrational situation arose in which, 'In legal terms the relationship between mainland Japan and the colonies was even more distant than that of the relationship between Japan and a foreign country, and thus the people of the colonies and corporations operating in the colonies were forced into an even more disadvantageous position than foreigners and foreign corporations'.[26] Clearly, this situation constituted an obstacle to smooth and efficient overall colonial governance. In order to address this problem, the 'Law of Mutuality' (*Kyōtsū-hō*) (Law No. 39) was promulgated on 16 April 1918, as an ordinance that facilitated the mutual contact of (that is, interaction between) both civil and criminal administrative processes in each imperial jurisdiction. This law became a very important legal mechanism during the imperial era.

The use of the term '*gaichi*' also related to concerns that the word 'colonies' (*shokumin-chi*) might easily create an impression of 'imperial exploitation' (*teikokushugi-teki sakushu*).[27] Authorities in Japan therefore tended to avoid the legal use of that expression when referring collectively to Taiwan, Korea and Karafuto. With the June 1929 establishment of the Ministry of Colonial Affairs (*Takumu-shō*) as the administrative organ with principal responsibility for colonial governance, the word '*gaichi*' was specifically adopted for legal use and came into common circulation both in official documentation and in materials produced by the private sector.[28] We should be mindful of the fact that the term '*gaichi*' was not limited to legal matters. Rather, this word, which as noted above literally meant 'outer territories' and which referred to those parts of the empire that were governed by other than mainland Japanese law, became a common-use word of convenience that functioned politically to gloss over the invasive nature of colonial control.

Korean koseki registration and being 'Korean'

As a result of the structure that saw the mainland legal system differ from that of each colonial holding, there was never an imperial era koseki registration law that operated uniformly across mainland Japan and its territories. It has been noted that rather than immediately assimilating the colonies into mainland Japan, the policy of the Japanese government was to assimilate them incrementally. Koseki registration in the colonies, too, was based on specific legal frameworks that differed for each territory.

Of the territories, Korea's koseki registration system was closest to that of the Japanese mainland. The indigenous Korean equivalent of the koseki registration system originated in the kingdom of Baekje (Kudara) as early as the seventh century, after which it was implemented by the successive Korean dynasties across the centuries. With the fundamental objective of enabling the state to tax and tithe its citizens, the system was based on a population survey which, with the aims of preventing failure to register, evading government control and avoiding status contamination, provided information on the family relationships of an individual, including the name of the household head, her or his address and changes to status.[29] Household survey regulations were promulgated in 1896, at the close of the Joseon Dynasty (*Ri-chō*), effecting a koseki registration system based on resident registration which recorded the household head and family members who spent their lives in the same domain as the head.[30]

On 4 March 1909, Korea became a protectorate of Japan, and the 'People's Registration Law' (*Minseki-hō*) was promulgated under the name of the government of Korea (Sunjong/Yunghui Year 3, Law No. 8). In addition, a people's registration system (*minseki seido*), which also operated after annexation, was implemented as the status registration system for the people of Korea. However, in terms of ensuring public order, this registration system could be maintained with its relatively simple content through a population survey conducted by the police.[31] Problems were created by the fact that the people's registration system did not work in conjunction with the koseki registration system of mainland Japan. This was an impediment to the exchange of lodgement information between Korea and mainland Japan when either making a new entry into or removing an entry from a koseki register record in the case of marriage between a mainland Japanese person and a Korean, or adoption for the purpose of continuing the family line.[32]

Essentially, these problems arose because family practices in Korea had special characteristics that did not accord with the koseki registration system that operated in Japan. A representative example of this was the *sei* family name. In the Confucianist-influenced society of Korea, the fundamentals of social order revolved around 'ancestor worship' (*sosen hōshi*), with the sibling ranking system giving greater respect to elder siblings. Accordingly, there was a focus on the eldest son as the individual who inherited the religious rites associated with the family. While prioritisation of male bloodline was similar to the tradition that operated in Japan, the special characteristic in Korea was the great respect accorded to the *sei* family name. This was in contrast to the Japanese system that bonded the family together through the *uji* family name. Since in Korea the *sei* family name provided proof of the father's bloodline, no change could be permitted. Furthermore, the adoption of a child with a different *sei* family name was prohibited (the principle of not adopting a child with a different surname – '*isei fuyō*'). In addition, in Korea great importance was placed upon the '*hongan*', the name given to the birthplace of the ancestors. Thus, even with the same surname, an individual could not be recognised as a blood relation without the same *hongan*. Initially, the Office of the Governor-General of Korea showed great respect to the unique characteristics inherent in the *sei* family name by acknowledging that 'the *sei* family name was not attached to a family, but to the single body of those with the same blood'.[33]

On 18 March 1912, the Office of the Governor-General of Korea proclaimed a regulation, as outlined above, announcing a Korean Civil Code (*Chōsen minji rei*) (1912, Regulation No. 7) that acknowledged the ethnic customs characterising the family system of Korea. This created a system whereby, rather than a direct application of Japanese homeland laws and ordinances, events related to the family relations and adoption procedures of Korean people were dealt with by the mainland Civil Code while also drawing on the regulations of the Korean Civil Code (this is referred to as legal 'appropriation', or '*eyō*' in Japanese). Eighteen December 1922 revisions to the Korean Civil Code saw the 'Korean

Koseki Registration Law' (*Chōsen koseki rei*) (1922, Ordinance of the Office of the Governor-General of Korea No. 154) promulgated to take effect from 1 July the following year. Koseki Registration Law administration in Korea was supervised by the District Justice General (*chihō hōin-chō*) or the Senior Sub-Prefectural Judge (*shichō jōseki hanji*), with Korean koseki registration maintained through justice governance administration.[34] Accordingly, the people's registration system that was little more than a police household (*kokō*) survey was abolished (information from the people's registration system, however, was carried over as valid into the Korean koseki registration system). The main objectives in creating a koseki registration system in Korea were given as follows: 'In both Japan and Korea even now it is the family system, a system that has developed equally in both places under the influence of Confucianism, which persists in providing the foundation of society'. As a result, 'there are many similarities in family relations and adoption procedures'. Furthermore, 'that fact that many Japanese have taken up residence in Korea following annexation [*Nikkan heigō*] and engaged in a common social life with Korean people has seen a sudden transplanting of Japanese systems and customs so that quite a few things have been assimilated and blended'. Thus, 'while there have been elements of difference between the customs of Korea [and Japan] since ancient times, there is no reason why we should particularly preserve these differences. Rather, *we need as far as possible to convert to a new system and progress this*' (emphasis added).[35] Ultimately, while the authorities intended 'as far as possible' to eventually assimilate the 'progressive' koseki registration system of Japan into local structures, there was an assumption that officialdom would for the time being respect the old customs and practices of the Korean people (*Chōsen minzoku*).

Thus, under the Korean Civil Code, Korean customary law was applied to fundamental matters related to the family such as marriage, the adoption of children to continue the family line and divorce by consent among Korean people.[36] For example, in the case of the adoption of a child for the purpose of continuing the family line, respect was shown to the previously mentioned principle of '*isei fuyō*' – literally 'the inability to adopt a child with a different *sei* family name'. Thus, as a condition of adoption in these circumstances, under Korean Koseki Law regulations, and with the general objective of defending any rupture of the patriarchal bloodline that was the foundation of the 'same *hongan*, same *sei* family name' principle (*dōhon dōsei*),[37] it was decided that the adopted child should share the *hongan* and *sei* family name of the adoptive parent. Accordingly, a Korean person could become the adopted child of a Japanese, but because of the surname difference, a Japanese was not permitted to become the adopted child of a Korean.[38] Conforming with the 'same *sei* family name, no marriage' custom that applied in Korea, marriage was also prohibited among relatives with the 'same *hongan* and same *sei* family name'.[39] In the case of a status change event involving a Japanese and a Korean, too, the Japanese would be administered according to the domestic (i.e. mainland Japanese) Civil Code, while the Korean was generally subject to local customary law. As discussed below, this was in contrast to the situation in Taiwan.[40]

The matters recorded in the Korean koseki registration system included: (1) the *sei* family name, place of origin and date of birth of the legal household head (*koshu*) and members of the family; (2) the *honseki* address of the legal household head; (3) the reason for and date of becoming the legal household head or becoming a member of his family; (4) the *sei* family name of the previous legal household head; and (5) the relationship between family members and both the legal household head and the previous legal household head. In the case of either the legal household head or the family being part of the Korean aristocracy, the aristocratic rank was also recorded. Among the above five points, special attention was given to the first and second. Concerning the first, in Korea the *sei* family name constituted proof of bloodline. Therefore, the *sei* family name of not only the legal household head but also of all family members was recorded. Since there was no change to the *sei* family name when an individual entered another family through marriage, people in a single family did not all necessarily have the same *sei* family name.[41] Furthermore, at the time that the Korean Koseki Registration Law came into effect, the Office of the Governor-General of Korea required those people without a *sei* family name to create such a name.[42] The *honseki* address referred to in the second point was not the previously discussed place of origin of a family. Rather, under the legislation the legal head of the household was newly required to stipulate a family *honseki* address as the unit around which the koseki register record was compiled.[43]

This legislation also saw the introduction into Korean society of the principle of lodgement (*todokede shugi*), which underpinned the regulatory function of Japanese koseki registration. The principle of lodgement that operated in the Japanese system decreed that once a person lodged a notice of a status event related to the Civil Code, that event came into legal effect. The Korean Koseki Registration Law introduced a lodgement principle that accorded with the Japanese procedure. It therefore became obligatory, as the 'sole process of recording information in the koseki register',[44] to lodge with the authorities that administered the relevant *honseki* address notice of events that related to civil affairs such as marriage, the adoption of a child for the purpose of continuing the family line, acknowledgement by a father of a child born outside formal marriage, divorce by consent, creation of a new register record (e.g. for a previously unregistered person) and creation of a branch family. It was also necessary to lodge this information with the authorities in the administrative district in which the person doing the lodging resided. There was little doubt that, in adopting this lodgement principle approach, authorities were seeking to ensure voluntary koseki registration on the part of the people of Korea.

We need to pay attention here to the relationship between Korean koseki registration and the Citizenship Law. As noted in the third section of Chapter Two, the former Citizenship Law in mainland Japan featured the fundamental rule, grounded in the principles of the *ie* family system, that all members of a single family should have the same citizenship. It was therefore stipulated that, in the case of a life event involving a Japanese and a foreigner such as marriage or adoption, there must be a change of citizenship involving entry into or departure from an *ie* family (that is, a change in the koseki register record). However, this former Citizenship Law was never brought into effect in Korea. As a result, Korean people were never included in the expression 'Japanese' as applied in the provisions of the pre-war law of mainland Japan. Accordingly, when a Korean person married a foreigner, they did not leave a family and hence did not change their citizenship to that of their spouse.[45] That is to say, while Korean people were bound to the status of 'Japanese subject', they were nonetheless placed outside the parameters of the legislation regarding change of citizenship that was based on the principle of the *ie* family.

In addition, there were restrictions on the freedom of Korean people to move between Korea and the Japanese mainland. This was in spite of the fact that, in terms of Article 22 of the Meiji Constitution, 'Japanese subjects' had a right to freedom of residence and movement. The authorities mandated mobility restrictions on Korean people from two perspectives. The first was fear of an influx of people from Korea to the Japanese mainland, while the second involved maintaining social order among Korean residents abroad. Having lost their holdings of arable land through the previously mentioned 'Land Survey Project', Korean peasant farmers flowed into mainland Japan looking for migrant labour work. As a result, by 1929 the resident Korean population in Japan had risen to 300,000. Furthermore, following the shock of the 1919 March First Movement that ignited throughout the whole of Korea, the Office of the Governor-General announced in April of the same year 'Matters Relating to the Control of Travel by Korean People' (*Chōsenjin no ryokō torishimari ni kan suru ken*) as the third military police proclamation. This proclamation sought to crack down on domestic social unrest and to restrict border crossing by Koreans. Accordingly, Koreans who travelled outside Korea were required to apply for documentation issued by the chief of police under whose jurisdiction they fell which confirmed their right to travel. This was then presented to police authorities at their port of departure from Korea. Such documentation was approved only for those who held a certified copy of an entry in the Korean koseki registration system as proof of their being 'Korean'. The water police branch office in Pusan, the point of departure for the Shimonoseki-Pusan Ferry that ran between 1905 and 1945, conducted strict checks of the koseki register details and travel documentation of those departing on boats carrying Korean labourers.[46]

In response to the outcry over the crackdown on the 1919 uprising, however, Japan's administrative control of Korea switched from oppressive 'military governance' (*budan tōchi*) to the more conciliatory 'cultural governance' (*bunka seiji*). The proof of travel documentation system also underwent various iterations until, in accordance with the 'Issues on the Policy of Korean Immigration' (*Chōsenjin ijū taisaku no ken*) determined at a cabinet meeting on 30 October 1934, 'a further reduction in the numbers of Koreans having passage to the Japanese mainland' was confirmed as government policy.[47] It is common knowledge, however, that following the outbreak of all-out war between Japan and China, the Japanese government needed to supplement labour shortages on the Japanese mainland. As a result, the July 1939 'Issues of the Immigration of Korean Labourers to the Japanese Mainland'

Table 4.1: Breakdown of the population in Japan's colonial holdings (1949 national census)

Region/ territory	Mainland Japanese	Local population	People from the territories not subject to mainland Japanese law[a]	Foreigners	Total	Mainland Japanese (%)
Korea	707,742	23,547,465	226	70,892	24,326,327	2.9
Taiwan	312,386	5,510,259	2,376	47,062	5,872,083	5.3
Karafuto	394,605[b]	396	19,540	352	414,891	95.1
Kwantung Leased Territory	198,188	1,158,083	6,934	4,129	1,367,334	14.5
South Sea Islands	77,011	50,648	3,479	120	131,258	58.6

Note: [a] Excluding members of the local population; [b] Including Ainu.
Source: Ministry of Foreign Affairs Treaties Bureau (ed.), *Gaichi hōsei-shi, dai-7-bu, Nihon tōchi-ka no Karafuto* (Journal of the Legal System of the Territories Not Subject to Mainland Japanese Law, Part 7, Karafuto Under Japanese Rule), Tokyo: Ministry of Foreign Affairs, 1962, p. 7.

(*Chōsenjin rōmusha naichi ijū no ken*), issued as a Ministry of Home Affairs memorandum of the Vice-Minister of Welfare, saw the forced relocation of more than 700,000 Korean labourers to Japan.

Koseki registration in Karafuto: Differences among 'aborigines'

Karafuto featured complicated circumstances that differed from those of either Korea or Taiwan. Among the 12,361 people who made up the resident population of Karafuto at the end of 1906, 10,806 were mainland Japanese while 1,291 were Ainu people.[48] As these figures demonstrate, Karafuto's special-case status was a result of the overwhelming percentage of mainland Japanese among the island's residential population (refer to Table 4.1). Accordingly, as a means of gathering information related to the status conditions of mainland Japanese residing in Karafuto, the mainland Japanese Civil Code was brought into operation from 1907. Karafuto was also the single case where the mainland Koseki Registration Law operated in a Japanese colonial holding. That legislation came into effect in Karafuto on 16 April 1924, as Imperial Ordinance No. 86.

However, the application of mainland koseki legislation was restricted to those Japanese who had transferred their koseki registration from mainland Japan. Because of customary differences, matters related to civil issues concerning the indigenous people of Karafuto were dealt with in terms of traditional practice.[49] Rather than including this group in the application of the mainland Koseki Registration Law, status registration by the indigenous people in Karafuto was achieved through the administration of a household survey based on the 'Aboriginal People's Household Regulations' (*Dojin kokō kisoku*) of 1908 (1908, Karafuto Prefecture Proclamation No. 17).

Ainu people were the indigenous group in Karafuto that had been under Japanese control for the longest time. Although direct social interaction saw an increase in marriages between Ainu people and mainland Japanese, these marriages were never formalised because koseki registration did not apply to Ainu people. As a result, the children born of these marriages were treated as '*shiseishi*' (so-called 'illegitimate children', that is, those born outside a formal marriage). In order to address problems arising from this, the Japanese government quickly gave koseki registration to the Ainu people of Karafuto and introduced policies that gave them the same rights and brought them under the same policies as 'Japanese subjects'. There was, furthermore, a sense that many Ainu people had successfully assimilated. This was demonstrated by statements to the effect that, '[Ainu people] both understand the structure of the national polity (*kokutai*) of Japan and demonstrate respect towards mainland Japanese. They also have a level of culture that is comparatively advanced'.[50] For these and other similar reasons, Ainu people were regarded as fitting subjects for the application of the Koseki Registration Law.

With this objective in mind, a joint Ministry of Justice/Ministry of Colonial Affairs survey of the traditional customs of the Ainu people of Karafuto confirmed in April 1932 that civil matters among Ainu people were now almost entirely conducted 'according to the standards of mainland Japan' (*naichi-ka*).[51] As a result, there were revisions in December of the same year to 'Issues Related to the Special Circumstances of Laws to be Implemented in Karafuto' (*Karafuto ni shikō suru hōritsu no tokurei ni kan suru ken*) announced as Proclamation No. 373. In conjunction with revisions to the application of the Civil Code, 'Issues Related to Creating a

Koseki Register for the Ainu People of Karafuto' (*Karafuto Ainu no teiseki ni kan suru ken*) (1932, Ministry of Justice Proclamation No. 47) were also enacted. Accordingly, from January 1933, it became possible for Karafuto Ainu people to be entered into a koseki register in mainland Japan.[52]

In contrast, an August 1932 survey of the traditional customs of the other five ethnic groups excluding Ainu people living on Karafuto – the Nivkh, the Orok (Uilta), the Kiirin (Evenks), the Sandaa (Ulch) and the Yakut peoples – concluded that, since the customs of these people 'remained primitive',[53] it would be difficult for them to assimilate into Japanese society. These groups were therefore legally declared to be 'Karafuto aboriginal people'.[54] Accordingly, even in the previously mentioned 'Issues Related to the Special Legal Circumstances of Laws to be Implemented in Karafuto' of 1932, civil matters concerning 'Karafuto aboriginal people' were dealt with through traditional customary law. As a result, there was no application of mainland Koseki Registration Law to members of these groups. Instead, based on the previously mentioned 'Aboriginal People's Household Regulations' and the 'Aboriginal People's Household Lodgement Regulations' (*Dojin kokō todokede kisoku*) stipulated with revisions to the original Household Regulations (1921, Karafuto Proclamation No. 25), these groups were registered in a 'household register roll' (*kokōbo*). However, since this form of registration was only for 'Karafuto aboriginal people', no *honseki* address was created. In other words, while the 'household register' based on the 'Aboriginal People's Household Regulations' operated as a koseki registration system for 'Karafuto aboriginal people', we need to remain cognisant of the fact that these people had no *honseki* address in Karafuto.

Essentially, among the indigenous people residing in Karafuto, only Ainu people were regarded as 'mainland Japanese'. Yet, while not being granted koseki registration on the Japanese mainland, from the perspective of citizenship, the other indigenous groups (the 'Karafuto aboriginal people') were required to submit as 'Japanese subjects' to the administrative powers of Japan. In terms of domestic law, however, they remained '*gaichijin*', people of a territory not subject to mainland Japanese law.[55] The fact that mainland Japanese, including Ainu people, formed a majority of the population was a situation that did not apply in other colonial holdings. As a result, Karafuto was formally incorporated as part of mainland Japan from April 1943. The Karafuto example clearly demonstrates that granting 'mainland Japanese' status was not merely perceived as a technical matter administered in terms of the Koseki Registration Law. Rather, this was a political issue that saw the Japanese government assess how the customs and spirit of a given ethnic group might assimilate as 'Japanese'.

The twists and turns of the koseki registration system in Taiwan

Taiwan was the site that presented the greatest challenge in terms of Japan's need to transplant the koseki registration system into the empire's colonial holdings. The ceding of Taiwan to Japan after the first Sino-Japanese War was concluded before the Japanese military had fully occupied the island. This provided an opportunity for the local indigenous people to demonstrate entrenched resistance to the colonial administration. Kabayama Sukenori (1837–1922), the first governor-general of Taiwan, imposed military rule across the island as an initial means of securing pacification and maintaining social order. The authorities also undertook a household survey in order to gather information on the general population, numbers of different ethnic groups and places of residence of the island's indigenous people. On 1 August 1896, by which time the whole island had been largely subjugated, Governor-General Kabayama announced the 'Taiwan Residents Koseki Register Survey Regulations' (*Taiwan jūmin koseki chōsa kisoku*) (1896, Directive No. 8). In an expansion of these regulations, on 6 August of the same year Governor-General Kabayama announced Official Notification (*kokuji*) No. 8, 'Recommendations Related to the Koseki Registration Survey' (*Koseki chōsa ni kan suru yukoku*). These regulations stated, 'information will be collected from all residents. This will become the grounds for the compulsory compilation of koseki registers with the governor-general ordering military police and ordinary police to create local koseki registers in order to gather proof of confirmation of the residents of the island'.[56] In addition to explaining to the residents of Taiwan the significance of the koseki registration system to the nation-state, the statement indicates that the compilation of Taiwanese koseki registers was a mode of military governance achieved through the joint activities of the military and the police. In response to this directive, military police and ordinary police surveyed their jurisdictions from September 1896 through to the end of that year, resulting in the compilation of koseki register records for the residents of Taiwan.[57]

As noted above, the compilation of the Japanese Civil Code was completed in 1898. Since the survey into the traditional customs (*kyūkan chōsa*) of Taiwan had not been concluded at that time, it was not possible to apply the mainland code to the island. At a meeting of the Legislative Investigative Committee held to deliberate upon the draft of the Civil Code, one member observed as follows: 'Only a short time has elapsed since Taiwan entered into the sphere of Japanese governance. We are thus unable to make this site the subject of our deliberations. It is probably best, therefore, if some special law is developed for Taiwan' (recorded as the words of Assistant Vice-Minister Ume Kenjirō).[58] This statement reflected a general agreement in government circles that the traditional customs of the ethnic groups residing on the island of Taiwan rendered that site, for the time being, beyond the applicability of the Civil Code.

On 1 December 1902, the Japanese government stipulated the 'Law Related to a National Census' (*Kokusei chōsa ni kan suru hōritsu*) (1902, Law No. 49). In 1905, a move was made to conduct a census of all imperial territory including the colonial holdings. However, in February 1904, the Russo-Japanese War broke out. When this conflict dragged on for longer than expected, the holding of a national census was postponed on the Japanese mainland where large numbers of young men of the age of majority were mobilised for conscription. Only in Taiwan was a census conducted as planned. This was the 'First Interim Household Survey' (*Dai'ichiji rinji kokō chōsa*) implemented across the whole island on 1 October 1905. With the results available in December that year, 'Household Regulations' (*kokō kisoku*) (1905, Ordinance of the Office of the Governor-General of Taiwan No. 93) and 'Household Survey Rules' (*kokō chōsa kitei*) (1905, Directive No. 255) were promulgated, and household survey rolls were compiled for Taiwan. The previous Taiwan household survey roll (*Taiwan kokō chōsabo*) had been regarded by the police as a tool to manage social order. This had led to information with no direct relationship to an individual's legal status, including 'race', 'conduct', 'previous convictions' and 'whether or not the individual smoked opium', being recorded on the former roll. The relevant justice administration bodies in Japan were of the opinion that information of this nature was inappropriate in terms of koseki register content.[59]

Finalisation as the 'Taiwan koseki register'

In August 1898, the Taiwan Civil Code (*Taiwan minji-rei*), which took into account the special circumstances unique to Taiwan, was proclaimed as code (*ritsurei*) No. 11. While this law fundamentally appropriated the framework of the mainland Japanese Civil Code and applied this to civil matters relating to the people of Taiwan, there were in fact significant differences between the Taiwanese family system and that of mainland Japan. Accordingly, rather than applying the stipulations of the civil code, matters concerning family relations and inheritance in Taiwan were dealt with according to local custom. The policies of the Hara Takashi Cabinet, however, advanced the incremental assimilation of colonial holdings and lauded 'the principle of making the colonies an extension of the mainland' (*naichi enchō shugi*). In line with these policies, through the 'Issues Concerning the Implementation of Civil Affairs in Taiwan' (*Minji ni kan suru hōritsu wo Taiwan ni shikō suru no ken*), (1922, Imperial Ordinance No. 406), a civil code was implemented there from 1 January 1923, under Governor-General Den Kenjirō (1855–1930). Even following this development, however, matters concerning family relationships and inheritance were processed in Taiwan according to custom rather than mainland civil code regulations.[60] In practice, this 'principle of making the colonies an extension of the mainland' presented problems in terms of complying with Taiwanese traditional family practice.

With the growing movement of people between the mainland and the colonies, private events such as marriage, adoption and a father's acknowledgement of a child born to Taiwanese and Japanese parents became an everyday occurrence. Given the differences between the family customs that prevailed on mainland Japan and in Taiwan and the asymmetry of the koseki registration systems that applied to the people in question, problems inevitably arose. This was because there were no overarching administrative stipulations equipped to deal with either marriage or adoption in the case of one party being from the Japanese mainland and one from Taiwan.

Problems of this nature were largely due to the fact that quite a number of aspects of the Taiwan household survey roll were not recognised as elements of the formal (mainland Japanese) koseki registration system. For example, when a mainland Japanese woman married and entered the family of a Taiwanese man, her marriage notice was accepted only at the relevant municipal office on the mainland. In the absence of a mechanism for formal administrative contact with the relevant municipal jurisdiction in Taiwan, her removal from that original mainland koseki register could not effectively be processed. In other words, from the Japanese administrative point of view she could not be removed from her original mainland register record as there was no appropriate koseki registration system in Taiwan into which she could be entered. As a result, the details of the marriage would be recorded only in the woman's mainland koseki record, and she would not appear in the Taiwan household survey roll.

According to the Meiji Civil Code, furthermore, marriage was legally formalised through the lodgement of a marriage notice. In mainland Japan, the head of the municipal office at which a marriage notice was lodged – whose duties included the administrative oversight of koseki matters – was ultimately responsible for the correct processing of the notice. In Taiwan, on the other hand, there was no corresponding koseki processing mechanism. In the absence of administrative links between the mainland Japanese koseki registration system and the system in Taiwan, the only way in which a mainland Japanese resident of Taiwan could achieve lodgement related to koseki matters was to physically return to the mainland. Frustration at this sort of administrative inconvenience associated with formal marriage between mainland Japanese and local Taiwanese people led to a rise in the numbers of such couples who avoided lodging a formal notice by entering into a de facto marriage. By October 1930, 149 cases of formal marriage between mainland Japanese and Taiwanese people had been recognised in terms of koseki administration procedures. In contrast, there were 370 de facto marriage relationships. Regarding the numbers of children born to mainland Japanese and Taiwanese couples, 284 were 'legitimate children' while 423 children were legally categorised as 'illegitimate'.[61]

While Taiwanese people were regarded as 'Japanese subjects' in the same manner as people from mainland Japan, the absence of koseki administrative links between these two sites with different legal procedures resulted in a lack of effective bureaucratic means of dealing with matters such as marriage, adoption or acknowledgment of paternity. Of course, the Japanese authorities sought a swift resolution once the issue that was generally referred to as 'the problem of de facto marriage relationships' (*kyōkon mondai*) became apparent. To this end, Japan officially declared, 'Given the growing numbers of close relationships and friendships developing between mainland Japanese and Taiwanese, there is a need in terms of effective governance and administration to seek to amalgamate the koseki registration systems of each place in a manner that accommodates the processes of both Taiwan and mainland Japan'.[62] In Taiwan, too, there were growing demands for koseki legislation that would enable the local register to correspond to the mainland system.

On 25 November 1932, in relation to Taiwan, 'Issues Relating to the Koseki Registration of the People of This Island' (*Hontōjin no koseki ni kan suru ken*) (1932, Code No. 2) was therefore announced. This was followed on 20 January 1933 by the promulgation of 'Issues Relating to the Koseki Registration of the People of This Island' (*Hontōjin no koseki ni kan suru ken*) (1933, Governor-General Directive No. 8). Based on these two sets of regulations, the household survey roll, derived from the former Household Regulations, came into effect on 1 March 1933, after which it was regarded in terms of mainland justice and administration processes as the 'koseki register roll' for the people of Taiwan. That is to say, the new roll functioned to administer processes such as entry into and removal from a local household register, a document that corresponded to the mainland koseki register. In June 1935, following Governor-General Directive No. 32, the Household Regulations were once more revised and subsequently recognised as having effect also on the Japanese mainland.[63] As a result of the implementation of the 'Issues Relating to the Koseki Registration of the People of This Island' proclamation, 272 cases of marriage or adoption involving mainland Japanese and Taiwanese people were registered by the end of 1933.[64]

It should be noted, however, that there were two particular points of difference between koseki registration practices in Taiwan and Korea. The first was the fact that, as the nomenclature of the relevant proclamation suggests, the 'Taiwan koseki register' was ultimately only the 'koseki register of the people of this island'. The phrase 'the people of this island' was a form of address only for the residents of the so-called 'general governance regions' of Taiwan. The indigenous peoples such as the Ami, Tayal and Payuan, on the other hand, were derogatorily referred to as 'savage natives' (*banjin*). These people resided in the so-called 'land of savages' (*banchi*) outside the zone of general governance. Unlike the registration processes that applied to the 'people of this island', the household and status relationships of these 'savages' were recorded in the 'savages district register' (*bansha daichō*), a register compiled according to the 'Format of the Savages District Register' (*Bansha daichō yōshiki*) (1903, Imperial Ordinance No. 73). By the end of 1934, the indigenous population of Taiwan was a little less than 150,000. With a population of 47,000, the Ami people comprised the largest single indigenous group.[65] 'Savages' who relocated to reside in parts of the general governance region we re-categorised as 'mature savages' (*jukuban*). Permitted to have an entry in the Taiwanese koseki registration system, these people were distinguished from the 'innate savages' (*seiban*) who lived in the 'land of savages'.[66] It is apparent, therefore, that a koseki register entry was proof that an aboriginal person had naturalised and could be acknowledged as a 'Japanese'.

The second point of difference with Korea was the fact that the Taiwanese koseki registration system never totally abandoned its original policing function. That is to say, notwithstanding the new status given to koseki registration and the fact that administrative stipulations relating to civil code matters were now maintained by processes similar to those of mainland Japan, administrative oversight of the registration system remained the responsibility of the district chief of police. Unlike mainland Japan, where koseki administration was the responsibility of the head of the relevant municipality, the registration system in Taiwan maintained a policing function. This was also a significant difference in comparison to Korea. There, matters of koseki administration became the province of the justice system so that administrative oversight for a particular koseki register lay with the head of the relevant district court.[67]

The koseki registration system was the root and trunk of the *ie* family system of imperial Japan. As is evident from the above, in attempting to implement the system uniformly in the colonies Japan had no option but to introduce a variety of koseki registration systems that accommodated the traditional customs of each locale. We might thus conclude that even the almighty koseki registration system was unable to suppress the local customs in each of Japan's imperial holdings.

Koseki and control of 'ethnicity': *Ie* family over bloodline

The construction of 'ethnic membership'

We have seen thus far how the specific koseki register laws and ordinances for each of the different jurisdictions in the 'Greater Japanese Empire' were implemented, with varying status registration stipulations in each location. As a result, differences arose in the definitions of 'Japanese subjects' as registered in the respective locations of mainland Japan, Korea, Taiwan and Karafuto. Thus, having a record in one of these regional registers became an indicator of 'ethnicity' in the sense of denoting 'membership of an ethnic group' (*minzoku seki*).

Depending on the territory in which the *honseki* address was recorded, an individual was, for example, designated as 'Korean' or 'Taiwanese' and as being of 'Korean' or 'Taiwanese' ethnicity. The corollary to this was that those regarded as being of 'Korean' or 'Taiwanese' ethnicity were accorded, following imperial domestic law, the respective status of being 'Korean' or 'Taiwanese'. For example, the legal definition of a 'Korean' person was 'one to whom the Korean Koseki Registration Law applied' (or one to whom the People's Registration Law, '*Minseki-hō*', which preceded the Korean Koseki Registration Law had applied). As the following comment made at a meeting of the Imperial Diet demonstrates, the Japanese government took the position that, 'If you ask what a Korean is, we understand this principally to be a person of Korean ethnicity'.[68] In other words, the label of 'ethnicity' operated to distinguish between people in the same way as the various koseki registers functioned to distinguish between people in different sites of the empire.

Furthermore, regardless of whether or not one's *honseki* address was in mainland Japan or in one of the *gaichi*, even those who were similarly designated as 'Japanese subjects' and who technically held the same citizenship status were divided into 'mainland Japanese' (*naichijin*) and 'people of the territories not subject to Japanese law' (*gaichijin*). Since 'Koreans', 'Taiwanese' and 'Karafuto people' had their *honseki* address in the colonies, they were treated as members of the *gaichijin* group. On the other hand, those who had a *honseki* address on mainland Japan, that is, who were subject to the application of the mainland Japanese Koseki Registration Law – fundamentally those who were native Japanese – became *naichijin.* And although, as noted above, in terms of international law the people of the two regions of the South Pacific Mandate and the Kwantung Leased Territory were regarded as residents of protectorates of Japan, the Japanese authorities considered these sites to be part of imperial Japan's colonial holdings. Special ordinances were issued, however, regarding the koseki registration of the aboriginal people of those two territories.[69] These aboriginal people, nonetheless, were never granted Japanese citizenship. Therefore, rather than domestic Japanese law treating the indigenous groups from these two territories as *gaichijin*, they were put in the exceptional position of being treated externally as 'foreigners'.[70]

Even if a *gaichijin* came to reside in mainland Japan, legally, she or he remained a *gaichijin.* In accordance with the Koseki Registration Law of mainland Japan, if a person designated as a *gaichijin* was born or died on the mainland, there was an obligation to lodge a notice of that event with the head of the mainland municipality in which that person resided. In such cases, however, it was necessary for the head of the relevant municipality to process the lodgement as that of a 'person without a *honseki* address'.[71]

'*Gaichijin*' was a general use term. Ultimately, however, there were a range of designations given to people residing in the colonies. For example, while people in Korea were merely referred to as 'Korean people', Taiwanese people could be 'people of this island' or 'savages'. Indigenous people who resided on Karafuto, on the other hand, were referred to as 'Karafuto aboriginal people' (*Karafuto dojin*) or just 'aboriginal people'.[72]

Honseki address change prohibition: Fixity of the *ie* family

We begin this section by outlining once more the two possible instances of changing a koseki register entry that applied in terms of the pre-war koseki registration system. The first was the transfer of the *honseki* address, that is, of the specific point in a given municipality at which the koseki record was located. This applied in the case of a change in the location of an *ie* family through either transfer of the register record itself or the creation of a branch family. A register change of this kind could also include the case of a person who, lacking a *honseki* address and therefore having no family record into which they could be entered, created a new *ie* family. The second type of change occurred when one shifted from the current koseki register record to a new one. That is to say, with the departure from or entry into an *ie* family through marriage, adoption, recognition of paternity or similar event, a person would depart the koseki record of the current *ie* family to enter a different *ie* family and thereby acquire a new koseki entry. In contrast to the former, which involved either a change to or movement of the *ie* family, the latter featured a change to an individual's koseki register entry.

Of the two forms of koseki registration change outlined above, the former was forbidden in terms of movement between the various jurisdictions of imperial Japan. In other words, it was not possible for a family to move between any of the *gaichi* and the Japanese mainland, or similarly between any of the territories to which different koseki registration ordinances applied. This was because if an individual moved their *honseki* address between any of those territories that comprised the colonies and mainland Japan, in which different koseki registration ordinances operated, disruptions might occur to the ethnic designations of 'mainland Japanese', 'Korean' or 'Taiwanese'. For instance, if a Korean or Taiwanese person transferred their *honseki* address to the Japanese mainland, they would become a 'mainland Japanese' attached to a mainland koseki register. Therefore, as a matter of principle, any change of koseki registration at the individual's discretion between different imperial territories was prohibited. Since it forbade free choice of 'ethnic membership' as determined by the *honseki* address, this regulation was referred to as 'the principle of no free change of *honseki* address' (*honseki tenzoku fujiyū no gensoku*).[73]

This principle permeated all koseki registration precedents established by the pre-war authorities. For example, on 18 January 1916, in reply to an inquiry from the mayor of Niigata concerning the appropriate response to a Korean person (*Chōsenjin*) who wanted to establish an *ie* family on mainland Japan, the Director of the Ministry of Justice Legal Affairs Bureau replied, '*People newly incorporated into the empire* [*shinpu no tami*], *including Korean people, will not be permitted to change koseki register, establish a branch family or establish a new family in mainland Japan*, and accordingly, we are of the opinion that the head of the municipality should not accept lodgement related to these matters'[74] (emphasis added). Thus, the establishment of a *honseki* address on the mainland was not permitted by 'people newly incorporated into the empire', a term that referred to those born in a colonial holding. Similarly, a mainland Japanese was forbidden to transfer their koseki registration to one of the territories not subject to mainland Japanese law. To an inquiry on this point, the Justice Ministry ruled, 'A mainland Japanese cannot transfer to Korea, nor can a Korean transfer to mainland Japan, nor establish a new koseki register record, nor create a branch family, nor be entered into a koseki register record'.[75]

Even in the legal interpretation of the time, it was determined as follows:

> While the Koseki Registration Law is a law that operates in mainland Japan, there are Korean koseki regulations that similarly operate for Korean people and Taiwanese koseki regulations that operate for Taiwanese people. This results in koseki regulations that match the character of the groups for whom the given system operates. A grounding principle of the country's various koseki registration systems is that, while mainland Japanese people derive their status from their ancestors on mainland Japan, people resident in the various colonies derive their status from ancestors in those places. We therefore cannot permit any mingling or confusion of family registration or status registration.[76]

Through this clear distinction of ethnic groups, a dividing line was created among 'subjects of the empire' that differentiated between *naichijin* and *gaichijin*. This is evident from the data provided in Table 4.2.

Military service and suffrage for *gaichijin*

The principle that prohibited a transfer of *honseki* address between mainland Japan and the territories not subject to mainland Japanese law also had an important influence on the function of the Japanese citizenship of *gaichijin*. We might examine this influence by considering the issues of suffrage and military service. These two matters are arguably representative of the respective rights and responsibilities of the citizen that are the usual justification for citizenship.

Table 4.2: The division of the 'subjects of Japan': Borders of ethnicity based on koseki registration (Post-1933)

	Identification criteria (for ethnic membership)	**Legislative framework**
Mainland Japanese (*naichijin*)		
Japanese Karafuto Ainu	Mainland Japan koseki registration	Koseki Registration Law
People from territories not subject to mainland Japanese law (*gaichijin*)		
People of this island (*hontōjin*)	Taiwanese koseki registration	'Household Regulations', 'Issues Relating to the Koseki Registration of People of This Island'
Savages (aboriginal people)	Savages district registration	'Format of the Savages District Register'
Korean people	Korean koseki registration	People's Registration Law, Korean Koseki Registration Law
Karafuto aboriginal people (excluding Ainu people)	Karafuto koseki registration	'Aboriginal People's Household Regulations'

Military service was fundamentally implemented through what is referred to as the 'personal principle' (*zokujin-shugi*). Article 9, Clause 2, of the Military Service Law (1927, Law No. 47) declared, 'This law applies to those between the ages of seventeen and forty *who are subject to the Koseki Registration Law* and who have not served as a regular solider, reserve soldier, supply soldier or other personnel' (emphasis added). Since conscription legislation applied to individuals who were 'subject to the Koseki Registration Law', its application was initially limited to 'mainland Japanese'. Accordingly, those who were born in the colonies were placed outside the target group of young men with military service obligations. The justification given for this 'principle of service by mainland Japanese' was not only the fact that military service was a very serious duty related to the survival or death of the *kokutai* – the national polity – but also that it involved knowledge of military secrets. There was some suspicion that, unlike innate Japanese, people born in the colonies might display questionable devotion to the national polity.[77] Faced with the necessity of ensuring an ongoing supply of military personnel, the state therefore sought to intervene in and prevent any developments that might reduce the number of mainland bodies available for military conscription. In fact, one reason for forbidding free choice of koseki registration transfer from mainland Japan to the *gaichi* was 'a fear that among those mainland Japanese who have not yet undertaken military service there may be some who seek a free koseki registration transfer for the purpose of evading conscription'.[78]

However, the demands of Japan's commitment to a system of total war and the outbreak of all-out hostilities between Japan and China on 1 July 1937 saw an end to this principle of military service as solely the duty of mainland Japanese. Administratively, two avenues were considered in bringing this change to fruition. The first was the excision of the article relating to koseki registration from military service legislation, while the second was the possibility of implementing the mainland Koseki Registration Law in Taiwan and Korea. As a preliminary to the introduction of conscription, the 'Army Special Volunteer Forces Directive' (*Rikugun tokubetsu shigan-hei rei*) (1938, Imperial Ordinance No. 95) was promulgated in Korea in February 1938. Yet, since wording to the effect that, 'Men who are imperial subjects above the age of seventeen who are not subject to the operation of the Koseki Registration Law', was inserted into the first article of the ordinance, these preparations for the implementation of a volunteer soldier system for Korean men did not necessitate any 'unification of mainland Japanese and Korean people' through the Koseki Registration Law. According to a survey conducted by public security authorities, significant in the reaction of Korean people to this development was the request that, 'there be general recognition of the fact that Korean compatriots have deep feelings regarding the many everyday rights denied to them, which include the freedom to transfer koseki registration, the freedom to move to Japan and the freedom to express themselves'. In the eyes of the authorities, however, such a request 'merely exposed the bad character of Koreans who, given an inch, now wanted to take a mile'.[79] For the people of Korea, any hope of unrestricted koseki registration transfer remained a mere illusion.

Nevertheless, with the Korean Army High Command (*Chōsen gun shirei bu*) implementing a system of volunteer service, a proposal was made on 2 July 1937, to the following effect: 'It is necessary to take steps to swiftly implement the [mainland] Koseki Registration Law in Korea in order to have Korean registration, in both name and reality, of those mainland Japanese who are permanent residents of Korea and also to ensure that Koreans fulfil their obligations towards the state'. The document continued, 'If the authorities are serious about realising the "unity of mainland Japan and Korea", then swift steps should be taken towards achieving this objective through permitting the transfer of koseki registration to Korea by those mainland Japanese who are resident in Korea. In order for this to occur, furthermore, it would be necessary to implement [mainland] Koseki Registration Law in Korea'.[80] However, as discussed below, there were manifold obstacles facing any unification of the koseki registration systems of the colonies with that of mainland Japan, and this audacious proposal remained nothing more than an opinion for later reference.

In May 1942, a Tōjō Hideki (1884–1948) Cabinet decision saw the implementation of a conscription system for Koreans, with 1 March 1943 revisions to the Military Service Law (1943, Law No. 4) declaring, 'those who are subject to the application of Koseki Registration Law regulations and of the stipulations regarding the koseki registers that operate under the Korean Civil Code' were now required to meet conscription obligations. The conscription of Korean men became possible through the wording of these revisions, in spite of the fact that they remained outside the application of the mainland Koseki Registration Law.

These legislative revisions relating to conscription in Korea furthermore revealed an interesting play of political power. While the formal conscription age was stipulated as seventeen to forty years of age, Clause 2 of the appendices to the revised Military Service Law noted, 'Rather than people who have already reached conscription age or who have already matured, we are interested in targeting a younger group that has not yet matured in either body or mind and who will be of conscription age at some time in the future'.[81] In seeking to ensure the call-up of soldiers with a high degree of loyalty as 'imperial subjects', it was judged problematic to draw on those who had reached formal conscription age, by which time an individual's identity as 'ethnic Korean' was already ingrained. More appropriate, according to this narrative, was targeting and placing pressure upon younger age groups that still had the potential to be cultivated as 'subjects of the Emperor'. Here we see how the political authorities in Japan knowingly constructed a false discourse of the 'unity of mainland Japan and Korea'.

The development of matters relating to conscription took longer in Taiwan, with the Governor-General of Taiwan's 'Ruling on a

Training Centre for Volunteer Troops' (*Taiwan sōtokufu rikugun shigansha kunrensho kansei*) (1942, Imperial Ordinance No. 198) not proclaimed there until February 1942. An army volunteer troop system was established in April of the same year. In September 1943, the Tōjō Cabinet determined that a conscription system would be implemented in Taiwan from 1945. Following this decision, revisions were made on 1 November 1943 to the Military Service Law (1943, Law No. 110). These 1943 revisions saw the excision from the legislation of the previous Korea-specific wording – 'those who are subject to the application of Koseki Registration Law regulations and of the stipulations regarding the koseki registers that operate under the Korean Civil Code'. Yet, at the end of the day, nowhere in the colonies were the Japanese authorities daring enough to pick the forbidden fruit by implementing the mainland Koseki Registration Law. Instead, they devised means to impose the military service responsibilities to which the 'subjects of Japan' were beholden on both the Korean and Taiwanese people, neither of whom were subject to the application of the mainland Koseki Registration Law. With differences related to military service between mainland Japan and the colonies now completely erased, there was no meaning to Article 3, Clause 3 of the previously stated Law of Mutuality, which limited the transfer of mainland Japanese into koseki registers located in those territories not subject to mainland Japanese law for fear of individuals using this as a means to evade military service. Thus, with the 1943 Military Service Law revisions, this stipulation, too, was rescinded.

According to the records of the Ministry of Health and Welfare, the implementation of the conscription system in Korea and Taiwan saw military service by 232,341 Koreans and 207,183 Taiwanese, with 22,182 Koreans and 30,304 Taiwanese eventually classified as either dead or missing in action.[82] However, neither conscription nor recruitment for military service made even the slightest chink in the wall that the authorities constructed between the mainland and the colonies. Accordingly, there was no change whatsoever to the varying koseki registration processes that operated between the different regions of the empire.

Let us now consider suffrage. Unlike the issue of military service that was based on the personal principle of '*zokujin-shugi*', suffrage was not something for which the application of koseki registration was necessary. This right of the citizen was, in fact, implemented through the principle of territoriality, '*zokuchi-shugi*'. Although the 'Law on Elections for the House of Representatives and the House of Peers' (*Shūgi'in gi'in senkyo-hō*), promulgated on 11 February 1889, was not brought into effect in the *gaichi*, both mainland Japanese and those born in *gaichi* territories with a fixed residence on mainland Japan could exercise their right to suffrage. While Article 6, Clause 2 of the original bill stipulated a *honseki* address and residence for more than one full year in the metropolis or prefecture which maintained the relevant voter roll as necessary conditions to qualify as a voter, revisions in 1900 (1900, Law No. 73) made it sufficient for a voter to reside in an electoral district for one full year.

In reality, however, the need to reside for one full year in one place struck a fatal blow to the suffrage of those such as mine and factory labourers or seasonal workers who were required to move their place of work on a regular basis. Hovering in the background of the relevant regulations we can detect the machinations of a government, concerned about the rise of the proletarian movement, attempting to strip voting rights from the working classes.[83] The employment circumstances of Koreans who relocated to mainland Japan saw the vast majority working in areas such as industry, civil engineering, construction and mining. According to statistics from the Ministry of Home Affairs Social Affairs Department, a national survey conducted as of 1 May 1924 among 7,104 Koreans who were resident in Japan at that time[84] indicated that there were 4,217 (fifty-nine percent) who had worked for a period of less than one year in factories and mines and who effectively had an itinerant lifestyle. Following relocation to mainland Japan once the quality of their homeland life had been undermined, those who managed to create a living environment with stability of residence in one single setting were the exception.

Thus, even after the introduction of the so-called 'Universal Suffrage Law' (*Futsū senkyo-hō*) which, through May 1925 revisions to the 'House of Representatives Election Law' (*Shūgi'in gi'in senkyo hō*) (1925, Law No. 47), saw the abolition of the necessity for voters to be taxpayers (prior to the Universal Suffrage Law, payment of taxes was a necessary condition of suffrage), the number of those born in the colonies who were granted the right to vote did not rise appreciably. For example, at the end of September 1931, only 38,912 of the 303,622 Koreans resident in Japan held that right, less than twenty percent of all Korean males.[85]

As compensation for the implementation of the conscription system in the colonies as an obligation of the 'imperial subjects' in those places, 1 April 1945 revisions to the 'House of Representatives Election Law' (*Shūgi'in gi'in senkyo hō*) (1945, Law No. 34) saw that law also come into effect in Korea and Taiwan. To qualify as a voter, however, an individual was required to pay taxes of more than fifteen yen. Furthermore, there was a quota system that restricted available seats to twenty-three people per region in Korea, five in Taiwan and three for all of Karafuto. At the same time, a section of the legislation relating to appointments to the House of Peers was revised (1945, Imperial Ordinance No. 193), and ten from the House of Peers members nominated by the Emperor (*chokusen gi'in*) were to come from both Korea and Taiwan on seven-year terms. (In the case of mainland Japanese, however, such appointments were for life.) According to Prime Minister Koiso Kuniaki (1880–1950), the limited suffrage extended to residents of the colonies 'took into account the general level of education and culture among those who live in Korea and Taiwan and the current conditions of local self-government'.[86] Koiso's words confirm the theory that discrimination against the colonies was grounded in mainland perceptions of the 'low level of civic consciousness' (*mindo*) of those locations. Nevertheless, the war came to an end before a general election was held, and the suffrage rights of Korean and Taiwanese people were suspended in December 1945. This point will be discussed further below.

When we consider each of the points above as a whole, it becomes clear that imperial Japan deployed the koseki registration system, which confirmed one's status as a 'subject of Japan', and related citizenship matters as effective mechanisms of control. Residents in both mainland Japan and the *gaichi* were thus permanently attached (through the official record of ethnic group membership, '*minzoku seki*') to their respective societies. By effectively prohibiting any free change of ethnic group membership, the authorities distinguished between and discriminatively managed these different ethnicities. It was thought that this process might assist Japan to aim toward integration and stability in a multi-cultural, multi-ethnic state.

The principle of the '*ie* family' that eclipsed 'bloodline'

Table 4.1 provided information on the population distribution, based on ethnic group membership, between mainland Japan and the *gaichi*.

Nevertheless, this division between a mainland Japanese (*naichijin*) and a person of those territories not subject to mainland Japanese law (*gaichijin*) was not completely set in stone. The entity that had the power to dissolve this boundary was none other than the principle of the *ie* family. Even the state was not able to forcibly intervene in or control the workings of family formation through events such as marriage or adoption that transcended region or ethnicity. Naturally, when there was a change in status such as marriage, which invoked the Koseki Registration Law and which involved, for example, a person of the colonies and a mainland Japanese, or a Korean and a Taiwanese person (or other couples in which each partner was born in a different colonial location), the problem arose as to how to deal with changes such as entry into a new koseki register record and removal from the previous record.

In circumstances such as these, the previously mentioned Law of Mutuality was the mechanism stipulating the legal processes that ensured administrative cohesion in the management of the varying koseki register legislation that stipulated different legal processes in different regions of the empire. Article 2, Clause 1 of the Law of Mutuality stipulated, 'through the regulations of a region, a person who enters an *ie* family of that region shall thereby leave the *ie* family of a different region'. The 'region' cited here was stipulated in Article 1 of the Law to 'refer to mainland Japan, Korea, Taiwan, the Kwantung Leased Territory or the South Pacific Mandate'. Karafuto, where approximately ninety percent of the residents were mainland Japanese, was to be classified for legislative purposes as part of 'mainland Japan'.[87] However, the fact that, as we have seen, the mainland Civil Code also operated in Taiwan made this site, in effect, the same legal jurisdiction as the mainland. Therefore, the Law of Mutuality was never put into effect in Taiwan.

What, then, did Article 3, Clause 1 of the Law of Mutuality seek to establish? According to the principle of 'one *ie* family, one koseki register record' that was the basis of the Meiji Civil Code and which stipulated that all persons be attached to one *ie* family and be entered into one koseki record only, it was natural that a person could not have two or more *honseki* addresses.[88] Accordingly, in the case of either the entry into an *ie* family in the colonies of a person who had a *honseki* address on the mainland, or the entry into a mainland *ie* family by a person who had a *honseki* address in the colonies, the basic koseki registration practice was applied. That is, when the person in question left the original *ie* family, she or he entered the *ie* family of the other party.

In other words, the site of the *ie* family was both immutable and unmovable; and, it was only when people stepped across regions and departed or entered an *ie* family that their ethnic membership changed automatically. For example, regardless of actual ethnic background, when a person who was ethnic Korean married or became the adopted child of a mainland Japanese and entered that person's *ie* family, she or he also became a 'mainland Japanese'. Further, in the case in which a child born to a mainland Japanese mother was recognised as the child of a Korean father, that child would have their registration transferred to the record of their father, that is, to a Korean koseki register record, and would thus be transformed in legal terms into a 'Korean' (that is, into a *gaichijin*).

In the case of those people who entered into a previously mentioned '*kyōkon*' (de facto marriage relationship), the lines that divided 'mainland Japanese', 'Korean' and 'Taiwanese' were especially blurred. If through marriage or adoption a mainland Japanese entered an *ie* family in Taiwan, they became a 'Taiwanese' (or, in the reverse instance, a Taiwanese person became a mainland Japanese); but in 'de facto marriages', 'bloodline' was never the basis of defining 'mainland Japanese' or 'Taiwanese' for the parties involved.

Since a person from the colonies who was given the status of 'mainland Japanese' became subject to the application of the mainland Japanese Koseki Registration Law, she or he acquired the right to freely decide upon a *honseki* address on the Japanese mainland and to transfer their *honseki* address in the mainland. Moreover, if a 'former Korean' who had once become 'mainland Japanese' through marriage or being adopted by a mainland Japanese subsequently divorced or broke ties with their adopted family, she or he left the *ie* family of the other party. However, in terms of ethnic group membership, these people were unable to be re-registered with a Korean family and accordingly retained their status as 'mainland Japanese'. Since their departure from the previous family resulted in them no longer having a *honseki* address in mainland Japan, such persons were permitted to take a *honseki* on the mainland through establishing a new family.[89] Thus, the administrative procedures involved in entering an *ie* family became a 'ritual' that clearly nullified 'bloodline'.

Table 4.3: Increase in numbers of marriages between mainland Japanese and Koreans (1928–1937)

	Total numbers	**Mainland Japanese husbands / Korean wives**	**Korean husbands / mainland Japanese wives**	**Mainland Japanese wives / Korean husbands who entered their wife's *ie* family**	**Korean wives / mainland Japanese husbands who entered their wife's *ie* family**
1928	527	266	238	21	2
1929	615	310	277	27	1
1930	786	386	350	46	5
1931	852	438	367	41	6
1932	954	533	364	48	9
1933	1,029	589	377	48	15
1934	1,017	602	365	43	7
1935	1,038	601	391	40	6
1936	1,121	625	430	47	19
1937	1,206	664	472	48	22

Source: Chōsen sōtoku-fu, (The Office of the Governor-General of Korea), *Shisei sanjunen shi* (Thirty Years of Administrative History), Seoul: Chōsen sōtoku-fu, 1940, p. 475.

The *ie* family, however, was an entity deeply permeated with notions of male superiority. As noted in Chapter Three, since the party that departed a family through matters such as marriage was fundamentally the woman, of necessity those who had their ethnic group membership forcibly changed were also largely women. Accordingly, as demonstrated in Table 4.3, in marriages between mainland Japanese and Korean people, the vast majority involved the woman entering the *ie* family of the husband. Even so, because it was possible, although exceptional, for a male to be entered into a 'register of the territories not subject to mainland Japanese law' (*gaichi seki*) through marrying into a family in which the woman was the legal household head (*koshu*), or through being adopted as a son-in-law to continue the family name (*mukoyōshi engumi*), the rule of the *ie* family was subordinate to the state's demand for military service. As discussed above, Article 3, Clause 3 of the Law of Mutuality forbade a mainland Japanese who had not fulfilled military service obligations from transferring their record to a koseki register of territories not subject to mainland Japanese law.

Essentially, koseki registration was a mechanism by means of which the location of the *ie* family the individual was attached to remained interminably fixed. It was, in other words, the individual who was required to enter into or depart from the *ie* family (that is, the relevant koseki register record), the pivot supported by the great principles of feudalism around which all else revolved. In this way, shifts the individual had no control over also occurred in ethnic group membership. At the end of the day, rather than bloodline, it was in fact the *ie* family that reigned supreme over 'ethnic' demarcations. Accordingly, even in a population breakdown based on different ethnicities as presented in Table 4.2, we cannot assume that the various categories presented are purely based on ethnic background.

It was crucial for the Japanese state to work tirelessly to preserve the *ie* family, because the *ie* family was the mechanism that homogenised the people and thereby constructed them as 'imperial subjects'. Thus, even if the koseki transfer of an individual threatened to contaminate the 'ethnic purity' of a koseki record, this was permitted as consistent with *ie* family principles.

Border-crossing, imperial subjects and the 'Japanese'

'People with Taiwanese koseki registration': 'Japanese' in name only

Citizenship is not necessarily only acquired through formal legal procedures. There are also cases in which the acquisition of citizenship has no relationship to an individual's sense of attachment to the state. The fact that granting and rescinding citizenship was a discretionary act determined by the state through case-by-case assessment often resulted in what might be referred to as the 'nominal citizen'. Let us consider some examples.

The fact that imperial Japan operated different koseki registration systems in the various regions of the empire provided a number of relatively simple means by which foreigners could become 'Japanese'. Registration on a Korean koseki register or a Taiwanese koseki register, for example, entitled one to legally qualify as being 'Japanese'. While these people were only nominally Japanese and did not enjoy the same citizenship rights as those on the mainland, there were significant benefits particularly to the categorisation of Taiwanese people in this way. Following the ceding of Taiwan to Japan, growing numbers of especially continental Chinese persons were granted 'Taiwanese registration' by either the Japanese Consulate or the Office of the Governor-General of Taiwan. Many of these people had both a primary registration address and property in continental China. With no blood or land ties to Taiwan, they were distinguished in terms of ethnicity from 'Taiwanese' by being referred to as 'people with Taiwanese registration' (*Taiwan seki-min*). Effectively, given their background, the majority of these people were more precisely characterised as 'Chinese people with Taiwanese registration'. Those so categorised largely came from places such as Amoy, Fuzhou and Shantou that lay along the coast of China directly opposite Taiwan. Many, furthermore, had links more broadly to Shanghai, Guangzhou, Hong Kong or even South East Asia.

Although there was no uniform process by means of which Chinese people with Taiwanese registration collectively emerged, we can identify three main groups. First were those who acquired Taiwanese registration through the governance measures of a Japanese Consulate or the Governor-General of Taiwan. For example, certain people, who were not in Taiwan at the time of the citizenship selection process as stipulated in the Treaty of Shimonoseki (referred to above), were initially omitted from the koseki registration system in Taiwan. In October 1898, therefore, the Governor of Tainan County (in southwest Taiwan) granted registration to sixty such men and forty-eight women. In 1921, moreover, ten wealthy persons were permitted to register in Fuzhou.[90] The Lin Ben Yuan family, who were people of means in Taiwan, were initially registered in Fujian Province and returned to the continent following the Japanese acquisition of Taiwan. Cognisant of the financial power of the Lin family, however, the Japanese sought to embrace its members back into the Taiwanese community. It is generally accepted that, as occasion demanded and without any consideration for the stipulations of citizenship legislation, people such as the Lin were permitted to acquire Japanese citizenship.[91]

The second group involved those who were entered into a Taiwanese koseki register following private status events involving a Taiwanese person. Residence outside Taiwan notwithstanding, Chinese persons might marry or be adopted by a Taiwanese head of a family, or marry a woman who was the legal household head. Because these Taiwanese people were 'Japanese', the Chinese partner also became 'Japanese' upon being entered into the relevant Taiwanese koseki register. This was in accordance with the Citizenship Law principle of shared citizenship among family members.

The third group were those who illegally acquired a Taiwanese passport. Only Taiwanese people held Taiwanese passports, which were issued according to the 'Foreign Travel Passport Management Regulations' (*Gaikoku-yuki ryoken torishimari kisoku*) (1897, Governor-General Directive No. 2) brought into effect in 1897 by the Office of the Governor-General of Taiwan.[92] Some Chinese people, however, were able to purchase a passport from Taiwanese, have one transferred or create counterfeit passport documents as a means of acquiring Taiwanese koseki registration. Those who illegally acquired the status of being 'Japanese' in this way were referred to as 'falsely registered people' (*kabō seki min* – the characters for '*kabō*' mean 'deceit' or 'misrepresentation'). According to a 14 September 1907 report prepared by the Amoy Consul, Segawa Asanoshin, for the Ministry of Foreign Affairs, 1,300 people with Taiwanese registration resided in Amoy at the end of June 1907. Segawa concluded that 'although Japanese in name', given that the majority had no family or property in Taiwan, 'these people were not substantively Japanese'.[93] He went on to denounce those among them who, holding Taiwanese passports that had been either purchased or acquired by fraudulent means, then registered at the consul's office. To Segawa, 'those people who falsely represent themselves as having Japanese citizenship are no better than felons'.[94]

The desire for Japanese citizenship by these Chinese people registered in Taiwan arose from the fact that the 1896 'Sino-Japanese Commerce and Navigation Treaty' (*Nisshin tsūshō kōkai jōyaku*) gave Japan extraterritorial rights in China. This in turn gave Japanese people entitlements such as tax exemption and access to consular courts. Thus, if in Amoy and Fuzhou, where Japanese concessions had been established in 1898 and 1899 respectively, Chinese people with Taiwanese registration were found to be engaging in illegal business or tax evasion, they could flee to the jurisdiction of the Court of the Japanese Consul. The system of extraterritorial rights operated under the personal principle (*zokujin shugi*) and was therefore invoked even if a person was 'Japanese' in name only. Furthermore, those people who registered as Taiwanese were, in actual fact, holders of dual citizenship. That is, although they were able to draw on their status as 'Japanese' when necessary, they retained their Chinese citizenship and lived generally as 'Chinese'. This was often a cause of conflict in terms of jurisdictional rights between Japanese authorities and Chinese officialdom.

In East Asia where the Great Powers of Europe such as England, France and Holland clamoured and vied with each other over colonies, leased territories, concessions and open ports, self-interest was evident at every turn. Chinese people, too, sought to grab hold of the privileges that came with being a 'foreigner' in territories in which the legal powers of foreign nations applied. Because Japanese koseki registration gave them 'foreigner' status, overseas Chinese people who lived in the colonies or Chinese who moved in and out of the concessions and open ports of China had access to privileges that were denied to local residents of those sites. The Great Powers also made policy plans to further entrench their entitlements by opening, for example, consulate offices where they registered overseas Chinese and, in the interests of expanding the sphere of their 'own citizens', protected these Chinese in the same way in which they protected citizens of their own countries.

Even in the colonies of the Great Powers of Europe, Chinese people with Taiwanese registration profited greatly from their privileged position as 'Japanese'. With the opening in April 1908 of a Japanese consul office in the Dutch controlled East Indies (present-day Indonesia), Japan received 'most favoured nation' treatment. Regarding this as grossly unfair, overseas Chinese in the region strengthened their demands that the Qing authorities also establish a consul office in the Dutch East Indies.[95] In 1910, Takekoshi Yosaburō (1865–1950) published 'A Record of Southern Countries' (*Nangoku ki*), which recounted the author's observations throughout East Asia and the Pacific. Here, Takekoshi observed that overseas Chinese were concerned by the fact that in the Dutch East Indies, Chinese people with Taiwanese registration were given preferential treatment as Japanese over other overseas Chinese like themselves. Takekoshi noted that these people, too, hoped to become naturalised subjects of Japan.[96] In Siam (present-day Thailand), the Japanese legation registered Chinese people who self-identified as being born in Taiwan and granted them the status of being 'Japanese' as a means of entrenching Japan's strength in that location.[97] These people comprised but one of the various categories of Chinese people with Taiwanese registration.

Creating 'people registered as Taiwanese' via koseki registration

In Europe from the second half of the nineteenth century, citizenship law was enacted with the intention of unifying the 'nation-state'. With the successive inroads made into its authority by the Great Powers of the West, even the Qing authorities eventually awoke to the need to draft citizenship legislation as a means of self-reformation as a modern sovereign state. The direct motive for the Qing authorities to implement their own citizenship law was to deter the moves referred to above by the Western states to implement Western citizenship law in the colonies that they controlled, and thereby grant overseas Chinese citizenship of their own country. Against this, the Qing sought to establish legal boundaries around the entity of Chinese 'citizen' and thus regulate and control internal cases of 'falsely registered people' (*kabō sekimin*). In March 1909 the 'Regulations for Citizenship of the Qing Nation' (*Daishin kokuseki jōrei*) and 'Bylaws for the Implementation of the Regulations for Citizenship of the Qing Nation' (*Daishin kokuseki jōrei no shikō saisoku*) were both proclaimed as the first modern citizenship legislation in China. As in Japan, those regulations drew on concepts of patrilineal bloodline. However, the Qing strictly regulated those who wished to renounce their Chinese citizenship. In the case of fraud when either taking out foreign citizenship or losing Qing citizenship, the authorities stipulated sanctions of imprisonment for no less than six months and no more than one year.[98] This policy ensured that Japanese citizenship unlawfully acquired by some people registered as Taiwanese would be rendered invalid.

With this Qing citizenship legislation in mind, the Special Envoy to the Qing, Ijūin Hikokichi (1864–1924), reported as follows in a telegraph to the Minister of Foreign Affairs, Komura Jutarō (1855–1911), concerning the policy treatment of the legal position of Chinese people registered as Taiwanese. According to Ijūin, the desire for dual citizenship among this group could be understood as 'human nature that alternately asserts one of the two citizenships, as needed, depending on natural self-interest'. Seeking to avoid conflict with the Qing authorities, Ijūin went on to conclude that it would be very much in the interests of Japan to '*maintain the current ambivalent situation and treat those involved as naturalised Taiwanese guaranteeing their ownership and residential rights*' (emphasis added).[99] Accordingly, the position of people registered as Taiwanese remained undefined, although the Japanese authorities largely followed Ijūin's realistic policy suggestion of guaranteeing rights as Japanese citizens to those concerned.

The various consul offices understood that the 'Japanese citizenship' of Chinese people registered as Taiwanese arose from a sense of acute self-interest rather than patriotic feelings towards Japan. In a 14 March 1910 report to the Ministry, Amoy Consul representative Mori Yasusaburō (1880–1952) noted, '*Since these people were inextricably tied to the Qing nation*, taking citizenship with the Japanese empire was largely a form of expedience. There was, in fact, absolutely no likelihood of their ever turning their back on their own country to sacrifice themselves for Japan' (emphasis added). In other words, Mori expressed the clear opinion that the 'Japanese citizenship' of the Chinese people registered as Taiwanese was, after all, nothing more than personal convenience, and that any love of country felt by these people was directed entirely towards the Qing nation. Nevertheless, Mori realised the benefit of taking the long-term view by concluding, 'It is almost certain that the time will come when Japan will need as many people as possible whom we can use for our own ends residing in those regions'. In terms of policies for the 'opposite shores' (that is, the south coast of China directly opposite the west coast of Taiwan), he judged, 'those Chinese registered as Taiwanese are positioned in a way that will be most convenient in the future'. Given that they were Han Chinese, these people had built up a strong foundation in their home-base on the continent, something that would eventually be favourable to Japan. In February 1908, furthermore, the so-called 'Tatsumaru Incident' (*Tatsumaru jiken*) saw a Qing naval vessel seize the Japanese merchant ship *Tatsumaru II.* When Japan demanded an apology and reparation from Qing authorities, Japanese freight in Guangdong (Canton) was boycotted in retaliation in March of the same year. This action extended to South China, Hong Kong and the South Pacific. While engaging in backroom negotiations in an attempt to quell the outbreaks of anti-Japanese nationalism generated by this series of events, the Japanese authorities also expected Chinese people registered as Taiwanese to become 'agents of mitigation who would help to defuse anti-Japanese campaigns'.[100]

Chinese people registered as Taiwanese were clearly seen to have use-value as human resources in the context of Japan's advance into the continent. The Japanese authorities were therefore reluctant to thoroughly manage or regulate this group. That is to say, even though Japan was aware that Chinese who registered as Taiwanese were freeloaders who acquired Japanese citizenship without any sense of patriotism, the authorities permitted this group to hold dual citizenship. It is worth stating here that Japanese officialdom at all levels – from Ministry of Foreign Affairs bureaucrats down to lower order functionaries – was permeated with a realistic awareness of the need for this sort of citizenship acquisition as a formalistic and technical concept.[101]

With the objective of broadening the strength of the Japanese presence in the region, the Japanese authorities devised various policies that encouraged entry into the Taiwanese koseki registration system by Chinese located in South China. In March 1917, Gotō Shinpei (1857–1929), the then Minister of Home Affairs, issued a directive to the Office of the Governor-General of Taiwan entitled 'Issues Related to Giving Japanese Citizenship to Chinese People' (*Shinajin ni Nihon kokuseki wo shutoku seshimuru no ken*). Here, Gotō noted the existence of Chinese people who supported Japan by providing monetary donations or capital support to enterprises operated by Japanese in places such as Amoy, Fuzhou, Shantou and Guangzhou. These places would be future footholds in the Japanese advance to the south. He therefore encouraged the Japanese authorities in Taiwan to take measures to acknowledge and naturalise these people as Japanese by entering them into the Taiwanese koseki registration system.[102] At the discretion of the authorities, Taiwanese koseki registration could be granted through a Japanese consul office outside Taiwan. As demonstrated in Table 4.4, by 1922 in excess of 5,000 people had been granted Taiwanese registration in Amoy, with this number reaching 10,000 by the second half of 1930. The difference in numbers between people in this category and residents from mainland Japan in Amoy is evident.

Furthermore, the 11 August 1936 'Standards of National Policy' (*Kokusaku no kijun*) document, endorsed by the Cabinet of Hirota Kōki (1878–1948), referred to 'progressing the advance to the Southern Ocean' (*nanpō kaiyō ni shinshutsu hatten suru*).[103] In

Table 4.4: Shift in numbers of mainland Japanese and Chinese people registered as Taiwanese in Amoy (1916–1936)

	Mainland Japanese[a]	**Chinese people registered as Taiwanese**
1916	–	2,654
1917	–	2,883
1918	–	3,374
1919	–	3,516
1920	–	3,765
1921	281	4,423
1922	310	5,226
1923	297	5,816
1924	285	6,168
1925	281	6,539
1926	260	6,832
1927	271	6,660
1928	314	6,721
1929	347	7,058
1930	349	7,195
1931	–	7,352
1932	–	8,326
1933	–	9,496
1934	–	10,625
1935	–	10,326
1936	–	10,317

Note: [a] Numbers of mainland Japanese as at October each year.
Source: *Gaimushō keisatsu shi: Shina no bu: Amoi ryōjikan* (The History of Ministry of Foreign Affairs Police: China Section, Amoy Consulate), Tokyo: Gaimushō Gaikō Shiryōkan Shozō, SP–205–6.

other words, the empire's southern advance was established as national policy. Chinese people with Taiwanese koseki registration were expected to be the vanguard of this advance. In fact, members of this group were seen as crucial to breaking the strength and power of those resident overseas Chinese communities that had traditionally held sway in the societies of South East Asia. Following the outbreak of the second Sino-Japanese War, overseas Chinese in the Southern Ocean had organised under the leadership of the Chinese Nationalist Party into anti-Japan nationalist movements. Between 1938 and 1939 particularly, Japan sustained a heavy blow through boycotts of Japanese goods destined for export to South East Asia. These boycotts were mainly carried out by overseas Chinese in the Philippines, French Indo-China and the British Empire Straits Settlements.[104]

Given the need to remove any impediment to the progress of the southern advance, the matter of overseas Chinese in the Southern Ocean became a pressing policy issue. An information communiqué formulated in August 1938 and forwarded on 28 November by the Foreign Affairs Section of the Office of the Governor-General of Taiwan to the Ministry of the Army Secretariat, stated, 'Especially given the fact that their language and customs closely resemble those of the homeland of the overseas Chinese located in the Southern Ocean, we must from this point forward carefully consider the possibility of advance activities by the island people of Taiwan'.[105] In other words, there were strategic plans to train the Chinese people registered as Taiwanese as a rival force to pit against overseas Chinese in the Southern Ocean. Furthermore, the second Konoe Fumimaro (1891–1945) Cabinet ordered the occupation of the northern region of French Indo-China to commence in September 1940, in order to block the so-called 'Chiang Kai-shek Support Route' used by the Allies to provide supplies and other support for the Chinese Nationalists. This was to guarantee South East Asia's provision of resources such as coal required by wartime Japan. Given the urgency of southern advance policies, the Office of the Governor-General of Taiwan was charged with organising and despatching to the Southern Ocean Chinese people registered as Taiwanese. Just prior to the outbreak of the Pacific War in December 1941, more than 3,000 of these people were positioned in South East Asia, mainly in Dutch controlled Indonesia. Many, however, had no desire to bear the brunt of wartime anti-Japanese campaigns and activities, and therefore hid the fact that they were 'Japanese'.[106] As the war between Japan and China intensified, however, there was an expectation that Chinese people registered as Taiwanese would sacrifice themselves as 'subjects of the Emperor'. This was, however, only ever a faint, if not completely unrealistic, hope on the part of the Japanese authorities.

Regardless of their degree of commitment to Japan, as noted above, the numbers of Chinese people registered as Taiwanese expanded in Taiwan, China and South East Asia. Furthermore, overseas Chinese who were given an entry in the Taiwanese koseki registration system through the administrative procedures associated with marriage or acknowledgement of paternity also acquired 'Japanese citizenship'. In these ways, the numbers of people who were 'Japanese' in name only continued to expand and multiply. The nature of koseki registration for Chinese people who sought registration as Taiwanese was referred to in an information communiqué sent to the Ministry of Foreign Affairs on 5 December 1930 by the Amoy Consul, Terajima Hirobumi. Here, Terajima expressed the view that 'there was a tendency for [registration of this nature] to be used rather more frequently compared to the policies of the past'.[107] Nevertheless, there is little doubt that through this policy of nominally registering Chinese people as 'Japanese', imperial authorities successfully exploited colonial koseki registration practices as a means of expanding the numbers of 'Japanese' and entrenching the empire's presence in key locations overseas.

In the space of East Asia where legal rights around the 'citizen' intersected, Japan rode the wave of imperialism that promoted the outward expansion of the modern sovereign state in order to successfully capitalise on citizenship policies designed to bring national benefit to Japan. As a result, Chinese registered as Taiwanese were granted the privilege of being 'Japanese'. A special characteristic of the koseki registration system of imperial Japan was that by acquiring 'ethnic membership' of any of the sites throughout the empire one could easily acquire the status of being 'Japanese'. Thus, those Chinese people who registered in Taiwan were, temporarily at least, able to present themselves as Japanese. Here, we see how the koseki mechanism, disguised as the 'legal' selection of citizens, became a tool in a sovereign state's arrant exercise of power against a background in which any operation of individual free will had all but withered away.

'Korean' people without proof of identity: Unregistered Koreans

The problems of minority ethnicities, refugees and stateless people, which erupted throughout the world following the end of the First World War, destabilised notions of 'fixed abode' and 'equality among citizens' that, until that time, had been the self-evident principles of the modern nation-state. In fact, what Hannah Arendt (1906–1975) referred to as the 'end of the nation-state'[108] became a point of contention in international politics.

One of the factors at play was the unrestricted activity of people moving between various territories and citizenships, and thereby evading the koseki registration net. While the modern nation exerted its jurisdictional sovereignty over territory and citizens, the labour of individuals with the freedom to move for work was a necessary condition for the development of capitalism. From this perspective it is clear that the koseki registration system, which was administered by means of the principle of immobility inherent in the fixed *honseki* address, failed to respond to the dynamism of modern society.

The unregistered Korean person was an entity that embodied the contradictions involved in the collapse of the nation-state and the liberalisation of political society on the one hand, and the perverse state surveillance of the koseki registration system on the other. We have already noted how, through Japanese government policies that determined that citizenship legislation did not apply in Korea, Korean people continued to be nonetheless strictly constrained by Japanese citizenship. Koseki registration thus became the means of keeping Korean people who moved outside Japanese territory under surveillance. Without koseki registration, not only did these people effectively become 'stateless', there was no proof that they were, in fact, Japanese citizens. The Japanese state therefore lost any power to control, search for or pursue unregistered people from Korea.

In particular, regions of Manchuria became home to many unregistered Koreans. One reason for this was the fact that, as noted above, large numbers of Koreans had relocated to China's northeast even prior to the implementation of the 1909 People's Registration Law (*minseki-hō*) in Korea. Many then continued to live in that region rather than return to their homeland.[109] Based on the criteria of koseki registration as proof of 'conversion to the Emperor' (*ōka*), these unregistered Koreans were by all accounts 'people from benighted lands beyond the sphere of imperial rule' (*kegai no tami*). That is, they were outside the reach of imperial administrative structures. As a presence that completely compromised the concept of 'empire' (*kōkoku*), this group presented a challenge that the authorities were unable to ignore. Accordingly, the legal process of '*shūseki*', which enabled an unregistered person to establish a new koseki register record, assumed particular importance as a means of incorporating this group into the Korean koseki registration system. The authorities accordingly did their best to encourage unregistered Koreans to participate in this process.

The Governor-General of Korea had noted the failure of attempts to have unregistered Koreans resident in China's northeast create new koseki records prior to the Manchurian Incident of 18 September 1931. According to that office, this was because of 'issues arising in the territories of foreign powers opposed to Japan', with an accompanying 'instability of the social order'. Furthermore, 'the level of civic consciousness of Korean people resident in China's northeast is particularly low and they lack the knowledge necessary to initiate koseki registration'.[110] Following the rise of the May 4 Movement, anti-Japanese nationalist activities flourished during the 1920s in China, while in areas of China's northeast, now Manchuria, Communist activity became more prevalent. In May 1930, an armed uprising largely involving Korean Communists broke out in Jiandao. International tensions had also heightened in China's northeast, and the concentration there of unregistered Koreans who had not been subjugated by the civil protocol of koseki registration led the Japanese authorities to fear that these people were connected to both the anti-Japanese and Communist movements.[111] Unregistered Koreans who had slipped through the net of imperial governance and were wandering unchecked around a foreign territory were regarded as a dangerous presence in terms of social order and national defence. In this sense, the Japanese political powers were keenly aware that these Koreans had successfully disrupted the social order of koseki registration that was proof of being 'a subject of the empire'.

Following the Manchurian Incident of September 1931, citizenship issues regarding Korean residents in China's northeast quickly came to the attention of the international community and developed into a diplomatic dispute. These tensions came to a head in October 1932, following the release by the Lytton Commission of Inquiry of the *Report of the Commission of Inquiry into the Sino-Japanese Dispute*, the so-called 'Lytton Report', which was adopted by the General Assembly of the League of Nations in February 1933. Section 5 of Chapter 3 of that report, entitled 'Manchurian Issues Between China and Japan (Before September 18, 1931)', began with a section headed 'The Korean Problem in Manchuria'. Here it was argued that prior to the Manchurian Incident the problem of the citizenship of Korean residents in China's northeast had been one cause of conflict between Japan and China. Section 5 of the Lytton Report stated, 'The problem of dual nationality of the Koreans influenced the National Government of China and the provincial authorities of Manchuria generally to look with disfavour upon indiscriminate naturalisation of Koreans, fearing that they might, by temporarily acquiring Chinese citizenship, become potential instruments of a Japanese policy of acquiring agricultural land'. In other words, the issue of dual citizenship among Koreans resident in Manchuria was seen by the commission as a factor that had contributed to worsening Sino-Japanese relations.

These pre-Manchurian Incident tensions between China and Japan were at least partly due to the fact that citizenship legislation enacted by the Republic of China government in February 1929 permitted foreigners to apply for naturalisation without renouncing their original citizenship. The purpose of this legislation was effectively to increase the numbers of 'Chinese' people. In other words, it was now acceptable for a person who became a naturalised Chinese to hold dual citizenship. Accordingly, Koreans were able to acquire Chinese citizenship while also retaining their Japanese citizenship. It is furthermore reasonable to assume that, if the person was a Korean without koseki registration, then, as a 'stateless person or person without citizenship', it would be even easier for them to naturalise. It should be noted, however, that the Lytton Report left no doubt that the principle cause of conflict around the dual Japanese/Chinese citizenship of Koreans who were resident in China's northeast was the Japanese policy of incursion into that territory.[112]

How many unregistered Koreans, then, were in Manchoukuo? We have previously noted that the vast majority of Korean people who had departed Korea relocated to China's northeast. Even following the 1931 Manchurian Incident, there was no change in the direction of this flow. Table 4.5 gives a breakdown, based on surveys conducted by the Ministry of Foreign Affairs, of the location of Koreans resident outside Korea.

Since many people did not hold formal registration confirming them as Korean, it is difficult to say that these figures are totally accurate. Nevertheless, the table indicates that ninety percent of the 900,000 Koreans who had departed their homeland re-settled in China's northeast, Manchoukuo. Originally, it was understandably not possible to give accurate figures for unregistered Koreans. However, as shown in Table 4.6, the results of a survey conducted by the Consul of Japan in Manchoukuo between November 1933 and March 1934 confirm the presence of a little over 430,000 Koreans without registration. Based on these figures, we can

Table 4.5: Numbers of Korean people resident in regions outside Korea (excluding mainland Japan) (1935–1936 Ministry of Foreign Affairs survey)

	Manchoukuo	Kwantung Leased Territory	Nationalist China	United States	Soviet Union	Cuba	Others	Total
Men	460,046	1,988	6,377	4,691	847	218	218	480,395
Women	406,135	1,738	4,976	2,195	475	152	43	415,625
Total	866,181	3,726	11,353	6,796	1,322	370	261	896,020

Note: Figures for Manchoukuo, Kwantung Leased Territory and Nationalist China as at end of June 1936; other figures as at end of September 1935.
Source: Chōsen sōtoku-fu (The Office of the Governor-General of Korea), *Shisei sanjunen shi* (Thirty Years of Administrative History), Seoul: Chōsen sōtoku-fu,

assume that approximately half of all Koreans living outside their homeland had no koseki registration.

Strategies for dealing with unregistered Koreans in Manchoukuo

As will be explained in detail in the following chapter, in citizenship terms, Korean people in Manchoukuo were treated as 'Japanese subjects'. Based on the 1915 'Treaty Concerning Southern Manchuria and Eastern Inner Mongolia', 'Japanese subjects' in Manchoukuo were recognised as having extraterritorial rights which gave them access to consular courts and exempted them from taxation. Repealing the rights of 'Japanese subjects' as a means of demonstrating the new nation's 'independence' to the international community was an issue from the beginning of the Manchoukuo 'nation building campaign'. Closely related to this was the matter of whether or not to acknowledge the 'privilege' of the right to hold land that had been extended to Korean people in terms of the Jiandao Agreement (Gando Convention) (refer to the first section of this chapter).

On 29 September 1934, a four-way meeting was held between the Japanese Embassy and the Manchoukuo departments of foreign affairs, public welfare and justice. This meeting agreed to recognise the vested right of Korean people resident in areas of cleared land in Jiandao to hold or own land. However, a survey conducted by the office of the Japanese Consul revealed, as shown in Table 4.6, that there were up to 300,000 unregistered Korean people living in Jiandao.

Table 4.6: Consul of Japan survey results of numbers of unregistered Koreans in Manchoukuo (between November 1933 and March 1934)

Data collection date	Official with responsibility for survey	No. of households	No. of people
20 Nov. 1933	Mukden Consul, Hachiya Teruo	13,700	74,000
25 Jan. 1934	Jiandao Consul General, Nagai Katsuzō	60,000	300,000
31 Jan. 1934	Jilin Consul General, Morioka	901	10,771
1 Feb. 1934	Qiqihar Consul, Uchida	–	–
3 Feb. 1934	Andong Consul, Okamoto	7,000	36,000
5 Feb. 1934	Jinzhou Acting Consul, Gotō	–	–
8 Feb. 1934	Manzhouri Acting Consul, Izumi	18	33
8 Feb. 1934	Chifeng Consul, Kiyono	–	–
15 Feb. 1934	Harbin Acting Consul, Morishima	4,000	14,000
9 Mar. 1934	Dunhua Vice-Consul, Kusano	333	1,853
14 Mar. 1934	Chengde Vice-Consul, Nakane	–	–
Total[a]		89,952	436,657

Note: [a] The total excludes numbers that are unknown.
Source: 'The Korean situation' (*Ōno Rokuichirō Documents*: R-133), p. 139.

This figure represented more than sixty percent of the 450,000 Korean people residing in this area. Thus, it appeared that among the Korean people of Jiandao there were many who owned land and conducted business in spite of the fact that they were unregistered. However, various administrative matters related to land or business transactions could not be processed without the parties involved having koseki registration. Seeking to assist those who were unregistered to continue conducting business activities, the Ministry of Foreign Affairs, the entity responsible for ensuring legal compliance and social order, realised the necessity of 'urging a policy of creating new koseki records' for unregistered Koreans. In 1939, the Ministry entered into negotiations with the Office of the Governor-General of Korea in order to have these new registers created.[113]

To assist in this process, the Governor-General of Korea approved the simplification of procedures for unregistered Koreans who were resident in Manchoukuo to create new koseki records. A request for lectures on koseki registration administration, intended to facilitate the creation of new koseki records by Korean people, came from the Federation of Korean People Resident in Manchoukuo (*Zaiman Chōsen jinmin rengōkai*), which was the central committee of the Korean People Resident in Manchoukuo Protection Society (*Zaiman Chōsenjin hogo dantai*), officially recognised by the Japanese government as the representative body of Korean people in each area of Manchoukuo. Accordingly, these lectures were collaboratively organised by the Office of the Governor-General of Korea, the Ministry of Foreign Affairs and the Manchoukuo government and delivered in October 1935 in Mukden, Changchun and Harbin. Furthermore, the Federation of Korean People Resident in Manchoukuo initiated the 'Campaign for Enlightenment of Koseki Registration' (*Koseki keimō undo*), which undertook tasks such as the publication of explanatory information related to new koseki registration processes and the distribution of pamphlets explaining the political significance of koseki registration. Key in this respect was the distribution of an advertising brochure, 30,000 of which were printed in Hangul, entitled 'Announcement to Our Fellow Unregistered Korean People Resident in Manchoukuo' (*Zaiman museki Chōsenjin dōhō ni tsugeru*). This brochure urged Korean people to remember that 'failing to address one's status as an unregistered imperial subject who is resident in Manchoukuo is the most powerful shame of the people of Korea, a shame that also defames the honour of *the citizens of a leading power*' (emphasis added). In other words, Korean people were urged to create a new koseki register record as their duty as 'Japanese' who were 'citizens of a leading power'. The brochure also emphasised that the creation of new koseki register records by unregistered Koreans was crucial for the actualisation of 'the unity of Japan and Korea' (*naisen ittai*).[114]

In Jiandao, however, where there were the largest numbers of unregistered Koreans, the project of creating new koseki register records soon faltered. There were approximately 2,500 authorisations for new records given there in 1934. Of the 5,000 applications made in 1935, 3,000 were approved. This left over 400,000 unregistered Koreans in Manchoukuo, who remained not authorised as 'Japanese citizens'.[115]

In June 1937, with the numbers of unregistered Korean people resident in Manchoukuo continuing to rise, the Department of Justice of the Office of the Governor-General of Korea urged the mainland authorities to encourage the Manchoukuo authorities to conduct some sort of comprehensive population survey. Among the points of concern raised was the fact that 'It wasn't just a matter of *those who were Korean* formally creating a new koseki record; there was also a need to negotiate with the Manchoukuo authorities to have Manchoukuo adopt a policy to accurately survey the actual situation [of Koreans in that site]' (emphasis added).[116] Here, koseki registration had already degenerated into a type of 'formalism', with even the Office of the Governor-General of Korea acknowledging that it was not useful in ascertaining the status of itinerant Koreans.

It was noted above that in May 1942 the Japanese Cabinet took a decision to introduce a conscription system for Koreans from 1944. At a 28 September 1942 government Vice-Ministerial meeting, the Vice-Minister of the Army submitted information on preparations underway for the implementation of this system. This submission observed that 'the most difficult problem is ascertaining the situation regarding *those Koreans who are resident outside Korea*' (emphasis added). The submission went on to urge the necessity of conducting annual surveys of this situation. However, there were clearly difficulties involved in the administration of an annual survey. It was suggested, moreover, that 'ultimately, this problem will best be solved by maintaining the koseki registration system (that is, creating new koseki records for unregistered Koreans) and the thorough [implementation] of the Temporary Residence Law' (*Kiryū-hō*).[117]

The Temporary Residence Law had been enacted in 1914 on mainland Japan in order to record the names of those who resided at a place other than the *honseki* address. This law, however, did not apply in Korea. On 26 September 1942, therefore, the Office of the Governor-General of Korea promulgated the 'Korean Temporary Residence Law' (*Chōsen kiryū rei*, 1942, Regulation No. 32) and the 'Regulations for Administering Korean Temporary Residence' (*Chōsen kiryū tetsuduki kisoku*, 1942 Directive of the Office of the Governor-General of Korea No. 235), to be introduced from 15 October in the same year. This legislation stipulated that, in the event of having a fixed address for more than ninety days, those Koreans who lived at an address other than their *honseki* address, including people who were unregistered or whose *honseki* was unclear, were required to register on a roll for 'temporary residents' (*kiryū-sha*).

In December 1942, the Office of the Governor-General of Korea directed the respective heads of each local court and the judiciary of each court branch office to have Korean people resident in Manchoukuo use the temporary residence register forms, drawn up according to the Korean Temporary Residence Law, to record their *honseki* address as it appeared on the people's register (*minseki*) of Manchoukuo. It was pointed out that 'even if they are entered into the people's register of Manchoukuo, these people of course have a duty not to rescind their Korean koseki registration'.[118] As explained in the following section, the people's registration system (*minseki seido*) that operated as a status registration system in Manchoukuo was actually a mechanism that registered the place of residence as the *honseki* address. By ensuring that the Manchoukuo people's register connected and integrated with the Korean temporary residents register, the authorities were able to gain an accurate picture of both the status relationships of Korean people resident in Manchoukuo and their current residence. In this way, the Office of the Governor-General of Korea worked in tandem with the military to achieve wartime mobilisation.

In spite of the various strategies undertaken by the Japanese authorities to pursue and then eradicate unregistered Koreans in Manchoukuo, the desired outcome was never achieved. Immigrant Koreans in Manchoukuo had largely managed to throw off the yoke of colonial control. Official attempts to raise the consciousness of these people as 'imperial subjects' (*kōmin*) by lauding the power of Japan with slogans exhorting the moral worth of holding koseki registration as proof of being 'Japanese' were nothing but empty rhetoric.

Citizenship and koseki registration in Manchoukuo

Was there such a thing as a 'citizen of Manchoukuo'?

In this section we will examine the problem of koseki registration and citizenship relating to those 'Japanese' who were residents of former Manchoukuo.

On 1 March 1932, the 'Proclamation of the Formation of Manchoukuo' (*Manshū-koku kenoku sengen*) was promulgated by the so-called government of Manchoukuo. With the conclusion on 15 September of that year of the 'Japan-Manchoukuo Protocol' (*Nichiman gitei sho*), the Japanese government recognised Manchoukuo as an 'independent state'. The 'Outline Dealing with

External Relations Following the Establishment of the New State of Manchoukuo/Mongolia' (*Manmō shinkokka seiritsu ni tomonau taigai kankei shori yōkō*) gave the main challenges facing this new nation as, 'striving to accelerate the chance of future international recognition, while gradually preparing to create the actual conditions of an independent state'.[119] Accordingly, as a substantive condition of an independent state, it became necessary to establish citizenship legislation in order to determine the qualifications needed to be classified as a Manchoukuo 'citizen'.

In Manchoukuo legal documentation, the expression 'the people' (*jinmin*) was generally used when referring to citizens of the new state. For example, Article 1 of the 'Human Rights Guarantee Law' (*Jinken hoshō-hō*; Daidō Year 1, Provision (*kyōrei*) No. 2), stipulated that 'The people (*jinmin*) of the Manchoukuo state shall have no violation of personal freedom'. What exactly was the definition of this expression 'people of the Manchoukuo state'? There was no particular ordinance that formally stipulated who was or was not included in this group. Nevertheless, Paragraph 5 of the 'Declaration of the Founding of the [Manchoukuo] Nation' (*Kenkoku sengen*) lauded the fact that, 'in addition to *the original* ethnic groups of *Han Chinese, Manchus, Mongolians, Japanese and Koreans*, we give equal treatment to *those too from other places who wish to live [in Manchoukuo] for a long period of time*' (emphasis added). This theory of founding the nation on 'the harmony of the five ethnicities' (*gozoku kyōwa*) was often offered in the place of formal citizenship legislation as the logic that defined 'the people of Manchoukuo' (*Manshūkoku jinmin*). Takahashi Teizō (1898–1972), a professor at Hosei University in Xinjing (Shinkyō), theorised that if a person was either one of 'the Han Chinese, the Manchus or the Mongolians who had been the original inhabitants of the territory, or either Japanese or Korean', then that person satisfied the criterion necessary to acquire Manchoukuo citizenship. So, too, did 'people of other nations who desired to live in the territory on a permanent basis'.[120] Statements such as those by Takahashi rationalised the practice of making reference to the Declaration of the Founding of the Nation as a source of 'customary law' (*kanshū-hō*) in matters pertaining to 'Manchoukuo citizenship'.

However, in the words of South Manchurian Railway Research Economic Survey Committee member Hirai Shōichi, while

Manchoukuo proclaimed itself as an independent nation in both international and domestic circles, for some considerable time the new state was in 'the highly undesirable situation of having to deal with a nation-state format in which citizenship law, required as a constitutional element of a nation, operated on an unwritten basis'.[121] The process of confirming precisely the constitutional elements that defined its own citizens thus became a matter of great urgency for the Manchoukuo authorities. Accordingly, between 1932 and 1936 various drafts of Manchoukuo citizenship law were compiled by bodies such as the Kwantung Army Special Administration Office, the Manchoukuo government and the Economic Survey Committee of the South Manchurian Railway (*Mantetsu*).

One element that drew special attention was whether or not Japanese people who were resident in Manchoukuo should or should not be made to naturalise as citizens of the new state. Given that, according to the Japanese Citizenship Law, being naturalised elsewhere led to a loss of Japanese citizenship, becoming a citizen of Manchoukuo involved a huge risk for Japanese. Building the new nation created a widespread need for human resources in the form of bureaucrats from Japan, with most draft citizenship legislation drawn up at the time providing for Japanese nationals to take citizenship with Manchoukuo while retaining their Japanese citizenship. In other words, the drafts permitted dual citizenship. However, this position was not without problems. Based on the 1915 'Treaty Respecting South Manchuria and Eastern Inner Mongolia', Japanese people had extraterritorial rights that provided access to consular courts and exemption from taxation. There was concern that the capacity of Japanese in Manchoukuo to access these rights would damage the external (international) image of the country as an independent state.[122] As long as Japanese people resident in Manchoukuo enjoyed extraterritorial rights and the right to hold dual citizenship, the spotlight would fall on the fact that 'Japanese subjects' had special status among the 'five ethnicities' that comprised the new nation. This would effectively obstruct any shared national consciousness among these five ethnicities that might unite residents as the 'people of Manchoukuo' (*Manshūkoku jinmin*). In fact, it would expose the fact that the notion of the 'harmony of the five ethnicities' – a founding principle of the new state extolling the equal treatment of each ethnicity – was nothing more than a meaningless catchphrase.

Attitudes towards the privileged status of Japanese residents in Manchoukuo also influenced preference for one of the two key citizenship principles – *jus soli* or *jus sanguinis* – that are central to all citizenship law. For example, the draft citizenship law of the Manchoukuo government took the long-term view of administering Manchoukuo as a pluralist state comprised of migrant subjects. This draft therefore adopted the principle of *jus soli*, citizenship according to place of birth. Drafts drawn up by the Kwantung Army and *Mantetsu*, on the other hand, prioritised the relationship with the homeland of the Japanese immigrant. According to this thinking, adopting *jus sanguinis*, citizenship by bloodline, would make it possible even for descendants of Japanese people resident in Manchoukuo to have 'Manchoukuo citizenship'. No agreement was reached on which of the two should be adopted.

Other matters related to people of non-Japanese background also presented challenges. In the case of a Korean person who was a Japanese citizen naturalising in Manchoukuo, there was the problem – related to Japan's annexation of Korea – of whether or not to permit that person to hold dual citizenship in a manner similar to that being considered for Japanese people. There were also fears of worsening relations with the Soviet Union if deeply anti-Soviet White Russians were to be granted 'citizenship of Manchoukuo'. There was further the matter of whether or not 'Coolie labourers' (*kuurii*) should be treated as foreigners. Each issue hindered the development of coherent citizenship law and resulted in the various drafts ultimately falling through.[123]

While citizenship legislation was never enacted, the expression 'Manchoukuo citizenship' appeared here and there throughout documentation prepared by both Japanese and Manchoukuo authorities. For example, holding or not holding citizenship was important in terms of the governance procedures related to entering or departing the country. If a person entering or disembarking on the Japanese mainland held a *honseki* address in Manchoukuo, she or he was regarded as a 'Manchoukuo citizen'. Precedent established in Manchoukuo also gave eligibility for classification as a 'citizen of Manchoukuo' to those who were resident for a fixed length of time in that site. A 'foreigner' entering Manchoukuo needed to be issued with 'proof of entry', while, in compliance with the 'Foreign Passport Regulations' (*Gaikoku ryoken kisoku*; Kotoku Year 4, Concil Ordinance No. 31) promulgated on 22

December 1937, those who intended to travel overseas needed a passport issued by the Manchoukuo authorities. In this way, measures and terminology that camouflaged the lack of criteria defining 'Manchoukuo citizenship' featured regularly in official ordinances and notifications.[124]

Fundamentally, however, in the absence of Manchoukuo citizenship law, neither the category of 'Manchoukuo citizen' nor 'foreigner' had any clear legal foundation. Administrative bureaucrats were therefore forced to work within the parameters of a 'case-by-case basis' approach that drew on 'custom or precedence'. Legal scholars who wanted to ensure the orthodoxy of the founding of the state of Manchoukuo in terms of international law therefore highlighted the customary law related to 'Manchoukuo citizenship' in the wording of the Declaration of the Founding of the Nation referred to above. In this way, they constructed at least the impression of a 'sovereign state'. Ultimately, the motive that drove the political authorities of Japan and Manchoukuo to attempt to establish 'Manchoukuo citizenship' was a desire to avoid the condemnation of the new state by the international community as a tributary state of Japan. Yet, while creating the impression of independence, it was necessary to retain a means by which the power and privilege of Japanese people resident in Manchoukuo could be effectively stage-managed and maintained under the pretext of their equality with those from other ethnic groups.

The koseki registration of 'Japanese subjects' in Manchoukuo

From the outset, there was a need to enact laws relating to koseki registration in Manchoukuo. This was primarily related to law and order policing and the search for the 'bandits' (*hizoku*) who obstructed the governance of Manchoukuo. There was also, of course, the essential aim of implementing koseki registration to collect personal status information on those who resided in Manchoukuo in order to establish a precise definition of the 'citizen'. In September 1932, scholar of international law Ōhira Zengo (1905–1989) presented the 'Draft of Citizenship Law in Manchoukuo' to the Manchoukuo Department of Justice and the Legislation Bureau of the Manchoukuo National Council (*kokumuin*). This document stated, 'The range of those residing in Manchoukuo is exceedingly unclear [...] and without enacting legislation relating to koseki registration it will be wellnigh impossible to clarify this matter'.[125] Here we see the suggestion that the implementation of koseki register legislation in Manchoukuo was also indispensable in the process of legislating Manchoukuo citizenship law. However, Manchoukuo embraced many ethnicities, each of which had widely divergent family customs, and it would have been very difficult to enact koseki register legislation that unified these. Accordingly, the household surveys (*kokō chōsa*) conducted by the military and the police operated in reality as a koseki registration system and provided population statics and information on the residential circumstances of people resident in the Manchoukuo state.

On 25 August 1936, the Hirota Kōki Cabinet ratified the 'twenty years, one million households, five million people' (*Nijūka-nen, hyakuman-ko, gohyakuman-nin*) plan to develop and open up the Manchoukuo frontier. In December 1937, furthermore, the Manchoukuo/Mongolian Development Youth Volunteer Corps (*Manmō kaitaku seinen giyūgun*) was formed with a view to recruiting young men between sixteen and nineteen years of age. Training for this commenced on the Japanese mainland in 1938. Steps were also taken to include Korean people in development plans for Manchoukuo. In September 1936, the 'Korean Manchurian Reclamation and Colonisation Company' (*Senman takushoku gaisha*) was established in line with the policy of despatching migrants to undertake the planned opening of Manchoukuo land. These plans for migration as a means of developing national policy, actioned in April 1937 as a 'mission of the military defence of the nation' (*gunji-teki kokubō-teki shimei*), differed from the economic justification for previous Japanese migration to North America, South America, South East Asia and the South Sea Islands.[126] From 1937, there was an exponential annual increase in the numbers of 'Japanese subjects', both mainland Japanese and Korean people, who migrated to Manchoukuo (refer to Table 4.7).

The abolition of extraterritorial rights for Japan, a concern as noted from the time of the founding of Manchoukuo, assumed greater and greater importance with the rise in the number of 'Japanese subjects' resident in Manchoukuo. Following joint Japanese/Manchoukuo research, a decision was made to implement the abolition of these rights in stages. The first step was the conclusion on 10 June 1936 between Japan and Manchoukuo of the 'Treaty Between the Japanese and Manchoukuo Related to Manchoukuo

Table 4.7: Population shift among mainland Japanese and Koreans in Manchoukuo (1932–1943, figures as at end of administrative year)

	General population	No. of mainland Japanese	No. of Korean people
1932	29,968,837	(116,589)[a]	(27,956)[a]
1933	31,234,032	178,680	579,884
1934	33,135,296	241,804	690,716
1935	34,702,319	318,770	774,627
1936	35,870,573	392,742	894,744
1937	36,949,972	418,300	31,620
1938	38,623,640	522,189	1,056,308
1939	39,454,026	642,356	1,162,127
1940	41,660,672	862,245	1,345,212
1941	43,188,000	1,017,000	1,465,000
1942	44,462,000	1,097,000	1,541,000
1943	45,323,000	1,148,000	1,634,000

Note: [a] In the territory adjacent to the South Manchurian Railway only.
Sources: 1932–1940, Ishihara Iwao, 'Projected future population of Manchoukuo', in *Chōsa* (Survey), December 1941, p. 7; 1941–1943, Ōkurashō Kanrikyoku (Ministry of Finance Administrative Bureau), *Nihonjin no kaigai katsudō ni kan suru rekishiteki chōsa* (Historical Survey Related to Activities of Overseas Japanese), No. 22, Manchuria Vol. 1, Ministry of Finance Administrative Bureau, 1949, p. 210.

Taxation and the Residency of Japanese Subjects in Manchoukuo'. This was followed on 5 November 1937 by the 'Treaty Relating to the Abolition of Imperial Extraterritoriality in Manchoukuo and the Transfer of Governance of Land Adjacent to the South Manchurian Railway Line'. With the conclusion of these agreements, the abolition of extraterritoriality was technically complete, and thus 'Japanese subjects' in Manchoukuo should have become subject to the administrative power of the Manchoukuo government. This would have seen a marked increase in demands upon the legal governance of Manchoukuo in terms of dealing with status changes such as births, deaths or marriages, and an associated need for a koseki registration law to be implemented in Manchoukuo.

On 18 June 1937, however, the Japanese government took a cabinet decision concerning 'Matters of the Implementation Policy Related to the Abolition of Imperial Extraterritoriality in Manchoukuo and the

Maintenance and Transfer of Governance Power of Land Adjacent to the South Manchurian Railway Line'. As a result, extraterritorial rights were, in fact, retained in terms of governance related to the sense of being 'Japanese'. These extraterritorial rights included shrine administration, education and military matters, in addition to all issues concerning 'imperial subjects'. It goes without saying that each of these elements, especially military service, was inextricably related to koseki registration. In order to accurately and efficiently conduct the military administration relating to the conscription and subsequent discharge of 'Japanese subjects' resident in Manchoukuo, the Japanese authorities considered it necessary to retain the right to administer koseki registration matters for these people. By 1938, the abolition of extraterritoriality had seen the Japanese consul offices in Manchoukuo, excluding those in the national border zone, abolished and integrated into other administrative structures. Previously administered by these now defunct consul offices, the koseki registration of Japanese people resident in Manchoukuo became a matter for the police agencies under the control of the Japanese embassy. In other words, control of these matters in fact remained in the hands of the Japanese.[127] We can only conclude that, given that the koseki registration system provided genealogical evidence of being 'Japanese' through attachment to an *ie* family in Japan, the Japanese authorities considered it vital that administration of these processes remained in their hands.

Manchoukuo people's register: Inadequate 'proof of citizenship'

With barriers to the introduction of citizenship and koseki register legislation in Manchoukuo, steps were taken to enact a 'People's Registration Law' (*Minseki-hō*) as a status registration law appropriate for a society of multi-ethnic cultures and customs. The existence of such a law was regarded as an indispensable element of Manchoukuo national security policy. On 11 April 1940 (Kōtoku Year 7, Manchoukuo Imperial Ordinance No. 71), furthermore, the 'National Military Law' (*Kokuhei hō*) was promulgated. While this law proscribed the military conscription obligations of 'male imperial subjects' in Manchoukuo, the critical matter of precisely who these 'imperial subjects' were remained unclear. A concrete definition of this group was thus determined in terms of the special People's Registration Law. With plans to implement a

Table 4.8: Results of the first provisional national census in Manchoukuo (1 October 1940)

	Population	**%**
Total population of Manchoukuo	43,202,880	100.0
Manchurian people		
Total number	40,858,473	94.6
Han Chinese	36,870,978	90.2
Manchu	2,677,288	6.2
Mongolian	1,065,792	2.5
Muslim	194,473	0.5
Japanese people		
Total number	2,271,495	5.3
Mainland Japanese	819,614	1.9
Korean	1,450,384	3.4
Stateless people	69,180	0.2
Third country people[a]	3,732	0.0

Note: [a] Refers to people such as Americans and others who are neither Japanese nor Chinese.
Source: *Manshū-koku shi hensan kankō-kai hen* (Manchoukuo History Compilation Publishing Association, ed.), *Manshū-koku shi kakuron* (Manchoukuo History Itemised Topics), Tokyo: Manmō dōhō engo-kai (Manchurian Compatriot Relief Association), 1971, p. 58.

national conscription system from April 1941, a suitable 'temporary people's register roll' (*kari minseki-bō*) was established and a survey of conscription-age young men was initiated. Entry into the roll authorised one as a 'person of the Manchu Empire'. These initiatives established the framework necessary to administer military conscription.[128]

The 'Provisional People's Registration Law' (*Zankō minseki-hō*; Manchoukuo Imperial Ordinance No. 197) was promulgated on 1 August 1940. Taking a broader perspective, it is clear that the mission of this law was to incite a 'citizenship' consciousness among residents of Manchoukuo. It did this by permitting the registration of each of the various ethnicities that comprised the population and thereby compiling evidence of the status of the 'Manchoukuo people'. Accordingly, when the law came into force on 1 October 1940, the first Manchoukuo national census was conducted with those surveyed entered into the people's register as a general rule.

Although Japan may have regarded itself as the leading nation, as is clear from Table 4.8, more than ninety percent of residents in Manchoukuo were Han Chinese. 'Japanese citizens' (including mainland Japanese and Korean people) comprised less than ten percent of those surveyed.

The unit of entry into the people's register for those with a *honseki* address in a city, town or village (the administrative divisions in Manchoukuo) was the household ('*ko*', i.e. '*setai*'). Matters recorded included *honseki* address ('*seki-kan*', from the Chinese phrase meaning 'ancestor's original address'), residential address, place of birth, ethnicity, date of arrival in Manchoukuo and more. Since the people's register was more of a residential register, the format differed from the Japanese koseki registration system. As an immigrant nation, Manchoukuo was characterised by extraordinarily volatile population mobility patterns. Therefore, creating a register such as the Japanese mainland koseki register, in which the unit of entry was based on the concept of the *ie* family, would have been completely ineffectual.

Under the People's Registration Law, mainland Japanese and Korean people retained their respective *honseki* addresses in mainland Japan and Korea. If, in order to conform to Manchoukuo laws, these people had established a new *hoseki* address in Manchoukuo, they would have then held more than one *honseki* address. As already noted, the Koseki Registration Law prohibited this in Japan. This problem was solved when Japanese authorities categorised Manchoukuo as a 'foreign nation'. According to Shinzeki Katsuyoshi (1906–1994), a councillor with the Department of Justice in Manchoukuo who played a key role in drafting the People's Registration Law, 'Those of Japanese descent, including Koreans and Taiwanese as well as mainland Japanese, had a fully functioning koseki registration system. In one sense, doubling up with an entry in the people's register was completely superfluous'. He also expressed concerns that such a situation might confuse both those with the double registration and the authorities. Nevertheless, Shinzeki ultimately concluded that 'Because this register was the document that provided formal proof of the status relationships of a citizen of Manchoukuo, it was essential that it apply to all citizens, regardless of their ethnicity'.[129] In terms of the national policy of 'ethnic harmony' in Manchoukuo, it was not possible to officially approve any exceptional treatment that would have exempted

'Nikkei' (Japanese descendants) only from having an entry in the people's register.

On 31 December 1941, the Japanese government gave cabinet approval to the 'Second Manchoukuo Five Year Development and Opening Plan'. This expanded the original target of the Manchoukuo development plan to the recruitment of a further 220,000 households of mainland Japanese for development and frontier-opening activities over the coming five years. The massive scale of the increase in mainland Japanese and Korean immigrant numbers is apparent in Table 4.7. As a strategy to deal with the scale of this increase, plans were made to simplify people's register administrative processes. On 23 December 1942, the Manchoukuo government promulgated 'Matters Related to the Special Case of the Creation of New Koseki Records for Japanese People Resident in Manchoukuo' (*Manshūkoku ni zaijū suru Nihonjin no shuseki no tokurei ni kan suru ken*; Kōtoku Year 9, Manchoukuo Imperial Ordinance No. 254). This ordinance simplified the legal administration involved when Japanese people created a new record in the people's register.

However, the primary issue for Japanese people (mainland Japanese) in terms of making an entry in the people's register was the need to conform to the mainland Koseki Registration Law. For example, in July 1942, the Manchoukuo Department of Justice received an inquiry from the Undersecretary of Fengtian (Mukden) Province concerning the appropriate administrative response to requests to enter concubines (*mekake*) and their children into the people's register. In terms of the mainland Koseki Registration Law, these women and their offspring were not regarded as members of a 'family' (*kazoku*). The department's response was that the entry into the local register of people 'who were not recognised as family in the Japanese Koseki Registration Law' was contrary to the spirit of the People's Registration Law. In this way, the regulatory power of the *ie* family that operated in the mainland koseki registration system extended even into Manchoukuo.

Ultimately, an entry in this people's register became the formal proof that an individual qualified as one of 'the people of Manchoukuo' (*Manshūkoku jinmin*). However, there continued to be no stipulation regarding the definition of 'citizenship', or of the conditions of the acquisition or loss of this that should have been a central element of the Provisional People's Registration

Law. Essentially, since the people's register also had no relation to 'Manchoukuo citizenship', it was necessarily inadequate as proof of being a 'citizen' of Manchoukuo. This is also clear from the fact that a 'Japanese subject' did not lose Japanese citizenship upon entry into the people's register. Even after migration to Manchoukuo, both Japanese and Korean people remained 'Japanese subjects' who were bound to the mainland or Korean koseki registration system. In Manchoukuo, too, koseki registration provided inviolable proof that one was a 'Japanese subject'.[130]

The single-minded focus on favourable treatment for the Japanese in Manchoukuo saw notions of the 'citizen' and 'citizenship', elements that were critical to the sovereignty of a nation-state, consigned to limbo. It is impossible, therefore, to in any way classify this 'puppet state' as an 'independent nation'.

Koseki registration as crucial for imperialisation policy

'Creating Japanese names for Koreans' and the Korean koseki system

The overriding symbol of the 'imperialisation' policies targeting Korean people was the forcible 'creation of Japanese names for Korean people' (*sōshi kaimei*). As discussed in a previous chapter, a key feature of the Korean family system was the tradition of ancestor worship that pivoted around the *sei* family surname. One principle of this system was that, as proof of the correct bloodline of a particular family, the *sei* family name was taken for life. Even after implementing a koseki registration system in Korea, the Japanese authorities initially demonstrated a reluctance to interfere with *sei* family name practices. As the need for the state to optimise military mobilisation became more pressing, however, it became necessary to ensure unity among those being mobilised as tools of war. This was particularly important in the case of those of different ethnicities. During the Second World War, Britain, which had constructed the 'British Empire' (*Daiei teikoku*), conducted military mobilisation on an unprecedented scale among residents of the colonies and dependent territories such as India and South Africa. They were inevitably confronted, however, with displays of anti-imperial sentiment among these colonial troops.[131] In Japan, once the authorities took concrete steps to implement conscription in Korea, the decision was taken to assign Japanese-style 'names' (*shimei*, *uji* family name and last name) to Korean people as a means of heightening the spiritual dimension of mobilisation in the name of empire.

On 24 November 1939, 'Matters Concerning the Revision of the Korean Civil Code' (*Chōsen minjirei chū kaisei no ken*; 1939, Regulation No. 19) and 'Matters Related to the Names of the Korean People' (*Chōsenjin no shimei ni kan suru ken*; 1939, Regulation No. 20) were promulgated. These were brought into force in Korea on 11 February 1940, the date of the so-called 'Kigensetsu', the day on which imperial Japan celebrated the enthronement of Jimmu as the first Emperor. These two regulatory directives made it compulsory for Korean people to take a new *uji* family name. This involved changing their official name in their koseki register record from their previous Korean-style name with a *sei* family name to a Japanese-style name with an *uji* family name. The traditional *sei* family name was not, however, completely erased. Rather, this name was transferred to a newly established column on the person's koseki register record headed '*sei* family name and ancestors' place of origin' (*sei oyobi hongan*). Thus, the Japanese-style *uji* family name and the previous *sei* family name were recorded in parallel. This complete standardisation of the *uji* family name delivered a significant advantage to the ruling powers. Having a record of the *sei* family name and the '*hongan*' (the origin of the ancestors) which identified people from the 'same bloodline group' (*dōzoku*), may in one sense have been necessary in terms of the traditional Korean principle of 'same bloodline, no marriage' (*dōzoku fukon*). It also made a clear distinction between Korean people and mainland Japanese.[132]

Koseki registration procedures in Japan determined the *uji* as the distinguishing symbol of the *ie* family. Accordingly, enforcement of the *uji* family name signalled the submission of the individual to the *ie* family, which in turn elicited devotion to the 'national polity' (*kokutai*) that followed from the legal fiction of the *ie* family. Korean people were given from 11 February to 10 August 1940 to lodge a change of name. According to the Department of Judicial Affairs of the Office of the Governor-General of Korea, information received from various district courts and branch offices indicated that 2,680,050 households throughout the whole of Korea had lodged new family name notifications. At sixty-three percent of all registered households, the authorities expressed their satisfaction with this figure as 'the expected result'.[133]

However, as noted above, large numbers of unregistered people with no Korean koseki register entry resided in communities of Korean people who lived outside of Korea. Oversight of the policy that required a Korean person to create a 'mainland Japanese-style *uji* family name' (*naichijin-shiki uji*), however, could only occur if an individual and the family to which they belonged had a record in a Korean koseki register. In other words, there was no way of ensuring that unregistered people adopted a Japanese name. To rectify this anomaly and in tandem with the implementation of the Japanese names creation policy, the Office of the Governor-General of Korea attempted to encourage the creation of new koseki register records for those who were unregistered. A memorandum dated 22 April 1940, entitled 'Matters Relating to the Creation of an *Uji* Family Name and the Name Change of Korean People Without Koseki Registration' (*Mi-shuseki Chōsenjin no uji settei oyobi na-henkō ni kan suru ken*), was circulated to all district courts by the Department of Judicial Affairs of the Office of the Governor-General of Korea. This document stated that those Koreans with permission to adopt a new name were able to use 'a Japanese-style *uji* family name' when applying for the creation of a new register. The Governor-General's Office did not neglect to mandate, however, that 'in this case, the previous *sei* family name must also be recorded'.[134] Given that the Japanese names creation policy in fact worked to clearly distinguish between Japanese and Korean people, it embodied the goal of the Japanese authorities to exercise complete koseki registration control over the people of Korea.

Many Koreans, however, objected to the maintenance of this chasm between mainland Japanese and Korean people through rigorous koseki register distinction, noting that the implementation of the names creation policy cut across any realisation of the 'unification of mainland Japan and Korea' (*naisen ittai*). The direct opposition of Korean people to the policy is evident in comments such as the following: 'Even with this names creation policy a Korean person is unable to transfer her or his koseki register record to the mainland. This demonstrates that, fundamentally, the unification of mainland Japan and Korea has not been achieved'. It was also argued that 'Unification of Japan and Korea will not come about through the creation of an *uji* family name. This can only happen with the abolition of *discriminatory* treatment by mainland Japanese towards Korean people. Even after the implementation of this system of creating an *uji, the fact that Korean people will still be unable to take a* honseki *address on the Japanese mainland will create enormous problems*' (emphasis added).[135] Had the Japanese authorities really intended to bring into practice notions of 'universal benevolence' (*isshi dōnin*) both in name and reality, they would have responded to Korean voices calling for freedom to change one's koseki registration to the mainland by abolishing the distinction between 'mainland Japanese' (*naichijin*) and 'persons not subject to mainland Japanese law' (*gaichijin*).

Against 'racial mixing': Ban on registration transfer to mainland

With the outbreak of the Second World War, the Japanese system of total war demanded mobilisation of the people without exception. Expanding the scale of military conscription, the 'National Recruitment Order' (*Kokumin chōyō rei*; 1939, Imperial Ordinance No. 451) was applied in the colonies from May 1944. With this development, wartime mobilisation now equally applied to all subjects of imperial Japan.

Historian Edward H. Carr (1892–1982) has stated that the scale of wartime mobilisation throughout the contemporary world dissolved the old social and political regulatory order while creating a new order that determined the shape of society and politics for forthcoming eras.[136] Through its audacious declaration of all-out war, Japan, which had also propelled itself into the international order as an imperial state, was forced to initiate new means to tighten the links between empire and colonial holdings. The Pacific War assumed the form of a 'race war' (*jinshu no sensō*),[137] and the problem of race became one of the main points in the ideological conflict between the Axis Powers, Japan and the American and British Allied Powers. Japan, for example, argued that, with the aim of achieving reciprocal coexistence and co-prosperity, freedom and independence and the elimination of racial discrimination throughout the countries of 'Greater East Asia', it was taking the high moral ground by embarking on the 'Greater East Asia War' (*Daitōa sensō*). It is well known that in creating the 'New Order in Greater East Asia' (*Daitōa shin-chitsujo*), Japan sought to idealise its moral leadership over a pseudo-family style community of nations as a means of crushing the United States and Great Britain.

In a diary entry of 24 November 1943, the Minister of Foreign Affairs, Shigemitsu Mamoru (1887–1957), was highly critical of the 'fiercely discriminatory attitude [towards non-white races] of the British and Americans', emphasising in contrast the racial equality that was a fundamental ideal of the 'New Order in Greater East Asia'. Shigemitsu observed, 'without the elimination of racial discrimination, there can be no true emancipation in Asia, and it is impossible to aim for world peace'.[138] However, it was not long before America and Great Britain were in turn strongly criticising the discriminatory practices evident in Japan's colonial policies as issues of race. On 1 December 1943, the three Allied nations of America, Great Britain and China issued the Cairo Declaration (*Kairo sengen*). This document declared, 'The aforesaid three great powers, mindful of the enslavement of the people of Korea, are determined that in due course Korea shall become free and independent'. Here, the Allied Powers put forward the emancipation of the Japanese empire's colonial holdings as a matter of great importance in the war against Japan, and made a trenchant moral criticism of Japanese colonialism.

With the successful implementation of military service and labour mobilisation policies in the colonies, the reform of the political and social treatment of the colonies became a serious policy issue within Japanese government circles. Enacting reforms designed to ensure equal treatment of the people of the colonies was also seen, in terms of 'racial equality' and the justice of the 'New Order in Greater East Asia', as a means of pushing back against criticism of Japan's colonial project by the Allied Powers. In this context, consideration was given to enacting legislation that would permit the unrestricted transfer to mainland Japan of koseki registration for those born or registered in the colonies. For example, the Department of Judicial Affairs (*Hōmu-kyoku*) of the Office of the Governor-General of Korea devised the 'Draft Law Relating to the Transfer of Koseki Registration Between Mainland Japan and Korea' (*Naichi Chōsen kan no tenseki nado ni kan suru hōritsu-an*) dated 11 October 1944, which suggested that, conditional on three years of residence in mainland Japan and the ability to use standard everyday Japanese, permission could be given for koseki registration transfer from Korea to mainland Japan.

From the perspective of the Ministry of Home Affairs, however, any move to permit the transfer of koseki registration from the colonies to mainland Japan presented a serious challenge to the orderly rule of empire. In a document entitled 'Various Issues Associated with the Koseki Registration Transfer of People from

Korea and Taiwan' (*Chōsenjin oyobi Taiwan-jin no iseki ni kan suru sho-mondai*), dated 12 November 1944, the Ministry indicated that it was opposed to approving the 'transfer of koseki registration' (*iseki*) from the colonies as follows:

> It is difficult to accept that koseki registration transfer is a problem simply terms of koseki administration. *Encompassing [as it does] fundamental issues such as the mixing of races, assimilation and the maintenance of purity, [permitting such a transfer would give rise to] long-term policy fundamentals concerning both the future of the Japanese race and ethnic policies towards Koreans and Taiwanese.* Accordingly, such a suggestion should not be treated lightly as a convenient administrative measure. Rather, it should be investigated very prudently by comparing matters such as the racial nature, assimilation capacity, adaptability, reproductive capacity and the population of Korean and Taiwanese people with those of mainland Japanese. It is basically necessary to bear in mind the fundamentals of regulating race. (emphasis added)[139]

Here, far from being a mere administrative matter, the existence (or otherwise) throughout the empire of a boundary based on the koseki registration system was ultimately interpreted as a means of 'governing the races'. It was accordingly related to problems such as 'racial mixing, assimilation and the maintenance of purity'. Thus, according to the Ministry of Home Affairs, any move to approve unrestricted koseki registration transfer to mainland Japan, especially by Korean and Taiwanese people, would have a critical and long-term impact on 'the future of the Japanese race'. Such a move thus required the most extreme caution.

On 22 December 1944, under the Koiso Kuniaki Cabinet, a document was presented entitled 'The Outline of Improving the Treatment of Our Fellow Korean Brothers Who Are Resident on the Japanese Mainland' (*Naichi zaijū Chōsen dōhō ni tai suru shogū kaizen yōryō*). This considered the need to 'respond to the current stage of the war situation and, as a means of gaining the fruits of the "one hundred million, one mind" [*ichi-oku isshin*] policy and striving towards the completion of the sacred task of the construction of Greater East Asia, to perfect a more complete self-awareness by our Korean and Taiwanese brothers of themselves as imperial subjects'. Advocating the 'opening [of] a path to koseki registration transfer' (*iseki no michi wo hiraku koto*), the document expounded the worth of permitting the transfer of the *honseki* address to mainland Japan by residents of the colonies.[140] However, this policy draft for the liberalisation of koseki registration transfer was never progressed in any concrete policy form. As confirmed by the comments above by the Minister of Home Affairs, the priority for the Japanese government was maintaining the koseki register wall that acted as a means of 'governing each ethnicity' throughout the empire.

Once assimilation had been thoroughly enforced, logic suggests that there would have been a resultant unification of each of the varying koseki registration systems of the 'Japanese'. Since, however, the koseki registration system was a public demonstration of pure blood and ethnic superiority, the imperial authorities were reluctant to take any steps that would compromise the dominant position of the ruling mainland Japanese. Various ethnic groups had been subsumed from a putative perspective of reciprocal equality into the 'New Order in Greater East Asia', the ideal used to promote the high moral ground of the 'Greater East Asia War'. This 'Order', however, lacked anything like the strength necessary to overcome the unassailable sense of supremacy that prevailed among the 'Japanese' as the race that reigned over the colonies.

Thus, debate over whether or not to permit unrestricted koseki registration transfer from the colonies to the Japanese mainland was essentially a problem of whether or not the authorities should permit non-mainland Japanese access to the koseki registration system of mainland Japan. This is in spite of the fact that the 'purity of the Japanese race', the preservation of which was so insistently argued in the extract given above from the Ministry of Home Affairs, was clearly nothing but a fabrication constructed by a forced change of ethnic membership on a koseki register record when one entered into or departed from an *ie* family. Any authorisation of unrestricted koseki registration transfer within the empire carried the particular danger of promoting an erosion of this 'purity'. Regardless of the manifold attempts made by authorities to assimilate the colonies into the imperial fold, koseki registration procedures created 'fundamental problems' that inevitably worked against this possibility.

5 Post-war Reconstruction of the 'Japanese': Koseki Registration and the Citizenship of 'Subjects of the Empire'

Transforming former colonial people into 'foreigners'

Liberated ethnicities' post-war retention of Japanese citizenship

When Japan accepted the Potsdam Declaration's terms of unconditional surrender to the Allied Powers and signed the Instrument of Surrender on 2 September 1945, the country was stripped of any authority to govern its former colonial holdings. Building on the 1943 Cairo Communiqué's repudiation of Japan's colonisation policies, one objective of the Potsdam Declaration was to free 'all other territories taken by [the Japanese empire's] violence and greed'.

With the establishment of the position of Supreme Commander for the Allied Powers (SCAP/GHQ) under the control of General Douglas MacArthur (1880–1964), the indirect rule of the Occupation forces began. Notwithstanding the Potsdam emphasis on ending Japan's colonialist endeavours, however, neither SCAP nor the United States formulated any clear policy concerning the legal position of people from Japan's former colonial holdings. The State-War-Navy Three Ministry Coordinating Committee was formed on 1 November 1945. One week later, on 8 November, the Committee forwarded to MacArthur the 'Basic Initial Post Surrender Directive to Supreme Commander for the Allied Powers for the Occupation and Control of Japan'. Here, Korean and Taiwanese people were designated as 'liberated persons' (*kaihō jinmin*) rather than 'Japanese'. There was, nonetheless, a clear assertion that, since the people of former colonies were 'Japanese subjects' (*Nihon shinmin*), they could if necessary be dealt with as the 'enemy' (*tekikokujin*). In other words, in terms of official control, these 'liberated peoples' were to be treated expediently as 'citizens of Japan'. We can read the reason for this ambivalence, which gave no clear articulation of the citizenship of the people from Japan's former colonial holdings, as the GHQ's desire to take a practical approach at that time.[1]

Following defeat, the Japanese government's interpretation of the legal position of the people of its former colonies was that they would retain Japanese citizenship until their legal status was clarified after the return of territories that would eventually occur upon conclusion of a peace treaty with the Allies. In the records of the National Assembly, Clause 5 of the appendices to the revisions to the 'House of Representatives Election Law' (*Shūgi-in gi-in senkyo-hō*) (1945, Law No. 42) promulgated on 17 December 1945, stipulated, 'Those persons to whom the Koseki Registration Law does not apply are suspended from voting or standing for office for the time being'. This led to a suspension of the suffrage rights, only granted in April of that year (1945) and more correctly regarded as suffrage within the colonies only, of former residents of Japan's colonial holdings. In a 1 December 1945 explanatory summary of justification for this law given to the eighty-ninth meeting of the Imperial Diet, Horikiri Zenjirō (1884–1979), the Minister of Home Affairs, stated, 'Since, with its acceptance of the Potsdam Declaration, Japan lost colonial holdings such as Korea and Taiwan, we suppose that Korean and Taiwanese people in principle should lose imperial citizenship'. Horikiri nevertheless continued, 'Until the conclusion of a peace treaty, the imperial citizenship of these people should be considered as remaining intact'.[2] Given that their suffrage rights had been indefinitely suspended, however, it is obvious that any 'Japanese citizenship' held by Korean or Taiwanese people after the war had ended was completely invalid. Deprived in this way of fundamental suffrage privileges, including the right to both demand benefits and protest against government policies through the processes of parliamentary democracy, residents from the former colonies became one-sided citizens in the sense that they were subject to Japanese state control without any reciprocal benefit.[3]

It appears, however, that only bureaucrats and those in positions of political power regarded the people of former colonies as having valid legal status in Japan. In broader Japanese society immediately after the war, the average person tended to view these previous 'compatriots' as 'foreigners' (*gaikokujin*). With the spiritual sense of collapse experienced at the end of the war, former colonial people became subject to exclusionary sentiment.

For example, a report sent to the Ministry of Home Affairs by the head of the Niigata Prefecture Police Department noted 'a tendency by mainland Japanese to demean and regard [Korean people] with disdain'. The report found that, especially 'within this jurisdiction, there are cases of mainland Japanese students in national schools [*kokumin gakkō*] saying to Korean children, "The Americans made Korea an independent country so now you're the enemy. Get back to Korea as soon as you can"'.[4]

Notwithstanding what may or may not have been the legal position on citizenship matters, both Koreans, the 'second class citizens' (*nitō kokumin*) of the imperial era, and Japanese, the 'first class citizens' (*ittō kokumin*) of that time, were 'Japanese subjects'. Since Japan had lost the war, however, Koreans became 'people of a victorious nation' (*senshō kokumin*), while Japanese became 'people of a vanquished nation' (*haisen kokumin*). The hostility and chauvinism displayed towards Koreans came from the loss of ethnic pride experienced by the Japanese – who had a common consciousness of having once been 'first class citizens' – at the reverse of power relations between themselves and Koreans.

Defeat saw those in the provinces often adopt an instinctive group mentality that deemed people of the former colonies to be, in citizenship terms, no longer 'Japanese'. As a result, there was an ongoing stream of inquiries received by central authorities from regional departments of home affairs and municipal offices on how best to process the 'naturalisation' (*kika*) of Korean and Taiwanese people, in spite of continual insistence by the Attorney General's Office (*Hōmu-fu*, the present-day Ministry of Justice) that provincial and municipal administrations comply with previous policy and precedent on this matter. These included the 26 January 1949 announcement, 'There is no need for Koreans to naturalise' (Civil Affairs Notification No. 144), and the 28 December 1951 ruling, 'Until the conclusion of a peace treaty with the Allies, Korean and Taiwanese people do not lose Japanese citizenship' (28 December 1951, Civil Affairs Notification No. 2463).[5]

At a 6 February 1946 press conference, a SCAP spokesperson officially announced, 'Japanese law applies to foreigners who live in Japan and who are not Occupation forces officers or enlisted men or civilian personnel attached to the Occupation forces'.[6] The defeat had initially left the Japanese government uncertain as to the legal status of people of the former colonies. The official Occupation designation of those people as Japanese citizens, however, gave Japan the authority to exercise arbitrary administrative control over the people of the former colonies. The promulgation on 19 February 1946 of the SCAP memorandum entitled, 'Matters Relating to the Exercise of Criminal Jurisdiction' (*Keiji saiban-ken no kōshi ni kan suru ken*) (SCAPIN-756), confirmed that Japanese criminal jurisdiction and the right to arrest did not extend to Allied nation citizens or organisations. However, since Koreans were not designated as 'citizens of Allied nations', there was no impediment to Japan retaining criminal jurisdiction over people from Korea. On this matter, the Japanese authorities observed, 'It is deeply regrettable that Japan has been forced to forfeit criminal jurisdiction over occupation personnel. Nevertheless, we clearly hold such rights with respect to Korean and Taiwanese people and we will continue the thorough exercise of those rights towards these people into the future'.[7] While the Japanese state had its sovereignty curtailed considerably by SCAP, it is obvious that even as an occupied nation Japan retained the right to exercise judicial and law-enforcement authority over the people of its former colonies.

The original SCAP opinion that Korean people residing in Japan retained Japanese citizenship until the conclusion of the peace treaty remained constant throughout the Occupation. This is clear from two successive announcements: the 5 November 1946 'Announcement by the SCAP Civil Information and Education Section Regarding the Repatriation of Korean People' (*Chōsenjin no hikiage ni kan suru sōshirei-bu minkan jōhō kyōiku kyoku happyō*), and the 12 November 'Announcement by the SCAP Public Relations Bureau Regarding the Status and Treatment of Korean People' (*Chōsenjin no chi'i oyobi toriatsukai ni kan suru sōshirei-bu shōgai-kyoku happyō*). With respect to repatriation, SCAP declared, 'Those Korean people in Japan who decline to return to their homeland in accordance with the repatriation plan offered by SCAP will be regarded as retaining Japanese citizenship'.[8] This announcement was strongly opposed by Korean advocacy groups such as the 'Association of Korean Residents in Japan' (*Zai-Nihon Chōsenjin Renmei*). It was also condemned by public opinion on the Korean Peninsula. Both demanded that, as 'liberated people, Koreans be given the same status as citizens of the Allied nations'.[9] People of former colonies who were living in Japan, however, were never extended the privileges that applied to citizens of the Allied nations. Rather, the fundamental SCAP position that the legal status of these people was in principle that of 'Japanese citizens' remained unchanged.[10]

Dept. of alien registration: Nominal Japanese citizenship

Immediately after the war, the Occupation authorities and the Japanese government were faced with the huge problem of repatriating more than 2,000,000 people from former colonies who remained in Japan. In a 17 February 1946 memorandum to the Japanese government, entitled 'The Registration of Korean, Chinese, Ryūkyūan and Formosans' (*Chōsenjin, Chūgokujin, Ryūkyūjin oyobi Taiwanjin no tōroku ni kan suru oboegaki*) (SCAPIN 746), SCAP requested that 'all Koreans, Chinese, Ryūkyūans and Taiwanese [Formosans] living in Japan' register with the authorities by 18 March 1946.[11] There is no doubt that the purpose of the memorandum was to assist SCAP to calculate the numbers of people seeking to return to their homeland in order facilitate smooth repatriation processes. To the Japanese authorities, however, the SCAP request became an opportunity to create a registration regime for former colonial people for the purpose of maintaining social order.

We should never forget the power held by Yoshida Shigeru (1878–1967) and the influence wielded by this five-time prime minister of Japan on Occupation era policies concerning Korean people resident in Japan. In a 1949 letter to MacArthur, Yoshida's ethnic prejudice led him to notoriously declare that the majority of Korean people resident in Japan were 'illegal immigrants' (*fuhō imin*), and that all Koreans should be 'forcibly returned to Korea'.[12] In addition to being Minister of Foreign Affairs in the Shidehara Kijūrō (1872–1951) Cabinet, Yoshida was Director-General of the Central Liaison Office (*Shūsen renraku jimu-kyoku*), the key Japanese conduit for negotiations with Occupation authorities. Regarding the necessity of a registration system for people from former colonies, on 25 February 1946, the Chair of the Meeting of Regional Heads (*Chihō chōkan kaigi*) convened by the Shidehara Cabinet made the following statement.

> In order for the government to accurately conduct compulsory registration processes relating to [Koreans and other colonial groups] *we need to agree that those who wish to remain in Japan will not*

> *receive the same treatment as Japanese. Cognisant of the fact that we wish to sweep away undesirable, trouble-making elements*, we are currently in negotiation with SCAP. Given the importance of accurately registering Chinese, Taiwanese and Koreans from here on in, we must take every care and ensure every precision in the conduct of the forthcoming survey.[13] (emphasis added)

Thus, under SCAP auspices, the forcible registration of Koreans, Taiwanese and other people from former colonies was implemented from 18 March 1946. While the stated reason was to identify those who wished to be repatriated, the comments cited above make it clear that there was undoubtedly also a tacit public order and policing aim of 'sweep[ing] away undesirable, trouble-making elements'. The registration process identified 647,006 Korean people in Japan (3,595 of whom were in prison), with 514,060 of these (3,373 in prison) expressing a desire to return to Korea.[14] Yet, although the Japanese government commenced repatriation procedures based on these figures in April that year, political instability, food shortages in Korea and Japanese government restrictions on the amount of cash repatriated people were permitted to take out of the country resulted in many more than expected thinking twice about returning home. As a result, the repatriation process stalled. Upon its conclusion at the end of 1946, only 82,900 names had been recorded as repatriated.[15] Ultimately, more than eighty percent of those who initially registered opted to remain in Japan.

Parallel to the planned repatriation of Korean people, concrete plans were made to take what Yoshida considered to be the necessary legal steps to eliminate 'undesirable elements' among people from former colonies. To this end, the Ministry of Home Affairs and the Ministry of Justice, largely in collaboration with the Central Liaison Office, drafted ordinances on alien registration and immigration controls over foreigner mobility.[16] These developments occurred against the background of a dramatic increase in the numbers of Korean people illegally crossing to Japan by ship in the first half of 1946. The majority of those making these voyages, which resulted in 17,000 arrests, were people who had resided in Japan before the war. After repatriation to Korea, however, they sought to leave their homeland upon deciding that chances for building a decent life were, after all, better in Japan.[17] With the collaboration of the relevant agencies, a 'Draft Plan for Alien Registration' was compiled in

October 1946.[18] After six months of negotiation with SCAP, the 'Alien Registration Ordinance' (1947, Imperial Ordinance No. 207) was both promulgated and brought into force as the very last ordinance of the Emperor on 2 May 1947, the day prior to the implementation of the new Constitution.

Article 11 of the Alien Registration Ordinance stipulated, 'In terms of the applicability of this ordinance, Korean people and Taiwanese people as designated by the Ministry of Home Affairs shall be regarded as foreigners'. On 21 June 1947, a communiqué from the head of the Survey Bureau of the Ministry of Home Affairs ruled that the Korean people to whom the Alien Registration Ordinance applied were 'those persons to whom the Korean Koseki Registration Law applied'.[19] Clearly, these were those marked as 'Korean' on the membership of an ethnic group register (*minzoku seki*). On the matter of suffrage, it has been noted that a koseki registration provision was inserted into the 'Members of the House of Councillors Election Law' (*sangiin giin senkyo-hō*) (1947, Law No. 11) as a means of suspending the voting rights of Korean and Taiwanese people. This provision was carried across into Article 9 of the appendices of that law and also into Article 20 of the 'Regional Municipality Law' (*Chihō jichihō*) (1947, Law No. 67). In addition, Article 2 of the appendices to the '1950 Public Office Election Law' (*Kōshoku senkyo-hō*), which amalgamated elections for the upper and lower houses, also stipulated that 'the right to vote and to stand for public office is suspended for those persons to whom the Koseki Registration Law does not apply'. Clearly, people from former colonies held 'Japanese citizenship' in name only.

The appendices of the original government draft of the 26 August 1951 Immigration Control Ordinance of the cabinet, introduced by the Japanese authorities in anticipation of the conclusion of the peace treaty, also stipulated that 'those persons to whom the Koseki Registration Law does not apply are regarded in terms of the application of this law as foreigners'. SCAP, however, deemed the designation of Koreans and Taiwanese who had resided in Japan from before the war as 'foreigners' to be unfair and unreasonable and requested that the stipulation be revised. Accordingly, the Japanese authorities reluctantly removed the statement. There were concerns that legally designating Korean people to be 'Japanese' would make it impossible to conduct public order deportations of those regarded as undesirable.[20]

This official legitimisation of discriminatory treatment effectively invalidated the function of citizenship. Although defined as 'Japanese citizens', people of former colonies were denied voting rights. Above all, however, they were forced to register as 'foreigners' on the grounds that they were 'persons to whom the Japanese Koseki Registration Law did not apply'. This skilful use of the condition of the non-applicability of koseki registration procedures saw what was no more than a law of convenience successfully implement discriminatory policies while avoiding manifestations of racism through legal terminology such as 'ethnicity' or 'race'. This tactic revived a favourite pre-war era ploy of drawing on the membership of an ethnic group as a means of social control and was ultimately a product of the koseki registration system of the 'Greater Japanese Empire' (*Dai Nippon teikoku*).

Restoring the original 'citizenship' of the people of Korea and Taiwan

Both Taiwan and Korea were liberated from Japanese control. Accordingly, the governments of each set out to restore the citizenship of their 'own citizens'.

On 22 June 1946, during the Chinese Civil War (*Kokkyō naisen*, the Nationalist-Communist Civil War in China), the Nationalist government initiated citizenship policy by promulgating and implementing the 'Law Dealing with the Citizenship of Overseas Taiwanese' (*Zaigai taikyō kokuseki shoriben-pō*). This law stipulated that, from 25 October 1945 – the so-called 'Day of the Taiwan Reversion' (*Taiwan kōfuku-setsu*) which saw Taiwan removed from Japanese control and revert to being a territory of Nationalist China – Taiwanese living outside Taiwan had their Chinese citizenship restored and could be issued with proof of citizenship if they registered with a Chinese government overseas legation or diplomatic mission. In a move perhaps designed to force people to revive their Chinese citizenship, those who did not wish to register as Chinese citizens were required to inform an overseas legation of their decision by 31 December 1946. By the end of February 1947, approximately 20,000 Taiwanese people living in Japan had registered at the various Chinese government legations throughout Japan and had received 'Chinese citizenship' certifications.[21] As the hostilities in China intensified, the Nationalists were increasingly overwhelmed by Communist forces. This campaign to have Chinese people living outside China (*kakyō*) restore their citizenship may have been a Nationalist Party tactic to shore up support from overseas Chinese.

On 25 February 1947, in response to these measures by the Republic of China, SCAP recognised the validity of the 'Chinese citizenship' certification issued by Chinese legations in Japan in its 'Memorandum Relating to the Registration of Chinese Nationals' (*Chūgokujin no tōroku ni kan suru oboegaki*). Accordingly, those who held this documentation were to be treated as Chinese – that is, as 'people of the Allied Powers' (*rengō kokumin*) – and were thus exempt from Japanese legal jurisdiction.[22] In other words, those Taiwanese people residing in Japan who had restored their Chinese citizenship and who held documentation verifying this were to be treated as 'people of the Allied Powers'. In this sense, they were in a much more favourable legal position than people from Korea.

On 15 August 1948, the Korean Peninsula was divided along the thirty-eighth parallel north, leading to the formation of South Korea (the Republic of Korea, *Daikan minkoku*) and North Korea (the Democratic People's Republic of Korea, *Chōsen minshu-shugi jinmim kyōwa-koku*) on 9 September 1948. The 1947 North/South division and the creation of separate states rendered citizenship legislation which stipulated '*Chōsen*', the pre-war name for Korea, as a single citizenship impossible. Naturally asserting itself as a sovereign state, South Korea therefore drew up conditions to define its own 'citizens'. In November 1949, the 'Citizenship Law of the Republic of Korea' (*Daikan minkoku kokuseki-hō*) (1948, Law No. 16), based on principles of paternal *jus sanguinis* (bloodline), was promulgated and brought into force. Since this legislation also applied to Korean people who resided outside the Republic of Korea, a 'Registration of Overseas Citizens Law' (*Zaigai kokumin tōroku-hō*) (1949, Law No. 70) was promulgated in November 1949. This law stipulated that Koreans living at a fixed overseas address who applied for registration with a Korean government overseas foreign legation would be accorded rights as 'citizens of the Republic of Korea' (*Kankoku kokumin*).[23] Citizenship law in the Democratic People's Republic of Korea, on the other hand, was not formulated until October 1963. That law drew on the bloodline of both the mother and the father and stipulated that those who had held Korean citizenship in the pre-war era prior to the creation of the two Koreas who had not rescinded Korean citizenship prior to the day of the promulgation of the law, as well as the children of those people, were able to become citizens of North Korea.[24]

With the emergence of the two Koreas, Japan's foreigner register was modified to include a Republic of Korea register (*Kankoku-seki*) and a Korea register (*Chōsen-seki*). At that time, Korean people were entered into the Japanese foreigner register as '*Chōsenjin*' (notwithstanding the contradiction that they retained their Japanese citizenship at that time), and '*Chōsen*' was their designated country. However, a 13 December 1948 United Nations General Assembly meeting declared the Republic of Korea as the sole legitimate government on the Korean Peninsula. With this development, a Republic of Korea Diplomatic Mission in Japan (*Chūnichi kankoku daihyō-bu*) was established in January 1949. This office commenced negotiations with SCAP with a view to having the original Korean citizenship of Korean people resident in Japan automatically reinstated. A further request was made, on the grounds of the Republic of Korea's recognition by the United Nations, for discussions to be held regarding the possibility of Koreans in Japan receiving 'people of the Allied Powers' status. However, William J. Sebald (1901–1980), head of the SCAP Diplomatic Section, felt that this issue could not be resolved prior to the conclusion of a Japan/Allied forces peace treaty and would therefore not permit discussions to proceed.[25] In March 1949, the Republic of Korea requested that alien registration designation for people from Korea change from 'Korea' (*Chōsen*) to 'Korea or the Republic of Korea' (*Kankoku*). After SCAP approved this change in February 1950, the Japanese Cabinet approved the use of the terms 'Korea' or 'Republic of Korea', depending on the preference of those concerned, in all government documentation.[26] With the outbreak of the Korean War in June 1950, political conflict around the North/South divide intensified even further. Some in Japan (even people born in the Korean south), however, sought a neutral stance apropos of this confrontation and thus retained the pre-Korean war expression for the Korean register, '*Chōsen-seki*'. This led to the absurd situation of Korean people in Japan being required to register as foreigners in spite of the fact that they were legally Japanese citizens, and in doing so to state their 'citizenship' as either *Kankoku-seki* (South Korean) or *Chōsen-seki* (Korean).

'People of the territories not subject to mainland Japanese law'

What was the fate of the Korean and Taiwanese koseki registration systems following Japan's wartime defeat? Grounded in the *ie* family system and, above all else, operated on the basis of ordinances enforced only in the colonies, both the Korean and Taiwanese koseki systems had worked to sustain Japan's control of its colonial holdings. Military Ordinance No. 21 proclaimed by SCAP on 2 November 1945 ruled that all laws, edicts, pronouncements and other documentation and precedent operating on 9 August 1945, including regulations promulgated by the Office of the Governor-General of Korea, would remain effective until terminated by decree of the United States Army Military Government. The Japanese authorities understood this directive as confirming that the various laws relating to the colonies, such as the Law of Mutuality (*Kyōtsū-hō,* referred to in Chapter Four) and the Korean Koseki Registration Law, also remained in effect into the post-war era.[27]

From 1943, administration of the colonies became the responsibility of the Ministry of Home Affairs. When Japan was stripped of its authority to govern the colonial territories at the end of the war, however, these sites effectively became 'foreign countries' (*gaikoku*). As a result, with the post-war bureaucratic restructure that came into effect from 1 February 1946, the administration of all matters in relation to former colonies became the responsibility of the Ministry of Foreign Affairs (with the Bureau of Administration taking the lead). As an item of post-war business, this Ministry undertook the management of 'Research Matters Relating to the Reform or Elimination of Legislation of the Territories not Subject to Mainland Japanese Law' (*Gaichi hōrei no kaihai ni kan suru kenkyū jikō*). After consultation with the Cabinet Legislation Bureau, the Ministry of Foreign Affairs stipulated on 20 February 1946 that for the time being the bureaucratic system and various ordinances relating to the former colonies would remain effective.[28]

The post-war legal system naturally underwent profound change following the promulgation of the new Constitution of Japan on 3 May 1947. Article 24, Clause 1 of this Constitution, which stipulated respect for the individual and the essential equality of the sexes, swept away the notion of the *ie* family system that had been a key prop of the imperial era state. The new post-war Civil Code (1947, Law No. 222), reformed in line with constitutional ideals, confirmed the abolition of the *ie* family system and, further, drove koseki registration reform. With the promulgation of a new Koseki Registration Law (1947, Law No. 224), the various regulations that had operated under the auspices of the *ie* family system were either revised or abolished.

However, the Japanese government did not consider the various legal edicts pronounced in the former colonies, such as the Law of Mutuality or the Korean Koseki Registration Law, to be incompatible with the spirit of the Constitution. As a result, these remained valid until the peace treaty was concluded.[29] Japanese municipal governance, therefore, continued to acknowledge the Korean and Taiwanese koseki registration systems, which, in terms of citizenship, operated into the post-war era as the state record of 'Japanese citizens' from former colonies. Because of the differences between koseki registration practices in mainland Japan and the former colonies, it was also necessary for the Law of Mutuality to continue to operate, in spite of the fact that the logic of this law was based on the now defunct *ie* family system. The Law of Mutuality also enshrined the different legal status of 'mainland Japanese' (*naichijin*) and 'persons of the territories not subject to mainland Japanese law' (*gaichijin*). Thus, these divisions continued to function in the legal sphere even after the implementation of the new Constitution. On this point, a 29 January 1948 notification from the head of the Civil Affairs Bureau of the Ministry of Justice stated, 'In order that the partners of Koreans and Taiwanese who marry Japanese are not categorised as illegal immigrants, all processing relating to koseki register lodgement or notification of a marriage between a Korean or Taiwanese person and a mainland Japanese will occur as before'. On 15 October 1948, a statement by the head of the Civil Affairs Bureau (Civil Affairs Matter No. 660) of the Attorney General's Office (*Hōmu chō*) (inaugurated in place of the Ministry of Justice in February of that year) ruled that entries to or removal from a koseki register record of information concerning the relationship between either a Korean or Taiwanese person and a mainland Japanese in matters such as marriage, recognition of a child born outside a formal marriage, adoption, withdrawal from adoption and divorce would comply as previously with the Law of Mutuality.[30]

Yet, the 'Governmental and Administrative Separation of Certain Outlying Areas from Japan' (SCAPIN 677) sent by GHQ on 29 January 1946 had instructed the Japanese authorities to cease conducting administration related to the regulation or governance of territories, such as Korea, Taiwan and Karafuto, which had previously been Japan's 'territories not subject to mainland Japanese law' (*gaichi*). This included matters relating to the people in those territories. As a result, administrative contact ceased between mainland Japan and both Korea and Taiwan.

The cessation of administrative contact between Japan and its former colonies made it impossible to lodge the documentation necessary to change a koseki register record in relation to a status issue, such as marriage or adoption between a mainland Japanese and either a Korean or Taiwanese person, at an office that administered a *honseki* address in either Korea or Taiwan. This led to the anomalous situation of the necessary change only being made to mainland koseki documentation.[31] In post-war Japan, therefore, although a mainlander who had become the wife or adopted child of a Korean or Taiwanese person was removed from the mainland koseki registration system, there could be no administrative response from the former colony. People in this situation were dealt with by the Korean and Taiwanese koseki registration systems as 'persons who require a koseki register entry' (*nyūseki subeki toriatsukai o uketa mono*). On 6 December 1950, however, the head of the Civil Affairs Bureau issued a communiqué to the effect that even when a parent–child relationship between a mainland Japanese and a Korean or Taiwanese person had been recognised, there should be no change to the ethnicity register.[32] This was in line with the objective of the new Citizenship Law implemented in July 1950, which discontinued the practice of citizenship change that was once demanded by the *ie* family system. However, because changes to the ethnicity register for status matters apart from paternal acknowledgement were recognised as before,[33] there was a mismatch between this policy and other decisions made by the authorities.

The mode of koseki registration governance that came to operate during this time of administrative chaos exercised a strong influence on how the line between 'Japanese' and 'foreigner' was drawn in the post-war era. As explained above, those 'Koreans' to whom the alien registration ordinances (*gaikokjin tōroku-rei*) applied were defined as 'persons to whom the Korean Koseki Registration Ordinance is applicable', including those 'Japanese' (that is, former mainland Japanese) who were 'persons who require a koseki register entry' (*nyūseki subeki toriatsukai wo uketa*) in the Korean

Table 5.1: Numbers of Koreans and Taiwanese registered as foreigners (1947–1952, figures as at end of administrative year)

	Total no.	Korea	South Korea	China (Nationalist China)	Taiwan
1947	639,368	508,507	–	19,770	13,119
1948	648,045	601,772	–	21,488	15,444
1949	645,583	596,879	–	21,945	16,637
1950[a]	598,696	467,470	77,433	22,680	17,801
1951	621,993	465,543	95,157	24,430	18,947
1952[b]	593,955	413,122	121,943	42,147	–

Notes: [a] From 1950, people from Korea are divided into being from 'Korea' or 'South Korea'; [b] 1952 figures include Taiwanese in the 'Chinese' citizenship category.
Source: *Sōri-fu tōkei-kyoku hen* (Statistics Bureau of the Office of the Prime Minister, ed.), *Nihon tōkei nenkan* (Annual Statistics of Japan), *Nihon tōkei kyōkai oyobi Mainichi Shimbun-sha, Shōwa* 27 *nendo oyobi Shōwa* 28 *nendo* (1952 and 1953).

registration system. Table 5.1 provides information on the numbers of people registered as foreigners between 1947 and 1952, that is, from the time that registration commenced until the implementation of the San Francisco Peace Treaty. It should be noted that some persons who were Japanese by birth have also been included here as 'Korean' or 'Taiwanese'.

The voting rights of Korean and Taiwanese people resident in Japan were eroded in various ways. In addition to the previously cited House of Representatives Election Law, both the 'Members of the House of Councillors Election Law' (*Sangiin giin senkyo-hō*) (1947, Law No. 11) and the 'Local Autonomy Law' (*Chihō jichi-hō*) (1947, Law No. 67) stipulated that the right to vote for 'those to whom the Koseki Registration Law does not apply' (*Koseki-hō no tekiyō wo ukenai mono*) would, for the time being, be suspended. In this way, people born as Japanese but regarded as 'persons who require a koseki register entry' in the Korean or Taiwanese koseki registration systems also had their right to vote rescinded.[34] In contrast, Korean or Taiwanese people who had been entered into a mainland koseki register became 'people to whom the Koseki Registration Law applied' (*Koseki-hō no tekiyō wo ukeru mono*), and were thus exempt from registering as foreigners. They were also granted the right to vote. The power of the koseki registration system to transcend personal preference saw individuals categorised as either 'Japanese' or 'foreigner' through an immutable act of administrative decision-making.

'Loss' (*sōshitsu*) of Japanese citizenship for those born in the colonies

The intensification of the Cold War saw an international polarisation of East and West. The resolve of the United States quickly granted Japan a 'generous peace' and thus worked to incorporate this East Asian country into the Western camp. Against this backdrop, Japan and the Allied nations signed the San Francisco Peace Treaty on 8 September 1951. Absent from the signing ceremony were the Republic of Korea (South Korea), the Democratic People's Republic of Korea (North Korea) and the Republic of China (Taiwan). These, of course, were the very countries that had formerly been under Japan's colonial control. While Article 2, parts (a) and (b), of the Treaty stipulated that Japan would recognise the independence of Korea and relinquish all rights, title and claim to Korea and Taiwan, there was no reference to the citizenship of the people in Japan from Korea or Taiwan who had now been formally severed from Japanese jurisdiction.

Decisions relating to citizenship are the province of the relevant sovereign state, and appropriate administration of this (due process) is a function of state law. This is evident from Article 10 of the Constitution of Japan, which reads, 'The conditions necessary for being a Japanese national shall be determined by law'. In addition, as stated in the first section of Chapter Four, from the eighteenth century it had been the practice in the West to accord with the 'non-compulsory principle of citizenship' (*kokuseki hi-kyōsei no gensoku*) regarding changes to citizenship that might occur with geopolitical shifts. That is, strong respect for free will, rather than state imperative, was the logic that informed citizenship changes that resulted when the governance of a territory changed hands. This logic continued to operate internationally into the post-war era.[35]

Japan's post-war citizenship legislation, enacted in 1950, made no provision for any changes to the citizenship of residents that would arise from changes to territorial governance. There was no interest in constructing a legislative framework that would protect Korean and Taiwanese people from the citizenship changes that loomed with the soon-to-be-signed Peace Treaty, in spite of the fact that the daily lives of these people would be plunged into chaos with the abrupt change to domestic citizenship administration and koseki registration governance that would follow the conclusion of the Treaty.

Nine days prior to the Peace Treaty coming into effect on 28 April 1952, the head of the Civil Affairs Bureau of the Office of the Attorney General (*Hōmu fu*, the present-day Ministry of Justice) sent a notification entitled 'Concerning the Citizenship, and Related Administrative Matters, of those such as Korean and Taiwanese People upon the Coming into Effect of the Peace Treaty' (*Heiwa jōyaku hakkō ni shitagau Chōsenjin Taiwanjin tō ni kan suru kokuseki oyobi kokuseki jimu no shori ni tsuite*) (Civil Affairs Item No. 438, hereafter referred to as the 'Civil Affairs Bureau head's notification') to the heads of each regional and provincial department justice office.[36] The relevant extracts are as follows:

1. As a result of this notification, all Korean and Taiwanese people, including those who reside on the Japanese mainland, will lose their Japanese citizenship.
2. *Those people who were previously Korean or Taiwanese and who, for example, married or were adopted by a Japanese person prior to the Peace Treaty coming into effect and were therefore entered into a koseki register of mainland Japan remain mainland Japanese and continue to retain Japanese citizenship without the necessity for any additional administrative processing even after the Treaty comes into effect.*
3. *Those people who were previously mainland Japanese and who, for example, through marriage or being adopted by either a Korean or Taiwanese person, had cause to be removed from a koseki register of mainland Japan remain Korean or Taiwanese* and will lose their Japanese citizenship after the Treaty comes into effect.
4. [...]
5. Following the Treaty coming into effect, it will be necessary for any Korean or Taiwanese person who wishes to take Japanese citizenship to apply as per the procedure for foreigners in general and to naturalise according to the provisions of the Citizenship Law.

   Furthermore, in the case of such naturalisation, Korean or Taiwanese people (this precludes the former mainland Japanese referred to in point 3 above) do not meet the conditions *for 'people who formerly held Japanese citizenship' as per Article 5, Clause 2 of the Citizenship Law, or 'people who lost Japanese citizenship' as per Article 6, Clause 4 of that law.* (emphasis added)

To summarise the above, upon promulgation of the San Francisco Peace Treaty, people who until then had been processed as if entered into either the Korean or Taiwanese koseki registration systems would each lose their Japanese citizenship, while those who were entered into the mainland koseki registration system[37] would be regarded as 'Japanese' and continue to hold Japanese citizenship. On the day of proclamation, a copy of the notification was forwarded to the Chief Cabinet Secretary, each vice-minister, the Director-General of the Supreme Court and the Director-General of the National Personnel Authority.[38]

This Civil Affairs Bureau head's notification provides insights into the Japanese government's understanding of the Peace Treaty. The loss of territories as stipulated in Article 2 of the Peace Treaty also meant that Japan naturally no longer had any jurisdiction over the people attached to those territories. According to the Japanese authorities, these people reverted to whatever status they held prior to colonial governance. In other words, Japan's response assumed that these people once again acquired Korean or Chinese citizenship. However, the following administrative problems arose regarding policy that was based on that assumption.

Firstly, defining the standard by which citizenship changed according to the status indicated on the koseki registration system proved problematic. In other words, although citizenship was decided upon according to koseki registration principles (*koseki-shugi*), mainland Japanese had repeatedly entered, for example, the Korean koseki registration system, and Korean people had repeatedly been removed. As a result, there had been a cumulative effect of mixing 'blood'. This meant that the Korean koseki registration system no longer functioned, as it had prior to colonial rule, as providing evidence of Korean ethnicity. Any claim that people could 'revert to their original status' completely ignored the reality of the conditions created by several decades of interaction during Japanese rule.

Secondly, the notification did not grant to either the Korean or Taiwanese people that it targeted the right of choosing to preserve their Japanese citizenship. That is say, in spite of the fact that in formal constitutional terms people from the colonies were Japanese 'citizens' (*kokumin*), they were forcibly deprived of this citizenship status regardless of personal choice. It is clear from this that the 'sovereignty of the citizen' (*kokumin shuken*) that was so praised by the new Constitution was merely a token concept subject to the state's manipulation.

Thirdly, it was stipulated that those Koreans or Taiwanese who thereby lost their Japanese citizenship and wished to regain this following the promulgation of the Treaty would need to apply for naturalisation in the same manner as any other foreigner in general. In the case of people, and their children, who had formerly held Japanese citizenship, Articles 5 and 6 (currently Articles 6 and 8) of the post-war Citizenship Law stipulated less stringent naturalisation conditions – for example, settled residence of more than three years. However, according to the Civil Affairs Bureau head's notification, these provisions did not apply to Korean or Taiwanese people. That is, those people were denied the preferential treatment accorded to others in the same situation.

What was the attitude of the South Korean government at the time, especially concerning the lack of the right to choose citizenship as highlighted in point 2 above? Records of South Korean delegate notes made at the time of Japan/South Korea meetings were released to the public in 2005, and suggest that the South Korean government did consider raising the matter of citizenship choice. Among the South Korean government documentation prepared for preliminary discussions held between Japan and South Korea from October to December 1952 is an 8 October 1951 paper entitled 'Outline of Agreement of the Citizenship of South Korean People Resident in Japan' (*Zainichi Kankyō no kokuseki ni kan suru kyōtei yōkō*). This paper proposed two options. The first was the restoration of South Korean citizenship for all South Korean people resident in Japan. The second was for South Korean people resident in Japan to apply for South Korean citizenship within three years of the Peace Treaty coming into effect. Concerning the second option, the paper cited 'a precedent in international law concerning citizenship questions similar to the current situation of South Korea'. This referred to the provision made in the Treaty of Versailles following the end of the Great War for people resident in Poland and Czechoslovakia, countries which ceded from Germany after the war, to choose citizenship at that time'.[39]

We will need to wait for the release of the relevant papers to know Japan's response to this suggestion. However, an 11 October 1951 document entitled 'Three Proposals for Consideration in Negotiations with South Korea' (*Taikan sesshō ni tsuite kangaeru san'an*), prepared by the Ministry of Foreign Affairs, suggested that, once Japan assumed independence, the Japanese authorities would regard all Koreans resident in Japan as retaining South Korean citizenship. This was the position assumed in the 1965 'Treaty on Basic Relations Between Japan and the Republic of Korea' (*Nikkan kihon jōyaku*).[40] In a 5 November 1951 rejoinder to the Diet committee charged with consideration of the ratification of the Peace Treaty, Nishimura Kumao (1899–1980), head of the Treaties Bureau of the Ministry of Foreign Affairs, explained that because a Korean person wishing to have Japanese citizenship could be processed through naturalisation procedures, no particular request had been made to the Allies to include a provision in the Peace Treaty making citizenship a matter of choice.[41]

According to Ōnuma Yasu'aki, with the international shifts in territorial control that took place after the Second World War came a trend to cede the right of choice of citizenship to the residents concerned. England had previously controlled the vast colonial holdings of 'the British Empire'. Countries such as India and Pakistan, however, won post-war independence from Great Britain. Giving priority to the decisions of these newly independent former colonies in citizenship matters, the 1948 British Citizenship Law stipulated that former subjects of Great Britain who might have been excluded from the citizenship measures of the newly independent countries could become English citizens in order that no person be made stateless. Furthermore, with the 1947 promulgation of the 'Burma Independence Law' (*Biruma dokuritsu-hō*), care was taken in terms of the acquisition or loss of English citizenship for residents of that country to ensure that those born in English territories outside Burma had the freedom to choose English citizenship.[42]

Although in wartime Europe the people of Austria were forced to take German citizenship following the country's annexation by Germany, this decision was reversed after Austria's independence at the end of the war. With the 1956 introduction of the 'Act of Regulation of Citizenship Matters' (*Kokuseki mondai kisei-hō*), however, West Germany gave Austrian people resident in Germany the right to revert back to German citizenship.[43]

Given these international precedents, it is clear that the matter of citizenship for people from the former colonies demanded a careful democratic response that acknowledged the right of those concerned to relinquish attachment to their homelands and live as Japanese. The matter was nonetheless 'solved' by the Civil Affairs Bureau head's notification to the heads of regional justice offices. This notification, moreover, couched the situation purely in administrative terms. As if the Japanese authorities had been biding their time and lying in wait, 28 April 1952, the very day that the Peace Treaty came into effect, saw the promulgation of the 'Alien Registration Law' (*Gaikokujin tōroku-hō*; 1952, Law No. 125) and the 'Law Related to Measures Arising from Various Ministry of Foreign Affairs Ordinances Based on Matters Relating to Ordinances that Arose Following the Acceptance of the Potsdam Declaration' (*Potsudamu sengen no judaku ni shitagai hassuru meirei ni kan suru ken ni motozuku gaimushō kankei sho-meirei no sochi ni kan suru hōritsu*; 1952, Law No. 126) – legislation relating to matters of immigration and citizenship. These laws stipulated compulsory fingerprinting, effective from 1955, as a necessary condition of alien registration.

As noted by a previous Ministry of Justice bureaucrat, the fixing of ethnic background as 'Korean' or 'Taiwanese' according to the koseki registration system ensured that 'It was easy to identify socially those who should have been categorised as the people of an independent Korea'.[44] Even in the post-war era, citizenship management maximised the use of koseki registration procedures that had been the core of discriminatory governance during the age of empire.

The notion of koseki registration as the wellspring of 'ethnicity' (*minzoku*) arose from a belief that the koseki system of mainland Japan, which had carried over the original information from the old Meiji era Jinshin koseki registration system, provided special proof of being a legitimate 'Japanese'. We might refer to this as 'the idea of koseki as the core principle' (*koseki genri shugi*). However, as previously noted, this so-called legitimacy had crumbled with the mingling of ethnicities that had occurred through events such as marriage during the era of colonial control. Nevertheless, from the critical perspective of rebuilding Japan as a sovereign state, 'the idea of koseki as the core principle' became the key notion in the post-war reconstruction of the entity known as a 'Japanese'. This was in spite of the fact that this core principle conflicted with both the ideals of the new Constitution and international precedent.

'Settlement' through the 1961 Supreme Court ruling

Once the Peace Treaty had come into effect, however, the Civil Affairs Bureau head's notification was not necessarily the golden rule invoked in governance or judicial matters related to citizenship changes among mainland Japanese, Koreans or Taiwanese. Other official determinations also played a part.

On 29 February 1954, the Tokyo District Court ruled as follows: 'Concerning ethnic Koreans who achieved independence according to Article 2 (a) of the Peace Treaty, these are those who were Korean people, that is people who held Korean citizenship, at the time of annexation and the children of these people'. However, 'a woman who married a Japanese man after annexation did not become a Korean citizen at the time of the Peace Treaty', and as further illuminated by the condition that she 'must be a resident of Korea who is residing in Korea at the time of the Peace Treaty', a woman not residing in Korea at that time 'was not in essence a Korean resident'. She therefore 'cannot be regarded as having gained Korean citizenship and lost Japanese citizenship at the time that the Peace Treaty came into effect'. Against this was an alternate judgment that ruled that since at the time of the acceptance of the Potsdam Declaration and the 2 September 1945 signing of the Instrument of Surrender Korea and Taiwan were removed from Japanese control, both Koreans and Taiwanese at that point lost Japanese citizenship.[45]

These shifting legal rulings terminated, however, with a 5 April 1961 Supreme Court decision. This ruling concerned a woman who, although born as a mainland Japanese, lost her Japanese citizenship upon entry into the Korean koseki registration system. The Supreme Court dismissed her appeal against this loss on the assumption that a change of citizenship accompanied a change of territory. With the conclusion of the Peace Treaty, Japan 'lost all jurisdiction over people registered in Korea'. Accordingly, 'those registered in Korea lost Japanese citizenship'. The court further stated that 'a Korean person' was a 'person who had been registered in the Korean koseki registration' system, and ruled that this was consistent with the interpretation of the Peace Treaty based on 'koseki registration principles'.[46] Rather than the lived reality place of residence as given in the Tokyo court ruling cited above, this 'interpretation of the Peace Treaty' determined that legitimacy to reside was to be found in an entry in a koseki register. Here 'koseki register' was nothing more than a synonym for the *ie* family of the Meiji Civil Code. It is no exaggeration to say that this ruling was completely inconsistent with the legal principles informing the post-war democratic reforms that underpinned the post-war Civil Code, Koseki Registration Law and Citizenship Law, each of which had been revised in relation to the new Constitution.

Reference was made in this book's Introduction to the unsuccessful citizenship appeal lodged in the Japanese courts by Kim Myeonggwan. This appeal challenged both the Japanese government's treatment of Kim's case and the associated interpretation of the Constitution by the courts. The four key elements of the case can be summarised as follows.

1. The appeal questioned the validity of rulings that declared that an individual's right to be granted citizenship depended on her or his status as recorded in the koseki registration system. Kim argued that this ruling violated Article 14 of the post-war Constitution, which stipulated equality of all individuals under the law.
2. Kim further argued that the principle factor influencing pre-war government and in turn court rulings of the time was the *ie* family system, which required a person's legal status to relate to their family. This notion, the appellant noted, had been discredited by Article 24 of the post-war Constitution. The new post-war Citizenship Law, revised in accordance with the abolition of the *ie* family system as stipulated in Article 24, abolished the need for an individual to automatically change citizenship as a result of a change to koseki registration.
3. Citizenship, the appellant noted, conferred various rights such as suffrage, the right to work as a public servant and the right to receive public benefits. Until legal revisions that accompanied Japan's entry to the Convention Relating to the Status of Refugees (1981), most social security legislation, particularly the 'National Pension Act' (*Kokumin nenkin-hō*), determined the provision of benefits based on citizenship.[47] Accordingly, citizenship was the legal matter that ultimately determined the fate of the treatment of the people of Japan. Any disadvantageous ruling in this respect, particularly a ruling made without consideration of the wish of the individual involved, was therefore a monumental determination that

violated the right to the pursuit of happiness as stipulated in Article 13 of the Constitution.

4. The appellant argued that determining changes to the citizenship of an individual in a manner that did not accord with legislation was a clear violation of Article 10 of the Constitution. Furthermore, from the international perspective, such a ruling also violated Article 2 of the Hague Convention on Citizenship which stipulated that 'Any question as to whether a person possesses the nationality of a particular State shall be determined in accordance with the law of the State'. The Preamble to the Peace Treaty, furthermore, noted that 'Japan for its part declares its intention [...] And in all circumstances [...] To strive to realise the objectives of the Universal Declaration of Human Rights'. Article 15 of this Universal Declaration of Human Rights proclaims that 'everyone has the right to a nationality and that no one shall be arbitrarily deprived of his [sic] nationality nor denied the right to change nationality'. Since the Japanese government's citizenship (that is, nationality) processes ran counter to this proclamation, it was clear, Kim argued, that Japan had failed to meet its obligations under international law.

Various other contradictions were evident in rulings by the Japanese courts. For example, it is difficult to accept the Supreme Court's claim that the citizenship of Taiwanese people was lost on 5 August 1952, the day on which the Treaty of Taipei between Japan and the People's Republic of China was concluded (ruling of the Full Bench of the Supreme Court of Japan, 5 December 1962).[48] This ruling was based on the fact that the Treaty of Taipei stipulated that the citizenship of Taiwanese people would revert to that of the People's Republic of China. While there might be some logic in rescinding the Japanese citizenship of these people when citizenship of the People's Republic was restored, determining that this occurred in conjunction with the Treaty of Taipei contradicts the interpretation that Korean people lost citizenship concurrent with the Peace Treaty.

Once the Peace Treaty came into effect, it was argued that the previously cited Civil Affairs Bureau head's notification set a legal and governance precedent related to previous colonial holdings which provided 'a coherent interpretation established by our country [Japan]'.[49] Yet, the contradictions outlined above suggest that, rather than providing coherence, the Japanese government implemented a series of random policies based on the koseki registration of people of the former colonies. This inconsistent policy stance also influenced citizenship determinations. Opportunistic political decision-making of this nature ultimately produced a category of 'helpless people with no avenue of appeal to the state' (*mukoku no tami*). Clearly, koseki registration, a chief legal and governance restraint of the colonial era, continued to control the fates of Korean people, Taiwanese people and also Japanese people into the post-war era.

Post-war Japanese repatriation and koseki registration

Koseki registration and citizenship of Karafuto returnees

As noted above, unlike Korea and Taiwan, more than ninety percent of the Karafuto (post-war Sakhalin) population was made up of mainland Japanese, and thus, the mainland koseki registration system had operated there. As apparent from Table 4.2 on page 173, there was also a strong presence in Karafuto of people from other imperial territories such as Korea.

Karafuto came under Soviet control in the very last days of the Second World War. The repatriation of mainland Japanese from Karafuto, now Sakhalin, began in December 1946, following a Soviet-United States accord regarding repatriation from Soviet controlled precincts. The vast majority of those repatriated had their *honseki* addresses on Karafuto. How, then, was their koseki registration managed once this former colonial holding ceased to be a territory of Japan? Article 2, Clause C of the Peace Treaty stated that Japan renounced all titular rights and claims to the Kurile Islands and to former Karafuto. However, as with the people of Korea and Taiwan, no provision was made regarding citizenship for the residents of former Karafuto or the Kurile Islands. The 19 April 1952 Civil Affairs Bureau head's notification noted that, with Japan's loss of control over the Kurile Islands and Karafuto after the promulgation of the Peace Treaty, those with a *honseki* address in those sites would not lose their Japanese citizenship. They would, however, 'lose their *honseki* address and it would therefore be necessary to introduce a provision for them *to create a new koseki register record through the Koseki Registration Law*' (emphasis added).

In other words, as a result of the Peace Treaty coming into effect, the people of former Karafuto lost the legal efficacy of their previous

Karafuto *honseki* addresses and found themselves in the complicated situation of maintaining their Japanese citizenship while having no koseki registration. In other words, they held no documentary 'proof' (*shōmei*) of Japanese citizenship. As noted in the second section of Chapter Four, in terms of the mainland Koseki Registration Law, both mainland Japanese and Ainu people (also regarded in this instance as mainland Japanese) had held *honseki* addresses in Karafuto. While the Peace Treaty deprived these people of koseki registration, in terms of the mainland Koseki Registration Law they had the right to create a new koseki register record.

From its commencement at the end of 1946 until declared 'concluded' by the Soviet authorities in June 1949, the Karafuto/ Sakhalin repatriation process saw approximately 300,000 mainland Japanese return home. Given their special circumstances, the Family Court gave permission for a simplification of the usual application process for koseki record creation for those among the 300,000 former Karafuto residents whose koseki registration had been lost. In spite of having also been registered in Karafuto, however, Japanese women from Karafuto who had married Korean men prior to the promulgation of the Peace Treaty became 'Korean' through Law of Mutuality stipulations regarding 'membership of an ethnic group' transfer. In terms of the Civil Affairs Bureau head's notification, these people were treated as not having Japanese citizenship and therefore were unable to access the simplified processes available to other former Japanese for citizenship restoration.[50]

In addition to mainland Japanese, Ainu and other aboriginal people (the Karafuto *dojin* of the pre-war era) were also among those repatriated. Since Ainu people were subject to the application of mainland koseki procedures and dealt with in the same manner as mainland Japanese, they did not lose their Japanese citizenship when the Peace Treaty came into effect. As noted above, furthermore, those Ainu people who had lost their Karafuto *honseki* address were also given the right to create a new mainland koseki register record.[51]

Problems arose, however, in the case of the Karafuto *dojin*. As noted above, while Karafuto territories were not subject to Japanese law, under Japanese control these people were treated as *gaichijin*. Since they were therefore not subject to the application of the Koseki Registration Law, they were merely recorded in the 'aboriginal people's household roll' (*dojin kokōbo*) and denied the right to hold a *honseki* address either in Karafuto or on the Japanese mainland. Since also considered to be outside the application of the Japanese Citizenship Law, administrative decisions concerning the citizenship of these people were made on the grounds of custom and reason. This situation, however, changed on 2 and 3 February 1956, when the Ministry of Justice gave permission for repatriated aboriginal people from Karafuto to apply for the creation of a new koseki record on mainland Japan.[52]

Creation of a new koseki register record is an administrative process permitted to those who are not registered in spite of holding Japanese citizenship. We might interpret the Japanese government's concession that the aboriginal people of Karafuto were qualified to create a new koseki record as an attempt to avoid discriminating between these people and mainland Japanese or Ainu by acknowledging the right of Karafuto aboriginal people to hold Japanese citizenship after the promulgation of the Peace Treaty. However, the Civil Affairs Bureau head's notification referred to above stipulated koseki registration as the criterion for identifying the 'people who were attached' to the territories ceded by Japan as a condition of the Peace Treaty. Given that the aboriginal people of Karafuto were not registered in the mainland koseki registration system, they fell into the same koseki administrative category as Koreans and Taiwanese. Why, then, did the notification discriminate so unreasonably against only Koreans and Taiwanese by forcing them to relinquish their Japanese citizenship? Ultimately, the Japanese government's favourable treatment of repatriated aboriginal people from Karafuto, who were very few in number compared to Korean people, was nothing more than expedient opportunism.

Yet another problem that arose in the context of repatriation from Karafuto was the fact that many Koreans were abandoned there without any means of returning to their homeland. At the war's end, approximately 43,000 Korean people were resident in Karafuto, the majority of whom had been mobilised either through official mediation by government-sponsored labour agents (*kan assen*) or forced labour recruitment (*chōyō*) at the direction of the Japanese government. In spite of the fact that they continued to hold Japanese citizenship, these Koreans were excluded from the 1946–1949 repatriation of Japanese from Karafuto. In the Soviet-Japanese Joint Declaration of 1956, however, it was agreed that Korean men married to Japanese women could be repatriated with their wives at the time that Japanese citizens interned in Siberia were returned to their home country.

Although they lost Japanese citizenship on 28 April 1952, Korean people in this situation undoubtedly received favourable treatment as the 'spouses of Japanese' (*Nihonjin no haigū-sha*). The benevolent hand of the Japanese state, however, could in the final instance only be extended to Koreans who were members of a Japanese *ie* family.

The Chishima (Kuril) Archipelago presented the 'Northern Territories Dispute' (*Hoppō ryōdo mondai*), with the ownership of a number of islands in this chain remaining a subject of dispute between Russia and Japan today. As noted above, the four islands of Kunashiri, Etorofu, Habomai and Shikotan became Japanese territory following the 1875 conclusion of the Chishima-Karafuto Exchange Treaty between Russia and Japan. These territories, however, were occupied by the Soviets between August and September 1945, after which Soviet and then Russian authorities assumed effective control. The Japanese government, however, maintained that Peace Treaty conditions requiring Japan to withdraw from the Kurils did not apply to those islands referred to as the 'Northern Territories'.

Accordingly, the Habomai Archipelago (which includes Taraku Island, Shibatsu Island, Akiyuri Island and Suishō Island) is regarded as part of the City of Nemuro. In March 1969, the Ministry of Justice approved the establishment of *honseki* addresses in the Habomai region.[53] The Koseki Registration Law applies in those regions of Japan stipulated in the territorial principle (*zokuchi-hō*). Therefore, places in which a *honseki* address can be determined are, by definition, Japanese territory. Promulgated on 31 August 1982, on the assumption that 'Japan has ownership of the Northern Territories', the 'Law Relating to the Special Treatment for the Acceleration of a Solution to Matters Such As the Northern Territories Dispute' (*Hoppō ryōdo mondai tō no kaiketsu no sokushin no tame no tokubetsu shochi ni kan suru hōritsu*) (1982, Law No. 85) approved the establishment of *honseki* addresses on an additional three islands and six villages outside the Habomai Archipelago.[54] We can interpret the introduction of laws authorising koseki registration procedures in these territories as a declaration to the international community that ownership resides with Japan.

Koseki registration and citizenship of Manchoukuo returnees

On 17 August 1945, subsequent to the 9 August invasion by the Soviet military, the Manchoukuo National Council (*kokumuin*) moved the dissolution of Manchoukuo. The following day, 18 August, Emperor (*kōtei*) Puyi, declared both his own abdication and the dissolution of Manchoukuo. At the time, there were 1,550,000 Japanese people living in Manchoukuo, including 250,000 in the Kwantung Leased Territory.[55] As noted in the fifth section of Chapter Four, Japanese people resident in Manchoukuo retained Japanese citizenship in principle. They also continued to hold mainland koseki registration, which was, above everything else, proof of Japanese citizenship. This continued to be administered by Japan even after the abolition of Japan's extraterritorial rights in Manchoukuo. Japanese had been permitted to register in the people's register (*minseki*) that was the status record in Manchoukuo. They were, in fact, actively encouraged to register through the 1942 Manchoukuo directive entitled 'Matters Related to the Special Case of the Creation of New People's Register Records for Japanese People Resident in Manchoukuo' (*Manshū-koku ni zaijū suru Nihonjin no shūseki no tokurei ni kan suru ken*). This, however, did not provide proof of being a 'citizen of Manchoukuo'. In 1956, the Ministry of Justice Civil Affairs Bureau confirmed that an entry in the people's register of Manchoukuo had no influence on Japanese citizenship status.[56]

As a sovereign state protecting 'its own citizens' (*ji-kokumin*), Japan assumed responsibility for those Japanese who were repatriated following the dissolution of Manchoukuo. Repatriation commenced in 1946 when more than 1,000,000 people returned home from Huludao. However, with factors such as rising Cold War tensions and other international shifts, including the Chinese Communist Party victory in the civil war against the Nationalists, there was no formal recommencement of relations with the People's Republic of China after its establishment in 1949. Repatriation therefore became problematic from that point forward. Although not all Japanese had returned to their homeland, as stipulated in the 'Act on Special Measures for Unrepatriated Persons' (*Mi-kikan-sha ni kan suru tokubetsu sochi-hō*) (1959, Law No. 7), Japanese authorities declared the repatriation project closed in 1959. Based on Article 30 of the Civil Code, a system of 'Adjudication of Death at Wartime' (*Senji shibō senkoku*) was then adopted. This permitted the state (the Minister of Health and Welfare) to categorise all people who had not yet returned to Japan, and those whose status as living or dead was unknown, as 'deceased persons' (*shibōsha*).[57] As a result, approximately 14,000 migrants, who had previously been despatched to Manchoukuo as pioneers to open land, were classified as 'deceased persons'. These people received no assistance to return to their homeland and lost the protection of the Japanese state. Stripped of their status as 'Japanese' through erasure from the koseki registration system, these former pioneer immigrants effectively became 'abandoned people' (*kimin*).

Nineteen seventy-two saw the normalisation of relations between the People's Republic of China and Japan. Almost ten years later, in 1981, the Ministry of Health and Welfare (currently the Ministry of Health, Labour and Welfare), began to support the mass return of 'Japanese people left behind in China' (*Chūgoku zanryū hōjin*; referred to by the Japanese authorities as either '*zanryū koji*', orphans left behind, or '*zanryū fujin*', women left behind). Having lost Japanese koseki registration, these people were processed upon entry into Japan as 'foreigners'.[58]

Some among these returnees, declared as 'wartime dead', had been erased from the koseki registration system. To revive their 'Japanese' status, they needed to apply to the Family Court for the dissolution of their 'wartime deceased' status. Once validity was confirmed and their applications were approved, koseki registration was reinstated.[59] Some without proof of identity, however, had their applications declined. On the assumption that they did indeed hold Japanese citizenship, these people were able to apply to create a new koseki record. Once this was approved, Japanese citizenship was restored through reinstatement of koseki registration. Approximately 1,250 people had Japanese citizenship restored in this way.[60] Regardless of the method deployed, it was important for an applicant who had lost their koseki registration to confirm blood relations with a Japanese relative. The testimonies of those relatives became the foundation of confirmation of an applicant's identity.

In the context of the need for the testimony of next-of-kin, the state demonstrated reluctance to accept the 'Japanese' identity of 'Japanese left behind in the Philippines' (*Firipin zanryū Nihonjin*). These were often the children of Japanese men who had gone to the Philippines in the pre-war era and had a child with a Filipino woman. Since the father generally had either died during the war or had left no personal details upon returning to Japan and could therefore not be contacted, there was no way of confirming the relationship between the Japanese father and the child. The reliance on *jus sanguinis* and blood relations in the Japanese Citizenship Law resulted in these people being denied Japanese citizenship.

With no koseki record to prove a blood relationship with their father, members of this group sought approval to acquire Japanese citizenship through the creation of a new koseki record. This approval was eventually granted in 2006, and since then Filipino 'left behind' Japanese have had the right to apply to the Family Court for the creation of a new koseki record.

From a certain perspective, therefore, the problem of 'Japanese left behind overseas' (*zanryū hōjin*) was essentially a problem of the koseki registration of people who had been 'outside' Japan. When despatched as an instrument of national policy to open up a different land, these people were bound to the koseki registration system and regarded as 'Japanese'. It is highly ironic that the entity that excluded these people from the repatriation project and that stripped those who remained overseas of their koseki registration was the very Japanese government that had despatched the former immigrants 'outside' Japan in the first place. Citizenship was often considered the legal process that tied one politically and spiritually to the state. It is clear from this example, however, that the way in which citizenship decisions were made through the opportunistic mediation of koseki registration ensured that this was a fragile tie. Those bound in this way could easily be set adrift by the state in times of crisis.

Post-war Okinawa and koseki registration: 'Japanese' again

Post-war Okinawa as a site of different law

For almost three decades after the end of the war, Okinawa was governed by the United States. In other words, these islands were outside Japanese administrative control. What was koseki registration and what did it mean to be 'Japanese' in Okinawa during that period? Okinawa fell into the hands of the United States military in June 1945, following the United States victory in the land battle of Okinawa. On 31 March 1945, immediately prior to landing on Okinawa, the Americans issued the First United States Navy Military Government Proclamation (the so-called Nimitz Proclamation). This declared the cessation of Japanese governance of Okinawa and the assumption by a United States military government of all administrative powers related to the governance of and jurisdiction over the residents.

From the time that Japanese governance ceased until the 1972 reversion of the islands to Japan proper (*hondo*), 'Okinawa Prefecture' was officially known as 'Ryūkyū' (for convenience, however, the remainder of this chapter uses the term 'Okinawa'). The administration of Okinawa during the United States Occupation occurred indirectly through the hegemony of the 'United States Civil Administration of the Ryūkyū Islands' (*Ryūkyū Beikoku minseifu*, hereafter referred to as the 'Civil Administration'), established in October 1950 following a reorganisation of the United States military government. A Civil Administration ordinance of 11 April 1952 determined the 'Government of the Ryūkyū Islands' (*Ryūkyū seifu*) as the body governing the residents of Okinawa under the guidance of the Civil Administration.

Although when the San Francisco Peace Treaty came into effect on 28 April 1952 Japan resumed its status as a sovereign state, Article 3 of the Treaty declared Okinawa to be subject to continued United States governance. While the United States acknowledged Japan's 'latent sovereignty' (*senzai shuken*), this was merely a token gesture. It was the authority of the governing Americans that gave power to the laws and ordinances implemented in Okinawa during that time. In other words, the islands were in reality governed by the laws of the United States of America.[61]

Since Okinawa was a 'region with a different law' (*ihō chi'iki*), in which Japanese legal proclamations and governance rights had no validity, koseki administration in Okinawa, too, naturally came under the administrative systems of the United States. The Nimitz Proclamation had fundamentally acknowledged the continuation in Okinawa of the laws and regulations that operated at the time of its declaration. Therefore, the former Civil Code and former Koseki Registration Law, which operated in Okinawa at the commencement of the United States Occupation, remained in effect.[62] Following the January 1948 introduction of a new Civil Code and Koseki Registration Law in Japan proper (*hondo*), Okinawa's Koseki Registration Law became invalid in Japan proper. This saw municipal heads in Okinawa lose responsibility for the carriage of koseki registration matters in their jurisdictions.

On 15 July 1945, just prior to the end of the war, the 'Office for Dealing with the Administration of Each City, Town and Village Municipality in Okinawa Prefecture' (*Okinawa ken-nai kaku-shiyakusho oyobi chōsonyakuba jimu toriatsukai-sho*), had been established in Fukuoka. In October 1948, this became the 'Okinawa Related Koseki Register Administration Office' (*Okinawa kankei koseki jimusho*). Restructured with no name change in October 1953 – that is, after the Peace Treaty came into effect – this became the office that administered koseki registration matters of Japan proper residents who held a *honseki* address in Okinawa. In this way, the Japanese government took care not to loosen the koseki registration system as the tie that bound 'Japanese' to Okinawa, even while the islands were under occupied governance.

Okinawans' Japanese citizenship and the 'temporary register'

How, then, was citizenship managed for those who lived under the United States Occupation of Okinawa? In its 'Memorandum Related to the Registration of Korean, Chinese, Ryūkyūans and Taiwanese' (*Chōsenjin, Chūgokujin, Ryūkyūjin oyobi Taiwanjin no tōroku ni kan suru oboegaki*) issued on 17 February 1946 (SCAPIN-746), the Occupation authorities canvassed the possibility, in relation to repatriation and depending on the stipulations of a future peace treaty, of rescinding the Japanese citizenship of the residents of Okinawa. It was thought that this could be done by distinguishing 'Okinawan' (*Ryūkyūjin*) from Japanese proper in the same way as had occurred in relation to Koreans and Taiwanese. However, the consistent opinion of the Department of State and the United States government was that, before or after the promulgation of any treaty, the people who lived in Okinawa should retain Japanese citizenship.[63]

The opinion of the Japanese authorities, reaffirmed after the Peace Treaty's conclusion, was that the residents of Okinawa held Japanese citizenship. Unlike Korea or Taiwan, Okinawa had undergone no change of territorial jurisdiction. Therefore, the citizenship of people who held a *honseki* address in that location would not change regardless of Peace Treaty conditions. Acquisition or loss of Japanese citizenship in Okinawa was thus determined in accordance with Japanese citizenship legislation.[64] Even Article 3 of the previously discussed 19 April 1952 Civil Affairs Bureau head's notification stipulated that '[Those who hold a *honseki* address in Okinawa] will not lose their Japanese citizenship when the Peace Treaty comes into effect and may therefore continue to hold a *honseki* address in that region [Okinawa]'.

In Okinawa, however, the actual koseki register documentation that provided crucial proof of Japanese citizenship had been reduced to ashes. With the extensive war damage incurred during both the October 1944 bombing raids on Okinawa and the land battles that followed the United States invasion of April 1945, all originals and copies of the koseki register records of the main islands of Okinawa, with the exception of Miyako and Ishigaki, had been obliterated.

Given the imperative to manage and collect information from the people of Okinawa, and also to distribute rations, the Civil Administration undertook the task of reconstructing the Okinawan koseki registration system. Because there was an urgent need firstly to gather information on the actual whereabouts of Okinawan residents, the head of the Office of Administrative Services of the Civil Administration (*Minseifu sōmubu-chō*) sent a notice on 19 September 1946 entitled 'Outline of the Management of Administration of the Temporary Koseki Register' (*Rinji 'koseki jimu toriatsukai yōkō*), which led to the compilation of a 'temporary koseki register' (*Rinji koseki*). Although, like the original koseki registration system, the temporary register centred on the legal household head (*koshu*), with the 'household' (*ko*) as the unit of compilation, the focus was on shared residence and the people who lived in a certain administrative district. Thus, the temporary koseki registration system involved registration of a person regardless of whether or not they held a *honseki* address or even Japanese citizenship. Furthermore, in the case of the legal head of the household not currently being in residence, the register record was compiled around the head of the resident unit (*setai-nushi*) as a household roll. A notification sent on 5 March 1947 by the head of the General Administration Bureau of the Civil Administration, entitled 'Matters Concerning the Administrative Treatment of the Koseki Register' (*Koseki jimu toriatsukai ni kansuru ken*), also made a provision for the compilation of a household roll with the people in a residence (*setai*) as the unit, in addition to a koseki register record with the actual '*ko*' household as the unit. In this way, the Okinawan temporary koseki registration system was more a resident registration system than a status registration system.[65]

The compilation of the temporary koseki register in Okinawa arose from the realistic objective of creating a register to assist the United States military to distribute rations. The information was also needed to facilitate the military's conscription of labour. Since many Okinawan people had been reduced to living in reception camps, the authorities were forced to gather data according to residential location. These records also effectively became a register of those who remained alive after the war.[66]

In Okinawa, the devastation of total war had been even more acute than in Japan proper. The death or disappearance of many legal household heads disrupted notions of *ie* family and *honseki* address, making a record complied around the unit of the '*setai*', of people currently living together, the most effective means of gaining information about Okinawa's residents. The necessity of this adjustment also exposed the complete inadequacy of the notion of '*honseki* address' during times of crisis such as wartime devastation. Thus, those with no *honseki* address and even foreigners were recorded on the temporary koseki register of Okinawa, which held information that was completely contrary to the original intent of koseki registration in Japan.

Okinawan koseki register as the 'Ryūkyūan register'

In occupied Okinawa, residents were 'Japanese' in terms of citizenship. Regarding Okinawan laws and ordinances, however, they were referred to as 'Ryūkyūans' (*Ryūkyūjin*). If an Okinawan resident travelled overseas, the term 'Ryūkyūan' was recorded on their visa.[67] To whom did this term refer, exactly? A definition of the term 'Ryūkyūan' was made arbitrarily by the United States. On 29 February 1952, the Civil Administration announced Proclamation No. 6, entitled 'Provisions for the Government of the Ryūkyū Islands' (*Ryūkyū seifu shōten*), which stipulated the legal position of those residents of Okinawa over whom the United States exercised control. Article 3 stated as follows:

> *A Ryūkyūan shall be a natural person whose birth and name are recorded in a family register in the Ryūkyū Islands,* provided that no family register record shall be transferred into the Ryūkyū Islands without authority of the Deputy Governor and no person who is a national of any foreign state other than Japan or who is a stateless person may be registered except in accordance with the provisions of law. (emphasis added)[68]

For the time being, a person with a *honseki* address in occupied Okinawa was a 'resident of the Ryūkyū Islands' (*Ryūkyū jūmin*), who nonetheless retained Japanese citizenship. However, the 'family register in the Ryūkyū Islands' (*Ryūkyū no koseki-bō*) mentioned here referred to the 'temporary register' (*rinji koseki*). Thus, the range of 'residents of the Ryūkyū Islands' naturally expanded to transcend nationality.

What, then, was the response to people who held a *honseki* address in Okinawa while residing outside Okinawa Prefecture? Repatriation to Okinawa commenced in August 1946. Since the Meiji era, there had been a history of waves of migration from Okinawa to both North and South America and also to South East Asia. By 1938, there were 72,745 Okinawan people living as migrants overseas. This included 20,000 people in Hawai'i and 14,000 people in Brazil. These figures amounted to twelve percent of the total population of Okinawa.[69] According to the stipulations of 'Provisions for the Government of the Ryūkyū Islands', referred to above, having a *honseki* address in Okinawa was furthermore proof that a person who had been repatriated back to Okinawa was indeed a 'resident of the Ryūkyū Islands'.

With Okinawa under United States control, the coming and going of people between Okinawa and Japan proper of course gave rise to the need for a process of 'immigration control' (*shutsunyū-koku kanri*). There was particular urgency concerning the question of whether or not an individual could be legally regarded as a 'Ryūkyūan' (*Ryūkyūjin*). Thus, on 7 January 1953, the 'Ordinance for Control of Entry and Exit of Individuals Into and From the Ryūkyū Islands' (*Ryūkyū rettō shutsunyū kanri rei*) was proclaimed as a means of regulating the entry into and departure from the islands of 'non-Ryūkyūans' (*hi-Ryūkyūjin*). Article 4 of this ordinance defined a 'person who is a resident of the Ryūkyū Islands' (*Ryūkyū rettō kyojūsha*), that is a 'Ryūkyūan', as 'a person who has continuously resided in the Ryūkyū Islands south of the 29 degrees parallel north since prior to 2 September 1945 who has an address in the Ryūkyū Islands that was registered in the *koseki registration system*, or who has been permitted, or who will be permitted, by the Deputy Governor of the Civil Administration to be in the Ryūkyū Islands since 2 September 1945, with a view to permanent residence'.[70] That is to say, the definition of 'Ryūkyūan' given by the Civil Administration was fundamentally either that of a person who had resided in Okinawa since before the war, or one who had a fixed address in Okinawa with a view to future permanent residence. Whether or not one had a *honseki* address in Okinawa, without receiving approval to take up permanent residence from the Civil Administration, those repatriated either from Japan proper or overseas or those who resided in Japan proper were regarded as 'non-Ryūkyūan'. However, 11 February 1954 revisions to the Ordinance for Control of Entry and Exit of Individuals Into and From the Ryūkyū Islands (United States Civil Administration Ordinance No. 125) saw the definition of 'resident of the Ryūkyū Islands' modified to become persons who held a *honseki* address in Okinawa and also those who currently resided there. This definition rejected the fundamental principle of the Japanese koseki registration system, which saw only the *honseki* address, a fixed address with no necessary relationship to an individual's residential address, as the standard for registration. Through their insistence that in the Ryūkyū Islands a record of the residential address was as necessary as a record of the *honseki* address, the Civil Administration created the unique entity referred to as the 'Ryūkyūan'.

We can perhaps best understand the unusual characteristics of koseki registration in occupied Okinawa by considering the fact that a person who held a *honseki* address in Japan proper was restricted in transferring that address to Okinawa. According to Civil Administration Ordinance (*Minseifu shirei*) No. 6, based on Article 3 of the Provisions for the Government of the Ryūkyū Islands, a person registered in Japan proper who wished to transfer their registration to Okinawa, or a person registered in Japan proper who wished to decide upon a new *honseki* address through marriage with or adoption by a resident of Okinawa, required the approval of the Deputy Governor of the United States Civil Administration.[71]

These restrictions on the transfer of koseki registration from Japan proper to Okinawa were the result of the Civil Administration's desire to keep koseki transfer to a bare minimum as a means of managing population growth and economic issues.[72] From 1951 to 1954, the population of Okinawa increased by twenty-five to thirty percent.[73] In addition to the problem of food supply for a population in excess of 800,000 people, the Civil Administration was faced with the pressing issue in 1954 of 5,900 unemployed people with absolutely no prospect of work.[74] The policy can also be seen as a tactic, in response to heightening Cold War tensions, to prevent the entry of Communist activists into Okinawa.[75] From around 1953, the campaign calling for the reversion of Okinawa to Japanese jurisdiction began to gather momentum. In July 1954, two Amami-born members of the Okinawa People's Party, which was active in the reversion campaign, were designated as 'undesirable foreigners' (*konomashikarazaru gaikokujin* [*hi-Ryūkyūjin*]) and ordered to leave Okinawa.[76] There is no doubt that Cold War and reversion movement political tensions were instrumental in the development of koseki registration transfer policies of the time.

However, restrictions on transferring a Japan proper koseki register record to Okinawa led to the creation of people in Japan proper without koseki registration. Applications for a transfer of Japan proper registration to Okinawa were directed to Japan proper municipal heads. If the applicant was approved, the person in question was removed from the relevant Japan proper koseki register. However, for the transfer to be completed, it was necessary to have the permission of the Deputy Governor of the Civil Administration in Okinawa. If this permission was not granted, the head of the relevant municipality in Okinawa was unable to create a new koseki record and the transfer could not proceed. Having already been removed from the Japan proper koseki registration system, the individual became a person without koseki registration (*mukoseki-sha*).[77] In April 1959, there was a loosening of procedures for people who had previously been registered in Okinawa and who were currently registered in Japan proper. This change permitted applicants to transfer a *honseki* address after, rather than before, entering Okinawa and receiving permission to take permanent residence.[78]

The restrictions on koseki transfer between Okinawa and Japan proper bring to the fore the fact that no unified system of law connected the temporary koseki registration system of Okinawa and the koseki registration system of Japan proper. In territories under Japanese jurisdiction in which the post-war Koseki Registration Law was implemented, a Japanese person could arbitrarily transfer a *honseki* address to any place within that jurisdiction. The restrictions that operated between Okinawa and Japan proper, on the other hand, recalled the policies of the 'Greater Japanese Empire'. Koseki registration transfer between colonies, such as Korea or Taiwan, and the mainland (*naichi*) – that is, between different regions in which different koseki registration laws and ordinances applied – had been forbidden at that time. The Okinawan koseki registration system, too, operated according to a unique system, similar to the imperial era mainland koseki registration system. Each differed from the post-war koseki registration system.

Japan's power as a sovereign state to determine the qualifications of its own citizens did not extend to Okinawa. Thus, rather than providing proof of being 'Japanese', the Okinawan koseki registration system, in fact, provided proof that a 'Ryūkyūan' was subject to the governance of the United States. In other words, while the territory's record of status might have been referred to as the 'Ryūkyū register' (*Ryūkyū-seki*), the territory was effectively an independent state with the legal range of 'Ryūkyūan' being determined by United States initiative. In this sense, the koseki registration system in Okinawa failed to achieve its role of providing proof of being 'Japanese' based on the putatively sacrosanct notion of bloodline.

Reversion movement and Okinawan koseki system reconstruction

As noted above, the legal sphere of the 'Ryūkyūan' who was the subject of governance by the United States was fundamentally based on the information provided in the temporary koseki registration system. However, not only did the temporary registration system randomly record Okinawan residents in a manner that was unrelated to *honseki* address or nationality, there were also notable omissions and false entries that made it unreliable as a means of status authentication. Furthermore, the August 1953 Amami Archipelago Reversion Declaration created a need for the authorities to be able to clearly distinguish between Amami residents and residents of the Ryūkyū Islands. The Okinawan government therefore set about fundamentally reconstructing the Okinawan koseki registration system.

There was a further important motivation for the reconstruction of an Okinawan koseki registration system. The 'Act on Relief of War Victims and Survivors' (*Senshōbyōsha senbotsusha izoku tō engo-hō*), which came into effect in Japan proper from April 1952 (1952, Law No. 127), and laws relating to the support for war victims such as military pensions which were revived in August 1953, applied also to the people of Okinawa. Applications for funds such as pension and condolence monies called for proof of identity based on koseki register entries.[79] Okinawa had been a tragic theatre of war and there was a pressing demand for the reconstruction of a legitimate koseki registration system in order to facilitate receipt of benefit entitlements. Eligibility to apply for these benefits in terms of the Act on Relief of War Victims and Survivors stipulated the provision requiring koseki registration in addition to citizenship. In other words, this law only applied to those to whom the Koseki Registration Law applied. Once the Peace Treaty came into effect, therefore, those who were Korean or Taiwanese were denied the support for victims of war provided by this legislation. The issue arose in Okinawa, too, of whether or not the former Koseki Registration Law, which continued to operate in that territory at the time, would be problematic in terms of eligibility for benefits. However, the Japanese government determined that because the residents of Okinawa held Japanese citizenship, their applications would be approved. This was in spite of the fact that the koseki legislation that applied at that time in Okinawa was the former Koseki Registration Law that had ceased to operate in Japan proper. In this sense, the people of Okinawa were regarded in principle as 'persons to whom the Koseki Registration Law applied'.[80]

However, reconstructing the original contents of the Okinawan koseki documentation, which had been completely reduced to dust and ash, was a Herculean task. To this end, the 'Koseki Register Reconstruction Law' (*Koseki seibi-hō*) was promulgated on 16 November 1953 as Law No. 86 and implemented from 1 March 1954 as a special law based on the stipulations for koseki register reconstruction set out in Article 15 of the former Koseki Registration Law. Given the massive loss of materials that had occurred, the authorities set out to first establish an 'interim koseki register'. One strategy adopted by the authorities to help navigate the difficulties involved was the creation of a 'Koseki Register Survey Committee' (*Koseki chōsa I'inkai*) that received objections from concerned parties and inquiries from heads of municipalities. This committee adopted even more prudent and transparent procedures than those stipulated for reconstruction in the former Koseki Registration Law. In cases in which there was no remaining documentation, such as a copy of the koseki register record or lodgement document, reconstruction could only occur according to the evidence provided by the person involved. The complications that arose were compounded by the fact that many legal household heads (*koshu*), the very persons who knew the contents of specific koseki register records, had died during the war. In this unique set of circumstances, it was necessary to take steps to prevent false applications being made.[81]

In 1950s Okinawa, 'reversion [...] was clearly a heartfelt wish'.[82] As a result, both the Government of the Ryūkyū Islands and the Japanese government assumed the future 'unification of Okinawa and Japan proper'.[83] The restructure of the koseki registration system, too, proceeded on the expectation of reversion in the not-too-distant future. This expectation was manifested in the recorded content of the Okinawan register. Under American occupation, as noted, the official name of Okinawa was 'Ryūkyū' and the public use of the term 'Okinawa Prefecture' was taboo. Nevertheless, the Koseki Register Reconstruction Law referred to 'Okinawa Prefecture' in terms of *honseki* address, while dates were given in imperial rule (*nengō*) count rather than the Western calendar. Kugai Ryōjun, who, as the first head of the Civil Affairs Bureau of the Department of Justice of the Government of the Ryūkyū Islands, was given the task of reconstruction and maintenance of the Okinawan koseki registration system, noted that 'recording a *honseki* address as Okinawa Prefecture gave an emotional satisfaction that could restore in the people of Okinawa a sense of rights and the happiness of being reconnected to Japan proper as a prefecture of Japan'.[84] Through, for example, the annual despatch of a koseki specialist from the Ministry of Justice, the Japanese authorities gave positive support to the koseki register reconstruction project in Okinawa. Hiraga Kenta, who visited the islands in this capacity in 1958, recalled 'definitely feeling a kind of overwhelming joy' at the fact that the expression 'Okinawa Prefecture' was being used in the koseki registration system.[85] The political intent behind the restoration of the term 'Okinawa Prefecture' as a *honseki* address was, at least partly, to provide the psychological reassurance to the people of actually being able to anticipate Okinawa's return to Japan proper.

In an attempt to arouse public interest in koseki registration as a means of further accelerating the reconstruction and maintenance of the Okinawan koseki registration system, in 1953 and 1954 the Government of the Ryūkyū Islands conducted a mass media 'koseki register reconstruction campaign'. This included broadcasts from Ryūkyū Radio, the publication of over 10,000 leaflets entitled 'Booklet Concerning Application of Koseki Register Reconstruction' (*Koseki seibi shinkoku no shirori*), and the publication in the

'Okinawa Times' newspaper of both a 'Consultation Column Concerning Koseki' (*Koseki sōdan-ran*) and articles explaining koseki registration processes. In addition, under the name of the administrative head of the Government of the Ryūkyū Islands, on 22 February 1954 the Civil Administration issued a memorandum entitled 'Concerning Contacting those Responsible for External Notification Accompanying the Koseki Register Restructure' (*Koseki seibi ni tomonau zaigai shinkoku gimusha e no rennraku ni tsuite*). This memorandum, which discussed the process of making an application for the reconstruction of a koseki register record, was sent to various national governments and also to those associations of Okinawa Prefecture people (*Okinawa kenjin-kai*) that were outside the prefecture. The effectiveness of the latter was seen in the fact that application forms were received from people registered in Okinawa who lived in the United States, Canada, Peru, England, the Soviet Union, France and Taiwan.[86] Having had their various socio-political relationships with Japan proper severed through submission to a foreign race, it was the koseki registration system that was, predictably of course, entrusted with the mission of preserving the 'Japanese' identity of the people of Okinawa who until that time had seen this identity slipping away.

With the Okinawan Koseki Register Reconstruction Law, 149,000 Okinawan koseki register records were declared largely complete on 25 September 1962. On that day, a Completion of the Reconstruction of the Koseki Register Ceremony was held in Okinawa.[87] Both the Okinawan Koseki Registration Law (1956, Law No. 87) and the Okinawa Civil Code that was implemented on 1 January 1957 noted the necessity of ensuring that the new Okinawan koseki registration system 'be aligned with that of Japan proper' (*hondo-ka*). Both also noted that the format of the reconstructed Okinawa register should follow the stipulations of the post-war Koseki Registration Law as implemented in Japan proper. Yet, while the content of the legislation was the same as the 1947 Japan proper koseki legislation, administrative responsibility for the Okinawan register lay with the head of the Department of Justice of the Government of the Ryūkyū Islands. The revisions necessary to align the Okinawan koseki register with the Japan proper register began on 1 July 1967 and, with the exception of the registers for Naha City, were completed by the end of June 1971.[88] According to a July 1956 survey by the Fukuoka-based Okinawa Related Koseki Registration

Administration Office, there were 62,852 people, comprising 36,200 households (*setai*), registered in Okinawa who were resident on Japan proper.[89] Following a notification from the head of the Civil Affairs Bureau of the Ministry of Justice permitting the exchange of koseki registration lodgements between Okinawa and Japan proper, the unification of the two koseki registration systems occurred in reality as well as in name.[90]

Following the 5 February 1972 reversion to Japan proper, the mayors of each municipality in Okinawa once more took responsibility for koseki matters under the supervision of the head of the Naha Region Department of Justice, which was responsible for koseki administration throughout Okinawa. At the time of reversion, the 'Ordinance Relating to Special Measures for the Application of Ministry of Justice Related Laws and Regulations Following the Okinawa Reversion' (*Okinawa no fukki ni tomonau hōmu-shō kankei hōrei no tekiyō no tokubetsu sochi ni kan suru seirei*) (1972, Ordinance No. 95) was pronounced, and both the koseki register records and inactive koseki register records (*josekibo*) that were stored in Okinawa assumed the same status as those of Japan proper.[91] Eventually, the administration of the koseki registers of both Okinawa and Japan proper was merged and the Okinawan koseki registration system gained the same status as that of Japan proper.

Steps were taken, furthermore, to re-register those people who had lost their registration during the United States Civil Administration restrictions on koseki registration transfer to Okinawa. A provision for reviving the previous registration of those people was stipulated in Article 24, Clause 3 of the new Okinawan Koseki Registration Law.[92] Koseki registration under the United States Occupation had been reduced to chaos, and this was a key move in restoring the system's integrity. With the reversion invalidating the United States administration's imposed Ordinance for Entry to and Departure From the Ryūkyū Islands, the Japan proper 'Immigration Control Ordinance' (*Shutsunyū-koku kanri rei*) (1951, Ordinance No. 319) and 'Alien Registration Law' were also applied in Okinawa.[93]

During the post-war decades, all legal processes in Okinawa were in the hands of the United States administration. It was through the project of reconstructing the Okinawan koseki registration system, however, that the Japanese government was able to walk the path to future reversion and to incrementally prepare for the unification of Okinawa and Japan proper.

We are ultimately compelled to ask what motivated the Japanese government to be so prudent yet so flexible regarding the legal status of the people of Okinawa, while remaining completely intractable in its stance towards the citizenship of Korean and Taiwanese people? Japanese 'bloodline' as indicated by koseki registration was the benchmark used by the Japanese state in its implementation of discriminatory citizenship policies in both Okinawa and the former colonies. Yet, when we consider the situation in the years immediately following the war with respect to both *honseki* address and nationality that played out in the temporary koseki registration system in Okinawa, we can see that notions of bloodline were largely rendered invalid in the chaos that prevailed at that time. Ultimately, what the Japanese state did in Okinawa was to deploy koseki registration mechanisms as a convenient means to realise the desire of the sovereign state to have Okinawa revert to Japan proper and to have the residents of Okinawa reintegrate as 'Japanese'. In other words, the reconstruction of a koseki registration system in Okinawa was merely a process performed to confirm the political power of the 'citizen' of Japan.

6 Koseki as Distorted Reality: Towards an Open Institution

Koseki bias: Foreigners, children born outside marriage

A new management system for foreigners

On 28 April 1952, the day the San Francisco Peace Treaty came into effect, people from Japan's former colonies (former imperial subjects from Taiwan and Korea) and their descendants were classified overnight as foreigners. While the 1991 'Special Act on Immigration Control' (*Nyūkan tokurei hō*) eventually came to guarantee the right of residence and universal recognition of permanent residence eligibility for these people, they nevertheless remained 'outside the applicability of the Koseki Registration Law'. In other words, they were positioned beyond the bounds of the various institutions linked to the koseki registration system.

The xenophobia inherent in the koseki registration system was manifested, too, in the resident registration system. Like the pre-war and wartime systems, the draft resident registration system established in post-war Japan to replace the Temporary Residence Law (*Kiryū-hō*) initially required both foreigners and stateless persons to register as 'residents' (*jūmin*). However, the linking for administrative convenience of resident registration and koseki procedures, and the growing impact on legislative processes of the tense Cold War security situation, saw a shift towards managing Koreans and Taiwanese via alien registration. Accordingly, the 'Residency Registration Law' (*Jūmin tōroku hō*) (1951, Law No. 210) established in June 1951 applied only to 'persons subject to the Koseki Registration Law'. These conditions, which excluded the former residents of colonial holdings and foreigners, also applied to the later 'Basic Resident Registration Law' (*Jūmin kihon daichō hō*) (1967, Law No. 81).[1] As control over koseki procedures by the ruling powers strengthened, those without koseki registration were inevitably subject to even greater disadvantage. This also led to growing discrimination against foreigners in Japan.

In July 2009, however, amendments to the 'Immigration Control and Refugee Recognition Act' (*Shutsunyūkoku kanri hō oyobi nanmin nintei hō*) (2009, Law No. 79) saw a significant turning point in Japanese foreigner management policies. This was followed by the July 2012 abolition of the alien registration system that had regulated resident foreigners for more than sixty years. Rather than a alien registration card, 'mid- to long-term residents' residing in Japan for more than ninety days were now required to hold a 'resident card', while 'special permanent residents' were issued with a separate 'special permanent resident certificate'.

As a result of these reforms, foreign nationals were now entered into the basic resident registration system in the same way as 'Japanese nationals'. Formerly, households in which both foreign and Japanese nationals resided were respectively managed by the alien registration and resident registration systems. From July 2012, however, all members of a single household were entered into the relevant resident record (*jūminhyō*). As noted on the Ministry of Justice Immigration Bureau homepage, in addition to permitting 'an even more precise grasp of the circumstances of residents [in a jurisdiction] than was previously possible', the new residence management system was designed to 'enhance convenience for foreign nationals residing legally [in Japan]'. Nonetheless, since the foundational principle of not applying the Koseki Registration Law to foreign nationals remained unchanged, a spouse or child without Japanese citizenship still merely had their name noted among the status details recorded in a Japanese person's koseki register record. While, as noted in the fourth section of Chapter Two, modifications to koseki procedures now permitted a Japanese person to record a 'foreign surname' on their koseki record, fully opening the registration door that had been so firmly shut to foreign nationals in the past would have been tantamount to the 'death' of koseki registration as an institution.

Political elites, moreover, have always wielded a stick while offering a carrot. Firstly, there were notable disparities in the new immigration control system between the treatment of regular and irregular residents. Since eligibility to reside was not a factor in the previous alien registration system, registration was also open to irregular residents. Immigration Control Law amendments, however, now prevented irregular residents from being issued with a resident card, which in turn prevented them from having an entry in the resident register. Irregular residents, who according to Ministry of Justice figures numbered up to 62,000 nationwide in January 2012, thus lost access to any identification documentation. In other words, they came to no longer exist in the public record.

The old Alien Registration Law assumed the necessity of constant 'control' of foreign nationals. It is clear that residual influences of this law continue to operate unabated in that it remains compulsory, as it was with the alien registration card, for all foreign residents (including 'permanent residents') to carry a resident card at all times. Furthermore, failure to notify the authorities of, for example, a change of address continues to lead to cancellation of eligibility to reside.

Koseki record update problems: Gender and birth notification

In a democracy, legislation is expected to respect, as far as possible, social and personal diversity, and to respond flexibly to changes in values related to family structure. Koseki registration procedures that discriminate between 'legitimate' and 'illegitimate' according to the circumstances of a child's birth have led to confrontation in various forms. Two recent examples demonstrate this.

When submitting notification of the birth of their child to Tokyo's Setagaya Ward authorities, a couple in a de facto marriage refused, on the grounds that it constituted discrimination against the children of couples who were not legally married, to enter the term 'non-legitimate child' into the 'kinship' column of the documentation as required. Since staff at the ward office would not accept the validity of the form, no koseki register entry was made for the child. Accordingly, Setagaya Ward, the authority with responsibility for such matters, did not enter the child into the ward's koseki register. In 2006, the couple sued Setagaya Ward and sought a koseki record entry for their child on the grounds that the stipulation in Article 49 of the Koseki Registration Law to label a child as either 'legitimate' or 'illegitimate' when lodging a birth notification was both a violation of human rights and a breach of the Constitution. Although the Supreme Court dismissed the claim, the couple were undeterred and filed a second lawsuit in March 2011 with the Tokyo District

Court. In this second suit, the parents sought to have Setagaya Ward register the child as a resident and to have the state confirm that the child held Japanese citizenship.

In response, Setagaya Ward provided a stopgap measure that saw koseki registration remain as the hurdle that one needed to clear in order to be registered as a resident. With the notification of birth still deemed invalid, rather than entering the child in the koseki register record as the parents' demanded, Setagaya Ward gave special authorisation for the child to be entered into the mother's koseki record. With this koseki entry, the municipality could create an entry in the Setagaya Resident Record. Still, the legal point of contention was the breach of the Constitution by Article 49 of the Koseki Registration Law. By responding in a manner that sidestepped this, Setagaya Ward managed to evade any criticism on the grounds that the authorities had failed to act. There was, however, precedent for this case. In 2007, Tokyo's Adachi Ward exercised its authority to create an entry in the koseki register on humanitarian grounds for a child whose birth notification had been rejected because the infant had been fathered by a previous husband in accordance with the Civil Code '300-day rule' (see below for further details). Nevertheless, Setagaya Ward's actions made the public very aware of the absurdity of this Koseki Registration Law stipulation requiring parents to label a child 'legitimate' or 'illegitimate' when lodging an official notice of birth.

Values around sex and gender have also changed. There is now a wide body of evidence confirming that people subject to 'gender identity disorder' (GID) are caused profound mental anguish as a result of their physical gender not matching their mental gender. This has led to a growing number of people undergoing gender reassignment surgery (now referred to as 'gender confirmation surgery') as a means of establishing a new gender identity.

Koseki registration processes, however, initially did not permit any change in documentation of gender (entered in terms of the individual's relationship with her or his parents) for people who had undergone this medical procedure.[2] Article 113 of the Koseki Registration Law stipulates that 'in cases where a koseki register entry is discovered to be not permitted by law, or in the case of an entry error or omission', an application for correction can be lodged with the Family Court. Accordingly, people who wished to change a koseki register entry relating to gender were unable to do so without proof that this was an 'error'. We might speculate that, while longing to have the gender that enabled them to fully express their true selves, many people baulked at the barriers placed in their way by Koseki Registration Law stipulations and accordingly abandoned any thought of gender reassignment surgery.

In July 2004, however, the 'Act on Special Cases in Handling Gender for People with Gender Identity Disorder' ('GID Law') came into effect. Article 3, Clause 1 of this law stipulated that change of gender in the koseki register column listing matters such as an individual's relationship with her or his parents could now be made with approval from the Family Court. Ministry of Justice statistics indicate that this amendment saw an annual rise in the numbers of people seeking a change to their koseki register gender status. Of a total of 2,847 cases since 2004, 609 were recorded in the 2011–12 Japanese fiscal year. It might be noted that in 2004, however, amendments were also made to Article 39 of the Regulations for Implementation of the Koseki Registration Law so that 'Items relating to change of gender' became subject to transfer when a new koseki register record for the person in question was compiled. Political elites could not resist using koseki mechanisms to place those people who opted to change their gender under surveillance.

With the possibility of koseki register gender change, marriage between a man and a former man, or between a woman and a former woman, also became possible. There were, however, issues relating to the children of couples in which one or both parties were gender reassigned. One such case involved an Osaka man who, after having gender reassignment surgery and amending his koseki register record, had a child by artificial insemination. Upon receiving the birth notice lodgement, however, the ward office in question invoked its authority and made no entry in the 'father' column of the notice. The authorities justified this on the grounds that because the man's change of gender would be evident from his koseki register entry, the child would not be recognised as a 'legitimate child'. When the man withdrew the notification of birth, the child became unregistered (*mukoseki*). In February 2012, alleging a breach of Article 14 of the Constitution, the man lodged an appeal with the Tokyo Family Court on the basis that any failure to recognise the child of a married couple as 'legitimate' constituted discrimination. The claim was dismissed in November the same year. Arguing that a man who has undergone gender reassignment does not have a biological father–child relationship with his child, the Ministry of Justice enforced a policy requiring children in these circumstances to be registered as 'illegitimate'.

Children subject to the legal distinction between 'legitimate' and 'illegitimate' and marked by political powerbrokers as deviating from national standards of 'homogeneity' naturally bear a heavy psychological burden. Here, with no regard for the wishes of those concerned, the law seeks to determine what is 'proper' in the sphere of parent–child relations and, in doing so, enters territory into which it has no right whatsoever to venture. Such rulings, moreover, establish boundaries around the meaning of the entity, 'Japanese'. Accordingly, ongoing pressure is applied to those judged to have strayed outside those boundaries in an attempt to draw them back into the fold and to ensure proper 'assimilation'. This is the power inherent in koseki registration, a power that is surely incompatible with democratic principles that demand respect for the character and diversity of each individual who is a member of the state. On 4 September 2013, however, a historic decision was handed down by the Supreme Court. On this day, the court ruled that the stipulation in Article 900 of the Civil Code declaring the inheritance of a child born outside a legal marriage to be half of that of a 'legitimate' child – a matter regarded as the most significant point of legal discrimination against children born outside a legal marriage – was in breach of the Constitution in terms of failing to uphold 'equality under the law'. If the antiquated legal notions that have endured from the Meiji Civil Code are to be abandoned, surely the koseki registration system and the discrimination it engenders should be the next target for eradication.

Limits to eligibility: Questioning Japan's citizenship policy

Towards dual citizenship: Compulsory citizenship choice meaning

Since the Meiji era, the Citizenship Law in Japan has deemed dual citizenship to be illegal. In spite of the fact that the current Citizenship Law which was enacted in 1950 should have been subject to the stipulations of the new Constitution, this law violated Article 24 of the Constitution relating to gender equality by maintaining the patrilineal *jus sanguinis* ideology of that time. Justified on the grounds that a patrilineal system was considered effective in preventing dual citizenship, other countries also adopted this system at that time.[3] Article 5, Clause 5 of the current Citizenship Law stipulates that the condition of application for Japanese citizenship is 'not having a nationality or having to give up his/her nationality due to the acquisition of Japanese nationality'. This is a hangover from Article 7, Clause 5, Item 2 of the former law. Accordingly, those who have been declared stateless, or those whose original country of citizenship stipulates by law that upon acquisition of foreign citizenship the individual automatically loses their original citizenship status, are able to become naturalised Japanese. In other cases, it is mandatory that application for Japanese citizenship can only occur after renunciation of the applicant's original citizenship status. There are currently few countries around the world that so tenaciously oppose the concept of dual citizenship.[4] These stringent conditions undoubtedly act as a huge disincentive to the naturalisation of foreign nationals in Japan.

The system of compulsory citizenship selection is a further device that was introduced to prevent dual citizenship. With the May 1984 amendments permitting the bloodline of either a mother or father to be invoked, a child born to a foreign father and Japanese mother (including any child born before the introduction of the revised law) became eligible to acquire Japanese citizenship. Prior to the revisions, Japanese citizenship was already an option for second-generation children, such as those born to a Korean father resident in Japan and a Japanese mother. However, since the Republic of Korea's Citizenship Law also operates according to *jus sanguinis* (patrilineal *jus sanguinis* at that time), a child born to a Korean father and Japanese mother automatically became a dual citizen.

As a countermeasure to the anticipated creation of a large group of Japanese-Korean dual nationals, the 1984 revisions simultaneously introduced a system of compulsory citizenship selection. Article 14, Clause 1 of the Citizenship Law stipulated, 'A Japanese citizen with foreign nationality' must, in the case of having foreign and Japanese nationality prior to reaching the age of twenty, select one only of those nationalities before turning twenty-two; or, if this occurred after the individual reached the age of twenty, within two years of the date of acquiring Japanese citizenship. Thus, an individual can choose to confirm their Japanese citizenship by either 'renouncement of the foreign nationality' or by 'selecting Japanese nationality and declaring the renunciation of foreign nationality' (Article 14, Clause 2 of the same law). Unless a notification of selection of Japanese nationality is lodged within the set period, dual citizens lose Japanese nationality: dual citizens who are notified in writing by the Minister of Justice that any Japanese citizen with foreign nationality who has not selected Japanese nationality within the assigned time, if the selection of Japanese nationality is not made within one month of receiving the notice, lose Japanese nationality (Article 15 of the same law).

This system of compulsory citizenship selection was instituted in Japan with the fundamental aim of dissolving dual citizenship by ensuring automatic loss of Japanese citizenship for those who do not voluntarily endeavour to renounce their foreign citizenship and do not make the selection within the time specified in the Minister's notice.[5] Korea, too, had similar concerns. When 1998 legislative amendments in the Republic of Korea saw that country adopt a system of citizenship based on the lineage of either parent, children with one Korean and one Japanese parent became citizens of both places. This resulted in increasing numbers of individuals holding dual citizenship. As a comprehensive strategy to prevent dual citizenship, Korea introduced a system similar to that of Japan that forced the individual involved either to actively choose Korean citizenship or to lose that status.

The compulsory selection of citizenship system adopted by Japan is assumed to be based on the 1977 Council of Europe decision to prevent dual citizenship. However, even in Italy, the only country to ever act upon the 1977 decision, forced selection of citizenship was abandoned in 1992. Currently, only a handful of countries throughout the world operate a system of compulsory citizenship selection. In an increasingly integrated Europe, growth in migrant numbers and the liberalisation of movement between EU (European Union) member states saw the problems of dual citizenship become more prevalent. As a result, in 1997 the Council of Europe adopted the European Convention on Nationality, which came into effect in 2000. This convention granted dual citizenship as a right to a child who acquired different citizenships at birth. In fact, rather than dual citizenship, the European emphasis has increasingly been on the prevention of statelessness. While Europe continues to address the possible manner in which some exploit the benefits of dual citizenship, there is nonetheless a trend there to approve this status in specific cases based on the actual life circumstances of the person/s in question.[6]

Koseki register function of monitoring those with dual citizenship

In actual fact, however, the processes for compulsory citizenship selection in Japan are unable to completely erase dual citizenship events. Even if a person declares their selection of Japanese citizenship within the set timeframe, it is technically possible for that person to continue to hold a second citizenship. Thus, koseki registration becomes the mechanism that seeks and monitors dual citizens residing in Japan. The introduction of the compulsory citizenship selection system saw amendments to the Regulations for the Implementation of the Koseki Registration Law requiring a dual citizen who opts for Japanese citizenship to have this fact entered in the status column of their koseki register record. Moreover, selection of citizenship is now one of the mandatory transfer items in the case of the transfer of *honseki* address (*tenseki*) or the creation of a new koseki record.

As noted previously, koseki register administration is the responsibility of city, ward, town and village municipal heads. Should it come to the attention of a municipal head that a dual citizen who has failed to comply with citizenship selection procedures is registered within their jurisdiction, this person is obligated to notify the supervising regional or district Legal Affairs Bureau (Article 104, Clause 3 of the Koseki Registration Law; Article 65, Clause 2 of the Implementation Regulations of the Law). Since status actions such as marriage to or adoption by a foreign national, birth in a foreign country or the completion of citizenship selection processes must be entered into the relevant koseki register record, this mechanism acts as the perfect means to expose dual citizens. Furthermore, since an individual's residential address is recorded on their koseki register label (*koseki fuhyo*), dual citizens can thereby be tracked down and brought in for investigation. Should a person not be at the recorded address, the authorities can inquire with the municipality that held her or his previous registration information. In the case of a dual citizen residing outside Japan, some municipalities record in the register the destination in the foreign country the individual first went to after selecting Japanese citizenship.[7]

Why is the state so concerned about dual citizenship? Conventional wisdom has it that the most pressing problem caused by dual citizenship is the clash of state jurisdictions. This conflict is said to inevitably complicate matters such as the right to diplomatic protection by the state and the relationship between the citizen's legal rights and obligations, such as the right to vote and conscription. These issues, however, can be addressed through the 'principle of effective citizenship' which requires matters such as diplomatic protection to apply only in terms of an individual's state of permanent residence and occupational base, that is, in terms of the state to which she or he has the stronger substantive connection.

According to Ministry of Health, Labour and Welfare statistics, the number of cases of international marriage in the 2010–11 fiscal year accounted for approximately 4.3 percent of all marriages in Japan. The countries whose citizens most frequently marry a Japanese person are China, the Republic of Korea and the Philippines, each of which has *jus sanguinis* citizenship law. With the exception of China, which does not grant citizenship to the children of persons residing permanently outside China, the children of these unions will acquire dual citizenship at birth. Children who inherit the different nationalities and cultures of each parent typically have their character shaped by both as they grow. Japan needs to recognise these children, who have acquired multiple cultures and multiple languages while residing in the country, as a precious national resource. Yet, while their gift of diversity has the potential to act as an incentive to Japanese society and to make a valuable contribution to internationalisation, the citizenship selection system imposes a painful burden by effectively forcing these children to choose one parent over the other. To be deprived of the status of 'being Japanese' in a society that remains riven by citizenship-based discrimination is a huge disadvantage for the children concerned. Furthermore, it is surely a great loss at the most practical level of national interest and in relation to the pressure to maintain 'global human resources'.

In considering the obsessive nature of the measures adopted by Japan to prevent dual citizenship, we might recall the case of 'Chinese persons registered as Taiwanese' discussed in the fourth part of Chapter Four. In spite of questioning the 'patriotism' towards Japan of Chinese persons registered as Taiwanese with Japanese citizenship who were also citizens of China, the state nonetheless expediently protected the 'Japanese' status of this group as human resources to be exploited for the sake of the empire. In other words, pre-war authorities took a pragmatic approach to citizenship that permitted the flexible creation of members of this group as 'Japanese'.

How ironic, then, that Japan should now resist the international trend towards support for dual citizenship and insist on operating a system of enforced citizenship selection imposed with a rigidity seen in few other places around the world.

Is 'Japanese' eligibility opening? Maintenance of 'bloodline'

The continued distinction between 'illegitimate' and 'legitimate' children was the result of the tenor of the pre-war Koseki Registration Law being carried through to post-war citizenship legislation. This was apparent in the case of a child born to a couple in which one partner was Japanese and one non-Japanese.

Article 772 of the Japanese Civil Code stipulates that any children born within 200 days of the date of a marriage or within 300 days after the dissolution date of a marriage will be presumed to have been conceived within that marriage. Accordingly, a child born less than 300 days after the finalisation of a divorce decree is regarded as the child of the former husband. Known as the '300-day rule', this is a key element of the 'presumption of legitimacy' system that seeks to establish a child's status with early confirmation of the father–child relationship.

This 300-day rule also impacted upon the acquisition of Japanese citizenship by children born to a Japanese/non-Japanese couple. This is demonstrated by the following example from the period during which post-war citizenship legislation stipulated principles of patrilineal *jus sanguinis* (1950–84). Consider the hypothetical case of Japanese woman B, married to foreign man A, who, within 300 days of the finalisation of the couple's divorce, gives birth to Child C. If child C was registered as 'illegitimate', that is, if A was legally deemed not to be the father, then the child acquired the Japanese citizenship of the mother, B, and would accordingly be entered into the mother's koseki record as a 'Japanese citizen'. If C, on the contrary, was registered as 'legitimate', that is, in the case of A being legally recognised as the father, then according to the patrilineal *jus sanguinis* principle, C did not acquire Japanese citizenship and was given no koseki register entry.

A former Ministry of Justice bureaucrat testified that, in spite of the fact that they were the 'legitimate' children of a foreign father and Japanese mother, there were cases of children of

Japanese and non-Japanese parents being falsely reported as 'illegitimate' as a means of acquiring Japanese citizenship. There were also cases in which, while the birth notification initially listed the child as 'legitimate', the documentation was accepted by a municipal office and the child given a koseki register entry *after* the person making the notification amended the entry to read 'illegitimate'.[8]

Those who committed each of these fraudulent acts clearly regarded being 'illegitimate' as less disadvantageous than being a 'foreign national' in terms of the child's future life in Japan. It is hardly necessary to point out that this mindset is a product of the level of social discrimination against foreigners that is embedded in Japanese society. The real point here, however, is the implacable momentum of a legal system which, regardless of the will of the child, makes the life-altering decision of categorising that child as either 'illegitimate' or a 'foreign national'. Neither of these classifications, of course, carry the benefits that come with being the 'legitimate child' of a 'Japanese'.

With the law amended to accommodate *jus sanguinis* in relation to both parents, whether born to a legally married couple or not, the child of a foreign father and Japanese mother could receive Japanese citizenship from the mother's side. Yet, if the father–child relationship was not specified in the case of a child born outside a legal marriage to a Japanese father and foreign mother, the child would be unable to acquire Japanese citizenship. The current Citizenship Law as a rule did not recognise the acquisition of citizenship in terms of the acknowledgement of paternity by the father of a child born outside a legal marriage (*ninch*). The law did, however, stipulate that a child whose paternity was recognised prenatally by its Japanese father could acquire Japanese citizenship. In addition, according to the Civil Code, the status of a child born outside a legal marriage can be 'legitimised' (*junsei*) once the parents marry after the birth of that child. In the case of a legal marriage between a Japanese and a non-Japanese, regardless of which parent holds Japanese citizenship, the law permits the child to acquire Japanese citizenship at birth (Article 3, Clause 1).

The fact that, while 'illegitimate', only a child recognised by the father (*ninchi*) prior to birth was eligible for Japanese citizenship clearly contravened Article 14 of the Constitution which forbids discrimination based on 'social status'. Accordingly, on 4 June 2008, the Supreme Court ruled that Article 3, Clause 1 of the Citizenship Law was in breach of Article 14 of the Constitution. The court further required that the legislature revise the related elements of the Citizenship Law. This ruling resulted from a case involving a child born outside a legal marriage to a Japanese father and Filipina mother. In spite of the fact that the father had acknowledged paternity after the birth, the child had been unable to acquire Japanese citizenship. The court ruled that the child's status in this respect was related to the actions of the parents and 'was something that lay outside the power of the child to change'.[9]

In December 2008, in response to this ground-breaking confirmation of the fact that Japan's Citizenship Law violated the Constitution, the government made revisions to the law to come into force from January 2009. The amended Article 3, Clause 1, now permitted the acquisition of Japanese citizenship by any child under the age of twenty who was born outside a legal marriage and whose parentage had been acknowledge by either a Japanese mother or father. While this certainly expanded the range of those defined as 'Japanese' in terms of the Citizenship Law, the great Meiji era principle of *jus sanguinis* nonetheless remained intact. At the time of the 1984 revisions, the Ministry of Justice declared, 'Since [Japan] has one of the largest populations in the world in a confined territory, there is essentially no room to accept migrants, except where necessary for humanitarian reasons as in the case of refugees'. Having thus justified the retention of *jus sanguinis*, the Ministry concluded, 'It is not anticipated that this policy will change in the near future'.[10] In spite of the frequent outbreak of regional conflict that followed the end of the Cold War and the dramatic increase in human mobility, both voluntary and forced, that has recently accompanied the ongoing expansion of capitalism, Japan continues to focus solely inwards. The authorities are seemingly unaware that the country has been swept up in the maelstrom of international events and that any ability to pursue and achieve the age-old chimera of the 'nation-state' has long been lost.

In recent years, partly from a need to widen the definition of 'citizen' in response to the relentless reality of globalisation and thereby ensure a more flexible approach to citizenship, even states that formerly applied *jus sanguinis* principles have introduced legislation to recognise the relative importance of *jus soli*. Nineteen ninety-nine revisions to citizenship law in Germany, which traditionally operated a *jus sanguinis* system similar to that of Japan, granted German citizenship to any child born to at least one parent who had legally resided in Germany for a minimum of eight years as a permanent resident or had permission of an indefinite period of residence for more than three years. Children born in Germany during the previous ten years also acquired German citizenship. This change in German law aimed to integrate these children as 'German' citizens in line with the growth that had occurred in the number of migrants and the emergence in Germany of a more multicultural society.

Certainly, changes to German citizenship policy were politically motivated to the extent of promoting settlement and appeasing demands from the burgeoning numbers of migrants and foreign workers by facilitating their integration as German nationals. In other words, the changes largely prioritised national interest over humanitarian concerns. In spite of becoming an increasingly pluralistic society, Japan on the other hand is notable for the marked absence in its citizenship policies of any recognition of connectivity with the state on the part of foreign nationals through residence spanning many years and the accompanying mastery of language and culture. Neither is there any acknowledgement of a need to adapt to changing times by working to guarantee the rights of these people as members of the Japanese state. For, in the words of one judicial affairs bureaucrat, since the days of the ancient state, Japan has after all been '*constituted by a single ethnic group*' so that 'the *consciousness that places importance on the "bloodline"* that originates from this *tradition*' is deeply rooted in Japanese society (emphasis added). There appears, in other words, to be a perception among state functionaries that the issue of 'bloodline' underpins the identity of the Japanese people, a perception that perhaps explains the state's determined adherence to *jus sanguinis*.[11] It is precisely the idea of koseki registration and its formalisation of bloodline as discussed in this book that promotes the fabricated tradition of a 'mono-ethnic state' and which is, in fact, the final bastion that supports the faux 'Japanese identity' that is grounded in this fabrication.

Koseki system trends in East Asia: Korea and Taiwan

Abolition of koseki registration system in Republic of Korea

It has often been noted that in the post-war era the Republic of Korea and Taiwan introduced koseki registration systems similar to that of Japan. Certainly, in the sense that each had the household head as lynchpin and recorded only its own citizens (*kokumin*) in the register while excluding foreign nationals, there were commonalities with the Japanese system. With both places controlled until 1987 by authoritarian regimes supported by military dictatorships, a koseki registration system was deemed essential as a means of ensuring both regime stability and military mobilisation in each site. The success of the democratisation movements in each country, however, led to a maturing of Korean and Taiwanese civil societies. As a result, both became aware of the contradictions inherent in a Japanese-style koseki registration system and moved to modify their versions.

We will first consider the system in the Republic of Korea. In post-war Korea, while surnames altered by imperial Japan's '*uji* family name creation and name change' (*sōshi kaimei*) policy were restored, the Republic of Korea replicated the format of the Korean koseki registration system that operated during the time of Japanese rule. The Republic of Korea's Civil Code, implemented from January 1960, established a legal household head system, while also maintaining traditional customs such as the marriage ban on those people with the 'same *hongan* [ancestral place of origin] and same *sei* family name' and the preservation down the generations of the father's surname. Implemented at the same time as a new civil code, the Republic of Korea's Koseki Registration Law drew largely on the pre-war Korean Koseki Registration Law (*Chōsen koseki rei*) with an *ie* family unit controlled by a legal household head and the koseki register record compiled with the *honseki* address as the point of reference.[12] However, from the time of the enactment of the Civil Code, a family law reform movement, which became the seedbed for a grassroots women's movement in the Republic of Korea, demanded the abolition of the legal household head system as a symbol of gender inequality. This led to ongoing activism around that issue. Accordingly, from the time of the 1987 presidential election that marked the transition from military to democratic government, successive candidates made campaign promises that reflected popular opinion calling for the abolition of, or revisions to, the legal household head system.[13]

In February 2005, amid momentum regarding changing attitudes to the family and the recognition of the need to dismantle patriarchal traditions, the Constitutional Court of Korea ruled that the legal household head system was incompatible with the constitutional ideal of individual dignity and gender equality. In March of that year the Civil Code was amended accordingly and the legal household head system abolished. Modifications to the Koseki Registration Law occurred as a matter of course, with the task of drafting templates for the new individual registers given to the parliamentary legal department and chancery. Promulgated in May 2007, the Family Relationship Registration Law, which came into force on 1 January 2009, saw the Republic of Korea's Koseki Registration Law abolished.[14] The 'family relationship register roll' that replaced the official copy of the koseki register record (*koseki tōhon*) saw the individual become the unit of registration. Depending on the form of event being registered, the system issues five types of certificates: family relationship certificates, basic certificates, marriage certificates, adoption certificates and special adoption certificates. Individuals are free to change their registration address (*kijunchi*), and, unlike Japan's *honseki*, there is no need for all family members to share the same registration address.[15]

With the abolition of the Koseki Registration Law, the Korean family system also underwent significant change. As stated in Chapter Four, the patrilineal surname and ancestral seat had been handed down from generation to generation as the keystones of family custom in Korea. The abolition of the Koseki Registration Law made it possible through the mutual agreement of the parties involved in a marriage to change to the surname and ancestral seat of the mother's side. Traditionally, family matters such as marriage in Korean society had been bound by strict Confucian ethics. This change, however, was a major shift towards open individualism. Moreover, it is clear that 'democratisation' is now embedded in the Korean political system which, in response to calls for constructive social change based on individual dignity, took measures to dramatically revise the country's legal conventions.

Transformation of Taiwan's Koseki Registration Law

In Taiwan, the Koseki Registration Law, enacted in December 1931 by the Nationalist government based in Nanjing at the time, continues to operate. There have, however, been numerous amendments.

Under the control of the Chinese Nationalist Party (*Kuomintang/ Guomindang* or KMT), which fled China in 1949 following defeat in the 1945–1949 Nationalist-Communist Civil War, Taiwan entered a 'period of mobilisation for the suppression of insurgency'. The imposition of martial law by the Chiang Kai-shek regime in May of that year saw the emergence of an authoritarian government that promulgated the ideology of '*Dalu fangong*' (counterattacking against 'Continent China', or reclamation by force of 'Continent China's' sovereignty). At that time, koseki registration procedures played a major security role in keeping the population under surveillance. This is evident from the fact that 1973 amendments to the Koseki Registration Law saw koseki administration taken over by the police. This system of 'koseki and police as one' (*kokei dōitsu*) recalls the policy during Japan's imperial rule of Taiwan. Following the 1987 lifting of martial law, however, the country transitioned from military rule to democratic government. With the 1991 announcement of the end of the 'period of mobilisation for war', koseki administration came under the jurisdiction of a civilian body the following year.[16] That is, with democratisation, koseki registration in Taiwan once more became a civil matter.

Taiwan's current Koseki Registration Law differs considerably from that of Japan. The differences can be summarised in five points. The first relates to the concept of the 'household' (*ko*), which constitutes the unit of establishment. While a 'household' in Japan is defined as a married couple and their unmarried children who share the same *uji* family name irrespective of whether they actually cohabit, the 'household' in Taiwan is organised into three types of registers: persons who cohabit ('cohabiting households'); persons who conduct a joint enterprise in the same location under the same entrepreneur, including schools and temples ('joint-enterprise households'); and persons who live alone ('solitary-living households'). The 'household head' is the person who leads one of these three kinds of 'households'. In other words, the Taiwanese koseki registration system is established with the 'resident' (including individuals and groups) as the unit of compilation. This is a different concept from the 'household head' of the Japanese *ie* family system, and there is no 'same household, same *uji* family name' rule that operates in the Japanese system.

Secondly, the Taiwanese koseki registration system has the dual function of status registration and resident registration. As Taiwan does not have an independent resident registration system, relocation or change of address is recorded in the koseki registration system as a transfer of registration. In comparison to Japan, moreover, there is a limit to the items listed in the status record, including birth, marriage, adoption, divorce, dissolution of adoption (*rien*), recognition of paternity of an unborn child (*ninchi*), guardianship (*kōken*) and death.

Thirdly, registration basically follows a reporting (*hōkoku*) system. The only item that has no legal force without notification is divorce by mutual agreement, as in the Japanese system.

Fourthly, nationals of the Republic of China who are fourteen years of age and above and who have a koseki register entry are issued with a 'certificate of national status'. In addition to a photograph and a standardised number, each certificate records the holder's surname, parental or spousal surnames and place and date of birth. Carrying this certificate in card form is compulsory at all times.[17]

The fact that there is no need to enter the equivalent of the *honseki* address into one's koseki register record in Taiwan can be cited as the fifth point of difference. Under Taiwan's Koseki Registration Law, a person's province or prefecture (or major metropolis, a so-called 'direct-control municipality'), generally referring to the original domicile of an individual's ancestors, is given as the *honseki* address. There is, however, no rule, as there is in Japan, requiring every individual listed in a koseki register record to have the same *honseki* address. In fact, it is common for each person listed on a record to have a different *honseki* address.

In post-war Taiwanese society, however, a distinction did arise on the basis of *honseki* address between 'persons from this province' (*benshengren*, persons and the descendants of persons who had lived in Taiwan since the pre-war era) and 'persons from external provinces' (*waishengren*, persons and the descendants of persons who moved from the Chinese mainland during the post-war era). This was called the 'provincial register' (*shōseki*). The borderline between 'persons from this province' and 'persons from external provinces' led to differences in matters such as place of residence and education. In post-war Taiwan, this 'provincial register contradiction' (*shōseki mujun*)[18] led to an ethnic social cleavage. Under the control of the KMT regime, the members of which were largely 'persons from external provinces ', emphasis on the 'provincial register' and 'persons from external provinces' saw a championing of 'one China' and advocacy for the sovereignty of the Republic of China to extend to the Chinese mainland. In the Taiwanese political sphere, this became a mechanism for allocating greater benefits and rights to the minority 'persons from external provinces '.[19] However, with the dramatic rise in the movement of people between Taiwan and China's mainland that occurred with economic development, there was also a rise in the number of marriages between 'persons from this province' and 'persons from external provinces'. As ethnic boundaries became more ambiguous, the 'provincial register' handed down through families came to bear little relationship to the individual's lived experience or record of residence. Without any necessary connection to actual birthplace or residence, the 'provincial register' merely functioned as an axis of conflict that inhibited the emergence of a unified 'Taiwanese' identity.

In 1990, Lee Teng Hui became the first 'person from this province' to become President of Taiwan. In June 1992, as part of a policy of 'Taiwanisation', Lee amended the Republic of China Family Registration Law in order to address the 'provincial register contradiction'. Through this move, the *honseki* address, which had functioned merely as an unjust 'label' that reproduced Taiwan's social cleavage, was abolished from the koseki registration system. Instead, the individual entered their place of birth.[20]

As a result of these changes, Taiwan's Koseki Registration Law now operates as a realistic status registration system that accommodates the actual life circumstances of individuals. In concert with the progress of democratisation, the system has identified and eradicated the irrational political rifts that operated in Taiwanese society. The function of the current system thus differs markedly from that of Japan. Comparing Japanese koseki registration practices with the legal and political developments that have occurred in both the Republic of Korea and Taiwan clearly highlights the enduring conservatism of the system in Japan.

In Conclusion: 'Ethnicity', 'Bloodline' and 'Citizenship' as Fiction

Koseki system production of 'the Japanese'

What role has the koseki registration system played in modern Japan? The emergence and development of the modern nation-state has relied upon the legal fiction of a single 'nation'. We might consider the concrete means that enabled the nation, a legal fiction of the modern state, to operate as a 'reality' based on shared understanding.

In the late nineteenth century, British political philosopher Henry Sidgwick discussed the attributes of the modern nation-state. Sidgwick observed as follows.

> I can find no particular bond of union among those [implications] that chiefly contribute to the internal cohesion of a strongly-united society – belief in a common origin, possession of a common language and literature, pride in common historic traditions, community of social customs, community of religion – which is really essential to our conception of a Nation-State. [...] [I]t is often assumed that the members of a Nation are descended from the same stock. But this presumption in modern civilised countries is in palpable conflict with the facts: some of the leading modern nations – so called – are notoriously of very mixed race, and it does not appear that the knowledge of this mixture has any material effect in diminishing the consciousness of common citizenship.[1]

Different states have used different strategies to elide the 'mixture' within a nation, strategies which Sidgwick identified as official attempts to shape the shared consciousness of the 'citizens' (*kokumin*). Undoubtedly, the strategy deployed in Japan was the invocation of *ie* family mechanisms. As noted in Chapter Three, the *ie* family meant, in short, the koseki register record.

The role of the koseki registration system in modern Japan was not limited to the standard function of a status registration system designed to support state processes such as conscription, taxation, the gathering of population statistics and the maintenance of social order. The Meiji state justified its own construction in terms of the '*Jimmu sōgyō*', the myth of the founding of the original Japanese state by Emperor Jimmu. Accordingly, and as one means of countering the 'international society' that began to apply external pressure on Japan once the state opened its doors to the outside from the mid-1800s, this state invested in its 'living god' Emperor a centripetal force intended to awaken among the people a national consciousness of being 'Japanese'. In the midst of such momentum, the 1872 Jinshin koseki registration system was compiled as a social apparatus aimed at integrating the nation at both the political and emotional levels. Although their sense of identification began to diversify throughout the socio-political disruption that marked the end of the Tokugawa era, once the common people had been classified as the 'original Japanese' (*ganso Nihonjin*) the concept of 'Japanese citizenship' arose. This occurred in conjunction with a dismantling of the feudal status order and the construction of the populace as equal 'subjects' through the slogan '*ikkun banmin*' (one sovereign for all subjects). As a 'roll of subjects', the koseki registration system resisted the encroachment of Western civilisation. It was thus accorded symbolic value as the repository of information about the people of Japan who acknowledged their Emperor as the symbol of an independent state. This was the source of the logic that deemed the koseki registration system to essentially provide proof of a person being 'Japanese'.

As time passed, the koseki registration system became the foundation of the *ie* family system as promulgated in the Meiji Civil Code. In other words, a fixed form emerged of a 'Japanese' as a person (or subject) attached to one *ie* family and one koseki register record only, and who shared a surname with other *ie* family members. This created a powerful moral standard that promoted voluntary submission to the koseki registration system by judging a person without an entry in a koseki register record as not 'Japanese'. Notwithstanding diversity in matters such as occupation, family relationships and customs and values, this sort of judgment enforced compliance with the fixed forms that normalised the people of Japan as 'subjects'. Other ethnic groups that had been incorporated into

Japanese territory, including people from the Ryūkyū Kingdom and Hokkaido Ainu, were also uncompromisingly integrated into this fixed form and incrementally forced to adapt as 'subjects'. While on the one hand the koseki registration system branded persons who submitted to Japan's legal order as 'Japanese', on the other this mechanism coldly recorded differences in 'bloodline'. In this way, the koseki system demonstrated an ambivalence that discriminated against people from other ethnic groups who were 'newly incorporated into the empire' (*shinpu no tami*).

With the ideology of 'pure blood' as its unifying principle, the *ie* family demanded that all constituent members be 'Japanese'. Given that the worship of and respect for ancestors were now lauded as inalienably beautiful social customs of Japan, the *ie* family was swiftly constructed as a key plank in Japan's 'national polity' (*kokutai*). This 'inalienable beauty' was also expressed in the spurious notion of 'family state', with the Emperor as patriarch of an *ie* family comprised of 'Japan' and the 'imperial subjects' (*kōmin*) as his 'children' (*sekishi*).

The unifying principle of the *ie* family, which stated that 'legitimacy' came only through a purity of blood that confirmed the integrity of the *ie* family', also carried through to the citizenship legislation that determined one's legal eligibility to be a 'Japanese subject'. Modern Japan's choice of *jus sanguinis* as the cornerstone of citizenship was also based on the belief that 'pure blood' preserved the integrity of the *ie* family that was the foundation of the 'state' (*kuni*). Thus, if a foreign national entered a Japanese *ie* family through marriage to or adoption by a Japanese person, they acquired, regardless of personal intent, Japanese citizenship and thereby became 'Japanese'. Conversely, if a Japanese person left an *ie* family in Japan to become the wife or adopted child of a foreign national, that individual lost Japanese citizenship and became a 'foreigner'. The legal ruling that stipulated a change in citizenship as a function of leaving or entering a koseki register record, independent of the wishes of the person involved, contradicted the principle of individual choice in citizenship matters that emerged as the norm in Western societies in the wake of the modern valorisation of individualism. In the sense that koseki registration imposed restraints on individual citizenship choice, we can surely declare a master–slave relationship between the koseki system and citizenship matters.

Critical here is the fact that the blood-purity and integrity of the *ie* family was guaranteed solely by information that appeared on a formal document declaring that a group of persons were entered into the same koseki register record and shared the same *uji* family name. In other words, rather than having any physiological meaning, the *ie* family as expressed in the koseki registration system always formally operated as a technical device. The 'bloodline' that the koseki system putatively verified merely expressed a fictional 'Japanese' genealogy through a shared koseki register record. Even today, it is clear that the concept of '*jus sanguinis*', the fundamental criterion for eligibility to be 'Japanese' and the essence of the koseki registration system, functions like a religious belief.

Koseki fundamentalism and imperial Japan

Various methods for granting Japanese citizenship to different ethnic groups operated across the colonies of the 'Greater Empire of Japan'. These included selection (Taiwan, Karafuto), compulsion (Korea) and incremental approval (aboriginal peoples of Taiwan and Karafuto). Nevertheless, these people were all largely integrated as 'Japanese subjects'. Rather than the creation of a unified koseki registration system to manage this process, however, different systems were implemented for different ethnic groups. While for mainland Japanese, or *naichijin*, the authorities stipulated mainland koseki registration only for those with a mainland *honseki* address, Korea and Taiwan operated with a Korean-only koseki registration system and a Taiwanese-only koseki registration system respectively, based on a fixed *honseki* address in one of those places. This fixed address could not be moved to other parts of the empire. Thus 'membership of an ethnic group' (*minzokuseki*) based on *honseki* address came into being for the various groups that included 'mainland Japanese', 'Korean' and 'Taiwanese'. While from an external perspective, people from the colonies held Japanese citizenship and were therefore 'Japanese', from an internal perspective, these people were marked as being 'from the external territories', *gaichijin*, and thereby differentiated from mainland Japanese, *naichijin*, from birth.

Terms such as '*naichijin*', 'Korean' and 'Taiwanese' were not specifically articulated in legal documents. In other words, discrimination was not explicitly codified by the use of the names of ethnic groups. Nevertheless, the mere expressions 'person subject/

not subject to the application of the Koseki Registration Law' acted as an effective mechanism for the discriminatory governance of colonial people. In other words, the 'Japanese citizenship' granted to these people in no way guaranteed equality with mainland 'Japanese' and had no meaning beyond that of an external sign which permitted the management of these individuals as 'citizens' at the whim of Japan's ruling powers.

The colony-specific koseki registration system of the imperial era developed from the pragmatic realisation by the powerbrokers of Japan of the need to acknowledge the multiple ethnic communities with differing customs and traditions as components of the empire. This was seen as a more effective governance strategy than uniformly assimilating different ethnic groups into the workings of the mainland state. There was also a realistic need to compromise in the face of the failure to subjugate different ethnic groups. Since civilisation was naturally assumed at the time to be the province of the strong, no equivalent koseki register was compiled for aboriginal people. From the start, the colony-specific koseki registration system of imperial Japan operated to distinguish between ethnicities and to compartmentalise communities on the basis of physiological bloodline into ethnic categories such as '*naichijin*', 'Korean' and 'Taiwanese'.

In the discourse of the Japanese state, the individual entity was subordinate to the *ie* family. The unifying principle of the *ie* family saw koseki registration transfer follow events such as marriage or adoption. This was accompanied by assimilation into the integrity of the bloodline of the *ie* family into which a person entered when this transfer occurred. Such a system also operated in the colony-specific koseki registration systems. In the case of transfer from one imperial regional register to another, irrespective of the wishes of the individual concerned, there was also a transfer of ethnicity. As a result, '*naichijin*' could become 'Korean', while 'Taiwanese' could become '*naichijin*'.

Modern society witnessed the inexorable rise of individualism that moreover incorporated utilitarianism. The state, furthermore, was unable to stem the accelerating movement of migration across national boundaries, often driven by 'private' rather than 'public' factors. Manchuria, or Manchoukuo, for example, became home to an enormous number of quasi-stateless Koreans who thereby evaded the koseki registration system's network of control. As the imperial

Japanese state accelerated its expansion into the international society of East Asia, those Chinese who longed to cross over into Japan's legal sphere and acquire the privileged status of 'Japanese citizen' were able to transform themselves into 'Japanese' swiftly and easily by circumventing Citizenship Law protocols and creating an entry in the Taiwanese koseki registration system. Such examples confirm that the individual was in fact not always merely an object that was subject to koseki register whim. Thus, the paradox emerged of a borderless 'Japanese' community even in the face of the on-paper commitment to uphold at all costs the koseki = *ie* family principle with its insistence on 'pure blood'.

The political powerbrokers of imperial Japan could not help but be aware of the 'citizen' mix that was a feature of the territories into which the empire advanced. It was for this very reason that those in power constantly espoused a form of 'koseki fundamentalism' that took registration to be proof of being an authentic 'Japanese'. The insistence upon the ongoing division between each of the koseki registration systems of the colonies and that of the Japanese mainland (*naichi*) was a tactic to preserve at all cost the degree of pure blood in the koseki register records of *naichijin*, or mainland Japanese. In other words, the authorities consistently called upon the koseki registration system to provide a psychological guarantee of the superiority of the bloodline of the *naichijin* as the ruling ethic group. Nevertheless, the incessant marginalisation of colonial koseki registration systems impacted adversely upon the fictive legal ideology of a multi-ethnic imperial community. This ideology was touted at every turn with empty slogans such as '*Naisen ittai*' (the unity of Japan and Korea), '*Minzoku kyōwa*' (harmony between ethnic groups) and '*Daitōa shin chitsujo*' (the New Order in Greater East Asia). Even as they lauded these ideas, however, the authorities were faced with the contradictorily pressing need to minimise the infiltration of other 'blood' into 'the Japanese' and to insist at all times upon a form of 'koseki fundamentalism'. It was for this reason that the various colony-specific koseki registration systems were never unified.

When Japan regained post-war sovereign status, the presence of other 'ethnic groups' and 'bloodlines' was clearly apparent. Nevertheless, the post-war reconstruction of 'the Japanese' was driven – always with koseki registration as the principle criterion – by reclassifying those Koreans and Taiwanese who had previously been 'Japanese' as 'foreign nationals'. In a move that lacked the smallest trace of compassion, the ruling powers of post-war Japan recognised only those registered in a mainland koseki register as 'Japanese'. Accordingly, both native-born Koreans and Taiwanese who for various reasons had been transferred to a mainland koseki register were included among those defined as 'Japanese' at that time. Conversely, native-born Japanese who had been removed from a mainland koseki register and entered into a Korean or Taiwanese register (including persons who, while not actually being entered into either of these, had been designated as 'requiring a koseki register entry'), were omitted from the frame of the 'Japanese'.

A similar attitude is evident in the koseki policy that operated in Okinawa, which was effectively cut off from Japanese sovereignty during the immediate post-war period. In accordance with United States occupation policy, Okinawan residents were placed under the management of a special koseki registration system, the Ryūkyū register, which departed from the mainland concept of the *ie* family. Upon reversion, however, Japanese authorities assiduously drew the Okinawan koseki registration system back into the mainland order, forcing the people of Okinawa to 'return' to being 'Japanese'. This was achieved through the standardisation of the Okinawan register to ensure 'equivalence to mainland Japan'. Here, the meaning inscribed in the demarcation line between the *naichi* and colonial registers, a line that Japan had strictly maintained, was thrown into sharp relief. In short, this was an expression of 'koseki fundamentalism' that strove to defend to the last the 'basic purpose' of koseki registration as proof of being 'true Japanese'. It is surely unnecessary to note that the rationale behind this mechanism was the need for individuals to subordinate themselves to the *ie* family, which equated with the koseki register record.

Conflict between the koseki registration system and democracy

Without doubt, there is a need for a state-operated status registration system to ensure that citizens are protected by the state and also to guarantee effective rights and services. Particularly in the context of the modern welfare state, there is a clear imperative to gather information on each individual's status and place of residence in order to deliver the necessary services within the territory under a state's jurisdiction. However, we must keep in mind that the foundation of democracy lies in the modern state's acknowledgment that its power derives from a contract with its 'citizens' who, having been freed from a feudalistic social order, seek the guarantee of individual spiritual freedom as a natural right.

Problems with the koseki registration system relate to the fact that, in going beyond the role of civil identification in terms of recording an individual's current status, the operation of this register conflicts with democratic principles. The koseki registration system takes diverse individuals with varying ethnicities, culture and customs, occupations, perspectives on the family and sexual orientations and forces each into one rigid format, thereby creating the standardised 'Japanese'. The authority of the register ensures that any individual who refuses to conform to the demands of the Japanese state or to fit into the proscribed format is disparaged as an 'insubordinate person' or 'un-Japanese' (*hikokumin*). In the koseki register order, the individual is understood to the bitter end to be merely a single member of an *ie* family. Rather than being an autonomous citizen, the value of each individual lies only in their role as one of a homogenous collective of loyal and obedient 'subjects'.

The underside of this superficial homogenisation is that the koseki registration system reproduces social discrimination and disparity by creating a discourse around lines of demarcation. This demarcation has differentiated, for example, between the nobility/persons with samurai ancestry, commoners/new commoners, legitimate children/ illegitimate children and *naichijin*/*gaichijin*. Moreover, the status published in a person's koseki register record is not always theirs by choice. There is a negative history, even in the post-war era, of Japanese people with special familial connections to colonial holdings being stripped of their Japanese citizenship and thus being abandoned by the state purely on the basis of not having an entry in a mainland koseki register. In other words, the legal status of these people was opportunistically manipulated at the whim of the authorities as either 'foreigner' or 'Japanese citizen'. A nation imbued with the spirit of modern democracy would surely have long ago abandoned any record of status and origin that strictly classifies and thus discriminates against groups and individuals in this way.

When, despite the needs of a society, a single system becomes entrenched over a long period, the preservation of that system becomes a goal in itself. This book has demonstrated that the historical trajectory of the koseki registration system, which statistically records information on individuals according to a highly rigid format, has rendered it incapable of fully adapting to the current era characterised by the free movement of people and the diversification of the family. With regards to the family, there is no doubt that this institution has long collapsed as an apparatus of state control. The Japanese state, nevertheless, insists on maintaining the koseki registration system and valorising this system as proof of a person's status as 'authentic Japanese'. The state further continues to insist that it is common 'bloodline' that creates a close connection between each 'citizen' (*kokumin*).

Throughout the states of the world, there has been a trend to seek connectivity between individual and state at the level of everyday lived experience. In a globalised society, where individual identity is grounded in diversity and no longer depends upon family or state, it can be difficult for the state to build a shared identity or to aim for the political integration that constitutes a 'nation'. Yet, if in trying to achieve these ends, the state implements policies that superficially champion democratic processes and the sovereignty of the people while in fact seeking to crush members of minority groups that challenge an officially imposed group self-identity, then surely the term 'nation-state' will only invite mounting distrust and resistance.

As Katō Takashi points out, the principal democratic task facing the contemporary state is 'the revitalisation of those women and men who seek identity and freedom amid difference into true bearers of the sovereignty of the people'.[2] We must acknowledge the inevitable power relation between the state and the individual and the fact that the legal system manifests as the will of the state. Nevertheless, in a democracy (and we can only assume that to be our political environment) we must also implement as far as possible a system that respects the complexity of human society, and that accords with the goals of welfare and convenience in the daily life of each individual. In that sense, we have no option but to accept the challenge to implement drastic reforms to the koseki registration system, which, relentlessly intertwined with manipulative discourse of political power and dependent on fictive symbols of 'citizenship', 'bloodline', 'ethnic group' and '*ie* family', analyses, classifies and orders the 'Japanese'. Only through reform of the koseki registration system can we eliminate the legal restrictions that interfere in the conduct of family life. In achieving this end, Japan might emulate a system, such as that of the Republic of Korea, that has established the 'individual', the 'living person' (*seikatsusha*), as its unit of compilation.

Recession and stagnation are apt to generate an eruption of social chauvinism that targets and constructs a specific ethnic group as the common enemy of the true 'citizens'. This chauvinism can seek psychological unity and superiority by repudiating the targeted group's access to rights or even attempting to exclude its very presence. In recent years, we have witnessed the spectacle of xenophobic demonstrations that target 'Koreans' (*Chōsenjin*, Koreans aligned with North or South Korea, respectively) and 'South Koreans' (*Kankokujin*) in urban areas throughout Japan.

As demonstrated in the argument presented in this book, when we examine how citizenship, in tandem with notions of 'bloodline' and 'ethnicity', has been manipulated through the koseki registration system as a mechanism of state power, it becomes incontrovertible that the term 'Japanese' in no way signifies 'Japanese race' or 'ethnic Japanese'. If nothing else, the history of the koseki registration system teaches us the irrationality of remaining locked away within a shell of bigoted nationalism and being deluded by the manipulative power-elite discourses of 'ethnic group', 'bloodline' and 'citizenship'. Ultimately, these are discourses that lose sight of Japan's true 'national interest'.

Glossary

Notes on translation technique

Where possible, citations from documents originally written in English, e.g. the 1930 Hague Convention on Certain Questions Relating to the Conflict of Nationality Laws, cite the original English language text rather than a translation of the Japanese. Similarly, where possible, source texts of Occupation material, such as the so-called SCAPIN or SCAP instructions, have been used.

Given that the defining characteristic of the koseki registration system in Japan is that it does not, in fact, register a household in the common understanding of that word as a group of people who reside together, and given that the term 'household registration' is in common use with respect to the Chinese *hukou* system, the term 'koseki' given in the Japanese original is retained in the translation. Furthermore, given that, as discussed several times during the course of the book's argument, the 'family' registered is largely a political construction, the term 'family registration' has also been avoided.

Items listed in the glossary below are limited to terms that are repeated throughout the book or which have a particular pertinence to the main thesis of the argument presented. Throughout the text, the majority of translated key terms are accompanied by a Romanisation of the original Japanese. This is especially the case in Chapters Three, Four and Five which provide concrete background to the use of koseki and *kokuseki* as control mechanisms during the imperial era and also during the immediate post-war era when Japan sought to divest itself of all responsibility towards the people subsumed into the empire's colonial holdings.

Romanised Japanese	English translation	Commentary
Bunseki	The creation of a branch koseki register record	
Chōsenjin	Korean	In line with common usage, the term '*Chōsenjin*', which applies to people from the Korean Peninsula in the imperial and immediate post-war era, has been translated as 'Korean' and should not be confused with the current term for South Korean, '*Kankokujin*'.
Daijō daijin	Early to mid-Meiji term used in reference to the prime minister of an administration	
Dōrui ishiki	Consciousness of commonality	Proposed by political scientist Ōyama Ikuo (1880–1955) to explain how communities are formed by individuals with conflicting interests (in the case of the Japanese state, this has been through the fictional notion of 'bloodline').
Fuhō imin	Illegal immigrants	Notoriously, the term used in 1949 by two-time Prime Minister Yoshida Shigeru in relation to Koreans who remained in Japan into the post-war era.
Fukuseki	The return to a koseki register record from which one has previously been removed	
Gaichi	Literally, 'outside lands'	The term used for colonial holdings in which the legal system differed from that of mainland Japan. In other words, in addition to a geographic distinction, the term implies a legal and administrative distinction in a system designed to mark certain groups as non-mainland Japanese. The term gives rise to derivative words such as that listed immediately below.
Gaichijin	People of the '*gaichi*'	People of those places during the imperial era who were not subject to mainland Japanese law.
Ganso Nihonjin	Authentic (original) Japanese	Literally 'founder' Japanese and used to distinguish those of 'pure' Japanese ethnicity from other imperial subjects.

Romanised Japanese	English translation	Commentary
Honseki	The address included in koseki register documentation	This is often different to a residential address, with permission given for citizens of Japan to enter Mt Fuji or the Imperial Palace as a *honseki* address on a koseki register record.
Hōten chōsa-kai	Legislative Investigative Committee	Convened in 1892 following the repudiation of the original Civil Code, to discuss the new draft Civil Code.
Ikka isseki	One family, one record	Requirement that all members of a single family should be entered into a single koseki register record.
Jinshin koseki	Jinshin koseki register	The first modern koseki register, compiled in 1872, following the promulgation of Japan's first Koseki Registration Law.
Josekibo	Inactive koseki register record	A previously existing koseki register record from which all members have either been removed through, for example, death, marriage or the creation of branch register records.
Kegai no tami	Literally 'subjects beyond the reach of imperial rule'	Term from *Nihon shoki* to refer to those people from lands over which the Emperor had no jurisdiction. To retain the ancient sense of this term, it is generally translated in this discussion as 'people from benighted lands beyond the sphere of imperial rule'. Variously translated in other places as 'people whom the Emperor's teachings had not reached' or 'people outside of shogunal control'.
Kettō	Bloodline	
Kettō shudan	Bloodline group	
Kettō-shugi	*Jus sanguinis*, principle of blood	Along with *jus soli*, one of the two principal means of determining citizenship and the option valorised in Japanese legal systems.
Kika	Naturalisation	Literally 'domestication' and also implying, from ancient times, 'subjugation'.
Kikajin	A naturalised Japanese	That is, a foreigner who has taken out – been granted – Japanese citizenship.

Romanised Japanese	English translation	Commentary
Kimin	Literally 'abandoned people'	Used in reference to former immigrants from Japan to Manchoukuo who, unable to return to Japan in the post-war repatriation processes, were stripped of their status as Japanese.
Kiryū	Temporary residence	The expression gives rise to several derivative expressions such as those immediately below.
Kiryū-hō	Temporary Residence Law	
Kiryū-rei	Temporary Residence Directive	
Kokuseki	Citizenship, nationality	In this translation, *kokuseki* is largely translated as 'citizenship', e.g. *Kokuseki-hō*, 'Citizenship Law', unless the term 'nationality' is used in an original English document.
Kōminka	Imperialisation policy	Term used to refer to policy urging the spiritual subjection of the individual to the virtue of the Emperor.
Koseki	Original retained	See 'Notes on translation technique' above.
Koseki-shugi	Koseki register principle/s	The set of principles arbitrarily constructed by the state that enabled koseki register procedures to create a clear division between 'Japanese' and 'non-Japanese' and which largely operated to exclude foreigners from the registration process.
Kyōkon mondai	Problem of de facto marriage relationships	Refers to the fact that the complexity of lodging koseki registration information between colonial holdings led people, particularly those who had come to Taiwan from Japan, to avoid the administrative inconvenience of entering into a legal marriage.
Kyōtsū-hō	Law of Mutuality	Since each imperial holding had a separate koseki register system that differed from that of the mainland and from that in other holdings, the Law of Mutuality was introduced to facilitate administrative links between each site.
Manshūkoku	Manchoukuo	This expression is used in preference to, for example, 'puppet state Manchuria' or 'Mănzhōuguó'.

Romanised Japanese	English translation	Commentary
Mindo	Level of civic consciousness	Used, for example, to judge the 'worthiness' of an 'ethnic' group or individual to be granted Japanese citizenship.
Minpō	Civil code	The body of legislation related to civil matters.
Minseifu	Civil government	The administrative arm of the Ryūkyūan government during the Occupation period.
Minseki	People's register	While same term is used in both the Korean 1909 system and the 1940 Manchoukuo system, those are different systems.
Minzoku	Ethnicity	
Minzoku seki	Membership of an ethnic group	Used to distinguish those from Japan's colonial holdings from '*gansō Nihonjin*' – authentic Japanese.
Mukoseki (*sha*)	(Person) without koseki registration	
Naichi	Literally 'inner lands' – used during the imperial era to refer to mainland Japan	Rather than denoting a mere geographical distinction, the term marked those areas of the empire that were subject to mainland Japanese law. The term gives rise to derivative words such as those listed immediately below.
Naichi-ka	To domesticate and make similar to a mainland Japanese	Used, for example, in the sense of 'domesticating Hokkaido policy'.
Naichijin	Mainland Japanese	
Naimin-ka	Japanisation, literally 'transforming an individual into a person of the inside'	Transforming a person into a mainland Japanese through entry into a mainland koseki register.
Naisen-ittai	Unification of mainland Japan and Korea (*Chōsen*)	The term is significant in that it was used merely as window-dressing, with the authorities of the time repeatedly rejecting moves to take the necessary administrative steps in terms of koseki registration procedures to facilitate unification.
Ninchi	Literally 'recognition' or 'acknowledgement'	Term used to refer to a father acknowledging paternity of a child born to a couple who were not legally married.

Romanised Japanese	English translation	Commentary
Nyūfu kon'in	Marriage to a woman who is a legal household head	In the patriarchal *ie* family system of pre-war Japan, once such a marriage took place, the new husband became legal household head of the family.
Rinji koseki	Literally 'temporary koseki register record'	Term used for the register record initially compiled during the reconstruction of the Okinawan koseki registration system, records for which were largely destroyed during the Battle of Okinawa and the bombing that preceded the land invasion.
Riseki	Separation from a koseki register record	The power to enact this removal was bestowed on the legal household head and was often used to discipline a recalcitrant *ie* family member.
Ryūkyū seifu	Government of the Ryūkyū Islands	Term used for the United States administration of Okinawa throughout the Occupation and until the 1972 reversion of the islands to Japan.
Ryūkyū shobun	Generally translated as 'Ryūkyū Disposition'	The various administrative processes by means of which the Japanese state assumed control of the Ryūkyū Kingdom.
Ryūkyū-jin	Ryūkyūan person/people	Term used to refer to Okinawan people during the period of governance discussed immediately above.
Sekishi	Literally 'children of the Emperor'	
Shinpu no tami	Literally 'newly ruled subjects'	Term entered into Meiji era koseki register records to refer to, for example, a person of Ainu background and which immediately distinguished an individual as non-mainstream Japanese.
Shiseishi	In pre-war Japan, a child born outside a legal marriage whom no man acknowledged paternity of	
Shoshi	In the former Civil Code, a child born outside a legal marriage who was entered into the koseki register record of the man who acknowledged paternity	

Romanised Japanese	English translation	Commentary
Shūseki	The creation of a koseki register record by a person without koseki registration	
Shusshōchi-shugi	*Jus soli*, right of soil	Along with *jus sanguinis*, one of the two principal means of determining citizenship.
Sōshi kaimei	Literally 'creation of an *uji* family name and change of name'	Process by means of which various groups during the imperial era were required to adopt a Japanese-style name in contrast to the naming culture of their own society. Sometimes translated as 'forced name change'.
Soson ittai	Unity of ancestors and descendants in family	Fictional concept glorifying family-line (and therefore bloodline) that bound members of a family entered into the same koseki register record across past and future generations.
Taiwan seki-min	Literally, people in the Taiwanese koseki register	This term refers to people, largely from the southern coastal areas of China, who registered in the Taiwanese koseki registration system in order to access the advantages accorded to those with Japanese documentation in places such as treaty ports. While Japan generally rejected giving legal status to 'outsiders', this group was exempt as they were seen to entrench Japanese influence in sites that would be key to the empire's southern advance.
Todokede shugi	Principle/s of lodgement	Refers to the fact that the koseki registration system required lodgement of information in order to function as intended and also to the fact that, once lodged, information assumed irreversible legal status.
Tokubetsu eijū-sha	Special permanent resident	The name given since 1991 to those born in, or descendants of those born in, imperial Japan's former colonial holdings and which permanently marks these people as not 'Japanese'.
Uji	Surname of members of the same family	The family name of the group of individuals entered into a single koseki register record.

Romanised Japanese	English translation	Commentary
Zokuchi-shugi	Literally 'principle of territoriality' or 'territorial principle'	
Zokujin-shugi	Literally 'personal principle'	

Notes

Introduction

1 Maruyama Masao, 'Kenryoku to dōtoku' (Power and morality), in *Maruyama Masao shū: dai 4 kan* (Collected Works of Maruyama Masao, Vol. 4), Tokyo: University of Tokyo Press, 1995, p. 272.

2 At the close of the nineteenth century, Sir John Robert Seeley stated that in no previous age had governments been so severely criticized for arbitrary intervention into private matters or for oppressive governance. John R. Seeley, *Introduction to Political Science: Two Series of Lectures*, London: Macmillan and Co., 1896, pp. 144–145.

3 Robert M. MacIver, *The Modern State*, Oxford: Oxford University Press, 1928, pp. 181–182.

4 Harold J. Laski, *The State in Theory and Practice*, London: G. Allen and Unwin, 1935, p. 104.

5 Ernest Freund, a noted scholar of policing governance by the nation-state, saw this as an issue not merely related to regulation, but also to the control exerted through both the exercise of regulatory power and its normalisation. Ernst Freund, *The Police Power, Public Policy and Constitutional Rights*, Chicago: Callaghan and Company, 1904, p. 40.

6 A statement made by secretariat councillor Watanabe Kiyoshi (1835–1904) at an 1882 meeting of the Council of Elders (*genrō-in*). See Fukushima Masao, *Ie seido no kenkyū: shiryō-hen II* (Researching the *Ie* Family System: Document Collection II), Tokyo: University of Toyko Press, 1962, p. 163.

7 Response given by government member Suzuki Kisaburō (1867–1940) on 2 March 1914, during the fourth plenary session of the Lower House. *Koseki-hō kaisei kiryū-hō seitei riyū* (Reasons for Creating a Temporary Residents Law and Koseki Registration Legislative Revisions), Tokyo: Hōritsu shimbun-sha, 1914, p. 66.

8 Yokoyama Minoru, 'Koseki-hō shikō 50 nen ni yosete: watashi no sengo koseki monogatari (jō)' (Fifty years of the implementation of the Koseki Registration Law: My post-war koseki register story, Part 1), *Koseki* (The Koseki Register), no. 669, January 1998, pp. 9–10.

9 Bertrand de Jouvenel, *On Power: The Natural History of Its Growth*, Indianapolis: Liberty Fund, 1993, p. 107.

10 Yamanushi Masayuki, 'Kazoku-hō to koseki ishiki' (Family law and koseki consciousness), in *Minpōgaku no sho-mondai* (Issues in the Study of Civil Law), Nihon daigaku hōgakukai-hen (ed.), Tokyo: Nihon daigaku hōgakukai, 1962.

11 Toshitani Nobuyoshi, 'Josetsu: koseki to mibun shōsho' (Introduction: The koseki register and status documentation), in *Koseki to mibun tōroku* (The Koseki Register and Status Registration), Tokyo: Waseda University Press, 2005, p. 4.

12 Shimada Tetsukichi, *Koseki-hō seikai* (Interpreting Koseki Registration Law), Tokyo: Hōrei shingi-kai jimukyoku, 1920, p. 6.

13 Katō Takashi, *Seiji to ningen* (Politics and People), Tokyo: Iwanami shoten, 1993, p. 67.

14 Ōyama Ikuo, 'Kokka seikatsu to kyōdō rigai kan'nen' (Life under the nation-state and notions of mutual interest), in *Ōyama Ikuo chosakushū, dai 1 kan* (Collected Writings of Ōyama Ikuo, Vol. 1), Tokyo: Iwanami shoten, 1987, pp. 381–382.

15 Oguma Eiji, *'Nihonjin' no kyōkai: Okinawa, Ainu, Taiwan, Chōsen shokuminchi shihai kara fukki undō made* (The Boundaries of the 'Japanese': From the Colonial Control of Okinawa, Ainu People, Taiwan and the Korean Peninsula to the Reversion Campaign), Tokyo: Iwanami shoten, 1998.

16 Endō Masataka, *Kindai Nihon no shokiminchi tōchi ni okeru kokuseki to koseki: Manshū, Chōsen, Taiwan* (Citizenship and Koseki Registration during the Era of Colonial Rule in Modern Japan: Manchoukuo, Korea and Taiwan), Tokyo: Akashi shoten, 2010.

17 See, for example, the work of Wagatsuma Sakae, *Ie no seido: sono rinri to hōri* (The *Ie* Family System: Ethics and Legal Principles), Tokyo: Kantō-sha, 1948; Fukushima Masao, *Nihon shihon-shugi to ie seido* (Capitalism in Japan and the *Ie* Family System), Tokyo: University of Tokyo Press, 1967; and Kano Masanao, *Senzen ie no shisō* (The Ideology of the Pre-war *Ie* Family), Tokyo: Sōbun-sha, 1983.

Chapter 1

1 Maruyama Masao, 'Kenryoku to dōtoku' (Power and morality), in *Maruyama Masao shū, Dai-4-kan* (Maruyama Masao Collection, Vol. 4), Tokyo: University of Tokyo Press, 1995, p. 272.

2 Murakami Tomokazu, *Koseki (jō)* (Koseki Registration, Part 1), Tokyo: Seirin-shoin, 1954, pp. 54–55.

3 Hiraga Kenta, 'Koseki seido ni tsuite' (On the koseki registration system), *Mibun-hō to koseki: Koseki seido hachi jū nen kinen ronbun shū* (Identity Law and Koseki Registration: A Collection of Essays for the Eightieth Year of the Koseki Registration System), Zenkoku rengō koseki jimu kyōgikai (ed.) (National League of Koseki Register Administrative Councils), Tokyo: Teikoku hanrei-hō shuppansha, 1953, p. 301.

4 Shihōshō Minjikyoku (Ministry of Justice, Civil Affairs Bureau), 'Shiseishi no meishō haishi' (The abolition of 'child born independently' nomenclature), Cabinet Information Department *Tsūhō No. 283* (Report No. 283), 11 March 1942, p. 26.

5 Notification of the Director of the Ministry of Justice Civil Affairs Bureau, Civil Matter No. 90, 18 February 1942. Koseki Registration Law Precedent Research Society (ed.), *Koseki senrei zenshū (2)* (Collected Koseki Registration Law Precedent (2)) (with insertions and deletions), Tokyo: Gyōsei Corporation, pp. 217–218.

6 Response of government delegate Suzuki Kisaburō to the fourth Lower House plenary session (2 March 1914). See *Koseki-hō kaisei kiryū-hō seitei riyū* (Reasons for Temporary Residence Regulations in Koseki Registration Law Reform), Tokyo: Hōritsu Shimbun-sha, 1914, p. 86.

7 Response of House member Shimada Toshio to the fourth Lower House plenary session (2 March 1914). See *Koseki-hō kaisei kiryū-hō seitei riyū* (Reasons for Temporary Residence Regulations in Koseki Registration Law Reform), Tokyo: Hōritsu Shimbun-sha, 1914, p. 86.
8 Sōri-fu tōkei-kyoku (Statistics Bureau of the Prime Minister's Office) (ed.), *Sōri-fu tōkei-kyoku hachi-jū nen shikyō* (Eighty Years of Statistics in the Prime Minister's Office), Sōri-fu tōkei-kyoku (Statistics Bureau of Prime Minister's Office), 1951, p. 52.
9 Response of the Director of the Ministry of Justice Civil Affairs Bureau, Civil Issue No. 629, 45 May 1916. *Koseki kankei hanrei sōran* (Complete Collection of Legal Precedents Concerning Koseki Registration), pp. 58–59.
10 Response of the Director of the Ministry of Justice Civil and Criminal Affairs Bureau, Civil and Criminal Issue No. 1442, 5 August 1899. *Koseki senrei zenshū (1)* (Collected Koseki Registration Law Precedent (1)), p. 1.
11 Murakami (ed.), *Koseki (jō)* (Koseki Registration, Part 1), p. 300.
12 Seki Kōjirō, *Koseki seido* (Koseki Registration System), Tokyo: Jōban shobō, 1933, p. 262.
13 Wagatsuma Sakae et al., *Koseki (1): Shusshō* (Koseki Registration (1): Birth), Tokyo: Yuhikaku Publishing, 1958, p. 22.
14 Response of the Director of the Ministry of Justice Civil Affairs Bureau, Civil Matter No. 1361, 4 April 1921. *Koseki senrei zenshū (4)* (Collected Koseki Registration Law Precedent (4)), p. 1169.
15 Yokoyama, 'Koseki-hō shikō 50-nen ni yosete: watashi no sengo koseki monogatari (jō)' (Fifty years of Koseki Registration Law implementation, Part 1), pp. 18–19.
16 Nakano Magoichi, 'Meiji 5-nen shiki koseki' (Concerning the Meiji 5 Form koseki register (Jinshin koseki register)), *Koseki* (Koseki Registration), Vol. 252, February 1968, p. 4.
17 *Taiwan-jin kankei zakken: Kengen oyobi Chinjō kankei* (Miscellaneous Information on the People of Taiwan: Proposals and Petitions), Gaimushō gaikō shiryōkan shozō A.5.3.0.3-5 (Ministry of Foreign Affairs Diplomatic Archive A.5.3.0.3-5).
18 Seki, *op. cit.*, p. 55.
19 'Honseki-jin hanzai meibo seibi-kata' (Method of compiling and maintaining a roll of criminals with a given *honseki* address), *Ministry of Home Affairs Directive 1*, 12 April 1917. See *Koseki*, Vol. 232, October 1966, p. 59.
20 *Ministry of Home Affairs Directive 3*, 29 January 1927. See *Koseki*, Vol. 232, p. 60.
21 Naruge Tetsuji, *Koseki no jitsumu to sono riron* (The Theory of Koseki Register Administration), Tokyo: Nihon kajo shuppan, 1956, p. 60.
22 Ebihara Yoshimune, 'Genkō hō ka ni okeru koseki no kōkai seigen ni tsuite' (On the limits to public access to the koseki register under current law), *Koseki*, Vol. 354, June 1975, p. 2.
23 Wada Mikihiko, *Ie seido no haishi* (The Abolition of the *Ie* Family System), Tokyo: Shinzansha, 2010, see particularly Chapter Five. According to Wada, in the context of Civil Code and Koseki Registration

Law revisions, both the GS (Government Section) of the GHQ and the Civil Code Drafting Committee, the members of which were Japanese, focused exclusively on the reform or abolition of the *ie* family system in the Civil Code and a concomitant reform or abolition of this concept in the Koseki Registration Law. GS presented no opposition to the data collection or information provision functions of the koseki registration system, and the Committee showed almost no interest in this matter. As a result, even after the abolition of the *ie*, those functions were strengthened. See Wada, *op. cit.*, pp. 420–421 and p. 424.

24 *Ibid.*, p. 421.

25 Amino Yoshihiko, *'Nihon' to ha nani ka* (What is 'Japan'?), Tokyo: Kōdansha, 2000, pp. 115–116.

26 Yanagita Kunio, 'Ie kandan: kamei shōkō' (Talking of the family: Some thoughts on family names), *Teihon Yanagita Kunio Shū, dai 15 kan* (Standard Edition: Yanagita Kunio Collected Works, Vol. 15), Tokyo: Chikuma shobō, 1963, p. 294.

27 Toyoda Takeshi, *Myōji no rekishi* (The History of the Surname), Tokyo: Chūkō shinsho, 1971, pp. 139–146.

28 Tono'oka Mojūrō (ed.), *Meiji zenki kazoku-hō shiryō, dai 1 kan, dai 2 satsu* (Documents on Early Meiji Era Family Law, Vol. 1, Book 2), Tokyo: Waseda University, p. 305.

29 *Ibid.*, pp. 348–349.

30 *Ibid.*, p. 366.

31 *Ibid.*, pp. 529–530.

32 Toyoda, *op. cit.*, p. 153.

33 Inoue Kowashi, 'Koseki iken an' (Koseki position paper) (1878), *Inoue Kowashi den: shiryō Dai 1* (Biography of Inoue Kowashi: Documentation No. 1), Inoue Kowashi denki hensan I'inkai (ed.) (Inoue Kowashi Biographical Compilation Committee), Tokyo: Kokugakuin University Library, 1966, p. 163.

34 Kameyama Sadayoshi, *Minpō seigi: jinji hen maki-no-ni* (*ge*) (Civil Code Justice: Civil Affairs, Vol. 2, Part 2), Tokyo: Shinpō chūshaku kai, 1891, pp. 12–13.

35 Wagatsuma Sakae (ed.), *Sengo ni okeru minpō kaisei no keika* (The Stages of Post-war Civil Code Reform), Tokyo: Nihon hyōronsha, 1956, p. 303.

36 *Ibid.*, p. 133.

37 Miyazawa Toshiyoshi, 'Ie yaburete uji ari' (The *ie* may have vanished but the family name remains), *Hōritsu taimuzu* (The Legal Times), Vol. 1, No. 7, p. 25.

38 Hiraga, 'Koseki seido ni tsuite' (On the koseki registration system), p. 308.

39 Hisatake Ayako, *Uji to koseki no josei shi* (A Women's History of the Koseki Register and the Family Name), Tokyo: Sekai shisō sha, 1988, p. 146.

40 *Ibid.*, pp. 189–191.

41 For further information on the Chinese family system and Chinese family surnames, see Shiga Shūzō, *Chūgoku kazoku-hō no genri* (The Fundamentals of Chinese Family Law), Tokyo: Sōbunsha, 1967.

42 Ueda Masa'aki, *Kika-jin* (Naturalised People), Tokyo: Chūkō shinsho, 1965, p. 14.
43 Hirano Kunio, *Kika-jin to kodai kokka* (Naturalised People and the Ancient State), Tokyo: Yoshikawa kōbundō, 1993, p. 1.
44 Ueda, *op. cit.*, p. 30.
45 Ōmori Kazuhito, 'Kokuseki jimu no sūsei to kongo no dōkō' (Trends in citizenship administration and future directions), *Minji geppō* (Civil Affairs Monthly Bulletin), Vol. 24, No. 10, October 1969, pp. 64–65.
46 Kidana Shōichi, *Chikujō chūkai kokuseki-hō* (Point-by-Point Annotations to Citizenship Law), Tokyo: Nihon kajo shuppan, 2003, p. 254.
47 Kimura Mitsuo, 'Moto-Chōsenjin kikasha to koseki no kisai' (Naturalised former Koreans and the koseki register record', *Koseki jihō* (Koseki News), Vol. 200, January 1975, p. 41.
48 Tashiro Aritsugu, *Kokuseki-hō chikujō kaisetsu* (Point-by-Point Commentary on Citizenship Law), Tokyo: Nihon kajo shuppan, 1974, pp. 6–7.
49 *Ibid.*, p. 71.
50 *Ibid.*, pp. 71–72.
51 Nakamura Shingo, 'Waga kokuhōjō gojin ga nihonjin naru koto wo shōmei suru koto wo uru ya' (Based on the laws of our land, is it possible to receive documentation which proves that one is Japanese?), *Hōgaku shinpō* (Legal Studies News), Vol. 12, No. 3, p. 58.
52 Tashiro, *Kokuseki-hō chikujō kaisetsu* (Point-by-Point Commentary on Citizenship Law), pp. 14–19; Kidana, *op. cit.*, p. 63.
53 Tokyo High Court ruling, 14 May 1959, Saikō saibansho hanrei chōsa kai (Supreme Court of Japan Casebook Survey Committee), *Kōtō saibasho hanji hanrei shū* (Appellate Court Judiciary Precedent Collection), Vol. 8, No. 1, p. 529.
54 *Ibid.*
55 See p. 2 of *ibid.*, 'Kōryō' (Charter) and Foreword. This draft outline was based on a document drawn up initially by Tokyo Appellant Court Judge Hayashi Tōru, and finalised by Tokyo University professor Suehiro Izutarō, Ōkura Institute for the Study of Spiritual Culture researcher Shinmi Kichiji, Chūō University professor Kainō Michitaka, Waseda University professor Yusa Yoshio and Manchurian Ministry of Justice Councillor Chigusa Tatsuo (all titles current at the time of publication).
56 A number of scholars have made this point, particularly Satō Bunmei in *Koseki ga tsukuru sabetsu: josei, minzoku, burakumin, soshite 'shiseiji' sabetsu wo shitte imasu ka* (The Discriminatory Effects of Koseki Registration: Are You Aware of Koseki Register Discrimination Against Women, Ethnic Groups, Burakumin-Background People and Illegitimate Children?), Tokyo: Gendai shokan, 1984. Other studies into this issue include Okuda Yasuhiro, *Shimin no tame no kokuseki-hō/ koseki-hō nyūmon* (Layperson's Introduction to the Koseki Registration Law and Citizenship Law), Tokyo: Akashi shoten, 1997, and Ninomiya Shūhei, *Kazoku to hō: Kojinka to tayōka no naka de* (Family and the Law in a Time of Individualisation and Diversification), Tokyo: Iwanami Shinsho, 2007.

57 Suzuki Rokuya, 'Kakkoku no mibun tōroku seido' (Identity registration systems across nations), in Nakamura Zen'nosuke et al. (eds) *Kazoku mondai to kazoku-hō VII: Kaji saiban* (Family Issues and Family Law: The Legal Response to Domestic Affairs), Tokyo: Sakai shoten, 1957, pp. 280–281.
58 For information on the family record system in Germany, see Wakao Yūji, *Kindai Doitsu no kekkon to kazoku* (Marriage and the Family in Modern Germany), Nagoya: University of Nagoya Press, 1996.
59 Suzuki, *op. cit.*, p. 294.
60 Aoki Yoshihito, 'Koseki-hō no hanashi: Ritsuan no kei'i wo fukumete' (Talking of the Koseki Registration Law: With reference also to the stages of drafting), *Koseki jihō* (Koseki News), Vol. 194, July 1974, p. 9.
61 For information on changes to family registration systems in China from ancient to modern times, see Wang Weihai, *Zhonguo hùjí zhìdù: lìshǐ yǔ zhèngzhì de fēxī*, (The Household Registration System in China: A Historical and Political Analysis), Shanghai: Wenhua chubanshe, 2006.
62 *Zhōng huá rén mín gòng hé guó hu kǒu dēng jì tiáo lì* (Regulations of Household Registration in the People's Republic of China), Beijing: Qunzhong chubanshe 1958, pp. 2–8.
63 Luo Ruiqing, 'Guanyu Zhōnghuá rénmín gònghéguó hukǒu dēngjì tiáolì cǎoàn de shuōmíng' (On an explanation of the draft regulations of household registration in the People's Republic of China), *ibid.*, pp. 12–13. At that time Luo was the head of China's Ministry of Public Security.
64 Wagatsuma Sakae, *Ie no seido, sono rinri to hōri* (The *Ie* Family System, Its Ethics and Jurisprudence), Tokyo: Kanchōsha, 1948, p. 121.
65 Roscoe Pound, *The Spirit of the Common Law*, Boston: Marshall Jones and Co, 1921, p. 37.
66 Aoki, *op. cit.*, p. 13.
67 Wagatsuma (ed.), *op. cit.*, p. 21.

Chapter 2

1 Kidana Shōichi, *Chikujō chūkai kokuseki-hō* (Point-by-Point Annotations to Citizenship Law), Tokyo: Nihon kajo shuppan, 2003, p. 24.
2 Hosokawa Karoku, *Shokumin-shi* (Colonial History), Tokyo: Tōyō Keizai shinpō-sha, 1941, pp. 22–23.
3 Hiraga Kenta, *Kokuseki-hō, jōkan* (Citizenship Law, Part 1), Tokyo: Teikoku hanrei-hōki shuppansha, 1950, p. 36.
4 Paul Weiss, *Nationality and Statelessness in International Law*, London: Stevens, 1956, pp. 5–6.
5 Itō Yukinori, *Shutsunyū-koku kanri ni okeru ryoken no toriatsukai ni kan suru kenkyū* (Research on Passport Management in the Context of Emigration and Immigration), Hōmu kenkyū hōkokusho, Vol. 72, No. 2, Tokyo: Hōmu sōgō kenkyūjo, 1985, p. 1 and pp. 4–5.

6 *Ibid.*, p. 7.

7 Sir Frederick Pollock and Frederic William Maitland, *The History of English Law before the Time of Edward 1*, Cambridge: Cambridge University Press, 1895, p. 442.

8 William Bennett Munro, *The Government of the United States: National, State, and Local*, New York: Macmillan, 1919, p. 75.

9 Roscoe Pound, *The Spirit of the Common Law*, Boston: Marshall Jones Co, 1921, pp. 100–101.

10 Hiraga Kenta, *Kokuseki-hō, gekan* (Citizenship Law, Part 2), Tokyo: Teikoku hanrei-hōki shuppansha, 1951, p. 200.

11 Prentiss Webster, *Treatise of the Law of Citizenship in the United States*, Albany: M. Bender, 1891, pp. 105–106.

12 Tashiro Aritsugu, 'Kokuseki-hō (Kokuseki tōroku=koseki) no shinzoku-hō, sōzoku-hō ni oyobosu eikyō ni tsuite' (The influence of citizenship law (citizenship registration = koseki registration) on family law and inheritance law), in *Nihon koseki no tokushitsu ni tsuite* (On the Special Characteristics of Japan's Koseki Registration System), Zenkoku rengō koseki jimu kyōgikai (ed.) (National League of Koseki Register Administrative Councils), Tokyo: Teikoku hanrei-hōki shuppansha, 1972, p. 439.

13 Egawa Hidefumi and Yamada Ryōichi, *Kokuseki-hō* (Citizenship Law), Tokyo: Yuhikaku, 1973, pp. 8–9.

14 *Ibid.*, p. 8.

15 *Ibid.*, p. 12.

16 John B. Moore, *American Diplomacy: Its Spirit and Achievements*, New York: Harper & Brothers, 1905, pp. 171–172.

17 Ninomiya Masato, *Kokuseki-hō ni okeru danjo byōdō* (Gender Equality in Citizenship Law), Tokyo: Yuhikaku, 1986, p. 28.

18 Francis T. Piggott, *Nationality: Including Naturalization and English Law on the High Seas and Beyond the Realm*, Vol. 1, London: William Clowes and Sons Limited, 1907, p. 135.

19 Tanaka Yasuhisa, 'Nihon kokuseki-hō enkaku shi (3)' (History and development of citizenship law in Japan (3)), *Kokuseki* (Citizenship), No. 456, June 1982, p. 4. Furthermore, prior to this, Clause 26 of the 'Dai Nippon teikoku kenpō gairyaku mikomisho' (Proposed outline for the future constitution of the Empire of Japan), compiled as a draft around February 1881 by the Fukushima Prefecture initiated *Chizuzen kyōaikai* (Association of Mutual Brothers of Chikuzen), stated 'A person born and raised in Japan is Japanese. However, if that child's father and mother are foreigners, the child also has that status'. The document gave detailed stipulations of six points concerning the acquisition and loss of citizenship that drew on *jus sanguinis* and bloodline. Tanaka, *Ibid.*, pp. 3–4.

20 'Kokumin-ken naigai-jin sabetsu ni tsuki Roesureru-shi Mosse-shi iken' (The views of Messrs Roesler and Mosse on civil rights and discrimination towards nationals and foreigners), Itō Hirobumi (ed.), in *Hisho ruisan: hōsei kankei shiryō jōkan* (Secretarial Classification: Documents Related to Legislation), compiled by Osatake Takeki and Hiratsuka Atsushi, Tokyo: Hisho ruisan kankō-kai, 1934, p. 473.

21 Nevertheless, Clause 8, Section 2, stated, 'When the child of a foreigner, too, is born in Japan', this child would be recognised as holding Japanese citizenship. The acknowledgement in this case of *jus soli* and the significance of place of birth resulted from a desire to avoid creating stateless children, that is, children without citizenship.
22 Kumano Toshizō, *Minpō seigi: jinji-hen kan no ichi* (*jō*) (Civil Law and Justice: The Original Civil Code, First Volume (Part 1)), Tokyo: Shinpō teishaku sha, 1893, p. 47.
23 *Ibid.*, p. 48.
24 *Ibid.*, p. 74.
25 *Ibid.*, pp. 85–86.
26 'Hōten chōsa-kai kokuseki-hō narabi ni Meiji 6-nen dai-103-gō fukoku kaisei-an giji soku-kiroku' (Stenographic Notes of the Legislative Investigative Committee Proceedings for Draft Amendments to Citizenship Law and Meiji Year 6 Ordinance Proclamation No. 135), in *Nihon kindai rippō shiryō sōsho, dai 26 kan* (Modern Japan's Legal Document Series, Vol. 26), Hōmu daijin kanbō shihō hōsei shōsa-bu kanshū (ed.) (Editorial Board of the Justice and Legislation Survey Department of the Minister of Justice Secretariat), Tokyo: Shōji hōmu kenkyū-kai (Japan Institute of Business Law), 1986, p. 11.
27 Sanekata Masao, *Kokuseki-hō* (Citizenship Law), Tokyo: Nihon hyōron-sha, 1938, p. 12.
28 Yamaguchi Kōichi, *Nihon kokusai shihō-ron* (A Discussion on International Private Law in Japan), 1938, p. 143.
29 Rogers Brubaker, *Citizenship and Nationality in France and Germany*, Cambridge: Harvard University Press, 1992, pp. 85, 93.
30 For further information on the anti-Japanese movement and the dual citizenship of Japanese people resident in the United States, see Chapter 1, Part 1, of Endō Masataka, *Kindai Nihon no shokuminchi tōchi ni okeru kokuseki to koseki: Manshū, Chōsen, Taiwan* (Citizenship, Koseki Registration and Colonial Governance in Modern Japan: Manchoukuo, Korea and Taiwan), Tokyo: Akashi shoten, 2010.
31 'Hōmu daijin kanbō shihō hōsei shōsa-bu kanshū (ed.), *op. cit.*, p. 13.
32 *Ibid.*, p. 32.
33 Sanekata, *op. cit.*, p. 31.
34 Taikakai (ed.), *Naimushō-shi, dai 3 kan* (History of the Home Ministry, Vol. 3), Tokyo: Hara shobō, 1980, p. 600.
35 Tameike Yoshio, 'Tsuma no kokuseki ni tsuite' (Concerning the citizenship of wives), *Hōgaku ronsō* (Kyōto Law Review), Vol. 58, No. 1, January 1952, pp. 45–48.
36 Hiraga, *op. cit.*, p. 109.
37 Sanekata, *op. cit.*, p. 18.
38 Tameike, *op. cit.*, p. 53.
39 *Ibid.*, p. 48.
40 *Ibid.*, p. 54.
41 Hiraga, *op. cit.*, p. 134.
42 'Gaikokijin o yōshi mata wa nyūfū to nasu no hōritsu' (Law on foreigners becoming adopted children or marrying into a wife's *ie* family), (1899, Law No. 21).

43 Ōmori Kazuhito, 'Kokuseki jimu no sūsei to kongo no dōkō' (Trends in citizenship administration and future directions), *Minji geppō* (Civil Affairs Monthly Bulletin), Vol. 24, No. 10, October 1969, pp. 71–72.
44 Sanekata, *op. cit.*, pp. 52–55.
45 *Ibid.*, pp. 25–26.
46 Kuroki Tadamasa and Hosokawa Kiyoshi, *Gaijihō, Kokuseki-hō* (External Affairs Law and Citizenship Law), Tokyo: Gyōsei, 1988, p. 263.
47 13 April 1898. 'Kokuseki hō narabi-ni Meiji 6-nen dai-hyakusan-gō fukoku kaisei-an giji sokukiroku' (Transcript of the Proceedings of Proposed Revisions to Citizenship Law and Meiji Year 6 103rd Ordinance'). Hōmu daijin kanbō shihō-hōsei chōsa-bu kanshū (Minister of Justice Secretariat Justice Administration and Legislation Survey Department, Gen. ed.). *Modern Japan Legislative Document Series, Vol. 6* (Kindai Nihon rippō shiryō sōsho, dai-rokkan), Commercial Law Research Society, 1968, p. 20.
48 *Ibid.*, p. 22.
49 *Ibid.*, p. 25.
50 *Ibid.*, p. 24.
51 'Hōten chōsa-kai minpō giji sokukiroku 6' (The Legislative Investigative Committee Civil Code Stenographic Notes Record 6), in *Nihon kindai rippō shiryō sōsho, dai 6 kan* (Modern Japan's Legal Document Series, Vol. 6), p. 77.
52 Koseki senrei kenkyūkai (ed.), *Koseki senrei zenshū: shōgai (1)* (Koseki Registration Precedent, Complete Edition: External/Internal Relations (1)) (addition and removal type), Tokyo: Gyōsei, 1952–, p. 18–19.
53 See Chapter 5 of Okuda Yasuhiro, *Kokuseki-hō to kokusai oyako-hō* (Citizenship Law and International Law Relating to Parents and Children), Tokyo: Yuhikaku, 2004.

Chapter 3

1 Kawakami Tasuke, *Nihon kodai shakai shi no kenkyū* (A Study of the History of Ancient Japanese Society), Tokyo: Kawade Shobō, 1947, pp. 152–154.
2 Nanbu Noboru, 'Nihon no kodai koseki to shi' (Japan's ancient household registers and the 'family surname'), in Toshitani Nobuyoshi, Kamata Hiroki and Hiramatsu Hiroshi (eds), *Koseki to mibun tōroku* (Household Register and Status Koseki Registration), Tokyo: Waseda Daigaku Shuppan Kai, 2005, p. 33.
3 Kishi Toshio, *Nihon kodai sekichō no kenkyū* (A Study of Japan's Ancient Population Registers), Tokyo: Hanawa Shobō, 1973, Chapter 5.
4 *Ibid.*, p. 280.
5 Ōishi Shinsaburō, *Kinsei sonraku no kōzō to ie seido zōho ban* (Early Modern Village Structure and the *Ie* Family System, Expanded Edition), Tokyo: Ochanomizu Shobō, 1976, pp. 339–341.
6 *Ibid.*, pp. 342–344.

7 According to Ōishi, *shūmon aratame* was systematically implemented by the shogunate government at a relatively late stage, probably in the late seventeenth century during the Kanbun period. *Ibid*., pp. 310–325.
8 Ōishi Shinsaburō, 'Edo jidai ni okeru koseki ni tsuite' (Koseki registration in the Edo era), in Fukushima Masao (ed.), *Koseki seido to 'ie' seido* (The Koseki Registration System and the *Ie* System), Tokyo: Tokyo Daigaku Shuppan Kai, 1959, p. 65. According to Ishii Ryōsuke, however, *shūmon aratame chō* and *ninbetsu chō* were always compiled separately in Edo and hence *shūmon ninbetsu chō* was never referred to by that name in Edo. In Osaka, on the other hand, *ninbetsu chō* developed from the *shūmon aratame chō* system and hence the two were referred to together as *shūmon ninbetsu chō*. Ishii Ryōsuke, *Ie to koseki no rekishi* (A History of the Family and Koseki Registration), Tokyo: Sōbun Sha, 1981, p. 244.
9 Nomura Kanetarō, *Goningumi chō no kenkyū* (A Study of the Five Households Group System), Tokyo: Yūhikaku, 1943, pp. 20–21.
10 Ōishi, *op. cit*., 1976, p. 399.
11 Ishii, *op. cit*., pp. 227–229.
12 *Ibid*., p. 136.
13 However, since the two developed for different purposes, there were many cases of separation between *shūmon aratame* and *ninbetsu aratame*. According to Shinmi Kichiji, there is some evidence that census procedures were carried out in Kumamoto Domain from the Bunka or Bunsei period and in Owari Domain from the Kaei period. Shinmi Kichiji, *Jinshin koseki seiritsu ni kansuru kenkyū* (A Study on the Compilation of the Jinshin Koseki Register), Tokyo: Nihon Gakujutsu Shinkō Kai, 1959, pp. 26–29. According to Tanaka Akira, in Chōshū Domain, a koseki registration system was enforced from 1825 (Bunsei 8) and so the two were conducted separately. Tanaka Akira, 'Meiji seiken shoki seisaku no genkei: Koseki chō wo ichirei toshite' (The prototype for early Meiji government policy: The example of the household register), *Nihon rekishi* (The Journal of Japanese History), No. 83, March, 1955.
14 Maruyama Masao, 'Chūsei to hangyaku' (Loyalty and rebellion), in *Kindai Nihon shisō shi kōza* (Lectures on the History of Modern Japanese Thought), Vol. 6, Tokyo: Chikuma Shobō, 1960. Also in Maruyama Masao, *Maruyama Masao shū* (Collected Works of Masao Maruyama), Vol. 8, Tokyo: Tokyo Daigaku Shuppan Kai, 1996, pp. 188–189.
15 No title. 'Homin koseki 2' (Protection of subjects and koseki registration), *Dajō ruiten* (Cabinet Archives of Japan), Book 1, Vol. 79.
16 Matsumoto San'nosuke, *Tennōsei kokka to seiji shisō* (The Imperial State and Political Thought), Tokyo: Mirai Sha, 1969, p. 177.
17 Fukuchi Gen'ichirō, *Bakufu suibō ron* (The Downfall of the Shogunate Government), Tokyo: Minyū Sha, 1892, p. 179.
18 'Kyūrai dappan tō no yakara kyūchi he fukkiseshimu' (Returning deserters to their former domains), 'Homin koseki 2' (Protection of subjects and koseki registers), *Dajō ruiten* (Cabinet Archives of Japan), Book 1, Vol. 79.

19 Fukushima Masao (ed.), *'Ie' seido no kenkyū shiryō hen I* (A Study of the '*Ie* Family' System, References Section I), Tokyo: Tokyo Daigaku Shuppan Kai, 1962a, pp. 8–30.

20 'Museki shobun kata Tokyo fu he tasshi' (Proclamation to Tokyo Prefecture on the handling of unregistered persons), 'Homin koseki 2' (Protection of subjects and koseki registers), *Dajō ruiten* (Cabinet Archives of Japan), Book 1, Vol. 79.

21 *Iwakura Tomomi kankei bunsho* (Documents Relating to Iwakura Tomomi), Vol. 1, Tokyo: Nihon Shiseki Kyōkai, 1927, p. 352.

22 Once the conscription and taxation systems based on the Jinshin koseki registration system were established, the tie between the land and people that had constituted the substrate of feudal society became obsolete. Accordingly, this 're-registration' rule lost its function and was abolished in practice in December 1877. Yamanushi Masayuki, 'Meiji koseki hō no ichi kinō' (One function of the Meiji Koseki Registration Law), in Fukushima (ed.), *Koseki seido to 'ie' seido*, 1959, p. 201.

23 Fukuzawa Yukichi, 'Seiyō jijō shohen' (Conditions in the West, Part 1), in Keiō Gijuku (ed.), *Fukuzawa Yukichi zenshū* (Collected Works of Yukichi Fukuzawa, Vol. 1), Tokyo: Iwanami Shoten, 1958, p. 290.

24 Katsuta Magoya, Ōkubo Toshimichi den chūkan (The Biography of Toshimichi Ōkubo, Vol. 2), Tokyo: Dōbunkan, 1910, p. 617.

25 Naikaku Kanbō Kyoku, *Hōrei zensho Meiji 2 nen* (Compendium of Civil Law, Meiji 2), Tokyo: Hara Shobō, 1974, p. 59.

26 Fukushima Masao (ed.), *'Ie' seido no kenkyū shiryō hen II* (A Study of the '*Ie* Family' System, References Section II), Tokyo: Tokyo Daigaku Shuppan Kai, 1962b, pp. 4–10. Quotes from the same source.

27 *Nanpaku Etō Shinpei ikō* (Posthumous Works of Shinpei Etō Final Collection), Tokyo: Yoshikawa Hanshichi, 1900, p. 52.

28 Quoted from *Hōrei zensho Meiji 4 nen* (Compendium of Civil Law, Meiji 4).

29 According to Garner, these activities of a state to legitimise itself include maintaining domestic peace, order and security, protecting individuals and properties and securing external security, which are essential and primary functions even for an immature developing state. James W. Garner, *Introduction to Political Science: A Treatise on the Origin, Nature, Functions, and Organization of the State*, New York: American Book Company, 1910, p. 318.

30 Fukushima (ed.), *op. cit.*, 1962b, p. 165.

31 *Ibid.*, pp. 95–96.

32 The treatment of monastics varied depending on the era and domain. For example, this group was subject to koseki registration in *machikata ninbetsu aratame* in Bishū Domain during the Kyōho period. Ōishi, *op. cit.*, 1959, p. 62.

33 *Hōrei zensho Meiji 4 nen* (Compendium of Civil Law, Meiji 4), p. 337.

34 Fukushima Masao, *Nihon shihon shugi to ie seido* (Japanese Capitalism and the *Ie* Family System), Tokyo: Tokyo Daigaku Shuppan Kai, 1967, p. 123.

35 *Hōrei zensho Meiji 4 nen* (Compendium of Civil Law, Meiji 4), pp. 269–270.

36 Shinmi Kichiji, *Ie to koseki* (The *Ie* family and Koseki Registration), Tokyo: Nihon Hōri Kenkyū Kai, 1942, p. 21.
37 Fukushima, *op. cit.*, 1967, p. 93.
38 See Takagi Hiro'o, 'Gōsha teisoku to koseki hō' (Village shrine precepts and the Koseki Registration Law), in Fukushima (ed.), *Koseki seido to ie' seido*, 1959.
39 'Naimu shō dai 1 kai nenpō yori Meiji 8 nen 7 gatsu itaru Meiji 9 nen 6 gatsu 1' (The Ministry of the Interior Annual Report No. 1 from July Meiji 8 to June Meiji 9, 1), in Obinata Sumio (ed.), *Naimu shō nenpō hōkokusho dai 1kan* (The Ministry of the Interior Annual and Other Reports Vol. 1), Tokyo: San'ichi Shobō, 1982, p. 69.
40 *Kessai roku Minpō 12 Meiji 10 nen 1 gatsu yori 6 gatsu* (Records of Civil Code Resolutions 12 from January to June, Meiji 10). In the possession of Kokuritsu Kōbunshokan.
41 'Dajōkan tasshi' (Proclamation of the Grand Council of State) No. 20 made on 5 February 1877, *Hōrei zensho Meiji 10 nen* (Compendium of Civil Law, Meiji 10), p. 164.
42 An address by Sufu Kōhei, Assistant Secretary of *Sanji in* (Legislative Advisory Council) to a Council of Elders meeting held on 31 March 1882. Fukushima (ed.), *op. cit.*, 1962b, p. 159.
43 'Naimu kyō dai 4 kai nenpō furoku 2' (Ministry of Home Affairs Annual Report No. 4, Appendix 2), in Obinata Sumio (ed.), *Naimu shō nenpō hōkokusho dai 6 kan* (Ministry of Home Affairs Annual and Other Reports Vol. 6), Tokyo: San'ichi Shobō, 1983, p. 348–357.
44 Yamagata Aritomo, with explanatory notes by Matsushita Yoshio, *Rikugun shō enkaku shi* (History of the Ministry of War), Tokyo: Nihon Hyōron Sha, 1942, p. 236.
45 Fukushima, *op. cit.*, 1967, p. 31.
46 Fukushima Masao and Toshitani Nobuyoshi, 'Meiji igo no koseki seido no hattatsu' (Development of the koseki registration system after the Meiji period), in Nakagawa Zennosuke et al. (eds), *Kazoku mondai to kazoku hō VII kaji saiban* (Family Matters and Family Law VII: The Family Court), Tokyo: Sakai Shoten, 1957, pp. 318–319.
47 Kobayakawa Kingo, *Zoku Meiji hōsei sōkō* (The Sequel to Notes on the Meiji Legal System), Tokyo: Yamaguchi Shoten, 1942, pp. 246–249.
48 Council of Elders meeting held on 3 July 1882. Fukushima (ed.), *op. cit.*, 1962b, p. 160.
49 Kameyama Sadayoshi, *Minpō seigi jinji hen maki no ni* (*ge*) (Annotated Civil Code, Civil Affairs Section Vol. 2), Tokyo: Shinpō Chūshaku Kai, 1891, pp. 5–6.
50 Seki Kōjirō, *Koseki seido* (The Koseki Registration System), Tokyo: Tokiwa Shobō, 1933, p. 4.
51 Kawashima Takeyoshi, *Ideorogī toshite no kazoku seido* (The Family System as Ideology), Tokyo: Iwanami Shoten, 1957, p. 33.
52 Watanabe Hiroshi refers to Tokugawa-era Japan as '*kashoku kokka*' (a family-business nation). Watanabe Hiroshi, *Nihon seiji shisō shi* (A History of Japanese Political Thought), Tokyo: Tokyo Daigaku Shuppan Kai, 2010, pp. 71–74.

53 Stenographic records of the 125th meeting of the Legislative Investigative Committee held on 16 October 1896. Hōmu Daijin Kanbō Shihō Hōsei Chōsa Bu (ed.), *Nihon kindai rippō shiryō sōsho* (Archival Collection of Modern Japanese Law-Making), Vol. 5, Tokyo: Shōji Hōmu Kenkyū Kai, 1984, p. 498.
54 *Ibid.*, p. 504.
55 Ueda Masa'aki, *Kika jin* (Naturalised Japanese), Tokyo: Chūkō Shinsho, 1965, pp. 15–19.
56 Hozumi Yatsuka, '"Ie" no hōriteki kannen' (Jurisprudential concept of 'family'), *Hōgaku shinpō* (Law Review), No. 85, 1898, p. 5.
57 Yanagita Kunio, 'Nōson kazoku seido to kanshū' (Farming village family system and customs), *Teihon Yanagida Kunio shū* (Collected Works of Yanagita Kunio, Revised Edition, Vol. 15), Tokyo: Chikuma Shobō, 1963, p. 356.
58 Monbushō (Ministry of Education) (ed.), *Kokutai no hongi* (Cardinal Principles of the National Polity), Tokyo: Monbushō, 1937, p. 44.
59 However, the title 'household head' was not used in the Jinshin koseki registration system. It appears that the person listed at the top of the koseki register record was determined as the 'household head'. Shinmi, *op. cit.*, 1959, p. 95.
60 Fukushima (ed.), *op. cit.*, 1962b, p. 166.
61 Hasegawa Takashi, member of the Committee, expressed his discomfort toward *riseki* as this was 'a completely new invention that was outside established custom'. He further declared, 'From the perspective of reason, this cannot be anything other than a punitive sanction'. Given that it was incompatible with reason, he requested the *riseki* rule be deleted. Stenographic records of the 127th meeting of the Legislative Investigative Committee held on 21 October 1896, Hōmu Daijin Kanbō Shihō Hōsei Chōsa Bu (ed.), *op. cit.*, 1984, p. 563.
62 Stenographic records of the 125th meeting of the Legislative Investigative Committee held on 16 October 1896, *Nihon kindai rippō shiryō sōsho minpō shingi sokkiroku 5* (Archival Collection of Modern Japanese Law-Making Stenographic Records 5), pp. 505–506.
63 Wagatsuma Sakae, *Ie no seido sono rinri to hōri* (The *Ie* Family System: Ethics and Jurisprudence), Tokyo: Kantō Sha, 1948, p. 74.
64 Satomi Kishio, *Nihon Kokutai gaku* (Introduction to the Study of National Polity, Vol. 1), Nagoya: Nihon Kokutai Gaku Kankō Kai, 1950, pp. 146–147.
65 *Hōrei zensho Keiō 4 nen: Meiji gan nen* (Compendium of Civil Law, Keiō 4 to Meiji 1).
66 Maki Kenji, *Nihon kokutai no riron* (*zōho ban*) (Japanese National Polity Theory, Enlarged Edition), Tokyo: Yūhikaku, 1943, p. 229.
67 Hozumi, *op. cit.*, 1898, pp. 6–7.
68 A comment made by Miura Yasushi, member of the House of Peers, at the first reading of the koseki registration bill during the first Imperial Diet on 29 January 1891, Dainihon Teikoku Gikai Shi Kankō Kai (ed.), *Dainihon teikoku gikai shi dai 1 kan* (Imperial Diet Journals Vol. 1), 1926, p. 184.

69 James Bryce, *Studies in History and Jurisprudence*, Vol. II, New York: Oxford University Press, 1901, pp. 840–841.
70 For example, see Frank Sargent Hoffman, *The Sphere of the State: or, The People as a Body-politic. With Special Consideration of Certain Present Problems*, New York: G. P. Putnam's sons, 1894.
71 Maki, *op. cit.*, p. 407.
72 Hori Makiyo, *Nishida Mitsugi to Nihon fashizumu undō* (Mitsugi Nishida and Japanese Fascist Movements), Tokyo: Iwanami Shoten, 2007, pp. 251–252.
73 Endō Masataka, 'Taiji suru futatsu no shin chitsujo – "Daitōa shin chitsujo" and "Taiseiyō kenshō" ni okeru shokuminchi shugi no yukue' (The course of colonialism in two competing new orders: 'The New Order in Greater East Asia' and 'The Atlantic Charter'), in Matsumura Fuminori, Morikawa Yūji and Xu Xian Feng (eds), *Higashi Ajia ni okeru futatsu no sengo* (The Post-war Regional Order in East Asia), Tokyo: Kokusai Shoin, 2012.
74 Monbushō Kyōgaku Kyoku (Department of Education and Learning of the Ministry of Education) (ed.), *Shinmin no michi* (Path of Subjects), Tokyo: Naikaku Insatsu Kyoku, 1941, p. 59.
75 *Ibid.*, p. 75.
76 Hōmu Daijin Kanbō Shihō Hōsei Chōsa Bu (ed.), 'Hōten chōsa kai koseki hō dai 2 kai giji sokki roku' (Stenographic records of the minutes of the second meeting of the Legislative Investigative Committee), *Nihon kindai rippō shiryō sōsho* (Archival Collection of Modern Japanese Law-Making), Vol. 26, Tokyo: Shōji Hōmu Kenkyū Kai, 1986, p. 60.
77 *Ibid.*
78 Usui Mizuki, *Koseki hō shōkai* (Detailed Explanation of the Koseki Registration Law), revised by Kuratomi Yūzaburō, Tokyo: Myōhōdō, 1898, p. 388.
79 *Ibid.*, p. 387.
80 An explanation given by Yamauchi Kakusaburō (Ministry of Justice advisor) at the third meeting (28 Febuary 1914) of 'The Committee for the Revision of the Koseki Registration Law and Three Other Matters' during the House of Representatives sitting of the thirty-first Imperial Diet, Hōritsu Shinbun Sha, *Koseki hō kaisei kiryū hō seitei riyū* (Reasons for Temporary Residence Regulations in Koseki Registration Law Reform), 1914, pp. 129–130.
81 Shimada Tetsukichi, *Koseki hō seikai* (The Correct Interpretation of the Koseki Registration Law), Tokyo: Hōrei Shingi Kai Jimukyoku, 1920, p. 22.
82 An explanation given by Suzuki Kisaburō (Government representative) at the second meeting (26 February 1914) of 'The Committee for the Revision of the Koseki Registration Law and Three Other Matters' held during the House of Representatives sitting of the thirty-first Imperial Diet, Tokyo: Hōritsu Shinbun Sha, *op. cit.*, 1914, p. 41.
83 An address by Representative Arakawa Gorō to the second meeting (26 February 1914) of 'The Committee for the Revision of the Koseki Registration Law and Three Other Matters' held during the House of

Representatives sitting of the thirty-first Imperial Diet, Tokyo: Hōritsu Shinbun Sha, *op. cit.*, 1914, p. 41.

84 *Ibid.*, pp. 41–42.

85 A reply made by Justice Minister Okuda Yoshito at the fifth meeting (3 March 1914) of 'The Committee for the Revision of the Koseki Registration Law and Three Other Matters' held during the House of Representatives sitting of the thirty-first Imperial Diet, Tokyo: Hōritsu Shinbun Sha, *op. cit.*, 1914, pp. 129–130.

86 The second meeting of 'The Committee for the Revision of the Koseki Registration Law and Three Other Matters' held during the House of Representatives sitting of the thirty-first Imperial Diet, Tokyo: Hōritsu Shinbun Sha, *op. cit.*, 1914, p. 49.

87 The fifth meeting of 'The Committee for the Revision of the Koseki Registration Law and Three Other Matters' held during the House of Representatives sitting of the thirty-first Imperial Diet, Tokyo: Hōritsu Shinbun Sha, *op. cit.*, 1914, pp. 128–129.

88 *Ibid.*, p. 48.

89 Ōkura Shō (undated), *Kaitaku shi jigyō hōkokusho dai 1hen* (Development Commission Operation Report Section 1). In the possession of Kokuritsu Kōbunsho Kan, p. 579.

90 Tono'oka Mojūrō (ed.), *Meiji zenki kazoku hō shiryō* (Early Meiji Family Law Documents), Vol. 1-2-1, Tokyo: Waseda Daigaku, 1969, p. 72.

91 Tono'oka Mojūrō (ed.), *Meiji zenki kazoku hō shiryō* (Early Meiji Family Law Documents), Vol. 2-2-1, Tokyo: Waseda Daigaku, 1969, pp. 191–192.

92 Kaiho Yōko, *Kindai hoppō shi: Ainu minzoku to josei to* (The Modern History of the Northern Regions: The Ainu People and Women), Tokyo: San'ichi Shobō, 1992, pp. 48–49.

93 *Ibid.*, pp. 75–76.

94 Takakura Shinichirō, *Ainu seisaku shi* (A History of Ainu Policy), Tokyo: Nihon Hyōron Sha, 1942, pp. 418–419.

95 *Ibid.*

96 *Ibid.*, p. 419.

97 A reply from the Director of the People's Affairs Bureau, Ministry of Justice, People's Affairs 1393 dated 18 January 1912. Ōchi Shintarō and Uotani Motozō (eds), *Koseki hō jitsurei taizen* (A Complete Book of Practical Examples of the Koseki Registration Law), Tokyo: Jichikan, 1938, p. 960.

98 *Ibid.*, p. 419.

99 *Kaitaku shi jigyō hōkokusho dai 1hen* (Development Commission Operation Report Section 1), pp. 550–551.

100 Kinjō Masaru, 'Kindai Okinawa ni okeru koseki seido no ittan' (An aspect of the koseki registration system in modern Okinawa), in Nakamatsu Yashū Sensei Sanju Kinen Ronbun Shū Kankō Iinkai (ed.), *Kami, mura, hito: Ryūkyū ko ronsō Nakamatsu Yashu sensei sanju kinen ronbun shū* (Gods, Villages, People: Collected Essays on the Ryūkyū Archipelago: Commemorating the Eightieth Birthday of Professor Yashū Nakamatsu), Tokyo: Daiichi Shobō, 1991, pp. 448–450.

101 'Ryūkyū han naimu shō nite kanri' (Ryūkyū Domain under the jurisdiction of the Ministry of Home Affairs), *Dajō ruiten dai 2 hen dai 129 kan chihō 35 tokubetsu no chihō Ryūkyū han 1* (Cabinet Archives of Japan Book 2, Vol. 129, Province 35, Special Province Ryūkyū Domain 1).

102 'Naimu kyō dai 4 kai nenpō furoku 2 koseki kyoku dai 4 kai nenpō' (Ministry of Home Affairs Annual Report No. 4, Appendix 2, Koseki Registration Bureau Annual Report No. 4), in Obinata Sumio (ed.), *Naimu shō nenpō hōkokusho dai 6 kan* (The Ministry of the Interior Annual and Other Reports Vol. 6), Tokyo: San'ichi Shobō, 1984, p. 357–362.

103 Ryūkyū Seifu (ed.), *Okinawa ken shi 12 shiryō hen* (The History of Okinawa Prefecture 12, Resources Section), Naha: Ryūkyū Seifu, 1966, p. 220.

104 Tono'oka Mojurō (ed.), *Meiji zenki kazoku hō shiryō* (Early Meiji Family Law Documents), Vol. 2-1, Tokyo: Waseda Daigaku, 1969, p. 34.

105 Kinjō, *op. cit.*, p. 457.

106 Ryūkyū Seifu, *op. cit.*, pp. 526–528.

107 Kinjō, *op. cit.*, pp. 465–468.

108 Asakawa Akihiro, *Kindai Nihon to kika seido* (The Naturalisation System of Modern Japan), Tokyo: Keisuisha, 2007, pp. 46–47.

109 'Ogasawara tō jū gaikokujin kika no ken' (Regarding the naturalisation of foreigner residents on the Ogasawara Islands), *Kiroku zairyō gian bo Meiji 15 nen 4 gatsu dai 3 naimu shō no bu* (Recorded Materials and Registers of Bills, April Meiji 15, No. 3, Ministry of Home Affairs Section), Tokyo: Kokuritsu Kōbunsho Kan archive 2A.35-2, p. 629.

110 According to Higashionna Kanjun's discussion of the relationship between the family name and surname, the former was '*kouji*' (small surname), while the latter, indicating consanguinity, was '*ōuji*' (large surname). Higashionna Kanjun, 'Ryūkyū jinmei kō' (A study of Ryūkyū personal names), in Ryūkyū Shinpō Sha (ed.), *Higashionna Kanjun zenshū 6* (Collected Works of Higashionna Kanjun 6), Tokyo: Daiichi Shobō, 1978a, p. 361.

111 *Ibid.*, p. 364.

112 As '*karana*' was assumed after one had reached a certain age or rank, it seems that persons with no official rank had few opportunities to use this form. *Ibid.*, pp. 363–364.

113 Higashionna Kanjun, 'Ryūkyū no rekishi' (The history of Ryūkyū), in Ryūkyū Shinpō Sha (ed.), *Higashionna Kanjun zenshū 1* (Collected Works of Higashionna Kanjun 1), Tokyo: Daiichi Shobō, 1978b, pp. 139–140.

114 People belonging to a class without a *nanori* were referred to by '*warabena*' in both private and public. According to Higashionna, this *warabena* was originally the only 'given name' for Ryūkyūan people. Higashionna, *op. cit.*, 1978a, p. 364.

115 Ōta, Chōfu, *Okinawa kensei gojū nen* (Fifty Years of Okinawa Prefectural Government), Tokyo: Kokumin Kyōiku Sha, 1932, p. 55.

Chapter 4

1 See Chapter Two of Endō Masataka, *Kindai Nihon no shokiminchi tōchi ni okeru kokuseki to koseki: Manshū, Chōsen, Taiwan* (Citizenship and Koseki Registration During the Era of Colonial Rule in Modern Japan: Manchuria, the Korean Peninsula and Taiwan), Tokyo: Akashi shoten, 2010.

2 Yasui Katsuji, 'Seibanjin no kokuhō-jō no chi'i ni tsuite' (On the legal position of savage indigenous peoples), *Taiwan kanshū jijō* (The State of Customs in Taiwan), Vol. 7, No. 1, January 1907, pp. 14–16.

3 Ikoma Takatsune, 'Naitai-jin kyōkon mondai to Karafuto dojin koseki mondai' (The problem of de facto marriage between mainland Japanese and Taiwanese people and the problem of koseki registration among the aboriginal peoples of Karafuto), *Takumu jihō* (Colonial Affairs Times), Vol. 22, January 1933, p. 17. At the time, Ikoma was the Director-General of the Department of Colonial Affairs.

4 *Ibid.*, p. 18. Furthermore, Nakano Magoichi makes an argument that contrasts with the view held by the authorities. See 'Karafuto dojin no kokuseki oyobi koseki no toriatsukai ni tsuite' (Concerning the treatment of the citizenship and koseki registration of the aboriginal peoples of Karafuto), *Minji geppō* (Civil Affairs Monthly Bulletin), Vol. 21, No. 3, March 1966, p. 40. Refer to Mukai Hidehiro, *Shokai kyū-gaichi-hō* (Interpreting the Laws of the Former Territories Not Subject to Mainland Japanese Law), Tokyo: Nihon kajo shuppan, 2007, pp. 61–67.

5 Sanekata Masao, *Kokuseki-hō* (Citizenship Law), Tokyo: Nihon hyōron-sha, 1938, pp. 40–41.

6 Scholar of international law Tatsu Sakutarō argued, 'Once annexation occurs, *Korea will no longer exist as an entity in international law*, and current Korean territory will become territory of Japan, while those with Korean citizenship will become citizens of Japan' (emphasis added). Tatsu Sakutarō, 'Kankoku heigō kokusai-hō kan' (The annexation of Korea from the viewpoint of international law), *Hōgaku kyōkai zasshi* (Journal of the Jurisprudence Association), Vol. 28, No. 11, October 1910, pp. 1–2. As a follow-up to this argument, see Egawa Hidefumi and Yamada Ryōichi, *Kokuseki-hō* (Citizenship Law), Tokyo: Yuhikaku, 1973, p. 98.

7 Minobe Tatsukichi, *Chikujō kenpō seigi* (Point-by-Point Analysis of the Constitution), Tokyo: Yuhikaku, 1927, p. 342. Sanekata Masao, *Kyōtsū-hō* (Law of Mutuality), Tokyo: Nihon hyōron-sha, 1937, p. 27. Kiyomiya Shirō, *Gaichi-hō josetsu* (Introduction to the Law of Territories not Subject to Mainland Japanese Law), Tokyo: Yuhikaku, 1944, pp. 9–10.

8 Administrative Bureau of the Ministry of Colonial Affairs, *Inin tōchi seido no kokusai-hō jō no seishitsu* (*Shōwa 6 nen, 2 gatsu*) (The Nature of the Mandated Territory System from the Point of View of International Law (February 1931)), Tokyo: Kokuritsu kōbunsho-kan shozō (Record of the National Archives of Japan), p. 6.

9 *Ibid.*, pp. 23–24.

10 *Ibid.*, p. 24.

11 Ministry of Foreign Affairs Treaties Bureau (ed.), *Gaichi hōsei-shi, dai-5-bu, Inin tōchi-ryō Nanyō Guntō zenpen* (Journal of the Legal System of Territories Not Subject to Mainland Japanese Law, Part 5, Prequel to South Pacific Mandated Territory), Tokyo: Ministry of Foreign Affairs, 1962, p. 59.

12 Ōmori Kazuhito, 'Kokuseki jimu no sūsei to kongo no dōkō' (Trends in citizenship administration and future directions), *Minji geppō* (Civil Affairs Monthly Bulletin), Vol. 24, No. 10, October 1969, p. 72

13 *Terauchi Masatake monjo* (Documents of Terauchi Masatake), 439-4. Kokuritsu kokkai toshokan kensei shiryōshitsu shozō (Records of the Constitutional Government Collection of the National Diet Library), pp. 71–72.

14 Yasui, *op. cit.*, pp. 14–16.

15 Minobe Tatsukichi, *Kenpō teiyō* (Summary of the Constitution), Tokyo: Yuhikaku, 1931, p. 151. Miyazawa Toshiyoshi, *Kenpō ryakusetsu* (Outline Summary of the Constitution), Tokyo: Iwanami shoten, 1943, p. 46.

16 Hiraga Kenta, *Kokuseki-hō, jōkan* (Citizenship Law, Part 1), Tokyo: Teikoku hanrei-hōki shuppansha, 1950, p. 133.

17 Mukai, *op. cit.*, p. 102.

18 For details of the issues associated with the implementation of the Koseki Registration Law in Korea, see Endō, *op. cit.,* Chapter 1, Section 3.

19 This citation comes from 'Chōsen shisei hōshin oyobi shisetsu kei'ei' (The administrative policies and the management of facilities in Korea), *Tera'uchi Masatake monjo* (Documents of Terauchi Masatake), 439-27-i. Kokuritsu kokkai toshokan kensei shiryōshitsu shozō (Records of the Constitutional Government Collection of the National Diet Library) pp. 71–72.

20 Chōsen sōtoku-fu gaiji-ka (The External Affairs Section of the Office of the Governor-General of Korea), *Dai-51-kai teikoku gikai setsumei shiryō* (Fifty-first Explanatory Document for the Imperial Diet), Kokuritsu kōbunsho-kan shozō (Records of the National Archives of Japan), 2A-34-7, Unit 2351.

21 Hosokawa Karoku, *Shokumin-shi* (History of Colonisation), Tokyo: Tōyō Keizai shimpō-sha, 1941, p. 348.

22 Wang Jian, 'Dōng-sān-sheng Rìběn yímín de guòqù hé jiānglái' (Past and present of Japanese immigrants in the three eastern provinces) *Dōngfāng Zázhì* (Eastern Journal), Vol. 30, No. 17, 1 September 1933, p. 47.

23 Walter M. Holmes, *An Eye-witness in Manchuria*, London: M. Lawrence, 1932, p. 3.

24 According to Konvitz, stripping an individual of citizenship was not originally designed as a political means. However, in times of emergency such as the Russian Revolution and the First and Second World Wars, it was used to assist in the expulsion and elimination of those who presented a threat to the political system of relevant nations. Milton R. Konvitz, *The Alien and the Asiatic in American Law*, Ithaca: Cornell University Press, 1946, p. 118.

25 Kiyomiya, *op. cit.*, p. 29.

26 Yamada Saburō, 'Kyōtsū-hō ni tsuite' (About the Law of Mutuality), *Kokusai-hō gaikō zasshi* (The Journal of International Law and Diplomacy), Vol. 16, May 1918, p. 6.
27 Kiyomiya, *op. cit.*, p. 2. However, according to Kiyomiya, there appear to be no examples of the term '*gachijin*' actually being used in a legal sense. Kiyomiya, *op. cit.*, p. 38.
28 The first use of the term '*gaichi*' in the title of an ordinance occurred in the document entitled, *Gaichi denwa tsūwa kisoku* (Regulations Relating to Telephones and Communication in the Territories Not Subject to Mainland Japanese Law; 1934, Ministry of Communications Edict No. 51), after which the expression '*naigaichi*' (mainland Japan and the territories not subject to mainland Japanese law) also came into use, as per the '*Shotoku-zei hōjin-zei naigaichi kanshō-hō*' (The Law Relating to Income Tax and Corporation Tax Between Mainland Japan and the Territories Not Subject to Mainland Japanese Law; 1940, Law No. 55). Ministry of Foreign Affairs Treaties Bureau (ed.), *Gaichi hōsei-shi, dai-2-bu, Gaichi hōrei seido no gaiyō* (Journal of the Legal System of Territories Not Subject to Mainland Japanese Law, Part 5, Outline of the Legal System of Territories Not Subject to Mainland Japanese Law), Tokyo: Ministry of Foreign Affairs, 1957, p. 2.
29 In the Goryeo era, a koseki register was created for the '*jōmin*' (ordinary people), for the purpose of conscription for military service and forced labour. There was also a register for the Yangban gentry to record the bloodline of the household head and the birthplace of family members. Kim Yong-han, *Kankoku no koseki seido to koseki-hō* (The Koseki Registration System and Koseki Law in Korea), Tokyo: Nihon kajo shuppan, 1977, pp. 1–2.
30 *Ibid.*, pp. 6–7.
31 Nomura Chōtarō, *Chōsen koseki rei gikai* (Explanation of Korean Koseki Registration Ordinances), Tokyo: Shōsanbō, 1923, p. 16.
32 For example, a mainland Japanese woman who married a Korean man would be entered into the relevant Korean people's register. However, she would not be removed from the relevant mainland koseki register. Reply given by government delegate (The Office of the Governor-General of Korea) Arai Kentarō at the sixth meeting (4 March 1914) of the 'Committee Examining Three Matters Including Revisions to the Koseki Registration Law' (*Koseki-hō kaisei hōritsuan hoka sanken i'in-kai*), during the thirty-first sitting of the Imperial Diet Lower House. *Koseki-hō kaisei kiryū-hō seitei riyū* (Reasons for Revisions to the Koseki Registration Law and the Introduction of the Temporary Residents Law), Tokyo: Hōritsu Shimbun-sha, 1914, p. 41.
33 Chōsen sōtokufu chūsū-in (The Central Council of the Office of the Governor-General of Korea), *Chōsen no seimei shizoku ni kan suru kennkyū chōsa* (Investigative Survey into the Korean *Sei* Surname/ Name and Clan), Keijō, 1934, p. 78.
34 *Ibid.*, pp. 36–39.
35 Nomura Chōtarō, *op. cit.*, p. 287.
36 In 1922 revisions to the Korean Civil Code, the application of the mainland Japanese Civil Code to matters associated with blood relatives

and inheritance among Korean people was restricted to administrative issues such as marriage age, marriage authorised by the courts, recognition of a child born outside marriage and acknowledgement of inheritance. Nomura Chōtarō, *op. cit.*, p. 288.

37 *Ibid.*, p. 46.

38 Response of the Director of the Ministry of Justice Civil Affairs Bureau on 28 December 1921, Civil Matter No. 4031. Shimoyama Sei'ichi, *Shinzoku sōzoku senrei ruisan* (Collection of Precedents on Family Inheritance), Tokyo: Ganshodō shoten, 1931, p. 229. Sanekata, *Kyōtsū-hō*, p. 46.

39 Nomura Chōtarō, *op. cit.*, p. 287.

40 Sanekata Masao, 'Kyōtsū-hō' (The Law of Mutuality), *Shin-hōgaku zenshū dai-27-kan* (New Jurisprudence, Collected Works, Vol. 27), Tokyo: Nihon hyōron-sha, 1937, p. 20.

41 Nomura Chōtarō, *op. cit.*, p. 64–65.

42 *Chōsen sōtoku-fu chūsū-in* (The Central Council of the Office of the Governor-General of Korea), *op. cit.*, p. 78.

43 Many *honseki* addresses established according to the Korean koseki registration ordinance carried over the *honseki* address that had been recorded on the people's register. At the time that the People's Registration Law came into operation, those without a *honseki* address were expected to create one by applying for registration. Nomura Chōtarō, *op. cit.*, p. 47.

44 *Ibid.*, p. 152.

45 In addition, when a foreigner entered the *ie* family of a Korean person through marriage or similar, that foreigner did not acquire Japanese citizenship. Nomura Chōtarō, *op. cit.*, p. 346.

46 Kawakami Iwao, 'Shutsu-nyū-koku kanri no ayumi (2)' (Progress of the management of immigration control, 2), *Gaijin tōroku* (Alien Registration), Vol. 90, January 1965, p. 33–34.

47 Morita Yoshio, *Zainichi Chōsenjin shogū no sui'i to genjō* (Changes and the Current Situation in the Treatment of Korean People Resident in Japan) (Hōmu kenkyū hōkoku-sho dai-43-shū dai-3-gō – Judicial Affairs Research Report, Collection 43, No. 3), Tokyo: Hōmu kenkyū-jo, 1955, p. 31.

48 Ministry of Foreign Affairs Treaties Bureau (ed.), *Gaichi-hō seishi, Dai-7-bu, Nihon tōchi-ka no Karafuto* (Journal of the Legal System of Territories Not Subject to Mainland Japanese Law, No. 7, Karafuto under Japanese Rule), Tokyo: Ministry of Foreign Affairs, 1969, p. 5.

49 Mukai, *op. cit.*, p. 118.

50 Ministry of Foreign Affairs Treaties Bureau (ed.), *Gaichi hōsei-shi, dai-2-bu, Gaichi hōrei seido no gaiyō* (Journal of the Legal System of Territories Not Subject to Mainland Japanese Law, Part 5, Outline of the Legal System of Territories Not Subject to Mainland Japanese Law), p. 21.

51 Ikoma Takatsune, *op. cit.*, p. 19.

52 The expression '*teiseki*' – settling a koseki register record – here has the same meaning as the Koseki Registration Law expression '*shūseki*' – establishing a koseki register record. Seki Kōjirō, *Koseki seido* (The Koseki Registration System), Tokyo: Jōban shobō, 1933, p. 8.

53 Ikoma Takatsune, 'Naitai-jin kyōkon mondai to Karafuto dojin koseki mondai', p. 19.

54 The 'Karafuto aboriginal people' comprised five different ethnic groups referred to as the Uilta (Orok), the Niv, the Kiirin (Evenks), the Sandaa (Ulch) and the Yakut peoples. Among these, the Uilta had the largest population. The Yakut people were the smallest in number, with only one person from this group being confirmed at the end of December 1943. Ministry of Foreign Affairs Treaties Bureau (ed.), *Gaichi hōsei-shi, dai-7-bu, Nihon tōchi-ka no Karafuto* (Journal of the Legal System of Territories Not Subject to Mainland Japanese Law, Part 7, Karafuto under Japanese Rule), pp. 8–10.

55 Response of the Director of the Ministry of Justice Civil Affairs Bureau on 22 March 1926, Civil Matter No. 1963. Koseki senrei kenkyū-kai hen (Koseki Precedent Research Society, ed.), *Koseki senrei zenshū, shōgai* (3) (Collected Koseki Register Precedents (3)) (Loose-leaf format), Tokyo: Gyōsei, pp. 3: 101–3: 102.

56 *Taiwan sōtoku-fu keisatsu enkaku shi II* (Journal of History of Police Policies in the Office of the Governor-General of Taiwan II) (Facsimile reprint), Tokyo: Enin shobō, 1986, p. 661.

57 Endō, *op. cit.*, pp. 137–138.

58 Stenographic records of proceedings on the Civil Code from the 139th meeting of the Legislative Investigative Committee (Hōten chōsa kai) held on 22 November 1896. Hōmu daijin kanbō shihō hōsei chōsa-bu kanshū (Legal and Legislative Survey Department of the Secretariat of the Minister of Justice, ed.), *Nihon kindai rippō shiryō sōsho, hōten chōsa-kai*, Dai-6-kan (Legislative Documents of Modern Japan Series: Code of Law Survey Society, Vol. 6), Tokyo: Shōji hōmu kenkyū-kai, p. 87.

59 Endō, *op. cit.*, refer to Chapter 2.

60 Eighteen September 1922, 'Taiwan ni shikō suru hōritsu no tokurei ni kan suru ken' (Matters Relating to Legal Exceptions Implemented in Taiwan) (1922, Imperial Ordinance No. 407). In addition, concerning civil matters relating to '*banjin*', or barbarians (the name given to the indigenous peoples), this was not originally based on legal terminology, instead arising through practice and ideas. Endō, *op. cit.*, p. 160.

61 Ikoma Takatsune, *op. cit.*, p. 3.

62 Tsuzumi tsutsumi, 'Koseki ni kan suru sho-hō seitei ni tsuite' (Concerning various legal statutes related to koseki registration), *Taiwan jihō* (Taiwan Times), Vol. 20, March 1921, p. 87.

63 Adding to this point, in Taiwanese custom neither divorce nor withdrawal from adoption involved any lodgement of notice. Rather, for practical purposes (these changes were regarded as having been decided by agreement), they were dealt with through Taiwanese customary law. As a result, there was a fear that those cases in which a 'Taiwanese' who was formerly a mainland Japanese either divorced or withdrew from an adoption agreement and was reinstated in the register record of their mainland *ie* family would disrupt mainland Japan's koseki administration which was based on notions of lodgement. As a result, revisions were made to the previously referred to ordinance entitled

Taiwan ni shikō suru hōritsu no tokurei ni kan suru ken (Matters Relating to Legal Exceptions Implemented in Taiwan), Imperial Ordinance No. 360, issued in November 1932, which stipulated that status changes involving Taiwanese would fall under the conduct of customary law. Accordingly, the following was added to Article 14, Part 2: 'When there is a mutually agreed divorce or withdrawal from an adoption agreement of *the person who entered the Taiwanese family following marriage or adoption between a mainland Japanese and an island person*, this will come into effect through lodging a notice with the head of a local municipality, district police chief or other government branch office' (emphasis added). The 'special exception' (*tokurei*) here was the notion of lodgement that was used to ensure stability in the status relations of mainland Japanese. Sanekata, *Kyōtsū-hō*. Refer to p. 23.

64 Ide Kiwata, *Taiwan chiseki-shi* (A Record of Administrative Achievement in Taiwan), Taiwan: Taiwan Nichi-nichi shinbun-sha, 1937, p. 879.

65 *Ibid.*, p. 189.

66 Endō, *op. cit.*, pp. 164–165.

67 An independent office that corresponded to the Legal Affairs Department of the Office of the Governor-General of Korea was never established in the Office of the Governor-General of Taiwan. As a result, both civil and criminal matters remained the province of the police and other local government offices. Endō, *op. cit.*, pp. 163–164.

68 Statement on 7 March 1918, by government delegate Yamada Saburō, to the Shūgi-in kyōtsūhō an shingi I'inkai (Lower House Law of Mutuality Draft Committee) of the fortieth Imperial Diet. *Teikoku gikai shūgi-in I'inkai roku 17* (Record 17 of Committees of the Lower House of the Imperial Diet), Tokyo: Rinsen shoten, 1983, p. 275.

69 Because the Koseki Registration Law applied to Japanese people (mainland Japanese) who resided in the Kwantung Leased Territory and the South Pacific Mandated Territory, lodgements related to the status of these people were processed, in the case of the latter, by the governmental branch office or nearest police station (a similar procedure applied in the Kwantung Leased Territory). Seki, *op. cit.*, pp. 158–159.

70 Kōzuma Arata, 'Heiwa jōyaku hakkō-mae ni okeru naichijin to gaichijin kan no "seki" no hendō (1)' (Changes to the 'registration' of mainland Japanese and persons not subject to mainland Japanese law prior to the coming into effect of the Peace Treaty (1)), *Koseki*, Vol. 271, January 1969, p. 23.

71 Response of the Director of the Ministry of Justice Civil Affairs Bureau on 30 August 1929, Civil Matter No. 8185. Koseki senrei kenkyū-kai hen (Koseki Precedent Research Society, ed.), *Koseki senrei zenshū, shōgai* (2) (Collected Koseki Register Precedents (2)) (Loose-leaf format), Tokyo: Gyōsei, p. 449.

72 Kiyomiya, *op. cit.*, p. 38.

73 Mukai, *op. cit.*, p. 131.

74 Sakamoto Ayarō (ed.), *Gaichi hōjin zairyū gaijin koseki kiryū todoke-sho kiseirei shiki nami kisai ruisan* (Collection of Statements and Written Form Lodgements for Japanese Residing in the Territories not Subject

to Mainland Japanese Law and Foreigner Koseki Registration and Temporary Residence), Tokyo: Meirinkan, 1938, p. 513.

75 Response of the Director of the Ministry of Justice Civil Affairs Bureau on 15 May 1922, Civil Matter No. 3236. Koseki senrei kenkyū-kai hen (Koseki Precedent Research Society, ed.), *Koseki senrei zenshū, shōgai* (3) (Collected Koseki Register Precedents (3)) (Loose-leaf format), Tokyo: Gyōsei, pp. 3–101.

76 Sanekata, *Kyōtsū-hō*, p. 51.

77 Tashiro Aritsugu, Yoshida Kazuo and Hayashida Satoshi, 'Kyōtsūhō-3-jō-3-kō to hei'eki-hō to no kankei (2)' (The relationship between Article 3, Clause 3, of the Law of Mutuality and the Military Service Law (2)), *Koseki*, Vol. 272, February 1969, p. 11.

78 Minobe Tatsukichi, *Kenpō satsuyō* (Outline of the Constitution), Tokyo: Yuhikaku, 1923, p. 158.

79 *Tokkō gaiji geppō* (Special Higher Police External Affairs Monthly), Vol. 13, No. 1, p. 111.

80 'Chōsenjin shiganhei mondai ni kan suru ken' (Matters relating to the issue of Korean volunteer soldiers), *Shōwa 13 nen Mitsudai-nikki dai-2-satsu* (1938 Secret Military Journal, 2nd Volume), Bōei-shō Bōei kenkyūjo shozō (Archives of the Defence Research Centre, Ministry of Defence).

81 Tashiro Aritsugu, Yoshida Kazuo and Hayashida Satoshi, 'Kyōtsūhō-3-jō-3-kō to hei'eki-hō to no kankei (1)' (The relationship between Article 3, Clause 3, of the Law of Mutuality and the Military Service Law (1)), *Koseki*, Vol. 270, December 1968, p. 6.

82 Tanaka Hiroshi, *Zainichi gaikoku-jin, dai san pan* (Resident Foreigners in Japan, Third Edition), Tokyo: Iwanami shoten, 2013, p. 118.

83 Matsuo Takayoshi, *Futsū senkyo seido seiritsu-shi no kenkyū* (Research into the History of the Establishment of Universal Suffrage), Tokyo: Iwanami shoten, 1989, p. 329.

84 Naimushō shakai-kyoku dai-1-bu, 'Chōsenjin rōdō-sha ni kan suru jōkyō' (The situation relating to Korean labourers), (July 1924), Pak Kyonshiku (ed.), *Zainichi Chōsenjin kankei shiryō shūsei dai-1-kan* (Collection of Documents Related to Koreans Resident in Japan, Vol. 1), Tokyo: San'ichi shobō, 1976, pp. 461–463.

85 Tsuboi Toyokichi, *Zai-Nihon Chōsenjin no Gaikyō* (*zenpen*) (The General Situation of Koreans Resident in Japan (Part I)), Tokyo: Kōan chōsa-chō (Public Intelligence Security Agency), 1953, p. 172.

86 *Teikoku gikai shūgi-in giji sokki-roku 80* (Handwritten Proceedings 80 of the Lower House Meeting of the Imperial Diet), Tokyo: University of Tokyo Press, 1985, pp. 128–129.

87 Ministry of Foreign Affairs Treaties Bureau (ed.), *Gaichi hōsei-shi, dai-2-bu, Gaichi hōrei seido no gaiyō*, pp. 20–21.

88 Nakagawa Zen'nosuke, *Koseki-hō oyobi Kiryū-hō* (The Koseki Registration Law and the Temporary Residence Law), Tokyo: Nihon hyōron-sha, 1941, p. 17.

89 Response by the Director of the Legal Bureau (Hōmu-kyoku), 7 September 1921, Civil Matter No. 1954. Shimoyama Sei'ichi (ed.), *Shinzoku sōzoku senrei ruisan* (Collection of Precedents on Family Inheritance), Tokyo: Ganshodō shoten, 1931, p. 15.

90 Ide, *op. cit.*, pp. 24–25.
91 Xu Xueji, 'Lizhi shiqi de Banjiao Lin jia: yi ge jiazu yu zhengzhi de guanxi' (The Lin family of the Banjiao district under Japanese occupation: The relationship between one family and politics), Zhongyang yanjiuyuan jindai-shi yanjiusuo bian (Institute of Modern History, Academia Sinica, ed.), *Jinshi jiazu yu zhengzhi bijiao lishi lunwenji* (Collection of Essays on the Comparative History of Families and Politics in the Modern Era), Taipei: Zhongyang yanjiuyuan jindai-shi yanjiusuo (Institute of Modern History, Academia Sinica), 1992, p. 670.
92 Concerning the Taiwanese passport system, see Endō, *op. cit.*, pp. 80–87.
93 Classified Communiqué Forwarded to the Minister of Foreign Affairs, Hayashi, from the Amoy Consul, Segawa, on 14 September 1907. 'Amoi zairyū Taiwan sekimin no jikkyō hōkoku sōfu no ken' (Matter of remitting a report on the situation regarding Chinese people with Taiwanese registration in Amoy), *Nanbu Shina zairyū Taiwan sekimin meibo chōsei ikken, 1* (An Incident in the Maintenance in South China of the Roll for Chinese People Registered in Taiwan, 1), Tokyo: Gaimushō gaikō shiryōkan shozō (Ministry of Foreign Affairs Diplomatic Document Archive), pp. 3, 8, 7–18.
94 *Ibid.*
95 Amry Vandenbosch, *The Dutch East Indies: Its Government, Problems and Politics*, Grand Rapids: Wm. B. Eerdmans, 1933, pp. 309–310.
96 Takekoshi Yosaburō, *Nangoku-ki* (Record of the Southern Lands), Tokyo: Nisei-sha, 1910, pp. 177–181.
97 Kawashima Shin, 'Taiwan-jin wa "Nihon-jin" ka', in Kishi Toshihiko (ed.), *Kindai Ajia no jigazō to tasha* (The Self-Image of Modern Asia and the Other), Kyoto: Kyoto University Press, 2011. Refer to Chapter 8.
98 *Seifu kanpō* (Government Gazette), No. 509, Xuantong 1 (1909), 10 February (intercalary).
99 The Fifty-fourth Secret Communiqué sent to Foreign Minister Komura by Qing Special Envoy Ijūin, 17 May 1909, entitled 'Nanshin chihō ni okeru kika Taiwan-jin toriatsukai ni kan suru ken' (Matters concerning the treatment of naturalised Taiwanese in the South China region). *Shinkoku kanken ga Taiwan sekimin kōkin no ken. Fu Taiwan sekimin no jōtai ni kan shi zai-Fukushū teikoku ryōji no hōkoku* (The Issue of Internment of Chinese People Registered as Taiwanese by the Qing Authorities. Appendix Report of the Imperial Consul in Fuzhou on the Situation of Chinese People Registered as Taiwanese), Tokyo: Gaimushō gaikō shiryō-kan shozō (Diplomatic Archives of the Ministry of Foreign Affairs), A, 4, 1, 5, 9.
100 Fifth Secret Communiqué sent to Foreign Minister Komura by Acting Amoy Consul Mori, 14 March 1910, entitled 'Taiwan sekimin no jōtai hōkoku no ken' (Matter of report of the situation of Chinese people registered as Taiwanese), *Nanbu Shina zairyū Taiwan sekimin meibō chōsei ikken 1* (The Case of the Maintenance of the Roll of Chinese People Registered as Taiwanese Residents in South China, 1).
101 Endō Masataka, 'Taiwan seki-min wo meguru Nihon seifu no kokuseki seisaku no shuttatsu: Nijū kokuseki mondai to Shinkoku kokuseki-hō e no taiō wo chūshin ni' (The beginning of Japanese government

citizenship policies regarding the people registered as Taiwanese: With a focus on the issue of dual citizenship and the response to Qing citizenship law), *Waseda seiji-keizai-gaku zasshi* (Waseda Journal of Political Science and Economics), No. 376, December 2009. See in particular the second section.

102 Endō, *op. cit.*, pp. 137–101.

103 *Teikoku no tai-shi gaikō seisaku kankei ikken, dai-6-kan* (An Issue Related to the Empire's Diplomatic Policies Towards China, Vol. 6), Tokyo: Gaimushō gaikō shiryō-kan shozō (Diplomatic Archives of the Ministry of Foreign Affairs), A, 1, 1, 0-10.

104 Endō, *op. cit.*, pp. 137–109.

105 Takaya Tameo, 'Nanyō kakyō jijō' (The situation of overseas Chinese in the South Pacific Islands), *Shōwa 13 nen, Dai-nikki otsushū* (1938, Dai-nikki Collection B), Tokyo: Bōei-shō Bōei kenkyūjo shozō (Archives of the Defence Research Centre, Ministry of Defence), p. 152.

106 Endō, *op. cit.*, pp. 137–110.

107 'Taiwan sekimin kankei jikō chōsa-hō ni kan suru ken' (Matter concerning survey issues related to Chinese people registered as Taiwanese), 566th Secret Communiqué sent to Foreign Minister Shidehara from Amoy Consul Terajima, 5 December 1930, *Taiwan-jin kankei zakken: Zaigai Taiwan-jin jijō kankei* (Various Matters Relating to the Taiwanese: Concerning the Situation of Taiwanese Residents Overseas), Tokyo: Gaimushō gaikō shiryō-kan shozō (Diplomatic Archives of the Ministry of Foreign Affairs), A, 3, 3, 0-3.

108 Hannah Arendt, *The Origins of Totalitarianism*, New York: Harcourt, Brace, 1951, pp. 269–270.

109 Gon Taizan, 'Manshū ni okeru museki Chōsenjin no hiai' (The sorrow of unregistered Koreans in Manchuria), *Zenman Chōsen jinmin-kai rengō-kai kaihō* (Bulletin of the Federation of Korean People in Manchuria), No. 27, May 1935, pp. 9–10.

110 'Chōsen no jōkyō' (The situation in Korea), *Ōno Rokuichirō monjo* (The Writings of Ōno Rokuichirō), Kokuritsu kokkai toshokan kensei shiryōshitsu shozō (Records of the Constitutional Government Collection of the National Diet Library), R-133, pp. 120–121.

111 Endō Masataka, 'Manshūkoku no Chōsenjin shūseki mondai: chigai-hōken teppai to museki Chōsenjin taisaku' (The problem of creating koseki register records for Korean people in Manchoukuo: The abolition of extraterritoriality and policies towards unregistered Korean people), *Ajia keizai* (Asia and Economics), Vol. 52, No. 10, October 2010, p. 41.

112 Endō, *Kindai Nihon no shokuminchi tōchi ni okeru kokuseki to koseki*, pp. 64–65.

113 Gaimushō tōa-daini-ka (Ministry of Foreign Affairs East Asia Section 2), '*Saikin shina oyobi manshū kankei shomondai tekiyō (Dai-68-gikai yō)*' (Outline of Various Recent Problems Concerning China and Manchoukuo), Kokuritsu kokkai toshokan kensei shiryōshitsu shozō, *Gaimushō monjo* SP-200 (Records of the Constitutional Government Collection of the National Diet Library).

114 Endō, 'Manshūkoku no Chōsenjin shūseki mondai: chigai-hōken teppai to museki Chōsenjin taisaku', p. 57.

115 *Ibid.*, p. 58.
116 'Chōsen no jōkyō', p. 127.
117 Shihōshō minji-kyoku (Civil Affairs Bureau, Ministry of Justice), 'Naichi oyobi Karafuto zaijū Chōsenjin ni danshi no koseki oyobi kiryū seibi kankei shorui' (Documents related to the establishment of koseki registration and temporary residence for Korean males), *Kōbun ruijū, shōwa 17, dai-15-kan, kanshiki 11-kansei 11* (*Kaigunshō*) (Collection of Public Documents, Vol. 15, Civil Service 11-Government System 11 [Ministry of the Navy]), National Archives of Japan, 2A-12, *rui* (class) 2573.
118 Hōmin otsu dai-619-gō hōmu-kyoku-chō tsūchō (Notification by the Director of the Department of Legal Affairs of the Ministry of Justice, Legal Matter B No. 619), 'Manshūkoku zankō minseki-hō ni yoru nyūseki tsūchi-sho no toriatsukai-kata' (Treatment of the registry entry notification documents relating to Manchoukuo's Provisional People's Registration Law), *Shihō kyōkai zasshi* (Journal of the Society of Justice), Vol. 22, No. 2, February 1943, p. 57.
119 Inaba Masao et al. (ed.), *Taiheiyō sensō e no michi: Kaisen gaikō-shi, bekkan* (The Path to the Pacific War: The Diplomatic History of the Outbreak of War, Additional Volume), Tokyo: Asahi shinbun-sha, 1963, p. 179.
120 Takahashi Teizō, *Manshū-koku kihon-hō* (Fundamental Law of Manchoukuo), Tokyo: Yuhikaku, 1943, pp. 86–87.
121 Hirai Shōichi, 'Manshū-koku no kokuseki mondai' (The citizenship problem in Manchoukuo), (September 1934), Mantetsu Keizai chōsa-kai hen (Economic Survey Department of the South Manchurian Railway, ed.), *Manshū-koku kokuseki narabi ni kaisha kokuseki oyobi shihon hōsaku* (*Ritsuan chōsa shorui dai-26-hen dai-1-kan*), Citizenship in Manchoukuo and in Companies and Capital Policy (Draft Survey Documents 26/1), Tokyo: Mantetsu Keizai chōsa-kai, 1935, pp. 52–53.
122 Asano Toyomi, *Teikoku Nihon no shokuminchi hōsei: hōiki tōchi to teikoku chitsujo* (The Legal System in the Colonies of Imperial Japan: Jurisprudence Governance and Imperial Regulation), Nagoya: University of Nagoya Press, 2008. Refer to Chapter 2 of the 4th edition.
123 Endō, *Kindai Nihon no shokuminchi tōchi ni okeru kokuseki to koseki*. Refer to Chapter 3, Section 2.
124 *Ibid.*
125 Ōhira Zengo, 'Manshū-koku no kokuseki mondai' (The citizenship issue in Manchoukuo), Tōkyō shōka daigaku kokuritsu gakkai hen (Tokyo Commercial College Nation Study Association, ed.), *Tōkyō shōka daigaku kenkyū nenpō: Hōgaku kenkyū* (Tokyo Commercial College Annual Legal Research Report), No. 2, 1933, p. 306.
126 Hosokawa Karoku, *op. cit.*, p. 486.
127 Endō, *Kindai Nihon no shokuminchi tōchi ni okeru kokuseki to koseki*, p. 270.
128 Manshū-koku chian-bu jōhō-ka (Information Section, Manchoukuo Public Order Bureau), 'Manshū-koku kokuhei hō to wa nan zo ya' (What is Manchoukuo's National Conscription Law?), *Tesshin* (Iron Core), January 1940, p. 83.

129 Shinzeki Katsuyoshi, 'Waga-kuni minseki seido no kakuritsu ni tsuite' (Concerning the establishment of the people's register system in our country), *Hōsō zasshi* (Legal Journal), Vol. 7, No. 7, July 1940, p. 31.
130 Endō, *Kindai Nihon no shokuminchi tōchi ni okeru kokuseki to koseki*, pp. 314–320.
131 Kibata Yōichi, *Shihai no daishō* (Compensation of Control), Tokyo: University of Tokyo Press, 1987, pp. 84–94.
132 Miyata Setsuko, Kim Yŏng-dal and Yang T'ae-ho, *Sōshi kaimei* (The Creation of Japanese Names for Korean People), Tokyo: Akashi shoten, 1992, p. 61.
133 *Keijō nippō* (Seoul Daily), 14 August 1940.
134 'Kakuchi hōin-chō oyobi shichō no jōseki mata wa hitori no hanjiho ate hōmukyoku tsūchō' (Communiqué by the Director of the Legal Affairs Bureau to Court Heads and Senior Officials of Government Offices in all areas and one Assistant Judge), dated 22 April 1940. *Shihō kyōkai zasshi* (Legal Society Journal), Vol. 19, No. 5, May 1940, p. 47.
135 Miyata, Kim and Yang, *op. cit.*, p. 99.
136 Edward H. Carr, *Conditions of Peace*, London: Macmillan, 1942, p. 3.
137 Hugh Tinker, *Race, Conflict and the International Order: From Empire to United Nations*, London: Macmillan, 1977, p. 42.
138 '"Mosuko-" kaidan to kokusai jōsei' (The 'Moscow' Conference and the international situation), (23 November 1943 [Shōwa 18]), by Shigemitsu Mamoru (Shigemitsu Memorial Museum; compiled by Takeda Kazumi), *Shigemitsu Mamoru gaikō iken-shū dai-2-kan* (*Chūka taishi, gaimu daijin jidai*) (Collected Diplomatic Opinion Statements of Shigemitsu Mamoru, Vol. 2 (Period of Ambassador to China and Foreign Minister)), Tokyo: Gendai shiryō shuppan, 2007, p. 315.
139 *Honpō naisei kankei zassan: shokuminchi kankei dai-3-kan* (Miscellaneous Collection Related to Our Country's Domestic Governance: Related to the Colonies, Vol. 3), Gaimushō gaikō shiryō-kan shozō (Diplomatic Archives of the Ministry of Foreign Affairs), A, 5, 0, 0-1-1.
140 *Honpō naisei kankei zassan: shokuminchi kankei dai-2-kan* (Miscellaneous Collection Related to Our Country's Domestic Governance: Related to the Colonies, Vol. 2), Gaimushō gaikō shiryō-kan shozō (Diplomatic Archives of the Ministry of Foreign Affairs), A, 5, 0, 0-1-1.

Chapter 5

1 Morita Yoshio, *Zainichi Chōsenjin shogū no sui'i to genjō* (Changes and the Current Situation in the Treatment of North Korean People Resident in Japan), Hōmu kenkyū hōkoku-sho dai-43-shū dai-3-gō (Judicial Affairs Research Report, Collection 43, No. 3), Tokyo: Hōmu kenkyū-jo, 1955, p. 31.
2 *Teikoku gikai shūgi-in giji sokki-roku 81* (Hand-written Proceedings 81 of the Lower House Meeting of the Imperial Diet), Tokyo: University of Tokyo Press, 1985, p. 66.

3 Koshikawa Junkichi, Gifu District Court Judge, argued that 'Korean and Taiwanese residing in Japan "could not participate in the Japanese state as its constituents" anymore at the time when their suffrage rights were suspended; it follows that their Japanese citizenship was then legally suspended'. Koshikawa Junkichi, *Nihon ni zaijū suru hi-Nihonjin no hōritsujō no chii: tokuni kyōtsūhō jō no gaichiiin nit tsuite* (Legal Status According to the Law of Mutuality of Non-Japanese Residing in Japan: Especially Concerning the People of Territories Not Subject to Mainland Japanese Law), Tokyo, Shihō shūshūjo, 1949, p.78.

4 *Naisen kankei shorui hensatsu, Shōwa 20nen, Shumushō hōkoku, tokkōka* (File of Documents Concerning Mainland Japan and Korea, 1945, the Report by Competent Ministry, Special Higher Police Division), Kokuritsu kōbunsho-kan shozō (Record of the National Archives of Japan), 2A-34-7, Unit 2351.

5 Mukai Hidehiro, *Shōkai kyū-gaichi-hō* (Interpreting the Laws of the Former Territories Not Subject to Japanese Law), Tokyo: Nihon kajo shuppan, 2007, p. 268.

6 *Asahi Shimbun*, 7 February 1946.

7 'Shitsumu hōkoku' (Office Report), No. 2, 15 April 1945. Ara Takashi (ed.), *Nihon senryō: gaikō kankei shiryō-shū ikki, dai-3-kan* (The Occupation of Japan: Initial Stage Diplomatic Documents Collection, Vol. 3), Tokyo: Kashiwa shobō, 1991, p. 31.

8 *Zainichi Chōsenjin kanri jūyō bunsho-shū* (Collection of Important Documents on the Management of Korean People Resident in Japan), Tokyo: Kohokusha, 1978, pp. 14–15.

9 Pak Kyong-sik, *Kaihōgo zainichi Chōsenjin undo-shi* (The History of Koreans Resident in Japan Following the Post-War Liberation), Tokyo: San-ichi shobō, 1989, pp. 105–106.

10 Edward W. Wagner, *The Korean Minority in Japan, 1904–1950*, Vancouver: UBC Press, 1951. Translated into the Japanese by the North America and Asia Section of the Asia Bureau of the Ministry of Foreign Affairs as *Nihon ni okeru Chōsen shōsū minzoku, 1904–1950*, Tokyo: Ministry of Foreign Affairs, 1961, p. 81.

11 *Zainichi Chōsenjin kanri jūyō bunsho-shū*, pp. 10–11.

12 Tanaka Hiroshi, *Zainichi gaikokujin, dai san pan* (Resident Foreigners in Japan, 3rd Edition), Tokyo: Iwanami shoten, 2013, pp. 72–74.

13 'Chihō chōkan kaigi kiroku' (Records of the meetings of provincial heads), *Naikaku/Sōri-fu ikan kōbunsho (Shōwa 57 nendo ikan) sono-ta shiryō, ryaku-shiki kakugi* (Public Documents Relating to Cabinet and Office of the Prime Minister Transfer of Control [1982 Transfers] and Other Related Documents, Simplified Meetings of Cabinet). Kokuritsu kōbunsho-kan shozō (Record of the National Archives of Japan), 2A-029-04.

14 Morita, *op. cit.*, p. 58.

15 *Ibid.*, p. 67.

16 Kawakami Iwao, 'Shutsunyū-koku kanri no ayumi (6)' (Progress of Management of Immigration Control, 6), *Gaijin tōroku* (Alien Registration), Vol. 94, May 1965, p. 28.

17 Morita, *op. cit.*, p. 85.

18 Kawakami Iwao, *op. cit.*, p. 30.
19 1947 nen 6 gatsu 21 nichi chōsakyoku 4-hatsu dai-833-gō, Naimushō chōsakyoku-chō yori chiji-ate (Sent to prefectural governors on 21 June 1947, from the head of the Survey Bureau of the Ministry of Home Affairs, Survey Bureau Notification 4, No. 833), 'Gaikokujin tōroku jimu toriatsukai yōryō no sōfu ni tsuite' (Concerning the Sending of Points on the Administrative Management of Alien Registration). Morita, *op. cit.*, p. 80.
20 *Ibid.*, p. 124.
21 28 February 1947 Announcement by the SCAP Public Relations Office (Shōgai-kyoku). Supreme Court Administrative Bureau, Public Relations Section (Saikō saibansho jimu-kyoku shōgai-ka), *Shōgai shiryō dai-7-gō: Taiwanjin ni kan suru hōken mondai* (Public Relations Documents, No. 7: The Issue of Jurisdiction in Relation to Taiwanese), May 1950, p. 7.
22 *Zainichi Chōsenjin kanri jūyō bunsho-shū*, p. 12.
23 Morita, *op. cit.*, p. 107.
24 The full text of the Citizenship Law of North Korea (the Democratic People's Republic of Korea) is available in Koyanagi Minoru, 'Tainichi heiwa jōyaku ni yoru kokuseki no hendō wo megutte' (Concerning the change of citizenship arising from the Peace Treaty with Japan), *Minji Geppō* (Civil Affairs Monthly Bulletin), Vol. 46, No. 8, August 1991, pp. 50–51.
25 Morita, *op. cit.*, p. 108.
26 *Ibid.*, p. 83.
27 Machiya Yūji, 'Kyū-gaichijin, naichijin kan no ninchi to kokuseki' (Citizenship and the acknowledgement of paternity between a former person from the territories not subject to mainland Japanese law and a mainland Japanese), *Minji geppō* (Civil Affairs Monthly Bulletin), Vol. 28, No. 8, August 1973, p. 183.
28 Ministry of Foreign Affairs Treaties Bureau (ed.), *Gaichi hōsei shi dai-1-kan, gaichi kankei hōrei seiri ni kan suru zengo sochi ni tsuite* (Journal of the Legal System of the Territories not Subject to Mainland Japanese Law, Vol. 1: Settlement Measures Related to Concluding the Laws and Ordinances of the Former Territories not Subject to Mainland Japanese Law), 1955, Tokyo: Bunsei shoin, 1996 facsimile edition, p. 105.
29 *Ibid.*, pp. 7–10 and 20–24.
30 Murakami Tomokazu (ed.), *Koseki (jō)* (Koseki, Part 1), Tokyo: Seirin shoin, 1954, p. 50.
31 Mukai, *op. cit.*, pp. 230–231.
32 Koseki senrei kenkyūkai-hen (Koseki Precedent Research Society, ed.), *Koseki senrei zenshū (1)* (Collected Koseki Precedent, 1), (addition/deletion type), Tokyo: Gyōsei, p. 474.
33 1951 nen 3 gatsu 6 nichi Minji-kō dai-423-gō, Hōmu-fu Minjikyoku-chō kaitō (Response of the head of the Civil Affairs Bureau of the Attorney General's Office, Civil Matter No. 423, 6 March 1951). *Koseki senrei zenshū* (1), p. 476.
34 1948 nen 10 gatsu 11 nichi Minji-kō dai-3134-gō Hōmuchō Minji-kyoku chō kaitō (Response of the head of the Civil Affairs Bureau of the Attorney General's Office, Civil Matter No. 3134, 11 October 1948). 1949

nen 11 gatsu 15 nichi Minji-kō dai-2666-gō (2) 549 gō Hōmufu Minji-kyoku chō kaitō (Response of the head of the Civil Affairs Department of the Attorney General's Office, Civil Matter No. 2666, (2) No. 549, 15 November 1949). *Koseki*, No. 6, February 1950, p. 20.

35 Miyazawa Toshiyoshi, *Kenpō Tai'i* (Outline of the Constitution), Tokyo: Yūhikaku, 1949, p. 98.

36 Agawa Kiyomichi and Watanabe Tamotsu (eds), *Koseki kankei hanrei sōran* (Complete Collection of Judicial Precedents Concerning Koseki Registration), Tokyo: Teikoku hanrei-hō shuppansha, 1960, p. 5.

37 In reality, this was not limited to those with an entry in the mainland register. Mukai, *op. cit.*, p. 215.

38 *Koseki*, No. 40, July 1952, p. 37.

39 Yi Yangsu (translation and commentary), 'Kankoku-gawa bunsho ni miru Nikkan kokkō seijōka kōshō, dai-3-kai, Zainichi kankoku-jin no kokuseki' (Third negotiations for the normalisation of relations between Japan and South Korea: The South Korean documents), *Kikan sensō sekinin kenkyū* (Researching Responsibility for the War Quarterly), No. 55, Spring 2007, pp. 80–81.

40 Yoshizawa Fumitoshi, 'Nikkan kokkō seijōka kōshō ni okeru kihon kankei kōshō' (Fundamentals of basic negotiations related to the negotiations for the normalisation of relations between Japan and South Korea), in Yi Jongwon, Kimiya Tadashi and Asano Toyomi (eds) *Rekishi toshite Nikkan kokkō seijōka 2: Datsu-shikuminchi-ka hen* (Normalisation of Relations Between Japan and South Korea as History 2: Decolonisation Volume), Tokyo: Hōsei University Press, 2011, p. 99.

41 Tanaka Hiroshi, *op. cit.*, pp. 72–74.

42 Ōnuma Yasu'aki, *Zainichi Kankoku Chōsenjin no kokuseki to jinken* (The Citizenship and Human Rights of Resident Korean People in Japan), Tokyo: Tōshindō, 2004. Refer to Chapters 2 and 3.

43 See Kawakami Tarō, 'Nishi-doitsu no kokuseki mondai kisei-hō' (The Act of Regulation of Citizenship Matters in West Germany), *Koseki*, No. 367, May 1976.

44 Ikegawa Yoshimasa, *Koseki shūhen no zakkō* (Various Aspects of Matters Related to Koseki Registration), Tokyo: Teihan, 1980, p. 137.

45 Tanaka Kato'o 'Shōgai-teki koseki teisei' (Revisions to the koseki register on public relations), in Takanshi Masayuki (ed.), *Kazoku to koseki no sho-mondai* (Issues Concerning the Family and Koseki), Tokyo: Nihon kajo shuppan, 1966, pp. 169–170.

46 *Saikō saibasho keiji hanrei-shū* (Criminal Precedent from the Supreme Court), Dai-15-kan, dai-3-gō, p. 657.

47 Tanaka Hiroshi, *op. cit.*, Refer to Chapter 4.

48 *Saikō saibasho keiji hanrei-shū* (Criminal Precedent from the Supreme Court), Dai-16-kan, dai-12-gō, p. 1661.

49 Hiraga Kenta 'Chōsenjin no kokuseki' (The citizenship of Korean people in Japan), *Minji kenshū* (Studying and Training Civil Matters), No. 117, January 1967, p. 19.

50 Yokoyama Minoru, 'Karafuto kikokusha no kokuseki mondai ni tsuite' (Concerning the citizenship problems of Karafuto returnees), *Minji geppō* (Civil Affairs Monthly Bulletin), Vol. 13, No. 3, March 1958, pp. 7–8.

51 Nakano Magoichi, 'Karafuto dojin no kokuseki oyobi koseki no toriatsukai ni tsuite' (Concerning the treatment of the citizenship and koseki registration of the aboriginal people of Karafuto), *Minji geppō* (Civil Affairs Monthly Bulletin), Vol. 21, No. 3, March, 1965, p. 43.

52 *1956 nen 2 gatsu 28 nichi-zuke Minji (2) hatsu dai-71-gō Hōmushō Minji-kyoku dai-2-ka chō no kaitō* (Response of the head of the Civil Affairs Bureau, Second Section, Ministry of Justice, Civil Matters (2) Announcement No. 71, 28 February 1956). *Dōnen 3 gatsu 13 nichi- zuke Minji (2) hatsu dai-116-gō Hōmushō Minji-kyoku dai-2-ka chō no kaitō* (Response of the head of the Civil Affairs Bureau, Second Section, Ministry of Justice, Civil Matters (2) Notification No. 116, 13 March 1956). Nakano, *Ibid.*, pp. 44–45.

53 *1969 nen 3 gatsu 11 nichi Minji-kō dai-422-gō Hōmushō Minji-kyoku chō kaitō* (Response of the head of the Civil Affairs Bureau, Ministry of Justice, Civil Matter No. 422, 11 March 1969). Fukutomi Tomi'o, 'Hoppō ryōdo no koseki (3)' (Koseki registration in the Northern Territories, 3), *Koseki*, No. 444, December 1981, p. 20.

54 Mukai, *op. cit.*, pp. 222–223.

55 Manshū kaitaku-shi kankōkai hen (The publishing association of the history of the development of Manchuria, ed.), *Manshū kaitaku-shi* (History of the Development of Manchuria), Tokyo: Zenkoku takuyū kyōgikai, 1980, p. 437.

56 *Koseki senrei zenshū (4)*, pp. 1086 No. 3 to 1086 No. 9.

57 When those who did not return home from war areas were declared deceased, it was decided that 30,000 yen would be awarded in consolation monies to the remaining family members. Articles 3 and 6 of the 'Act on Special Measures to Unrepatriated Persons' (*Mi-kikan-sha ni kan suru tokubetsu sochi-hō*).

58 Explanation by Ōtaka Hiroshi (1928–2001), committee member from the Ministry of Justice Immigration Control Bureau to the Justice Committee (*Hōmu i'inkai*) of the Lower House of the 95th National Assembly. 'Dai-95-kai kokkai shūgi-in hōmu i'inkai kaigi-roku dai-4-gō' (No. 4 of Records of Lower House Justice Committee of the 95th National Assembly), *Kanpō gōgai, shūgi-in kaigi-roku, dai-95-kai kokkai* (Official Records Additions, Records of Lower House Meetings of the 95th National Assembly).

59 See Chapters 2 and 5 of Okuda Yasuhiro, *Kazoku to kokuseki, hoteiban* (The Family and Citizenship, Expanded Edition), Tokyo: Yuhikaku, 2003.

60 Ōyama Takashi, 'Jūkokuseki to kokuseki yui'itsu no gensoku: Ōshū no taiō to waga kuni no jōkyō' (Dual citizenship and the principle of single citizenship: The European response and the situation in Japan), *Rippō to chōsa* (Legislation and Survey), No. 295, August 2009, p. 107.

61 Hiraga Kenta, 'Okinawa fukki ni tsuite no oboegaki' (Memorandum concerning the Okinawa reversion), Zenkoku rengō koseki jimu kyōgikai hen (National alliance of koseki registration administration, ed.), *Nihon koseki no tokushitsu* (The Special Characteristics of the Koseki Registration System in Japan), Tokyo: Teikoku hanrei hōki shuppansha, 1975, p. 609.

62 Nishihara Sunao, 'Koseki hōsei no hensen to mondai-ten' (Changes and problems in the koseki registration laws), Miyazato Seigen (ed.), *Sengo Okinawa no seiji to hō: 1945–1972* (Politics and Law in Post-War Okinawa: 1945–1972), Tokyo: University of Tokyo Press, 1975, p. 609.
63 *Ibid.*, pp. 629–630.
64 Hōmushō Minji-kyoku dai-5-ka (5th Section Civil Affairs Bureau, Ministry of Justice), 'Okinawa no fukki to Minji-kyoku no shoshō jimu (8) kokuseki jimu' (The reversion of Okinawa and the jurisdiction administration of the Civil Affairs Bureau (8) Citizenship Administration), *Minji geppō* (Civil Affairs Monthly Bulletin), Vol. 27, No. 6, June 1972, p. 171.
65 Fukutomi Tomi'o, 'Okinawa no fukki to koseki' (The reversion of Okinawa and koseki registration), *Koseki*, No. 311, June 1972, pp. 6–8.
66 Ōwan Chōken, 'Fukki-go no Okinawa koseki no seibi' (Maintenance of the Okinawan koseki register after reversion), Koseki-hō 50 shūnen kinen-ron bunshū hensan i'inkai hen (Committee for the Compilation of Essays to Mark the 50th Anniversary of the Koseki Registration Law), *Genkō koseki seido 50 nen no ayumi to tenbō* (The Path and Future of 50 Years of the Current Koseki Registration System), Tokyo: Nihon kajo shuppan, 1999, p. 276.
67 Explanation by Yamano Kōkichi (1916–1998) (administrative official of the Office of the Prime Minister (*sōri fu*) and head of the Special Regional Contact Bureau (*tokubetsu chi'iki renraku-kyoku chō*)) to the 1st Sub-Committee of the Lower House Budget Committee of the 48th Meeting of the National Assembly on 24 February 1965. *Dai-48-dai kokkai shūgi-in yosan i'inkai dai-1-bun kakai dai-3-gō* (No. 3 of the 1st Sub-Committee of the Lower House Budget Committee of the 48th Meeting of the National Assembly), p. 2.
68 Ryūkyū seifu rippō-in jimu-kyoku hen (Administrative Bureau of Legislature of the Government of the Ryūkyū Islands, ed.), *Ryūkyū hōrei-shū* (Collected Laws and Ordinances of the Ryūkyū Islands), 1953, p. 132.
69 Ryūkyū seifu bunkyō-kyoku kenkyū chōsa-ka hen (Government of the Ryūkyū Islands Education and Culture Bureau Research Survey Section, ed.), *Ryūkyū shiryō, dai-4-shū* (Ryūkyū Historical Record, Collection 4), 1959, p. 31.
70 *Ryūkyū hōrei-shū* (Collected Legislation of the Ryūkyū Islands), p. 132.
71 Hōmushō Minji-kyoku dai-2-ka (Ministry of Justice Civil Affairs Bureau, 2nd Section), 'Okinawa no fukki to Minji-kyoku no shoshō jimu (3) koseki jimu' (The Reversion of Okinawa and the Jurisdictional Administration of the Civil Affairs Bureau 3, Koseki Register Administration), *Minji geppō* (Civil Affairs Monthly Bulletin), Vol. 27, No. 6, p. 76. Fukutomi, 'Okinawa no fukki to koseki', pp. 9–10.
72 Response to the governance head of the Government of the Ryūkyū Islands (Ryūkyū seifu gyōsei shuseki) from the Office of the Deputy Governor of the United States Civil Administration of the Ryūkyū Islands (Gasshūkoku Ryūkyū shotō minsei-bu fuku-chōkan jimusho) on 11 October 1955, 'Ryūkyū ni okeru gaikokujin no kika' (The Naturalisation of Foreigners in the Ryūkyū Islands). *Koseki senrei zenshū (4)*, pp. 1058 No. 4 to 1058 No. 5.

73 *Ryūkyū shiryō, dai-4-shū*, p. 19.
74 *Ibid.*, p. 25.
75 Nishihara, *op. cit.*, p. 624.
76 Arasaki Moriteru, *Sengo Okinawa shi* (The History of Post-War Okinawa), Tokyo: Nihon hyōronsha, 1976, p. 111.
77 Hōmushō Minji-kyoku dai-2-ka (Ministry of Justice Civil Affairs Bureau, 2nd Section), 'Okinawa no fukki to Minji-kyoku no shoshō jimu (3) koseki jimu', p. 86.
78 Nishihara, *op. cit.*, p. 623.
79 Ōwan, *op. cit.*, p. 277.
80 Explanation by Nishimura Kenjirō (Committee member and head of the 3rd Bureau of Legal Opinion (*Hōsei iken dai-3-kyoku chō*) to the Lower House Budget Committee, 2 April 1952. *Dai-3-kai kokkai shūgi-in yosan i'inkai kaigi-roku dai-24-gō* (24th Record of the Meeting of the 3rd National Assembly Lower House Budget Committee), p. 27.
81 Hōmushō Minji-kyoku dai-2-ka (Ministry of Justice Civil Affairs Bureau, 2nd Section), 'Okinawa no fukki to Minji-kyoku no shoshō jimu (3) koseki jimu', p. 74. Fukutomi, 'Okinawa no fukki to koseki', p. 8.
82 Hiraga, 'Okinawa fukki ni tsuite no oboegaki', p. 286.
83 Kugai Ryōjun, 'Minji-kyoku to watashi to Okinawa no koseki seibi' (The Civil Affairs Bureau, myself and the Okinawa koseki register reconstruction), *Minji geppō* (Civil Affairs Monthly Bulletin), Vol. 27, No. 7, July 1972, pp. 25–26.
84 However, according to Kugai, if the Americans saw the expression 'Okinawa Prefecture' there was a strong possibility that they would veto the legislation, so they were not to use the term in drafts of the Koseki Reconstruction Law or when explaining the draft to the Civil Administration. Kugai, *op. cit.*, pp. 26–26.
85 Hiraga, 'Okinawa fukki ni tsuite no oboegaki', p. 287.
86 Kugai, *op. cit.*, pp. 26–28.
87 Ōwan, *op. cit.*, p. 277.
88 Hōmushō Minji-kyoku dai-2-ka (Ministry of Justice Civil Affairs Bureau, 2nd Section), 'Okinawa no fukki to Minji-kyoku no shoshō jimu (3) koseki jimu', p. 77.
89 *Ryūkyū shiryō, dai-4-shū*, p. 28.
90 Ōwan, *op. cit.* , p. 278.
91 Hōmushō Minji-kyoku dai-2-ka (Ministry of Justice Civil Affairs Bureau, 2nd Section), 'Okinawa no fukki to Minji-kyoku no shoshō jimu (3) koseki jimu', p. 82.
92 Notification from the head of the Civil Affairs Bureau of the Ministry of Justice to the head of the Naha Regional Legal Affairs Bureau, Civil Affairs Matter No. 1783, 15 May 1972. Hōmushō Minji-kyoku dai-2-ka (Ministry of Justice Civil Affairs Bureau, 2nd Section), 'Okinawa no fukki to Minji-kyoku no shoshō jimu (3) koseki jimu', p. 89.
93 Hōmushō Minji-kyoku dai-5-ka (Ministry of Justice Civil Affairs Bureau, 5th Section), 'Okinawa no fukki to Minji-kyoku no shoshō jimu (8) kokuseki jimu' (The Reversion of Okinawa and the Jurisdictional Administration of the Civil Affairs Bureau (8) Citizenship Administration), *Minji geppō* (Civil Affairs Monthly Bulletin), Vol. 27, No. 6, June 1972, p. 173.

Chapter 6

1 See Endō Masataka, 'Jūmin tōroku seido no seiritsu ni okeru "gaikokujin" no shogū' (The treatment of 'foreigners' in the establishment of the resident registration system), *Waseda seiji kōhō kenkyū* (Waseda Study of Politics and Public Law), No. 77, July 2004.
2 Ōshima Toshiyuki, *Seidōitsusei shōgaisha to hō* (Persons with Gender Identity Disorder and the Law), Tokyo: Nihon hyōronsha, 2002.
3 Kuroki Tadamasa and Hosokawa Kiyoshi, *Gaiji hō; kokuseki hō* (External Affairs Law and Citizenship Law), Tokyo: Gyōsei, 1988, p. 267.
4 Egawa Hidefumi and Yamada Ryōichi, *Kokuseki hō* (The Citizenship Law), Tokyo: Yūhikaku, 1973, p. 40.
5 Muranaga Gōji, 'Sentaku seido ni tsuite' (On the selection system), *Minji geppō* (Civil Affairs Monthly Bulletin), Vol. 40, No. 2, February,1985, p. 34.
6 Kidana Shōichi, *Chikujō shōkai kokuseki hō* (Point-by-Point Commentary of Citizenship Law), Tokyo: Nihon kajo shuppan, 2004, p. 402.
7 Explanation given by government committee member Biwata Taisuke (Director of the Civil Affairs Bureau of the Ministry of Justice) at the Lower House Judicial Affairs Committee on 17 April 1984. See Biwata Taisuke, cited in *Shūgiin hōmu iinkai kaigiroku dai-10-gō* (Minutes of Lower House Judicial Affairs Committee, No. 10), 1984, p. 10.
8 Ebihara Yoshimune, 'Kokuseki to koseki' (Nationality and koseki registration), *Koseki*, No. 541, November 1988, p. 4.
9 *Hanrei jihō* (Law Cases Reports), No. 2002, p. 3.
10 Hosokawa Kiyoshi, 'Kaisei kokuseki hō no gaiyō' (Outline of revised citizenship law), in Hōmushō minjikyoku naihōmu kenkyūkai (ed.), *Kaisei kokuseki hō; koseki hō no kaisetsu* (Commentary on Revised Citizenship Law and Koseki Registration Law), Tokyo: Kin'yū zaisei jijō kenkyūkai, 1985, p. 8.
11 *Ibid.*
12 Kim Yong-Han, *Kankoku no koseki seido to koseki* hō (The Republic of Korea's Koseki Registration System and Koseki Registration Law), Tokyo: Nihon kajo shuppan, 1977, pp. 11–13.
13 Moon Heung Ann (trans. Kim Yang Wan), 'Kankoku ni okeru mibun tōroku seido no kaihen to kadai' (Changes to the civil status registration system in the Republic of Korea, and problems), in Ajia kazoku hō kaigi (ed.), *Koseki to mibun tōroku seido* (Family Registration and the Civil Status Registration System), Tokyo: Nihon kajo shuppan, 2012, pp. 134–139.
14 On the processes of the abolition of the Koseki Registration Law and the enactment of the Family Relationship Registration Law in the Republic of Korea, see Sin Yŏng-ho and Bae Hun, *Kankoku kazoku kankei tōroku hō* (The Republic of Korea's Family Relationship Registration Law), Tokyo: Nihon kajo shuppan, 2009, pp. 11–13.
15 *Ibid.*, p. 19.
16 Huang Zongle, 'Taiwan ni okeru koseki to mibun tōroku ni tsuite' (On Koseki registration and civil status registration in Taiwan), *Koseki jihō*, No. 510, January 2000, p. 6.

17 *Ibid.*, pp. 7–15.
18 Wakabayashi Masahiro, *Taiwan: Bunretsu kokka to minshuka* (Taiwan: A Divided State and Democratisation), Tokyo: Tōkyō daigaku shuppan kai, 1992, pp. 58–60.
19 Huang Zongle, 'Taiwan no koseki hō to sono keisei (ge)' (Taiwan's koseki registration law and its revision (part 2 of 2), *Koseki jihō*, No. 426, May 1993, p. 25.
20 Huang, *op. cit.*, 2000, p. 9.

Conclusion

1 Henry Sidgwick, *The Elements of Politics*, London: Macmillan, 1897, p. 223.
2 Katō Takashi, *Seiji to ningen* (Politics and People), Tokyo: Iwanami shoten, 1993, p. 124.

Index

www.ingramcontent.com/pod-product-compliance
Lightning Source LLC
Chambersburg PA
CBHW060142280326
41932CB00012B/1598